The Seven Liberal Arts
in the Middle Ages

EDITED BY

David L. Wagner

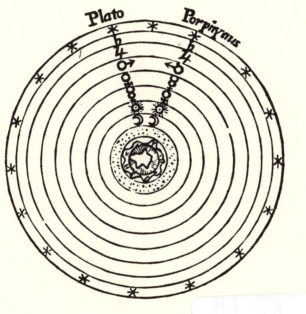

Indiana University Press • Bloomington

Manufactured in the United States of America

Library of Congress Cataloging in Publication Data
Main entry under title:

The Seven liberal arts in the Middle Ages.

Includes index.
1. Education, Medieval—Addresses, essays, lectures. 2. Education, Humanistic—Curricula—History—Addresses, essay, lectures. 3. Learning and scholarship—Addresses, essays, lectures. I. Wagner, David L. (David Leslie)
LA93.S48 1983   370'.9'02   83-47660
ISBN 0-253-35185-5
1 2 3 4 5 87 86 85 84 83

*The Seven Liberal Arts
in the Middle Ages*

To Nan and Les

Contents

Illustrations

Preface

The present book represents the culmination of a project that began several years ago when Linda Caruthers, Jim Peavler, and I designed a course that would satisfy a new requirement for interdisciplinary study that was to be part of the general education program at Northern Illinois University. In developing this course, "Introduction to Medieval Studies," we adopted the seven liberal arts as the theme not only because it allowed examination of the basic curriculum of medieval education but also because it provided a springboard for the study of many other facets of medieval culture. We established a format that combined classroom discussion with public lectures by scholars from other universities who were specialists in the various medieval arts.

During the first semester that the course was taught, we came to recognize that there was need for a book synthesizing the extensive contemporary scholarship devoted to the medieval arts. Since this task seemed beyond the scope of any single scholar, we decided that the public lectures could well serve as the basis for such a work. Because of a variety of unforeseen circumstances, however, I had to assume responsibility for carrying out this project.

The lecture series on which this book is based was put together in 1977. Professor Morrison's lecture and those devoted to the individual arts were delivered during the academic year 1977-78. The series concluded the following November with Professor McInerny's lecture. All the speakers from the previous year returned to Northern for that address, which also served to open a conference, "The Medieval Arts and the Modern World." This conference provided a unique opportunity to coordinate the various lectures. It included both public and private meetings, with two working sessions devoted to discussing the original lectures, copies of which had been sent to each participant. The present essays incorporate the revisions decided on at that conference, with one exception. When the lecturer on rhetoric found it necessary to withdraw from the project, Martin Camargo generously agreed to write an essay specifically for this volume.

The original plan was to concentrate on the High Middle Ages. It became clear in the course of the lecture series, however, that the medieval arts could be understood only against the background of classical scholarship. Therefore, at the conference, we decided that I should write a historical survey of the relation between the liberal arts tradition and ancient learning. We also decided that my essay should discuss the standard topics in each art. I found it difficult to accomplish both tasks in a single essay. Instead, I have analyzed the standard topics in the chapter headnotes, which are designed to be read together as a brief essay on the formal structure of the seven arts.

That this volume is based on a series of public lectures has affected its character in certain evident ways. In the first place, the essays are written at the level of the general educated reader. We decided at the conference, however, to use the footnotes to provide a basic bibliography suitable for scholars. In the second place, because each essay concentrates on a particular art, there is little consideration of the interrelations between the various arts. Finally, the various authors adopt diverse approaches to their subjects. At the conference, we considered and rejected the idea of imposing greater uniformity on the essays, believing that the variety of interpretations would provide a more comprehensive view of the history of the liberal arts.

The editor of a book such as this has an especially wide variety of debts to acknowledge. I am grateful above all to the contributors—who were willing to revise their contributions, often more than once. The lecture series and the conference were supported by the former and current presidents of NIU, Richard J. Nelson and William R. Monat, as well as by the Graduate Colloquium Committee. A grant from the Illinois Humanities Council made possible the conference on "The Medieval Arts and the Modern World." Daniel Wit, dean of International and Special Programs, supported the project in innumerable ways. Two deans of the College of Liberal Arts and Sciences, Paul S. Burtness and James D. Norris, also lent their support, as did J. Carroll Moody, chairman of the history department. Elaine Kittleson somehow always arranged for the departmental secretaries to have my copy ready "yesterday"—as I so often seemed to need it. The Phi Beta Kappa Association of Northern Illinois cosponsored both the lecture series and the conference and contributed to the congeniality that characterized the entire project. For all this support, I express my sincere thanks.

Most university professors are indebted to their students in any book that they write, but the contribution of students who participated in the interdisciplinary course was perhaps unique. They read critically both the original and revised versions of the essays and helped me clarify my ideas as I worked out the history of the liberal arts. Whatever stylistic clarity I have achieved in my contributions has depended to a great extent on the editorial assistance of Ann Bates Congdon; for this and for her general support I owe a debt that is beyond thanks. And finally, as I near the completion of this project, I recall with gratitude the contributions of those who were the core of the original Medieval Studies Program: Linda Caruthers, Jim Peavler, and Thomas Blomquist.

The Seven Liberal Arts
in the Middle Ages

1 The Seven Liberal Arts and Classical Scholarship

David L. Wagner

The seven liberal arts consist of the verbal arts (the trivium) — grammar, rhetoric, and logic or dialectic—and the mathematical arts (the quadrivium) —arithmetic, music, geometry, and astronomy. In a strict sense, the term designates those arts as they were codified by the Latin encyclopedists of the fifth and sixth centuries A.D., whose works provided the basic content and form of intellectual life for several centuries.

The emergence and evolution of the liberal arts may be viewed as an aspect of the history of education. Yet this process can best be understood if it is viewed in the total context of intellectual history. In this essay, I shall analyze the development of the liberal arts in relation to the dominant cultural traditions of the ancient and medieval periods.

Classical scholarship plays an especially significant role in this development. For one thing, the classical tradition was the ultimate source for the Latin encyclopedists, whose writings mark the culmination of a process of simplification that began in the Hellenistic Age. For another, the recovery of classical learning in the twelfth and thirteenth centuries led to decisive changes in almost all of the arts.

The classical tradition established the formal features of the arts as well as their content. The following essay will discuss the structure of the arts as a whole. By the time of the Latin encyclopedists, the concepts of the quadrivium and the trivium, although not the names, had emerged; and the idea of a canon of liberal arts was already common, although the number seven would become traditional only through their writings.

Subsequent headnotes will consider the internal structure of each individual art.

I. THE HELLENIC AGE

The history of the Hellenic Age (the period from the eighth century B.C. to the death of Alexander the Great in 323 B.C.) is essentially the history of the Greek city-state (the *polis*), and the origins of the liberal arts can best be understood in terms of its cultural traditions. Although physical education and music—the core of early Greek education—were the most pervasive of these traditions, rhetoric and rationalism were of paramount importance to the development of the liberal arts.

While the influence of rhetoric on the liberal arts tradition would be felt only in the fifth century, that of rationalism was manifest almost from the beginning of Hellenic history. Commonly cited as the preeminent contribution of Greek civilization, rationalism can be defined abstractly as an attitude that emphasizes (at the very least) systematic unity and generality. This abstract definition can be made concrete by examining the role of rationalism in the origins of each liberal art.

The Quadrivium

Philosophy originated when the Greeks began to interpret the universe in rational terms.[1] Their cosmology probably grew out of Bronze Age creation myths, with Hesiod's *Theogony,* an extremely detailed and systematic genealogy of the gods, marking the transition between the two modes of thought.[2] The essence of the new rational spirit is found in the Greeks' identification of a concept of "nature."[3] They distinguished the natural realm from the divine and identified it as a "cosmos," i.e., a unified whole, deriving from a principle (or beginning point) and developing according to a law. Each of these elements— unified whole, principle, law—reflected the new rational spirit that distinguished Greek philosophy from Bronze Age mythology.

This development began at the end of the seventh century in Miletus, a prosperous trading center off the coast of Asia Minor, when Thales argued that all is water. His successors took up this search for a basic principle, proposing a series of alternatives to water. Aristotle argued that these philosophers were seeking a material principle that somehow subsumed the world of appearances. It would seem preferable, however, to view the Milesian school as seeking the generative principle of the universe, thereby emphasizing the derivation of their philosophy from the creation myths. The earlier genealogical approach, moreover, was replaced in the cosmologies of Thales' successors by a law of development.

Greek mathematics also manifested this new rationalist spirit.[4] The

Bronze Age cultures of Egypt and Mesopotamia had developed sophisticated procedures in mathematics (as well as in astronomy), but these were rules of thumb, perfected empirically by trial and error. The Greeks, however, established mathematics as an axiomatic-deductive science—i.e., an ordered system, the elements of which are necessary consequents of explicitly stated premises. Its essential features—ordered system, explicit premises, necessary connection—were analogous to the basic elements in the concept of the cosmos and like them reflected the spirit of rationalism.

According to tradition, Thales was also the first to prove a mathematical theorem. Since his contribution is as problematic today as it was in antiquity, however, it is customary to begin an account of Greek mathematics with Pythagoras or (because it is difficult to separate Pythagoras's contributions from those of his followers) with the early Pythagoreans. It is especially appropriate in an essay on the liberal arts to begin with the early Pythagoreans, since they were the first to link the four arts of the quadrivium.[5]

The central principle of the early Pythagoreans was that all is number. They modified Milesian cosmology by adopting number (apparently conceived as material) as a generative principle and interpreting law in terms of arithmetical order. Thus they understood nature in terms of number.

The early Pythagoreans emphasized number for yet another reason. Pythagoras, who was as much a religious leader as a philosopher, seems to have adopted the Orphic belief in the transmigration of souls. The soul, as a microcosm of the macrocosm, was understood in terms of mathematical harmonies, and the study of number was thought to be a means of purifying the soul. Society also was analyzed in numerical terms; thus number was considered the basis of morality and justice as well as of nature.

Given the preeminent role of number in their philosophy, it is not surprising that the early Pythagoreans emphasized the study of arithmetic and geometry. It is perhaps surprising to find them analyzing music in terms of number, although according to one tradition it was Pythagoras's discovery of the mathematical basis of musical consonances (the fourth, the fifth, and the octave) that gave rise to his mathematical philosophy. The Pythagoreans also assumed a tie between number and reality in astronomy, arguing that the order of the universe reflected musical or mathematical harmonies.

The early Pythagoreans thus linked the four disciplines that would come to make up the quadrivium, although the earliest surviving statement of this fourfold curriculum comes only from the fourth century B.C., when mathematics had already entered a second stage. Its author,

Archytas, who is best known for his musical theory, was a contemporary of Plato and very possibly influenced Plato's adoption of the mathematical arts as the core of his curriculum. The list of mathematical arts varied in different Platonic dialogues, sometimes including stereometry—the study of motionless spheres (in contrast to the moving spheres of astronomy), which we label spherical geometry—and sometimes omitting music. But as the Platonic-Pythagorean tradition became established in Hellenistic thought, the four disciplines we call the quadrivium became canonical.

While the medieval belief that mathematics reveals the order of the universe was rooted in Pythagoreanism, Plato provided it with a metaphysical justification. Plato believed that to be is to be intelligible and that this reality is apprehended through reason. He identified the "really real," the realm of intelligible Being that was eternal and unchanging, with the Forms and distinguished this realm of Being from that of Becoming, known through the senses. He believed one could grasp the world of Forms only after a long program of study and argued, most famously in the *Republic,* that this progressive comprehension required the study of mathematics. Thus arithmetic and geometry became essential disciplines in the Platonic curriculum.

It is often argued that Plato's idealist metaphysics thwarted any possibility of scientific progress. It is true that Plato's interest in mathematics derived more from his philosophy of Being than from a desire to analyze the empirical world. Yet he did believe that in some sense the sensory realm participated in Being, though the exact nature of this participation is perhaps the chief problem in the interpretation of his philosophy. Since the tie between the two realms was most evident in music and astronomy, these disciplines too were essential in the Platonic curriculum.

In fact, Plato's theory of music was more closely tied to actual musical experience than was that of the Pythagoreans; he supplemented their mathematical analysis with the interpretation, primarily in ethical terms, of the actual modes of Greek music.[6] In astronomy, he established both the basic empirical problem of classical astronomy (the explanation of planetary motion) and its basic assumption (that heavenly motion, being perfect, is circular motion at a constant velocity). Although both empirical and rational elements were present in his philosophy, the general effect of his view that science investigates the operation of reason in the universe was to emphasize the search for mathematical laws.

The full influence of the speculative Platonic-Pythagorean tradition on the liberal arts was to be postponed for two centuries, the most creative period in theoretical mathematics and pure science during antiquity. Theoretical astronomy, based on the problem and assumption of Plato, made notable progress, beginning with Eudoxus—a contemporary of Plato who first described the orbits of the planets (including the sun and moon) in terms of the mathematics of the circle. As the first mathematical astronomy, this theory ambiguously combined mathematical and physical concepts, a tension that was never resolved in classical or medieval science.

The history of the other mathematical arts is best understood in terms of the discovery of irrational numbers.[7] The arithmetic and musical theory of the early Pythagoreans clearly assumed that all numbers are rational—an assumption that in geometry entailed the belief that all lengths are commensurable. This phase of mathematics culminated in the late fifth century, when Hippocrates of Chios—according to tradition the first to compile an *Elements*—systematized plane geometry, providing the core for Euclid's later synthesis. But he (or a contemporary) also set the stage for the next phase with the discovery that the hypotenuse of an isosceles right triangle could not be represented as a rational integer—i.e., that the length of the hypotenuse was not commensurable with the sides.

The discovery of irrational numbers affected the various mathematical arts in different ways. In arithmetic, the Greeks apparently were unable to abandon the concept of rational number; thus the Pythagorean approach continued to dominate the art and was transmitted to the Middle Ages by the Latin encyclopedists. Nor were the Greeks willing to accept irrational number in their mathematical analysis of music, a failure that was to lead musical theory further and further away from the analysis of music as actually heard.

Geometry, however, could not avoid the problem of incommensurability; the square root of two clearly exists geometrically—as the hypotenuse of an isosceles right triangle. Perhaps the chief interest of Greek mathematics was the comparison of two or more mathematical entities; thus the central problem became the discovery of a theory that would encompass both rational and irrational numbers. This problem was solved by Eudoxus, equally famous in antiquity as a mathematician and as an astronomer. His generalized theory of proportion provided the capstone for Euclid's treatment of plane geometry.

Eudoxus solved the problem of irrationals by treating numbers as magnitudes rather than as integers—i.e., in terms of greater generality. As a result, however, geometry could no longer be viewed as commensurate with arithmetic. Moreover, this solution ensured that algebra would be treated geometrically, a tendency apparent even among the early Pythagoreans. Thus problems that are today posed in algebraic symbols were represented and solved geometrically throughout antiquity, an approach that persisted through the Middle Ages and the Renaissance and was even employed by Newton in the *Principia,* despite his invention of the calculus. Finally, although mathematics could still serve to describe nature, as Eudoxus's mathematical astronomy demonstrated, the clear-cut tie between number and nature that had been the basis of early Pythagoreanism could no longer be maintained.

This brief analysis of irrational number can serve to conclude the discussion of the quadrivium. Aristotle did make important contributions to Greek science and mathematics, but from the point of view of this essay only two features of his philosophy need to be noted. First, he provided a philosophic justification for the separate treatment of different sciences, maintaining that each science had its own distinctive principles and methods.[8] Second, he viewed mathematics not as a part of philosophy but as preparatory to its study. In the early development of the trivium, however, Aristotle's was the major role.

The Trivium

The development of the verbal arts, with roots going back to the early fifth century, reflected certain fundamental changes in the cultural traditions of the polis.[9] Physical education retained its central role in Greek life, but following Athen's defeat in the Peloponnesian War at the close of the fifth century, music became the exclusive province of the professional performer. With music no longer central to the curriculum, rhetoric emerged as the cornerstone of secondary education and vied with philosophy as the focus of advanced education.

Though its educational preeminence was new, rhetoric had deep roots in Hellenic culture. Indeed, the significance of oratory antedated the classical city-state, the frequent speeches in the *Iliad* attesting to its importance in the society portrayed by Homer. Oratory continued to play an important cultural role in the centuries following Homer— in the Homeric hymns, and in the works of the dramatists and historians.[10]

With the growth of democracy in the fifth century, oratory took on an increased importance in the assembly and in the courts, leading to the appearance of a new professional class, the sophists. Although the sophists taught other subjects, including the mathematical arts, they were best known for their claim to teach the oratorical skills necessary for success in the new political environment. With the systematic treatment of oratory, one may speak of rhetoric.

This development culminated in the establishment of a school of rhetoric by Isocrates at the beginning of the fourth century. (While Plato viewed him as a sophist, and founded the Academy in conscious opposition to his school, Isocrates rejected this label.) Although his school grew out of the practical needs of the polis, Isocrates' influence was to make rhetoric the cornerstone of education for the next several centuries in both Greece and Rome, long after the political decline of the Greek city-state.

The rationalist tradition too entered a new phase in the fifth century, as the emphasis in philosophy shifted from the cosmos to man. Socrates, Cicero remarked in a famous passage, "was the first to call philosophy down from the heavens."[11] Plato's interest in mathematics had in fact grown out of his concern with epistemology, which in turn reflected his—or Socrates'—determination to establish the existence of objective and eternal moral truths in contrast to the moral relativism of the sophists.

Rhetoric was established as an art as a result of these changes in oratory and philosophy. Although the sophists' teaching was generally based on experience (Plato characterized them as merely empirical), they developed several types of rhetorical handbooks: teaching manuals, collections of commonplaces or *topoi* (i.e., examples of rhetorical devices that could be woven into a speech), treatises on rhetorical rules, and collections of actual speeches. This effort to treat oratory systematically can be viewed as the first step in the rationalization of the art.

The next step, Plato's attempt to treat rhetoric systematically, led to the development of dialectic—a term he was the first to use in a technical sense. Originally it meant simply "discussion." The precise origins of the art are obscure, but perhaps the most plausible explanation is that it grew out of the sophists' analysis of opposing arguments.[12] Their willingness to argue on both sides of a question, with its implications of moral relativism and its emphasis on persuasion rather than truth, provoked Plato's antagonism—another example of that deep-rooted opposition to sophistry that characterized his thought.

In an early work, the *Gorgias,* Plato characterized rhetoric, in contrast to philosophy, as a pseudoart. In the *Phaedrus,* however, he appeared to treat rhetoric more sympathetically. In this and certain subsequent dialogues, he sought to establish the principles of a true, or philosophical, rhetoric—which he equated with dialectic and opposed to the false rhetoric of the sophists. While Plato failed to formulate a systematic theory of dialectic, the Socratic dialogues exemplified his concept of the art and served as a model for Aristotle's systematic treatment in the *Topics.* In equating dialectic only with "true" rhetoric, however, Plato in essence maintained the distinction between the two arts.

In contrast, Aristotle viewed rhetoric as the counterpart of dialectic and treated each art in a completely systematic fashion. Thus, with

Aristotle, the rationalist and oratorical traditions clearly merged. His rhetoric took on a new rationalist orientation: while continuing to define rhetoric in traditional terms as the art of persuasion, he shifted the focus to proof, emphasizing the discovery, or invention, of arguments. His analysis of invention, moreover, was based upon his new conception of *topoi* (or commonplaces) developed in the *Topics.* Here too Aristotle's approach was clearly rationalistic since he treated *topoi* as strategies for the discovery of arguments rather than as rhetorical examples.[13]

But the most important influence of the rationalist tradition lay in Aristotle's concern for completeness and generality: rhetoric sought to discover the means of persuasion for all arguments; dialectic sought strategies that would work in any disputation. Most importantly, Aristotle subsumed both arts in a general theory of argument, which he later broadened to include demonstration (itself a general treatment of the laws of thought), and ultimately sophistical arguments.[14] Demonstration, based on true and indemonstrable premises, attains true and certain conclusions; dialectic, a disputative argument using question and answer, is based on premises that are readily believable and is often used to establish the indemonstrable premises of demonstration. Rhetoric, also based upon believable or probable premises, seeks to discover the means of persuasion for any argument.

Aristotle's theory of demonstration reflected the rationalist impulse not only in its impulse to generality but more importantly in its self-reflexive intent to justify the axiomatic-deductive system. Aristotle's claim to be the first to do this can be accepted, but his theory rested on a long tradition that included examples of deductive reasoning as well as preliminary attempts to analyze and justify this method.[15]

Probably the greatest stimulus to the development of Aristotle's theory of demonstration was the success of the axiomatic-deductive method in mathematics, but Plato's contribution was almost as important. Of most significance for this essay are the implications of Plato's metaphysics. His assumption that to be is to be intelligible provides the ground for a belief in necessary connections in reality, the existence of which makes valid inference possible; the correlative assumption that reality is apprehended by reason helps explain his philosophy of language. For Plato, words express the essences of things grasped in thought as concepts, a belief that led him to emphasize essential definitions. Words are combined into sentences (or propositions), the relations between words (or concepts) reflecting the necessary connections in reality.[16]

Plato's theory of language was worked out in that group of dialogues devoted to the theory of dialectic. He rejected the sophists' view that language was merely conventional in favor of the belief that words and things were integrally related; yet he never satisfactorily explained this relationship—a problem that presents much the same difficulty as the relation between the Forms and the realm of Becoming. Aristotle in general accepted this view of the tie between language and the world. Thus it is not surprising that Hellenistic scholars would arrange his logic in a way that presented it as a logic of terms.

The emergence of rhetoric and logic from the confluence of the rationalist and oratorical traditions reflected a general interest in language. While the tie between nature and number was being rejected in theoretical mathematics, a theory of language arose that stressed the tie between nature and the word. In this it was analogous to the speculative mathematics of the Pythagorean-Platonic tradition, which continued to equate nature and number. This fact perhaps helps explain the eventual association of the trivium and the quadrivium.

This concern with language also occasioned the first discussions of grammar. Many of the fundamental topics of grammar were first analyzed during the Hellenic period, but always in the context of rhetoric or logic.[17] Grammar would be treated systematically as a distinct art only in the Hellenistic Age.

II. THE HELLENISTIC AGE

The years following the death of Alexander the Great saw the cultural preeminence of the polis give way to a cosmopolitan culture extending throughout the lands ruled by Alexander's successors. From the perspective of intellectual history, the Hellenistic Age may be said to have continued through the first two centuries of the Roman Empire, the period of the Pax Romana.

The cultural traditions of this cosmopolitan society were more heterogeneous than those of the Hellenic Age. The most significant fact for the development of the liberal arts was the contrast—most striking in science—between creative scholarship and works of popularization. A contemporary scholar has emphasized what might be called the schizophrenic nature of the age:

> It is a curious phenomenon, and one that may have implications for other times and places, that the Hellenistic Age (323-30 B.C.), which is credited with producing the most significant achievements of the Greeks, is also to be debited with the full development of the popularization movement which, more than any other factor, was responsible for the subsequent decay of ancient science.[18]

While valid in regard to Greek scholarship, this judgment—if Roman thought is to be included in the Hellenistic Age—overlooks an important contribution of the popularization movement. Given the pragmatic nature of Rome's cultural traditions, it seems unlikely that theoretical science would have flourished in Rome. The popularization movement deserves credit for the transmission of Greek science to the Romans, and through them (though in even more elementary form) to the Middle Ages.

To speak of the works of scientific popularization in terms of the transmission of knowledge is suggestive. The Greek legacy to Rome was not limited to science; the contrast between scholarship and popularization can be construed in broader terms. In fact, three facets of Greek scholarship can be identified as significant for the development of the liberal arts. In the Hellenistic Age, in contrast to the Hellenic, philosophy and science developed separately. Athens remained the chief center for philosophy, while Alexandria emerged as the center for science. And at the same time that science flourished at the Alexandrian Museum, a new concept of literary scholarship was forged at the Alexandrian Library. The period of creativity in all three strands was quite brief. Philosophy lapsed into an age of eclecticism and scepticism, and Alexandrian science and scholarship gave way to an age of handbooks and encyclopedic compendia.

Thus the popularization movement was a general feature of the age. In part it grew out of the speculative Platonic-Pythagorean tradition that developed separately from theoretical mathematics and pure science; in part it grew out of the needs of primary and secondary education. In the Hellenistic Age the curriculum became more or less standardized and the concept of an *enkuklios paideia,* a circle of knowledge, became common.[19]

Greek Scholarship

Four major schools of philosophy flourished in Athens during the Hellenistic Age, after Stoicism and Epicureanism emerged in the third century as rivals to the schools originally founded by Plato and Aristotle. The philosophies of these schools, especially those of the two new ones, addressed the problems occasioned by the political collapse of the polis and the emergence of a new cosmopolitan society. Yet it was the Stoics' new interpretation of logic that most directly influenced the development of the liberal arts.[20]

In contrast to Aristotle—who viewed logic, like mathematics, as preparatory to philosophy—the Stoics regarded logic as a branch of philosophy, along with physics and ethics. They interpreted logic broadly as the verbal arts, a view they inherited from the Megarians—a school founded by Euclid of Megara, one of the disciples of Socrates. The Stoics divided logic into dialectic, grammar, and rhetoric, and were thus the first scholars to view the three disciplines of the trivium as a unity.

Stoic logic, a logic of propositions similar to the modern propositional calculus, had probably achieved its basic form by the time of Chrysippus, the leader of the school at the end of the third century. Though it differed markedly from Aristotle's logic of terms, it was nevertheless absorbed into Aristotelian logic under the rubric of the hypothetical syllogism.

The Stoics' logic of propositions was part of a more general theory of signification. They distinguished between the sign or "thing signifying," the significate or "thing meant," and the material object—roughly corresponding to the contemporary distinction between a sentence, its connotation, and its denotation. Significates (*lekta*) were further analyzed into incomplete lekta (subjects and predicates) and complete lekta, of which the most important were propositions. (Complete lekta also included such subtopics as questions and commands.) The analysis of "things signifying" included a discussion of the parts of speech, leading to a philosophic investigation of grammar. Thus, although grammatical issues had been raised in Hellenic treatises on rhetoric and logic, it was a Stoic, Crates, who in the first century B.C. wrote the first systematic grammar. This grammar was introduced to Rome when Crates, who had been injured while serving as an envoy to Rome, remained there as a lecturer.

The brilliant achievements in mathematics and science during the two centuries following Aristotle had only an indirect influence on the development of the liberal arts.[21] The mathematical analysis of planetary motion, the central problem of classical astronomy, was beyond the comprehension of the Latin encyclopedists and unknown during most of the Middle Ages. Even during the Hellenistic period, the most popular astronomical work, a Greek poem written early in the third century by Aratus of Soli, was simply a description of the constellations. A Latin translation of this poem would serve as one of the principal sources of the Latin encyclopedists. Yet the basically descriptive astronomy of the liberal arts tradition did incorporate certain discoveries of Hellenistic astronomy; of these, the most important were the size of the sun and moon and their distances from the earth. An analogous problem in geography, the size of the earth, also became part of the liberal arts tradition. Often treated separately by the Latin encyclopedists, geography was occasionally included in discussions of geometry

—compensating perhaps for the omission of Euclid's technical discussions.[22]

Of the three most important mathematicians of the third century, indeed of all antiquity, only Euclid played a significant role in the liberal arts tradition, and that of a peculiar kind. Euclid was perhaps less an original thinker than a systematizer of the received tradition. Yet, as a synthesis, his *Elements* was a work of genius—perhaps the most important handbook in European intellectual history—and remained the basic text for the study of geometry until the late nineteenth century. Although his geometry, like mathematical astronomy, was too complex to be understood by the Latin encyclopedists, they typically made some vague references to it. Geometry continued to be identified with Euclid throughout the Middle Ages, in artistic representations of the liberal arts as well as in the handbooks.

Perhaps the sustained association of Euclid with the liberal arts tradition throughout the Middle Ages can be explained by his tie with the Platonic-Pythagorean tradition. He was educated in the Platonic Academy in Athens; and the *Elements,* as a synthesis of that tradition, included both arithmetic and geometry. The sections on geometry, moreover, were based on the Platonic principle that only the compass and straightedge were to be used for geometric constructions. Thus the *Elements* omitted any consideration of a set of three related problems (trisecting an angle, squaring a circle, and doubling a cube) that could not be solved by these means. The investigation of these problems (which had exercised the Greeks from the fourth century B.C.) by Archimedes and Apollonius, the other two great mathematicians of the third century, gave rise to the geometry of conic sections. That the study of the *Elements* became the central concern of mathematics following the recovery of Greek learning in the twelfth and thirteenth centuries, while the full influence of Archimedes was not felt until the Renaissance, is perhaps explained by the continued association of Euclid's name with the liberal arts throughout the early Middle Ages.

Euclid's treatise on music is further evidence of his tie with the Platonic-Pythagorean tradition, with its broad conception of the mathematical arts. Probably based on Archytas, the *Section of the Canon* "contains our first preserved account of the complete system of Pythagorean harmonics."[23] This work of Euclid would be discussed centuries later by Boethius in his *De musica,* the central document in music theory in the medieval arts tradition. To modern musicologists, however, the most important musical theorist of the third century was Aristoxenes. While he too analyzed music in mathematical terms, his theory was based upon music as it was actually heard. Yet his theory had little subsequent influence. For whatever cause, musical theory became increasingly divorced from musical practice and dominated by the mathematical approach of the Pythagoreans. This mathematical approach, which went well with the Christian emphasis on divine order, continued to prevail in the musical theory of the Middle Ages.

Alexandrian scholarship, which took an empirical approach to grammar, influenced Roman and medieval grammatical theory more than did the philosophical grammar of the Stoics. The founders of the Alexandrian Library were poets who believed their art would benefit from the study of past poetry, especially that of Homer. Their recognition that the language of the Hellenic Age differed from contemporary usage and was in danger of becoming unintelligible forced them to become scholars as well as poets.[24]

Their scholarship involved several tasks—the editing of texts, literary criticism, investigation of the meaning of words, and antiquarian research—all with roots in the Hellenic past. Perhaps as a result of this complexity, toward the mid-second century scholarship broke off from creative writing. The interest in grammar arose within this context, but it was only in the first century B.C. that Dionysius of Thrax (influenced to some extent by the more philosophical approach of the Stoics) developed a plan for a systematic grammar.

The creative period of Alexandrian scholarship ended with the despotic rule of Ptolemy IV in the first century B.C. Dionysius fled to Rhodes, where this second grammatical tradition became known to Roman students. It is also probable that some of Dionysius's followers fled directly to Rome, carrying his theory with them.

With the suppression of learning by Ptolemy IV and the resulting dispersion of scholars, the great age of Alexandrian science and scholarship came to an end; compilers and popularizers increasingly dominated intellectual life. Yet the second century A.D., at the very end of the Hellenistic Age, saw a brief scholarly revival at Alexandria. Although Ptolemy, its best known representative, made substantial contributions to optics, geography, and music, his most influential work was the *Almagest*—the work that marked the culmination of mathematical astronomy in antiquity. His role in the history of the liberal arts was similar to Euclid's: while his mathematical astronomy was too complex to be understood during the early Middle Ages, his name was always associated with astronomy; as a result astronomers were quick to turn their attention to the *Almagest* following the recovery of Greek learning during the twelfth and thirteenth centuries.

If Ptolemy can thus be compared to Euclid, the most important mathematicians of this brief Alexandrian revival can be compared to Archimedes in that the impact of their thought would not be felt until the Renaissance. Diophantus was the first Greek to treat algebra arithmetically. Although verbal statements of algebraic problems were known in the time of Archimedes, Diophantus was the first to express them in a symbolic form that anticipated modern algebra.[25] Pappus, in the third century A.D., in his investigations of the three problems of higher geometry, systematized the theory of conic sections.

The Dissemination of Greek Learning

The Greek tradition of creative scholarship would contribute to the formation of the medieval arts through the handbooks and compendia of the popularizers. Since it is obviously beyond the scope of this essay to discuss these works exhaustively, I shall limit my discussion to those traditions and scholars that most influenced the development of the liberal arts.[26]

Prominent among the popularizers of Hellenistic science was the Greek encyclopedist Posidonius. The most influential Stoic of his age and one of its most characteristic scholars, he contributed substantially to the growing influence of Greek thought in Rome. Posidonius's school at Rhodes was especially popular with Romans, who (following their exposure to Greek culture in the second century B.C.) customarily sent their children to study in Greece. His thought evidenced the decaying fortunes of Greek philosophy; by the second century, Stoicism had become eclectic, incorporating elements of Platonism and Aristotelianism. Moreover, Posidonius belonged to the long-standing tradition of the polymath, or universal scholar. The term "polymath" was generally used pejoratively—of Pythagoras by Heraclitus and of the sophist Hippias by Plato—yet the tradition also included Aristotle, with whom Posidonius can be compared in influence. "Nothing less than that sort of comparison would be adequate to indicate the influence of Posidonius upon later compilers."[27]

It is, in fact, only through the works of these compilers that Posidonius's scientific thought can be known. Perhaps his most influential book was a commentary on Plato's *Timaeus*. This work was the direct source of a number of later commentaries, including those of Porphyry and Chalcidius; the latter's treatise would be the chief source during the Middle Ages for the knowledge of Plato.

Posidonius also helped stimulate a revival of Pythagoreanism in the first century B.C. For the history of the liberal arts, the most important contribution of this neo-Pythagorean movement, which lasted over two centuries, was the *Introduction to Arithmetic* of Nicomachus.[28] This work, basically a systematization of the arithmetical tradition inaugurated by the early Pythagoreans, displayed little originality. Yet it was probably the best of its kind, and Boethius did little more than translate Nicomachus's treatise in his *De arithmetica,* the central document for medieval arithmetic.

I have already discussed the roles of Crates and Dionysius of Thrax in the transmission of grammar to Rome. Cicero called attention to the similar dependence of Rome on Greek rhetoric:

> When our empire over all the races had been established and enduring peace made leisure possible, there was hardly an ambitious young man who did not think he should strive with all zeal for the ability to speak. At first, ignorant of the whole study, since they did not realize the existence of any course or exercises or rules of art, they did what they could with their own native ability and reflection. Afterwards, when they had heard the Greek orators and become acquainted with Greek literature and had studied with learned Greeks, our countrymen took fire with an incredible zeal for speaking.[29]

It is generally agreed that Hermagoras of Temnos shaped the tradition from which Roman rhetoric derived. Writing in the second century B.C., he developed the art as a complete system, establishing the topics that would be accepted as canonical throughout the long history of the rhetorical tradition.[30]

Roman Thought

The cultural traditions of Rome are usually described in such terms as "pragmatic" or "practical"; and its chief contributions are said to be in law and architecture (as well as engineering, military science, and politics—if one interprets the concept of culture broadly). The Romans contributed little to the development of theoretical science or mathematics; in keeping with their general pragmatic approach, they emphasized practical mathematics. But since their curriculum was based on the *enkuklios paideia* of the Greeks, it is probable that they studied the compendia and handbooks of the Greek popularizers (and perhaps even some more advanced texts, such as Euclid's *Elements*). In adapting Greek grammar to Latin, the Romans did improve on the inherited theory; but it was in rhetoric that they made their most substantial contribution to the liberal arts. Thus rhetoric should be given a prominent place in any discussion of Roman cultural traditions.[31]

Varro, one of the two leading intellectual figures of the first century B.C., introduced the Posidonian encyclopedic tradition to Rome. He is believed to have written more than seventy works, only two of which are extant. His encyclopedic *Nine Books of Disciplines* was especially important in the history of the liberal arts. For one thing, it first established a canon of the liberal arts, which for Varro included medicine and architecture; for another, it served as the basic source for Martianus Capella, one of the most influential of the Latin encyclopedists.

Varro contributed substantially to the development of grammar, establishing the theories of declension and conjugation for Latin, a task that had not yet been fully accomplished for Greek. He is better known, however, for his role in Roman science, for which his writings set the tone; he "became the prototype for a host of pedestrian Latin scholars who, through reading in many fields and digesting or excerpting the works of earlier scholars . . . expected to gain a reputation for learning."[32] Of such scholars, perhaps the most important for medieval intellectual history was Pliny the Elder, who deliberately set out to emulate Varro's vast learning. His work was much less theoretical than Varro's, reflecting a childlike but wide-ranging curiosity. The thirty-seven volumes of Pliny's *Natural History* became the major source for the knowledge of Roman science during the Middle Ages, and it is indicative of medieval taste that his work, rather than Varro's, was preserved. That Pliny was best known through a later single-volume abridgement is even more indicative of the lack of sophistication in medieval scholarship.

Cicero, the other leading scholar of the first century B.C., made his chief contribution to the liberal arts in rhetoric. Although his rhetoric derived from the philosophic tradition of Aristotle and the Stoics, he adopted the topics of Hermagoras, which would become standard in Roman and medieval rhetoric. His early treatise, the *De inventione,* and the anonymous *Rhetorica ad Herennium* (attributed to him by medieval scholars) became the basic sources for the study of rhetoric during the Middle Ages. His more mature rhetoric, the *De oratore,* would not be rediscovered until the Italian Renaissance.[33]

The most complete treatise on rhetoric, the *Institutes* of Quintilian, was written during the first century A.D., when political developments in the empire were already undercutting the practical importance of the art. Like Cicero's *De oratore,* this work was unknown during the Middle Ages and was rediscovered by Renaissance humanists. Nevertheless it played a crucial, if indirect, role in the development of the medieval arts. A synthesis of existing theory and practice, the *Institutes* was intended as a pedagogic handbook. It established a model that, despite its growing inappropriateness, would last throughout the Middle Ages and well into the Renaissance.

The *Institutes* included a lengthy discussion of grammar, which preceded rhetoric in both Greek and Roman education. Quintilian discussed both systematic grammar and the exposition of texts, reflecting contemporary practice. The Latin encyclopedists, however, restricted their discussions to systematic grammar—as did Donatus and Priscian, whose treatises served as the primary sources for the study of grammar throughout the Middle Ages. But these authors belong to the following age.

III. THE AGE OF TRANSITION

The military anarchy and economic crisis of the third century A.D. began a period of transition that saw the dissolution of the Roman Empire and the emergence of the medieval world. From the perspective of political, social, and economic history, the transition was gradual, extending over several centuries. Intellectually, however, the change was abrupt. The rational and this-worldly attitude that had characterized classical culture gave way almost overnight to its complete antithesis. Intellectual life came to be dominated by other-worldly philosophies and religions, characterized by a reliance on faith and revelation, by mysticism and magic. Yet classical traditions continued to shape popular culture, especially education, providing the matrix for the establishment of the canon of medieval arts in the fifth and sixth centuries.[34]

The Age of Handbooks

The strength of this new other-worldly attitude was evidenced during the third and fourth centuries by the rapid growth of Neoplatonism in philosophy and the triumph of Christianity in religion. Educational treatises, however, continued to reflect the intellectual climate of the previous age. These handbooks were almost wholly without originality so that Gibbon speaks of the "cloud of critics, of compilers, of commentators that darkened the face of learning."[35] The mediocrity of the handbooks in part reflected the fact that the creative intellectual energies of the age were absorbed in other-worldly pursuits and in part reflected the political decline of the empire. While rhetoric remained the cornerstone of education, and continued to be based upon Quintilian's *Institutes*, it was now divorced from practical affairs. The rhetoric of this age is usually described in terms of its emphasis on declamation, which had become little more than a rhetorical exercise, or in terms of the second sophistic, which stressed stylistic embellishment.

While these handbooks would provide the basic materials for the Latin encyclopedists, few were significant in themselves. A handful did, however, contribute substantially to medieval thought. Most important were the two fourth-century handbooks of Donatus, which became the standard texts for the study of grammar. The *De partibus orationis* (*Ars minor*), which would serve as the basic introductory text, was a very succinct treatment of the eight parts of speech; the *Ars grammatica* (*Ars maior*) was a more extensive and advanced treatment of the art.

Two other handbooks from this period remained quite influential throughout the Middle Ages. Both reflected the intellectual decay of the age in that they simplified previous works that were in themselves mere compilations. Solinus, accurately assessing the demands of the times, reduced Pliny's multivolume *Natural History* to a single volume that emphasized the most curious features of that work. Chalcidius's translation (with commentary) of the *Timaeus* was almost wholly derivative from the Posidonian tradition; yet it was the primary source for a knowledge of Plato during the Middle Ages.

The Latin Encyclopedists

The writings of the Latin encyclopedists constituted perhaps the most distinctive genre from the fifth through the early seventh century.[36] They combined the prevailing intellectual traditions of Neoplatonism and Christianity with the handbook tradition of popular culture— joining the two strands that had developed separately during the previous two centuries. Thus would the classical tradition be transmitted to the Middle Ages; and thus would the canon of the seven liberal arts be established at the center of medieval intellectual life.

Given the political chaos resulting from the Germanic invasions and the lack of communication with Greek scholars following the division of the Roman Empire, the danger was real that classical learning would disappear in the West. The Latin encyclopedists were motivated, at least in part, by a conscious effort to preserve this intellectual heritage. The task of preservation would seem to demand some interpretive or organizing principle; and for this the Latin encyclopedists adopted the concept of the seven liberal arts—a principle that would establish the basic organization of knowledge until the recovery of Greek learning. The encyclopedists used this organizing principle, however, in conjunction with the prevailing systems of knowledge and belief—Neoplatonism and Christianity.

Neoplatonism was itself an all-embracing system of knowledge. Neoplatonists often made a deliberate effort to incorporate all existing learning into their philosophy, perhaps to provide an alternative to Christianity. In the fifth and sixth centuries, several Latin Neoplatonists contributed substantially to the development of the liberal arts concept.

While Chalcidius is sometimes included among these scholars, I have preferred to treat him as part of the fourth-century handbook tradition. Priscian, who composed several treatises on grammar and rhetoric in the early sixth century, has also been included among the encyclopedists. The *Institutiones grammaticae,* his best-known work, served the Middle Ages as an advanced grammatical text, along with Donatus's *Ars maior.* However, the Neoplatonic encyclopedists who most influenced the development of the liberal arts were Macrobius and Martianus Capella.

Macrobius's *Saturnalia* and *Commentary on the Dream of Scipio* were known throughout the Middle Ages. While Macrobius did not use the seven liberal arts as an explicit organizing principle, these two works together touch on almost all the arts. The *Saturnalia* seems intended primarily as a display of Macrobius's wide scholarship. Its basic theme, an appreciation of Vergil, provided the opportunity for discussion of grammar and rhetoric, as well as of Vergil's knowledge of astronomy and philosophy. The *Commentary on the Dream of Scipio,* according to its modern translator, "is not so much a commentary as it is an encyclopedia of general information and an exposition of the basic doctrines of Neoplatonism." Almost half was devoted to astronomy; the remainder included discussions of arithmetic and music.

The *Marriage of Philology and Mercury* by Martianus Capella was explicitly organized in terms of the seven liberal arts. Based on Varro's *Nine Books of Disciplines,* it was the first work to set out the seven liberal arts as we know them, establishing the canon for medieval learning. The work is an elaborate allegory. The marriage symbolizes, at least according to the Carolingian commentators, the union of learning (Philology) and eloquence (Mercury), corresponding to the disciplines of the quadrivium and the trivium. The first two books set the scene; each subsequent book presents a speech by one of the seven bridesmaids, who personify the liberal arts. In these latter books the allegory plays a minor role, and the speeches are little more than digests of the handbook tradition.

The *Marriage of Philology and Mercury* was to have its greatest influence during the ninth and tenth centuries. It would not have attained this importance, however, had not certain Christian encyclopedists also adopted the liberal arts concept. And this development might seem surprising. The liberal arts, after all, derived from the pagan tradition; and one influential group of Christians believed that all pagan learning was a danger to the faith.[37] Since, however, Christianity was a "book" religion, as well as one that tended to incorporate opposing religions and philosophies, its acceptance of the curriculum of classical education was perhaps inevitable.

Of the church fathers, St. Augustine played the most important role in this process of assimilation. Although St. Augustine was ambiguous in his attitude toward the liberal arts, his early adherence to Neoplatonism and his training and experience as a rhetorician are clearly reflected in his writings. Thus his work reveals the influence of the most basic cultural traditions of his age. It is appropriate to include Augustine in a discussion of the Latin encyclopedists because he too adopted the liberal arts as an organizing principle, proposing to write separate treatises on each art (including architecture but not astronomy). While he completed only the treatise on grammar, his treatise on music (an early work in which the influence of Neoplatonism is especially clear) was nearly complete. In addition, Book IV of *On Christian Doctrine,* written late in his life, was a treatise on rhetoric from a Christian point of view.[38]

Boethius, a Roman who served in Theodoric's court, was, like St. Augustine, influenced by both Neoplatonism and Christianity; Boethius's best known work, the *Consolation of Philosophy,* written in prison while he was awaiting death for treason, would in fact seem to be more Platonic than Christian. His earlier proposal to translate the complete works of Plato and Aristotle seems clearly motivated by a desire to preserve classical learning. His imprisonment prevented the realization of this plan (if it were indeed possible), but his translations and original treatises were the most learned works available to medieval scholars until the recovery of Greek scholarship during the twelfth and thirteenth centuries. That he was the most significant encyclopedist will become clear to the reader of the essays in this volume, in almost all of which Boethius plays a central role.

Boethius would have his greatest impact in the High Middle Ages, during the period of intellectual revival that preceded the recovery of Greek learning. More influential in the period immediately following the Age of Encyclopedists was Cassiodorus—who, unlike Boethius, survived his service in Theodoric's court. His popularity is probably explained by the relative simplicity of his treatise, a short work incorporating brief, schematic summaries of each liberal art—a form that was particularly appropriate to a relatively backward age. (Martianus Capella, whose popularity peaked in the ninth and tenth centuries, had adopted a similar organization in the *Marriage of Philology and Mercury.*)

An Introduction to Divine and Human Readings consisted of two books, the first devoted to sacred knowledge, the second to the seven liberal arts. Cassiodorus's advocacy of the liberal arts as a necessary component of Christian education was decisive for the assimilation of the liberal arts within Christian culture. The library and the scholarly routine of the monastery he founded at Vivarium upon retiring from Theodoric's service also exemplified his recognition of the need for classical learning. Moreover, his organization of texts as a codex, a collection of various works devoted to a single art within a single manuscript, was "designed to promote and facilitate the study of the liberal arts."[39]

Pierre Riché has argued that the ancient educational system survived through almost the entire age of transition. The traditional schools of the grammarians and rhetoricians remained open—in Italy, Gaul, Africa, and Spain—following the barbarian invasions. And when the schools finally did close, the classical tradition was kept alive on the estates of the great aristocratic families. At the same time, classical education continued to exert a strong influence on Christianity. The final chapter of this confluence of classical and Christian cultures occurred in Spain during the first few decades of the seventh century. Isidore of Seville, the central figure of this "Spanish Renaissance," devoted the first three books of his *Etymologies* to the liberal arts. The last heir of ancient learning, he brought to a close the period of the Latin encyclopedists.[40] Along with the works of Martianus Capella and Cassiodorus, the *Etymologies* became one of the standard educational handbooks of the Middle Ages; and like Martianus and Cassidorus, Isidore was most influential in the age that immediately followed.

IV. THE CAROLINGIAN RENAISSANCE

If there is any period for which the term "Dark Ages" is appropriate, it is that time between the early seventh century and Charlemagne. The economic and political fragmentation that began in the third century resulted in an economy of self-sufficient estates and a decentralized political system. Given the disappearance of trade and urban culture, it is not surprising that intellectual life decayed.[41]

By the seventh century, Christianity had become the dominant, if not the exclusive, cultural tradition in the West; the literature of the next few centuries was characterized by theological controversy, biblical exegesis, and hagiography. In an age almost devoid of philosophy, in which the chief concern was to absorb and preserve a now foreign scholarly tradition, the liberal arts took on a preeminent role. And since Latin—the language of scholarship—was no longer a living language, grammar emerged as the central art.[42] If one peruses the relevant chapters in Laistner's *Thought and Letters in Western Europe: A.D. 500-900*, one observes that almost every scholar of this age was known for his grammatical studies. That scholarly activity was virtually limited to grammar at this time is in itself a commentary on the state of scholarship.

Ireland and Britain, however, stand out as exceptions to this general picture. In these lands, in contrast to continental Europe, intellectual life flourished during the seventh century; in fact, the greatest scholar of this age was an Englishman, the Venerable Bede. Bede is occasionally included within the encyclopedist tradition, but he more properly belongs to this age. His commentaries on the Old and New Testaments were quite remarkable for the period, and his *Ecclesiastical History of the English People* has justifiably become a classic of medieval historiography. His writings devoted to the verbal arts, however, were typical products of the age—compilations based upon the standard sources. Nevertheless, they would serve as essential building blocks for the cultural revival inaugurated by Charlemagne.[43] His treatises on ecclesiastical chronology, which grew out of his concern with the dating of Easter, were of even greater significance in the history of medieval astronomy.

At the end of the eighth century, the political fragmentation of Europe was temporarily checked by Charlemagne, who was able to establish limited centralized control. This political recovery led to a scholarly "Renaissance" when Charlemagne, turning to the Northumbrian Alcuin for leadership, actively promoted education in the monasteries and in his court.

The political centralization imposed by Charlemagne quickly collapsed following his death, in an epoch marked by civil war and new invasions. The intellectual revival continued, however, reaching its zenith during the ninth century. The liberal arts continued to play the predominant role in intellectual life, since the long-term neglect of scholarship made it necessary for all scholars to concentrate on the fundamentals of education. Grammar, including the study of literature as well as of language, remained the dominant art. Scholars typically prepared textbooks, based on standard sources, for the use of their own students. Instruction in rhetoric and dialectic was even more rudimentary; it depended largely on the extremely elementary treatises, in dialogue form, composed by Alcuin at the beginning of this educational revival. The quadrivium was almost totally ignored, contemporary scholars relying solely upon the encyclopedias of the previous period. The most characteristic work of the age was the commentary, with Martianus Capella's *Marriage of Philology and Mercury* by far the most popular subject for such treatment. In the ninth century, three such commentaries stand out as the central documents for a history of the liberal arts.[44] The author of one of these, John Scotus Erigena, is generally regarded as the only creative philosopher of the age; yet even he was first of all a grammarian.

V. THE HIGH MIDDLE AGES

The first three centuries of the second millennium, the culmination of the Middle Ages, form a distinct period in European history. The anarchy of the post-Carolingian age came to an end in the tenth century, and Europe entered a period of recovery that, once underway, continued unabated in all aspects of life until the end of the thirteenth century. The following age, whether it be identified as late medieval or Renaissance, clearly marks a new stage.

R. W. Southern sees the recovery in Western Europe as beginning with two events: the battle of Leche in 955, when Otto the Great—who would found the Holy Roman Empire—turned back the Magyar invasion of Europe; and Gerbert's journey to Rheims in 972 after he felt called to the study of logic. The latter event is especially significant for this essay since the shift from grammar to logic as the dominant art of the trivium is a central feature in the history of the liberal arts.[45]

In a later essay Southern uses a single, all-embracing concept, "medieval humanism," to identify a period from 1100 to 1320. For Southern, "humanism" connotes an emphasis on human dignity and rationality as well as a belief in the order and intelligibility of nature.[46] While this concept does call attention to certain dominant characteristics of the age, it slights the Christian worldview within which these features operated. If the term "humanism" is to be used, I would prefer it as an adjective, modifying "Christianity." The term "humanistic Christianity" would emphasize both the continued dominance of Christianity and the contrast to the asceticism of the early Middle Ages—a contrast that reflects an inherent tension within Christianity, illustrated most essentially by the dual nature of Christ.[47]

I also prefer to adopt Gerbert's journey to Rheims as the beginning of this period (i.e., 972 rather than 1100), not only because of its association with logic, but also because Gerbert—the most distinguished scholar of his time, and the future Pope Sylvester II—played a leading role in both the Twelfth Century Renaissance and the recovery of Greek learning. While these two movements are best understood as successive stages in the intellectual recovery of the High Middle Ages, they can also be viewed as two general aspects of this revival, with the roots of both going back to Gerbert in the late tenth century.

The Twelfth Century Renaissance

One of the principal features of the Twelfth Century Renaissance was a renewed interest in, and a more sophisticated understanding of, the liberal arts—including the mathematical arts, which had been neglected during the early Middle Ages.[48] Gerbert's newly awakened concern with logic may be taken to symbolize the beginning of this heightened appreciation. The study of the liberal arts continued to depend on the Latin encyclopedists, with Boethius playing an increasingly important role. Martianus's influence declined, except for his discussion of astronomy, the most informed section in the *Marriage of Philology and Mercury,* and the most satisfactory treatment of astronomy available before the recovery of Greek learning. Cassiodorus and Isidore of Seville also played less important roles during this period, as is evidenced by the apparent lack of manuscript copies of their works after the tenth century.

Gerbert's most direct contribution to this revival lay in his teaching. His curricular reforms were responsible for the increased importance of Boethius's logical works. Even more significant was Gerbert's influence on his students, who disseminated his thought through their own teaching. Many of these students founded or directed cathedral schools, the chief centers of learning in the eleventh and twelfth centuries.

Traditionally, Chartres has been viewed as the most eminent of the cathedral schools of the twelfth century.[49] At Chartres, noted for its contributions to both the verbal and the mathematical arts, the liberal arts attained their greatest prestige during the Middle Ages; at Chartres, also, Plato's thought attained its greatest influence. These two facts are probably related—for the liberal arts tradition, especially in the mathematical disciplines, had always been closely associated with Platonism.

While the liberal arts were regarded as preparatory studies, the scholarship devoted to them was as important as that devoted to theology; in fact, the philosophical and theological doctrines of such scholars as Anselm or Abelard can be understood only against the background of the liberal arts. The liberal arts were indeed more than merely preparatory:

> The seven liberal arts together give man both knowledge of the divine and power to express it. But, in so doing, they fulfill at the same time another purpose. They serve ad cultum humanitatis, that is, they promote the specifically human values, revealing to man his place in the universe and teaching him to appreciate the beauty of the created world.[50]

The Recovery of Greek Learning

The thirteenth century, a period of consolidation and increasing rigidity following the spontaneity and innovation of the twelfth century, marked the zenith of medieval Christianity, both for the church and in intellectual life. In this essay, with its focus on the liberal arts, I have often emphasized the recovery of Greek learning. Although this recovery was foreshadowed at the time of Gerbert, the Twelfth Century Renaissance stimulated a desire for knowledge beyond the rather rudimentary level it had attained with its limited sources. The recovery of Greek scholarship was actually but one aspect of a complex of interrelated events: thought became increasingly systematic, as evidenced by Scholasticism; Aristotle's influence clearly superseded that of Plato; and the university replaced the cathedral school as the center of learning. This complex development constituted the most decisive change in the liberal arts since the period of the Latin encyclopedists.[51]

During the early Middle Ages, when Greek scholarship was unavailable in the West, Moslem scholars had translated much of Greek philosophy and science into Arabic. Beginning in the tenth century, a few of these Arabic works were translated into Latin, a process that was accelerated following the military resurgence of Europe. Toledo, after its fall to the West in 1085, became the major center for translation; here translations were generally based upon Arabic sources, sometimes through the mediation of Spanish or Hebrew. Sicily, where ties with the Byzantine Empire had been maintained, became the chief center for translations directly from the Greek, following the victory of 1091 over the Arabs.[52]

With the rise of universities, the liberal arts clearly became subordinate to the study of philosophy and theology.[53] Yet the recovery of Greek learning led to significant changes in the arts. The curriculum itself was broadened—very possibly because the medieval arts had retained the formal structure of Greek scholarship and had kept alive the names of scholars such as Euclid and Ptolemy, even while their works were unknown. In fact, there was no longer the sharp division between the liberal arts and pure scholarship that had characterized the classical world; Euclid's *Elements,* Ptolemy's *Almagest,* and all of Aristotle's logic were now explicitly included in the liberal arts curriculum. For the liberal arts, the thirteenth century was perhaps less a creative age than one in which classical scholarship was relearned and mastered. Yet the reintroduction of Greek learning gave rise to problems, the solution of which would occupy the following age and contribute to the emergence of the modern world.

NOTES

1. The standard history in English of Greek philosophy is W. K. C. Guthrie, *A History of Greek Philosophy,* 3 vols. (Cambridge, 1962-69). For the Presocratics, see G. S. Kirk and J. E. Raven, *The Presocratic Philosophers* (Cambridge, 1957).
More useful for the development of the quadrivium are histories of Greek science: Marshall Clagett, *Greek Science in Antiquity* (New York, 1955); Morris R. Cohen and I. E. Drabkin, *A Source Book in Greek Science* (Cambridge, Mass., 1948); Giorgio de Santillana, *The Origins of Scientific Thought: From Anaximander to Proclus, 600 B.C. to 300 A.D.* (London, 1961); G. E. R. Lloyd, *Early Greek Science: Thales to Aristotle* (London, 1961); O. Neugebauer, *The Exact Sciences in Antiquity,* 2nd ed. (1957; repr. New York, 1969); S. Sambursky, *The Physical World of the Greeks,* trans. Merton Dagut (New York, 1956); George Sarton, *A History of Science,* 2 vols. (Cambridge, Mass., 1952-59); B. L. van der Waerden, *Science Awakening,* trans. Arnold Dresden (New York, 1961).
2. See the introduction by Norman O. Brown, trans., *Theogony,* by Hesiod (Indianapolis, 1953), which explicates Hesiod's myth in rationalist terms.
3. For discussion of this point, see Lloyd, *Early Greek Science,* pp. 8-10.
4. In addition to the general histories of science cited in note 1 above, see Sir Thomas Heath, *A History of Greek Mathematics,* 2 vols. (Oxford, 1921). An excellent general history of mathematics is E. T. Bell, *The Development of Mathematics* (New York, 1945).
5. Walter Burkert, *Lore and Science in Ancient Pythagoreanism,* trans. E. L. Minar, Jr. (Cambridge, Mass., 1972); J. A. Philip, *Pythagoras and Early Pythagoreanism* (Toronto, 1966).
6. The standard reference for Greek music is Isobel Henderson, "Ancient Greek Music," in *New Oxford History of Music,* vol. 1, *Ancient and Oriental Music* (London, 1957), pp. 336-403. See also Warren D. Anderson, *Ethos and Education in Greek Music* (Cambridge, Mass., 1964), and Edward A. Lippman, *Musical Thought in Ancient Greece* (New York, 1964). My understanding of music as a liberal art has profited from Curt Sachs, *Our Musical Heritage: A Short History of Music,* 2nd ed. (New York, 1955), and *The Practica musicae of Franchinus Gafurius,* trans. Irwin Young (Madison, 1969).
7. François Lasserre, *The Birth of Mathematics in the Age of Plato,* trans. Helen Mortimer and others (New York, 1966); Wilbur Richard Knorr, *The Evolution of the Euclidean Elements: A Study of the Theory of Incommensurable Magnitudes and Its Significance for Early Greek Astronomy* (Dordrecht, Holland, 1975).
8. See the discussion in ch. 3 below, pp. 78-79.
9. In addition to Guthrie, *History of Greek Philosophy,* vol. 3, see Werner Jaeger, *Paideia: The Ideals of Greek Culture,* trans. Gilbert Highet, 3 vols.; vol. 1, 2nd ed. (New York, 1943-45).
10. The standard reference in English for Greek rhetoric is George Kennedy, *The Art of Persuasion in Greece* (Princeton, N.J., 1963). See also Charles Sears Baldwin, *Ancient Rhetoric and Poetic: Interpreted from Representative*

Works (New York, 1924), and Donald Lemen Clark, *Rhetoric in Greco-Roman Education* (Morningside Heights, N.Y., 1957). The importance of oratory was explicitly recognized in the *Iliad* (9.442-3) when Phoenix remarked to Achilles that he had been sent by Achilles' father to make him both an orator and a man of action.

11. "Socrates on the other hand was the first to call philosophy down from the heavens and set her in the cities of men and bring her also into their homes and compel her to ask questions about life and morality and things good and evil." Cicero, *Tusculan Disputations,* trans. J. E. King, Loeb Classical Library (Cambridge, Mass., 1927), 5.10.

12. See G. E. R. Lloyd, *Magic, Reason, and Experience: Studies in the Origins and Development of Greek Science* (Cambridge, 1979), pp. 79-102.

13. See "Dialectic and Aristotle's *Topics,*" by Eleonore Stump, trans., *Boethius's De topicis differentiis* (Ithaca, N.Y., 1978), pp. 159-78.

14. With Aristotle's addition of a theory of demonstration, one may speak of logic rather than dialectic. The latter term is, however, used in the broad sense of logic in one medieval tradition. See ch. 5 below, pp. 126-28. The standard history of logic in English is William Kneale and Martha Kneale, *The Development of Logic* (Oxford, 1962). For medieval logic, however, see below, ch. 5, note 7.

15. Lloyd, *Magic, Reason, and Experience,* pp. 102-25.

16. In this and the following paragraph, I am following Edward A. Maziarz and Thomas Greenwood, *Greek Mathematical Philosophy* (New York, 1968), ch. 21.

17. Rudolf Pfeiffer, *History of Classical Scholarship: From the Beginnings to the End of the Hellenistic Age* (Oxford, 1968), part 1.

18. William H. Stahl, *Roman Science: Origins, Development, and Influence to the Later Middle Ages* (Madison, 1962), p. 30.

19. On the concept of *enkuklios paideia,* see H. I. Marrou, *Saint Augustin et la fin de la culture antique* (Paris, 1937), pp. 211-35; M. L. Clarke, *Higher Education in the Ancient World* (Albuquerque, 1971), pp. 2-7; Aubrey Gwynn, *Roman Education: From Cicero to Quintilian* (Oxford, 1926), pp. 82-92. Gwynn discusses changes in the terminology and content of the *enkuklios paideia.*

The standard history of classical education is H. I. Marrou, *A History of Education in Antiquity,* trans. George Lamb (New York, 1956). Kenneth J. Freeman, *Schools of Hellas* (London, 1907), is still the best work on Hellenic education, as is John W. H. Walden, *The Universities of Ancient Greece* (New York, 1910), on Hellenistic education.

20. On Stoic logic, see Benson Mates, *Stoic Logic* (Berkeley, 1953). For a more general treatment of Stoicism, see J. M. Rist, *Stoic Philosophy* (Cambridge, 1969). The history of philosophy begun in Guthrie, *History of Greek Philosophy,* is continued up to the twelfth century in *The Cambridge History of Later Greek and Early Medieval Philosophy,* ed. A. H. Armstrong (Cambridge, 1970).

21. Many of the works cited in notes 1 and 4 include Hellenistic science. In addition, see G. E. R. Lloyd, *Greek Science after Aristotle* (New York, 1973); S. Sambursky, *The Physical World of Late Antiquity* (New York, 1962); George Sarton, *Ancient Science and Modern Civilization* (New York, 1954).

22. J. Oliver Thomson, *History of Ancient Geography* (New York, 1965).

23. Lippman, *Musical Thought,* p. 156.

24. I am following the analysis of Pfeiffer, *Classical Scholarship.* On classical scholarship, see also Henry Nettleship, *Lectures and Essays on Subjects Connected with Latin Literature and Scholarship* (Oxford, 1885), and John E. Sandys, *A History of Classical Scholarship,* vol. 1 (Cambridge, 1903). On ancient and medieval grammar, see Robert Henry Robbins, *Ancient and Medieval Grammatical Theory in Europe with Particular Reference to Modern Linguistic Doctrine* (1951; repr. Port Washington, N.Y., 1971).

25. Jacob Klein, *Greek Mathematical Thought and the Origin of Algebra,* trans. Eva Brann (Cambridge, Mass., 1968).

26. Stahl, *Roman Science,* part 1.

27. *Ibid.,* p. 45.

28. Nicomachus of Gerasa, *Introduction to Arithmetic,* trans. Martin Luther D'Ooge, with studies in Greek arithmetic by Frank Egleston Robbins and Louis Charles Karpinski (New York, 1926). Nicomachus also wrote a treatise on arithmology, or number mysticism. Arithmology was generally mentioned briefly by the Latin encyclopedists. On number mysticism, see also Vincent Foster Hopper, *Medieval Number Symbolism: Its Sources, Meaning, and Influence on Thought and Expression* (New York, 1939).

29. Cicero, *De oratore,* 1.14, trans. Kennedy, *Art of Persuasion in Greece,* p. 310.

30. Kennedy, *Art of Persuasion in Greece,* and Baldwin, *Ancient Rhetoric,* include discussions of Hellenistic rhetoric.

31. On Roman science, see Stahl, *Roman Science,* chs. 5-8; Lynn Thorndike, *A History of Magic and Experimental Science during the First Thirteen Centuries of Our Era,* 2 vols. (New York, 1923), bk. 1; Charles Singer, *From Magic to Science: Essays on the Scientific Twilight* (1928; repr. New York, 1958), ch. 1. On Roman education, see Stanley F. Bonner, *Education in Ancient Rome: From the Elder Cato to the Younger Pliny* (Berkeley, 1977).

32. Stahl, *Roman Science,* p. 74.

33. The standard reference in English is George Kennedy, *The Art of Rhetoric in the Roman World: 300 B.C.-A.D. 300.* See also Clark, *Rhetoric in Greco-Roman Education.* On the influence of Roman rhetoric during the Middle Ages, and the history of medieval rhetoric in general, see James J. Murphy, *Rhetoric in the Middle Ages: A History of Rhetorical Theory from St. Augustine to the Renaissance* (Berkeley, 1974).

34. Two important studies of the influence of classical learning on the Middle Ages (and beyond) are: R. R. Bolgar, *The Classical Heritage and Its Beneficiaries* (Cambridge, 1958), and Ernst Robert Curtius, *European Literature and the Latin Middle Ages,* trans. Willard R. Trask (New York, 1953).

35. Edward Gibbon, *The History of the Decline and Fall of the Roman Empire,* ed. J. B. Bury, 7 vols. (London, 1909), vol. 1, p. 63. Gibbon is describing the Age of the Antonines, but his characterization is even more appropriate for the following two centuries. On these centuries, see Stahl, *Roman Science,* ch. 9.

36. Pierre Courcelle, *Late Latin Writers and Their Greek Sources,* trans. Harry E. Wedeck (Cambridge, Mass., 1969); M. L. W. Laistner, *Thought and Letters in Western Europe: A.D. 500 to 900* (London, 1931). Pierre Riché, *Education and Culture in the Barbarian West: Sixth through Eighth Centuries,* trans. John J. Contreni from 3rd French ed. (Columbia, S.C., 1976), surveys the history of education in this period; in the terms developed in my essay, his

book can be viewed as an examination of the interrelations between the classical, Christian, and Germanic cultural traditions in education.

The works of the Latin encyclopedists pertinent to the history of the liberal arts have been translated into English, with extremely useful introductions: Macrobius, *The Saturnalia,* trans. Percival Vaughan Davies (New York, 1969) ; Macrobius, *Commentary on the Dream of Scipio,* trans. William Harris Stahl (New York, 1952) ; Martianus Capella, *The Marriage of Philology and Mercury,* trans. William Harris Stahl, Richard Johnson, and E. L. Burge (New York, 1977) , vol. 2 of *Martianus Capella and the Seven Liberal Arts,* by William Harris Stahl; *Boethius's De topicis differentiis,* trans. Eleonore Stump (Ithaca, N.Y., 1978) ; *Boethian Number Theory: A Translation of the De arithmetica,* trans. Michael Masi (Amsterdam, Holland, forthcoming) ; *Boethius: The Principles of Music,* trans. Calvin M. Bower (New Haven, Conn., forthcoming) ; Cassiodorus Senator, *An Introduction to Divine and Human Readings,* trans. Leslie Webber Jones (New York, 1946) . *An Encyclopedist of the Dark Ages,* trans. Ernest Brehaut (New York, 1912), contains extracts from the *Etymologies* of Isidore of Seville.

37. Riché, *Education and Culture,* chs. 3-4, discusses a strand of Christian education that rejected classical culture.

38. The best study of the philosophy of St. Augustine in English is Etienne Gilson, *The Christian Philosophy of Saint Augustine,* trans. L. E. M. Lynch (New York, 1960) . Two works that are especially valuable for understanding St. Augustine's relation to the liberal arts tradition are Marcia L. Colish, *The Mirror of Language: A Study in the Medieval Theory of Knowledge* (New Haven, Conn., 1968) , ch. 1, and Marrou, *Saint Augustin.*

39. Leslie Webber Jones, trans., *Divine and Human Readings,* by Cassiodorus, p. 41.

40. Riché, *Education and Culture,* ch. 7.

41. Laistner, *Thought and Letters,* and Riché, *Education and Culture,* are relevant for the Carolingian Renaissance. See also Wilbur Samuel Howell, *The Rhetoric of Alcuin and Charlemagne: A Translation, with an Introduction, the Latin Text, and Notes* (Princeton, N.J., 1941) .

42. Charles Sears Baldwin, *Medieval Rhetoric and Poetic (to 1400): Interpreted from Representative Works* (New York, 1928) , pp. 90-91, argues that the dominant art of the trivium shifted from rhetoric in antiquity, to grammar during the early Middle Ages, to logic in the High Middle Ages. Cf. Colish, *The Mirror of Language,* pp. 92-102.

On differing conceptions of the arts of the trivium and the relations between them, see three articles by Richard McKeon: "Rhetoric in the Middle Ages," *Speculum,* 17 (1942): 1-32; "Poetry and Philosophy in the Twelfth Century: The Renaissance of Rhetoric," *Modern Philology,* 43 (1946): 217-34; "Dialectic and Political Thought and Action," *Ethics,* 65 (1954): 1-33.

43. R. W. Southern, "Bede," in *Medieval Humanism and Other Studies* (Oxford, 1970) , pp. 1-8.

44. While these commentaries have not been translated, they have been edited, with very useful introductions, by Cora E. Lutz. See ch. 9, note 8, below.

45. R. W. Southern, *The Making of the Middle Ages* (New Haven, Conn., 1953) , pp. 11-12. On the shift from grammar to logic, see note 42 above. Colish, *The Mirror of Language,* accepts Baldwin's general thesis but places the shift in the twelfth century rather than the eleventh. Henri Focillon, "The Pope in the Year 1000," ch. 3 in *The Year 1000* (New York, 1969) , contains a good,

brief discussion of Gerbert's early career, emphasizing his teaching of both the trivium and quadrivium.

46. Southern, "Medieval Humanism," in *Medieval Humanism,* pp. 29-60.

47. On this dualism, see Gerd Tellenbach, *Church, State and Christian Society at the Time of the Investiture Contest,* trans. R. F. Bennett (Oxford, 1966), who distinguishes the ascetic concept of the church from the hierarchical-sacramental concept. Jeffrey Burton Russell, *A History of Medieval Christianity: Prophecy and Order* (New York, 1968), distinguishes the two strands that coexist in tension throughout the history of Christianity; see ch. 9 for a discussion of manifestations of the prophetic spirit during the High Middle Ages.

The term "humanistic Christianity" would have the further advantage of allowing a contrast with "Christian Humanism," the term usually used to identify Renaissance scholars such as Erasmus.

48. On the "Twelfth-Century Renaissance" and the school of Chartres, see Charles Homer Haskins, *The Renaissance of the Twelfth Century* (Cambridge, Mass., 1927); G. Paré, A. Brunet, P. Tremblay, *La renaissance du XIIe siècle: Les écoles et l'enseignement* (Paris, 1933); Raymond Klibansky, *The Continuity of the Platonic Tradition during the Middle Ages: Outlines of a Corpus Platonicum Medii Aevi* (London, 1939); Marshall Clagett, Gaines Post, and Robert Reynolds, eds., *Twelfth-Century Europe and the Foundations of Modern Society* (Madison, 1966), part 1.

Two of the most important original sources for the history of the liberal arts have been translated into English: *The Didascalicon of Hugh of St. Victor: A Medieval Guide to the Arts,* trans. Jerome Taylor (New York, 1961); and John of Salisbury, *The Metalogicon: A Twelfth-Century Defense of the Verbal and Logical Arts of the Trivium,* trans. Daniel D. McGarry (Berkeley, 1962).

49. Southern, "Humanism and the School of Chartres," in *Medieval Humanism,* pp. 61-85, questions this traditional interpretation of the preeminence of Chartres.

50. Raymond Klibansky, "The School of Chartres," in Clagett, Post, and Reynolds, eds., *Twelfth-Century Europe,* pp. 9-10.

51. On thirteenth-century philosophy, see *The Cambridge History of Later Medieval Philosophy,* ed. N. Kretzman, A. Kenny, and J. Pinborg; E. Stump, assoc. ed. (Cambridge, 1982). Of the many general histories of medieval philosophy, Etienne Gilson, *History of Christian Philosophy in the Middle Ages* (New York, 1955) can be highly recommended. The classic study of the rise of universities is Hastings Rashdall, *The Universities of Europe in the Middle Ages,* ed. F. M. Powicke and A. B. Emden, 3 vols. (1895; repr. Oxford, 1936).

On medieval science in general, see: A. C. Crombie, *Augustine to Galileo,* 2nd. ed., 2 vols. (Cambridge, Mass., 1961); Edward Grant, ed., *A Source Book in Medieval Science* (Cambridge, Mass., 1974); Edward Grant, *Physical Science in the Middle Ages* (New York, 1971); Charles Homer Haskins, *Studies in the History of Mediaeval Science* (1924; repr. New York, 1960); David C. Lindberg, ed., *Science in the Middle Ages* (Chicago, 1978); Thorndike, *Magic and Experimental Science,* bks. 2-5.

52. On medieval Arabic scholarship, see F. E. Peters, *Aristotle and the Arabs: The Aristotelian Tradition in Islam* (New York, 1968). On the recovery of Greek learning, see David C. Lindberg, "The Transmission of Greek and

Arabic Learning to the West," in Lindberg, *Science in the Middle Ages*, pp. 52-90.

53. Louis John Paetow, *The Arts Course at Medieval Universities with Special Reference to Grammar and Rhetoric* (Champaign, Ill., 1910), describes the neglect of grammar and rhetoric (except for the *ars dictaminis*) in the medieval universities.

SELECT BIBLIOGRAPHY
GENERAL STUDIES OF THE SEVEN LIBERAL ARTS

Abelson, Paul. *The Seven Liberal Arts: A Study in Medieval Culture*. New York, 1906.

Arts libéraux et philosophie au Moyen Age. Acts du quatrième Congrès de Philosophie Médiévale. Montreal, 1969.

De Rijk, L. M. "Ἐγχύχλιος παιδεία. A Study of Its Original Meaning." *Vivarium*, 3 (1965) :24-93.

Koch, Joseph, ed. *Artes liberales von der antiken Bildung zur Wissenschaft des Mittelalters*. Leiden, 1959.

Kristeller, Paul Oskar. "The Modern System of the Arts." In *Renaissance Thought II: Papers on Humanism and the Arts*. New York, 1965.

Kühnert, Friedmar. *Allgemeinbildung und Fachbildung in der Antike*. Berlin, 1961.

Martin, R. M. "Arts libéraux (sept)." *Dictionnaire d'histoire et de géographie ecclésiastique*, 4 (1930) :827-43.

Masi, Michael, ed. *Boethius and the Liberal Arts*. Bern, 1981.

Paetow, Louis John, ed. and trans. *"The Battle of the Seven Arts": A French Poem, by Henri d'Andeli, Trouvère of the Thirteenth Century*. Berkeley, 1914.

Parker, H. "The Seven Liberal Arts." *English Historical Review*, 5 (1890) : 417-61.

Rajna, P. "Le denominazione Trivium e Quadrivium." *Studi Medievali*, N.S. 1 (1928) :4-36.

Wise, John Edward. *The Nature of the Liberal Arts*. Milwaukee, 1947.

2 Incentives for Studying the Liberal Arts

Karl F. Morrison

The Latin phrase artes liberales *reflects the dependence of Roman education on Greek culture: it is the equivalent for* enkuklios paideia, *the Greek term most commonly used to characterize the curriculum of secondary education. The Roman tradition in turn became the model for Christian culture and education, although the attitude of Christians toward the pagan tradition was extremely ambiguous, as the following essay makes clear.*

The meaning of each word in this Latin phrase further clarifies the nature and significance of the liberal arts. The most likely derivation of liberalis *is* liber *(free). The liberal arts are the arts of the mind as opposed to the mechanical arts, the arts of the hand. For Cicero, they are the roots of one's* humanitas.

The term ars *is the Latin equivalent of the Greek* techne—*a systematic and complete body of knowledge deriving from a clear beginning point (or principle). These elements—completeness, clear principle, and system—parallel those of the cosmos and of the axiomatic-deductive system discussed in the previous chapter. Clearly the concept of a techne is another illustration of Greek rationalism.*

In subsequent headnotes, I shall analyze each of the seven arts as a techne. This will also make possible the identification of the various topics that had become conventional in each art by the time of the Latin encyclopedists. While not ignoring the contributions of the classical age, I have generally taken as normative Martianus Capella's Marriage of Philology and Mercury *and Cassiodorus's* Introduction to Divine and Human Readings—*both of which treat the seven arts in their entirety.* **D. L. W.**

Why study the liberal arts? This is a perennial question in western culture. Throughout the period covered by essays in this volume, position, wealth, and fame were incentives for the study of the liberal arts. By the twelfth century, the reconstitution of Europe after the collapse of the Roman Empire had been accomplished. Then these practical incentives came to be nurtured by newly formed professional classes. John of Salisbury derided those classes for their arid, self-justifying specialization and for desecrating the arts in the pursuit of lucre. Rooted in self-interest, such motives are easy to understand. However other incentives, rooted in self-doubt, were more complex, and these latter are the subject of the present essay.

Many scholars insisted that the liberal arts were essential to the work of scriptural interpretation. The same writers were also repelled by the moral standards of pagan antiquity, conveyed through the classic texts of the arts curriculum. They were pulled in two directions, attracted both by erudition, the prideful learning of the world, and by holiness, the humble simplicity of Christ. The continuity of this ambivalence as a cultural trait over the space of many centuries deserves comment.[1]

Ambivalence toward the arts has sometimes been portrayed as a conflict between two antitheses: Christianity and classical culture. Of course, it was not a confrontation between two alien cultures or even between two hostile groupings within the same society. The fascination, and the pathos, of the ambivalence was that it expressed the need of individual persons to integrate the tangled patchwork of their own experiences and hopes. Whether in the fourth or in the eleventh century, they yearned to find some common thread unifying their lives on two sides of a great watershed: conversion to ascetic Christianity. The passionate nature of conversion demanded that such an integration spring from the emotions perhaps even more than from the intellect.

I shall begin by analyzing a particular example of ambivalence toward the arts. This example, drawn from writings of an Italian ascetic and cardinal, Peter Damian (1007-72), has the advantage of presenting the trait of ambivalence fully formed. Damian crystallized but did not explain the trait. I shall therefore go on to consider thought in the age of the Latin Fathers, while the formation of the trait of ambivalence was still in flux and the methods for shaping it were consciously and deliberately exposed.

At first glance, the argument that Peter Damian set down in his treatise, *On Holy Simplicity*, appears to be a consistent, relentless tirade against the liberal arts. They belonged, he said, to "worldly and animal wisdom," the antithesis of heavenly and spiritual.[2] A teacher of rhetoric before his conversion to ascetic spirituality, Damian admonished his hearers to abandon secular learning for heavenly eloquence. There was no need for monks to seek a wisdom that the reprobate and the pagan also had, and no need for them to envy contemporaries who had stayed in the world, enhancing proficiency in the arts. The quest for holiness demanded other skills. Damian recalled the example of John the Evangelist, who learned almost nothing in the world before he went, while still young, to the simple foolishness of Jesus.[3] He invoked the models of ascetic masters—of Martin of Tours, who knew no letters; of Benedict, who was sent to the study of letters but recalled to the foolishness of Christ; and of Hilary of Poitiers, who rejected Plato and Pythagoras and withdrew to his cell as to a tomb.[4] Above all, Damian recalled how Jerome had corrected his ways. The Father dreamed that he had been dragged before the throne of God and savagely beaten for the crime of being a Ciceronian, rather than a Christian. To return to secular letters, Jerome realized, would be to deny Christ. Damian commented, "If he who had studied earthly lore was restrained from using it, how much more should he who never learned it be forbidden access?"[5]

However, there is a glaring contrast between these theories and Damian's own action. Damian's education and practice as a rhetorician are apparent in the careful construction of each sentence and each section, and in the logical progression of his argument toward its final comparison between earthly wisdom and the true wisdom imparted to man through sacramental unity with God. To stir the emotions and convince the minds of his hearers, Damian freely employed his mastery of rhetorical figures, including historical exemplars and contrasts. Paradoxically, his text exemplifies the very arts that Damian's teaching urged his hearers to avoid: grammar, rhetoric (including poetry), and philosophy.

There was an evident, logical conflict between thought and action; a covert alliance, at best, between holiness and erudition. However, we have to deal with an emotional paradox, rather than a logical contradiction. Incentives give a key to that paradox.

Damian tenderly held out incentives for following his exemplars of holiness. They were: companionship through love in sacramental union with Christ, of which Christ's patronage was one aspect; power, such as the ascetic masters displayed in commanding demons and raising the dead; glory, as in the triumphs of martyrdom and victory over spiritual adversaries; fame, as in the patterns of conduct that, centuries after their own deaths, the Fathers continued to set for believers; and vivifying wisdom, such as John the Evangelist preached when he proclaimed the mystery of the Word, thereby revealing the dark blindness of the philosophers' subtlety. Damian invoked all these incentives of love and dominance, urging his hearers to abandon both the fruits of the liberal arts and the arts themselves.

However, as so often happens (and not only with scriptural commentaries), there is an implied text within the explicit text. Plainly, Damian's incentives for the pursuit of holiness are spiritualized counterparts of worldly motives for the pursuit of erudition. Damian had not rejected the secular incentives of love and dominance (friends and patronage, power, fame, wisdom) that were open to rhetoricians, especially to those who went on, as he had probably done, to practice law. He sought rewards of spiritual, not worldly, love and dominance.

Furthermore, Damian, in quest of holiness, had not escaped the social connotations of the secular incentives for seeking erudition. Primarily, Damian did not avoid the issue of dominance. The motives for studying the liberal arts did not operate equally on everyone in ancient culture for the simple reason that the goals were not equally open to all. They were not open to slaves; some incentives, notably those requiring political office, were not open to women. The full range of incentives was open to free men who (perhaps marginally) belonged to classes who enjoyed freedom from the mechanical, or servile, arts. Only they could pursue the liberal arts. It is striking that all of Damian's models were men. Moreover, his patristic exemplars represented social orders in which the liberal arts of the time were rooted. Benedict and Gregory the Great belonged to the highest levels of the Roman nobility; Anthony, to a wealthy family of the urban patriciate; Jerome to a family of great landowners. Martin, "who knew no letters, but raised the dead," was both a soldier and the son of a soldier in the Roman army. The privileged circumstance of leisure enters in, even when Damian describes a contemporary, one of the unskilled rustics welcomed into the monastery. This man, "wisely untaught," exceeded grammarians and worldly philosophers in his knowledge of Scripture. Treading the world underfoot, he also deceived Satan, the prince of this world, by his devout philosophizing; for this man too enjoyed leisure, the *otium monasteriale*.[6]

Evidently, incentives for proficiency in spiritual discipline were a mirror image of those for proficiency in the arts. Motivations in the two segments of Damian's life, on either side of his conversion, paralleled each other.

The twin impulses of love and fear—understood as the love of Christ and the fear of hell—were crucial to the reorientation of his thinking about the arts. One trait to which they contributed was the habit of viewing the world through lenses of self-hatred. This habit is illustrated by the dual role of pain as deterrent from evil and as incentive for love. The unspoken context of Damian's remarks was the routine and ritual of monastic discipline, especially the form prescribed by St. Benedict in the sixth century. In his *Rule* for the monastic life, Benedict transferred the language of the schoolroom to the monastery. The monastery was "a school of the Lord's service," and the abbot ruled it as a schoolmaster, chastening the recalcitrant with the rod. (Benedict also described the corrective use of pain when he portrayed the abbot as a spiritual physician, applying remedies of cautery and amputation.) [7]

In *On Holy Simplicity*, Damian alluded to the pain of monastic discipline by using a metaphor of ritual to depict monks offering themselves as sacrificial lambs, as holocausts. The sum of monastic life was love of God and mortification of self.[8] To be sure, the self-immolation of the monks involved knowledge, of a particular kind: "knowledge bears sorrow. For we know that the knowledge that each of us has consists in recalling our years in the bitterness of our soul, and in lamenting our own sins with teeming rivers of tears."[9] Within the bond of love uniting abbot and monks, eloquence, "the rich colors of rhetorical art," and logic were to be used to serve contrition, even in the very words with which one disclaimed them as vain baubles, worth no more than dung.[10]

Here, as so often, Peter Damian appropriated an ancient rule of rhetoric: one should use art to conceal art. But he had applied as instruments of hatred for this life the tools that rhetoric employed for self-concealment. Expressed in the rhetorician's mortification and sacrifice of himself,[11] hatred of worldly wisdom (exemplified by the arts) was equivalent with hatred of this life. Just as carnal men projected their pleasures on the world and found it delightful, ascetics projected a radical self-denial on the world, realizing that they were locked in savage warfare for their own salvation. Victory in that bitter conflict was "more important than all natural affection."[12]

Damian alluded to a second strategy, that of introjection, by which he reconciled the evident contradiction between his negative judgment on the liberal arts and his expert use of them. At the climax of his treatise *On Holy Simplicity,* he employed a metaphor charged with ritual connotations of the Eucharist to describe it: the metaphor of nutriment. His hearers were to cast aside the grass (of earthly knowledge) that inebriates the mind to the point of madness and to eat the good grain (of Christian wisdom) that strengthens the soul with sober refreshment. Thus, God might pour into their hearts with the light of true wisdom and delight to rest in their bowels; and He might grant that they would abide in Him. (For had not the wisdom of Christ united the wise men of this world in the bowels of His body, the Church?) By this mutual introjection, or "convisceration," God's promise would be fulfilled and, like branches on the vine, Damian's hearers would continually produce buds of pious work.[13]

Damian embodied the liberal arts in the very moment when he argued that monks should not learn them. He employed a number of strategies that disguised non-Christian incentives of love and dominance for studying and using the arts. These strategies also resolved the apparent contradiction between what Damian said about the arts and how he used them by turning that contradiction into a far-ranging, but comprehensible, paradox, both disparaging worldly erudition and yet using it in the quest of holiness. All of these incentives were subsumed in an enterprise of symbolic meaning, richly served by Damian's repertoire of allegorical figures. Clearly, Christian simplicity was anything but uncomplicated, and fittingly so, for simplicity was a quality, not only of style, but also of God. Damian applied disguises of emotions that were traditionally used to legitimate the study of liberal arts by Christians. I can now attempt to identify the processes by which those disguises were constructed during the age of the Fathers. In fact, these processes formed the tradition of which Damian was one beneficiary.

Masking discrepancies between ideal and fact was not uncommon among the Fathers, especially in their thought about ascetic practices that were believed to enhance the glory of salvation. Their idealization of martyrdom provides one example. Even under persecution, some (such as the historian, Eusebius of Caesarea) who extolled "the perfection of martyrdom" deliberately evaded experiencing it. With the end of persecution, martyrdom at the hands of public executioners became virtually unattainable, and a new equivalence was established between the ideal and daily mortification of flesh and spirit by penitential exercises. The Fathers thus kept the ideal, but masked the discrepancy between it and actual practice from others as well as from themselves. Likewise, some authorities, notably Jerome and Augustine, praised virginity as an ideal of Christian life, one that youthful adventures had put beyond their own grasp. In this case, the Fathers tended to mask the discrepancy between ideal and fact by ignoring it. When accused of hypocrisy, Jerome admitted the strategy of disguise, asserting that he extolled virginity to the heavens, not because he possessed it, but because he admired what he did not have. It is an honest and true confession, Jerome added, to preach qualities in others that are lacking in oneself.[14] Disguising the difference between the Fathers' praise of simplicity, exemplified by the humble fishermen and laborers who followed

Christ, and their own learning and social status required more elaborate strategies. How could the Fathers camouflage the painful disparity from others and mask it from themselves?

The Fathers' concept of the arts as media of symbolic disguise was rooted in their assumption that the religious world was a world of hidden meaning. Still accustomed to dividing catechumens from baptized Christians, the Fathers recognized that Christianity taught some truths that were open to all and others that were disclosed to the initiate. Belief was the key. "If you do not believe," Ambrose wrote, "[Christ] did not descend for you; He did not suffer for you."[15]

Within the community of believers, there were further distinctions. Belief was proportionate to the believer, not to the object of belief, just as knowledge was proportionate to the abilities of the knower, rather than to the nature of the thing known. The distinctions between insiders and outsiders, between wise and simple, and among different levels of wisdom and simplicity were, in part, a legacy of Christian gnosticism transmitted through the Alexandrine scholar, Origen, and his followers. To some sects (such as the Priscillianists), the distinctions appeared to justify the wise in dealing with each other, with the simple, and with outsiders according to different standards of truth. The Fathers argued against variable standards, but they, too, held that esoteric truth was neither accessible to unbelievers, nor equally accessible to all the faithful. Their task was, first, to use the arts to disclose the hidden mysteries of Scripture; and, second, to express esoteric doctrine for the wise, while disguising it from the simple without falsifying it. There was a third aspect of their work; for, in so far as the arts gave them the tools that they needed, they also had to mask the disguise.

Writings by Jerome and Augustine provide examples of this complex task. Jerome specifically attacked the Origenists for their practice of concealing esoteric doctrines from ordinary believers.[16] And yet, under attack himself, he took refuge in the example of Christ, whose words Jerome paraphrased to describe his own thinking: "We speak one way to those outside and another to those within the household [of faith]. The crowd hears parables; but the disciples hear the truth."[17] Moreover, Jerome wrote, as they reached out to a wider audience, interpreters and preachers should use their arts to conceal their arts. Beneath their apparent crudeness of style, the Scriptures concealed a variety of meanings, some from the unlearned, others from the learned. Exegetes were well advised to follow the examples of scriptural authors—of Paul, notably, who warily cloaked the objects that he wanted to convey, making "his words seem simple, as though of a guileless, rustic man," only to confirm his skillful and carefully premeditated proofs. "He simulates flight," Jerome wrote of the Apostle, "but only to slay [his enemies]."[18]

Augustine, too, contended that some doctrines should never—or but rarely and with caution—be aired in the hearing of the people,[19] and that the Christian sage should use his rhetorical abilities both to teach and to disguise the very arts that he was using. Like Jerome, he invoked the examples of scriptural authority. Worldly men condemned Paul and the prophets, he wrote, not because they lacked eloquence, but because they did not show it ostentatiously. True, they had no training in rules of oratory. They exemplified a spontaneous combination of wisdom and of eloquence, rather than making studied, obtrusive oratorical displays. Indeed, obscurity and stylistic coarseness were part of their eloquence, inviting readers to ever deeper scrutiny of the texts.[20] Augustine felt that Christian teachers should follow the prophets' example, avoiding the malignant pride of those who gloried in their linguistic powers and who, dealing in slavery to carnal images, boastfully sold their skills to others.[21]

A Christian must realize that God put good speech in his mouth and made the hearts of others receptive to his words. Before he was to preach, "he should raise his thirsting soul to God in order that He may give forth what he shall drink, or pour out what shall fill him."[22] Sustained by the introjection of the Holy Spirit, the Christian should use his art both to delve into the deep mysteries of Scripture and to disguise his investigatory and expository methods. Disguise was an act of humility, simulating and perhaps achieving the unlearned eloquence that attended Paul and the prophets when the wisdom of God spoke through them.

When they turned from Scripture to the liberal arts, the Fathers found a different kind of concealment. As interpreters, their object was to disclose basic propositions of life, divinely revealed in the text of Scripture. As practitioners of the arts, their object was to examine, not propositions, but valid processes of reasoning, the operations of the mind itself.[23] God had established these in the order of nature, but they too were hidden, not by inspired words, but by the fallacious content and methods of instruction in the arts. Augustine observed that the curtains veiling entrances to grammarians' schools signified, not the emblem screening a mystery, but the cloak over an error.[24] It followed that incentives for learning processes of inference were also concealed beneath the cloak of error. The Fathers labored to disclose the divine truth that was both revealed and hidden in the text of Scripture and the dynamic of mental process that was both manifested in and disguised by the arts.

The accusations that the Fathers brought against the arts as practiced by pagans are summed up in one word: emptiness. The symbolic life that pagans sanctioned was menacingly void. The Fathers ceaselessly charged that the arts were part of the complex of vain things—empty cults, gods, doctrines, and glory—that constituted pagan life. Augustine depicted Christianity as the safe harbor of true philosophy. Profane wisdom, he wrote, was like a mountain luring sailors away from their true haven by its deceptive appearance of security; but its surface would collapse beneath their weight; they would be swallowed into the darkness of its hollow shell.[25]

Pagans in the age of the Fathers also criticized the arts. But the Christians' charge of symbolic emptiness went beyond the sense of their pagan contemporaries that the arts shared, and contributed to, a moral decline.[26] Christian writers also contended that the laws and ceremonies prescribed by the Old Testament were empty; they were prefigurations, drained of their reality when Christ established the sacraments and ways of life that they foreshadowed. Whether directed against pagan learning or Jewish doctrine, the charge of emptiness posited an act of recognition, an ability to read signs correctly, that Christians could perform but that lay beyond the grasp of others.

Christian remedies for the emptiness of the pagan arts, and of incentives for studying them, began with theories about mental process. The Fathers held pre-Christian doctrines that the human soul was a microcosm, a small-scale model of the hierarchic order of the world. Its lowest level was matter; its highest was intellect. Thus, they argued, thought advanced horizontally, at each level (at the level of sensory perception, for example), and vertically, as the soul reflected on individual sense impressions stored up in the memory and sorted them into categories of progressive generalization. In the passage from the most fleeting event—a physical sensation—to the most general predicate, the mind therefore imitated and recapitulated natural order. It progressed by natural sympathy with and imitation of the objects of knowledge, an affinity that reminded the Fathers of love.

Augustine's treatise *On Music* provides an outstanding example of how one Christian rhetorician believed that, armed with such ideas, he could transcend the emptiness of the mathematical arts as known to the pagans. Augustine himself delighted in singing. He recognized song as a powerful didactic tool.[27] But he also regarded it as a key to world order.

"Music," Augustine wrote, "is the science of moving well," that is, of modulating tones into rhythms that move in proportional harmonies.[28] As a science, music derives from nature. It is indistinguishable from the meter of spoken language. The sense of harmony (or dissonance) corresponds with natural faculties, especially with memory and the sense of hearing.[29] But music is not only a science, with rules to be understood; it is also an art, with instruments to be played, or steps to be performed. It requires both knowledge and physical dexterity. In this regard, the role of mimesis is decisive. For true music, as Augustine defined it, was not mere repetition. Nightingales could mimic, and elephants and bears could dance; singers and dancers could go through their routines; poets could reproduce ancient meters. But animals did their tricks without understanding;[30] with rare exceptions, theatrical performers merely went through their exercises by rote, gratifying the crowd for cash and glory,[31] and what antiquarian poets practiced was history, not art.[32] All were imitators; none achieved music.

As a science, music required the full and conscious exercise of reason. Though music might surely be hidden "in the most secret recesses" of the human soul—indeed in the natural powers of the senses[33]—only the gifted and the well-trained could draw it forth and subordinate imitation to reason. Certainly, Augustine wrote, the mind proceeded from images to the invisible forms of truth that they reflected, and so from lower truths to higher. But not all images were true. By some, the mind deceived itself or was deceived. There were dreams and fantasies that the mind drew out of nothing or that the memory fabricated out of its store of experiences. Reason detected the fraudulence of dreams yet proved that some represented an authentic, underlying truth; in dreams, images and truth actually mingled with one another. But men rarely exercised reason in this way. Augustine reserved his most scathing remarks for those who confused empty imitations with art. This was the error of theatrical performers who had nothing in the way of truth and pure understanding, however skilled and well-trained they might be,[34] and yet who, without science, pleased the ears of the people.[35] Thus, even great men confused imitation with art, by trusting in what was actually subject to luck and untutored judgment, following the common crowd that hardly differed from cattle.[36]

Thus far, Augustine had described music as a science and an art that demanded more than the imitation of external forms. Without an exercise of reason that detected the authentic structure beneath what the senses saw and heard, they were counterfeits, or parodies. Relatively few people could thus exercise reason. But the reality of music was beyond the grasp even of the rational few; it stood somewhere outside either the theory of a science or the practice of an art. In the last book of his treatise, Augustine disclosed that human reason imitated and thus depended upon a reality that it could not comprehend.

His entire discussion of music as movement and the elaborate review of poetic scansion (which occupies most of the work) prepared for this final section. Augustine dropped his rhetorician's mask. All that had gone before was an elaborate prologue to a theological summary. The principles of music as movement were also those of psychology and physics. In his review of "carnal letters," Augustine disclosed various numerical proportions (or rhythms) that he now applied to the soul and the world. The measurable rhythms that the soul sensed and expressed through the body in music were related to numerical proportions that ordered the highest spiritual reality. Moreover, a numerical progression passing downward through a continuously graded hierarchy of forms bound together the physical and the spiritual. The entire cosmos, temporal and eternal, was modeled on one archetype. When it mastered sensual movements, the reason detected the spiritual reality behind and above them. Passing from sensual images to mental ones, the soul recapitulated the hierarchy of being passing upward to the ultimate reality that the images reflected and expressed. It thus freed itself to unite in harmony with them, and finally with "the rational and intelligible harmonies of blessed and holy souls, receiving, without any intervening nature, the very law of God, without which no leaf falls from a tree, and by which our hairs are numbered. . . ."[37]

Still, the soul reached this vision, not by reason alone, but by reason enlarged with love. Love reformed the soul and exalted it to the place where there was neither time nor variability, to the supreme and immutable pattern in imitation of which time was composed. Ecstatic delight in beauty raised the soul to the archetype that governed the orbits of heavenly bodies and the passage of days and years, and that joined earthly things with heavenly in a harmonious song of the universe.[38]

Despite the theological climax with which Augustine crowned *On Music,* recognizable varieties of the disguise through symbolism expressed in that treatise were in fact taught by pre-Christian philosophers. To discover the specifically Christian content with which the Fathers sought to redress the symbolic emptiness of the pagan quest for erudition, we must go beyond the mathematical to the literary arts. We must add other elements to grasp the soul's correct reading of symbols in its quest for holiness. What lay behind the metaphors of appropriation invented by Jerome and Augustine? Surely, Jerome wrote, secular wisdom could be regarded as the foreign woman described in Deuteronomy, captured by the Israelites, submitted to ritual purification, and taken to beget servants for the Lord of Sabbaoth. Surely, Augustine contended, Christians were right to seize what was good and pious in the arts, as the Israelites had plundered the gold, silver, and raiment of the Egyptians, converting "to the obedience of Christ" what pagans had abused in the worship of demons. The Israelite users of "Egyptian wealth" were to be cleansed with the hyssop of humility, so that they could be "filled unto all the fulness of God."[39]

Rationalization of the sort represented by Augustine's *On Music* was the first step toward adaptation. It taught that man did not invent the arts, any more than he created the captive woman or the deposits of gold and silver that the Egyptians had mined. Man discovered the arts in nature and investigated them as ways of methodizing what was already present in the world. But more difficult steps of adaptation were implied by the violent metaphors of ritual purification and pillage set down by Jerome and Augustine.

Augustine wrote *On Music* soon after his conversion as part of a grand project (never completed) to compose a set of texts that could be used in teaching the arts to Christians. Throughout the decades of turmoil and responsibility that followed, he turned repeatedly to the subjects that he had raised in those early years, exploring again and again the power of the arts, whether used for good or ill. His most mature statement came toward the end of his life in the treatise, *On Christian Doctrine*. To the end, he remained convinced that, necessary as they were for ordered social life, the arts were not autonomous, self-justifying techniques, but rather that each practitioner bent them to serve the object of his love. As we have seen, love and art intersected. The Christian doctrine of conversion called for a redirection of love away from associations in the physical world to those in the spiritual, and the arts were important as means toward bringing about, explaining, and understanding the emotional displacements that ensued.

Family ties were vulnerable. As stated in the Gospel According to Luke, Christ said, "If any man come to me and hate not his father and mother and wife and children and brethren and sisters, yea and his own life also, he cannot be my disciple" (Luke 13:26). Discipline in the arts coincided with this precept. It is hard to evaluate the testimony of one (pagan) author that corporal punishment in school induced children to run away from home.[40] However, writings of Augustine and Jerome give clear instances of the role that literary arts played in transferring affection from the family to other relationships.

Augustine acknowledged that Patricius, his father, went beyond the norm for a man of his modest resources to pay for secondary stages of Augustine's education.[41] Still, he also recalled that both his parents had laughed at the savage beatings that he received in school and had forced him to immerse himself in the "torrent of hell," the mythological exercises through which he learned grammar and rhetoric.[42] They did so with different motives. In Augustine's childhood, his (as yet) unbaptized father had virtually no thought of God, and he wished that Augustine would prosper in the empty things of this world. Later, when he paid for Augustine's study at Carthage, his father gave no attention to his cultivation of God. His devoutly Christian mother, Monica, believed that formal studies would draw him nearer to God.[43] As his mind reviewed these long-past events, Augustine recalled how his mother had striven for God to displace Patricius as his father; and he was able to think of both parents as his brethren under God, the Father, in the catholic mother, the Church.[44]

Jerome sanctioned an overt displacement. His young, wellborn disciple, Heliodorus, weakened and left Jerome's company in the monastic life, taking refuge with his family. Professing to write in outraged affection, Jerome called him to return. Jerome recognized that Heliodorus's love had not been like his own; but the young man should picture to himself the terror of the Last Judgment, when Plato and his followers would be shown up as fools and Aristotle's subtleties would amount to nothing.

Just as Augustine's study of the literary arts belonged to his long process of conversion, so too Heliodorus's erudition had made him Jerome's companion, friend, and brother. Jerome pleaded with him, drawing from the studies that Heliodorus had pursued from early childhood the precepts of rhetoricians, the rules of logical exposition, a learned quotation from Virgil.[45] But what would such learning be worth in the eyes of Christ, the son of laborers?[46] To be sure, the Old Testament enjoined children to honor their parents, but the Gospel recognized natural affection as a defensive wall battered down by the faith.[47] When he joined Jerome, Heliodorus had sworn to spare neither father nor mother in the service of Christ, his King. He should heed Jerome's affectionate counsel. A double bond, love of Christ and fear of hell, led to the inescapable conclusion. If his mother entreated him to stay, he should ignore her. If his father cast himself down in his path, he should trample him underfoot; for "in such cases, to be cruel is a kind of [filial] piety."[48]

Outside the family, supplanting of affection occurred in friendships, notably in the estrangements that parted Ausonius from his disciple, Paulinus of Nola, and Jerome from his erstwhile companion, Rufinus of Aquileia. As in the cases of Augustine and Heliodorus, the literary arts contributed to Paulinus's conversion to Christian asceticism, and to his resulting separation from Ausonius. After he embraced ascetic Christianity, Paulinus abandoned his glittering political career, left the luxurious circles of Gaul, and went to Spain on the journey that eventually led him to Italy. He left behind Ausonius, a man who had been his and his father's friend, Paulinus's own tutor in the literary arts, and his patron in political advancement. Ausonius's version of Christianity caused no conflict with older ways, and he was mystified by Paulinus's long, painful silence. Possibly, he thought, the younger man's new wife was at fault. Eventually, Paulinus explained himself. He acknowledged the affection that he owed Ausonius, as to a father, for his education and political advancement. But he now understood that this obligation existed because Ausonius had formed in him what Christ could love. Christ was also Paulinus's father, and this paternity had radically changed Paulinus. He was no longer the man he once was. He could no longer join Ausonius in invoking Apollo and the Muses, or in delighting in fables, sophistries, rhetorical exercises, and poetic fictions. All these belonged to the emptiness of the present life, things that were foolish to God. Under the shadow of the Last Judgment, he could not live for this world. If Ausonius approved, well and good. If not, Paulinus would go on in his new life, seeking approval from Christ alone.[49]

The experiences of Augustine, Jerome, and Paulinus illustrate that, in the name of love (or friendship), the arts could be used against the pagan culture that gave them birth. For the future, however, it was crucial that the arts had also gained an important role in the displacements of affection among professed Christians. Falling out of love could be expected between those who entered the household of faith and those they left outside. Christian simplicity was arrayed against both pagans and heretics, the latter of whom were charged with hiding their wicked errors beneath rhetorical devices and dialectical tricks.

But the estrangement between Jerome and Rufinus of Aquileia illustrates emotional displacements within the household of faith, among Christian exegetes. While they were still friends, Jerome wrote to Rufinus anticipating the time when he could again embrace and "press kisses on that mouth which often used to join with me in error or in wisdom."[50] In those early days, Jerome and Rufinus shared an enthusiasm for scriptural commentaries by the great pioneer in scriptural exegesis, Origen; each translated some of his works. But Rufinus persisted in the study, translation, and defense of Origen's doctrines long after some of them had been denounced as heretical. He had also persuaded others that Jerome was an Origenist. As a result, Jerome engaged in bitter controversy, dissociating himself from his former friend and explaining in detail the principles that he followed as a translator, his rhetorical devices, and his justifications for using secular arts in the task of scriptural interpretation.

The objects were, first, to defend his own theological position and methods of reasoning; second, to expose Rufinus's "blasphemies"; and third, to discredit his mastery of the expository arts. The arts supplied both the cause and the mechanism of estrangement. Jerome followed advice that he gave on another occasion, using spiritual affection to quench physical; the idea that brothers could part may indeed have been in his mind when he had written, still hoping to snare Rufinus "in the net of love": "the friendship that can end was never true."[51]

Loving and being loved remained incentives for the study of the arts in the effort to restore man's likeness to God; but the Fathers argued that carnal affections diverted love from its proper goal. An impersonal doctrine resulted, quite different from the intensely personal obligations of the patron-client relation. One should love, not individual persons, but attributes of God in them, the virtues of justice, goodness, and truth. For, Augustine asked, "What did Christ love in us, except God?" By the same token, one should hate vices in others. Thus, one can love or hate persons whom one never knew and even unknowingly love a person whose company one abhors.[52] The arts could assist the displacement of love from carnal affinity (as in the family) to spiritual (as in the brotherhood of believers) and ultimately to God. Their study was legitimate in so far as it assisted the right ordering of love, the endurance of pain in resulting separations, and the willingness to cause pain when to be cruel was an act of piety.

In the love of God, all variability of relationships was cancelled out; there would be no pain of separation. Indeed, one would pass beyond relationship and beyond likeness, absorbed into the single glory and eternal love that was God.

In the passionate search for a restored freedom in God, the emotions of love and fear were closely linked. The love of Christ and fear of hell were twinned. This combination of apparently contradictory motives was certainly formed and reinforced in childhood. It is worth emphasizing that corporal punishment was as integral a part of training in the liberal arts as were any of the subjects. Evidently, its persistence from one generation to another throughout classical and patristic antiquity (not to mention more recent periods) reveals conscious standards of the communities in which it took place.[53]

Rarely during the centuries represented in this volume did writers object that the cultivation of fear and physical pain debased human souls into animality.[54] More frequently, it was accepted as a kinesthetic part of education and a sign of love between dominant and subordinate partners. "It is one thing," Jerome wrote, "to smite with the affection of a teacher and a parent, but another to rage with a cruel spirit against enemies."[55] Acknowledgements of flogging as a sign of love occur in Augustine's comments about his parents, and, much later, in Guibert of Nogent's (ca.1064-1125) recollection (modeled on Augustine's account) of his bruised and lacerated shoulders as proof of his tutor's "harsh love" for him.[56] As pain, corporal punishment was a deterrent; as a sign of love, it was an incentive.

At any rate, the infliction of physical pain and reactions to it permanently formed habits of thinking about incentives for the study of the arts. They also laid—and not only among Christians—the basis for hatred of the arts that was rendered into ambivalence, or sublimated and disguised in some of the mental strategies with which we are dealing.[57]

Evidently, the association of love and inflicted pain, formed in childhood, had its role to play in the formation of adult habits; for, behind the grief-filled experience of early manhood, Augustine eventually detected God, wielding a disciplinarian's rod and sometimes laughing, as Augustine's parents had laughed when he prayed to be delivered from floggings at school.[58] And he was also prepared to think that fear of God was the first step toward wisdom and toward right love of God, of one's neighbors, and, in mercy, of one's enemies.[59] The Fathers' doctrines concerning love enabled them to adapt one non-Christian incentive for the study of the liberal arts: the cultivation of loving relationships. Their doctrines of fear enabled them to adapt other secular incentives: victory, glory, wealth, pleasure, and fame. Certainly, on one level, writings of the patristic age indicate a reversal of those incentives in Christian asceticism. Instead of victory, they teach abasement; instead of glory, shame; instead of wealth, poverty; instead of pleasure, self-denial; instead of fame, obscurity. On every count, the incentives for aggression in military and civil life are counterbalanced by their opposites. And yet, on another level, ascetic writers did continue to invoke the incentives for aggression, transferring them to the arena of spiritual conflict. It was only natural that this was so in the lives of such writers as Augustine and Jerome, who had been educated for secular careers. Conversion spiritualized, but by no means effaced, motives of dominance. One element in this transference was the calculated use of fear in teaching the liberal arts.

Jerome made this connection repeatedly in his controversy-filled life. He described his literary conflicts—as well as his spiritual struggles—in metaphors of war and held out as incentives for perseverance exactly the rewards of dominance that we have mentioned. He himself was wounded, he once wrote; his life was in danger on the battlefield. He would not reckon his comrade-in-arms a victor until he saw him behead his opponent.[60] Undeniably, he related the ritualized aggression of theological dispute to ways of thinking engendered in school. He challenged a rival to combat: "Let him move his hand, use the stylus, bestir himself, writing whatever he can. Let him give a chance to reply to his learning. I can return bite for bite, if I like. Wounded, I can fix my teeth in my adversary. I too have studied a smattering of the arts—'we also have often withdrawn a hand from the master's rod.' "[61]

Like Jerome, Augustine imagined that the Christian scholar lived for conflict, as "the defender (*defensor*) of right faith and the conqueror (*debellator*) of error."[62] He described a complex association of ideas and feelings when he recalled the schoolmaster who beat him. Whenever the master was "conquered" by one of his colleagues in discourse, he was as much tormented by anger and envy as was Augustine when bested in a ballgame.[63] Sharpened by his love of rewards, as well as by fear of the master's rod, the spirit of competition remained with Augustine, as it had with the master, into manhood.[64]

The Father was able to think of the tools of his trade—figures of speech and rhetorical styles—as instruments of war, or as warriors. The subdued style, he wrote, was a naked fighter, "crushing the sinews and muscles of his foe and with his most powerful limbs overcoming and destroying falsehood."[65] Augustine portrayed the incentives that glittered before the combative expositor—the conquest of resistent minds and the persecutions of this world; glory in God; the reward of satiety in eternal things; the pleasure in truth's victory; the fame of those who lead exemplary lives, notably the Greek and Latin Fathers who "spoiled the Egyptians."[66]

The lessons of aggression associated with the schoolmaster's rod prepared the Fathers to believe that "unless you use force, you will never seize the kingdom of heaven."[67] Thus they accepted, and sought, pain as part of their spiritual formation, and they sensed an imperative to inflict pain as part of the spiritual formation of others. Dependence and aggression were two sides of the same lesson. Analogues with medicine, which Jerome and many others counted among the liberal arts, were invoked to justify the same way of thinking. In moral correction, Jerome wrote, "Cautery and the knife are the only remedies when mortification has once set in. . . . What causes much pain can only be cast out by inflicting greater pain."[68]

Curative pain might be inflicted by God. As Augustine reflected on the physical and psychological sufferings of his life, he perceived that God had been at work, with the hands of a physician, dressing and curing the wounds of sin, and breaking his bones with the rod of discipline to heal him.[69] When Jerome described himself flogged before the throne of God for being a Ciceronian, not a Christian, his calls for mercy resounding through the blows, he relived a childhood experience familiar to any schoolboy, one that, for Jerome, blended connotations of pain and love.[70] Curative pain might be inflicted on oneself as, with violence, one fought against the violence of the arrogant flesh by castigating the body and humbling the mind, laying down one's life for Christ, giving blood for blood in daily martyrdom.[71] Finally, it could be inflicted upon others, for their spiritual cure, whether those united in the same community or those outside. "I hate the enemies [of Scripture]," Augustine wrote. "O that Thou wouldst kill them with a two-edged sword, that they would not be its enemies. For I would love them to be so killed to themselves that they might live to Thee."[72]

After many years of conflict with the Donatists, Augustine was prepared to use the material, as well as the spiritual, sword against them. Terror, he wrote, was the first step in the educational process, inflicted by fathers on sons, and by masters on students. In the same fashion, fear and pain were useful first steps toward conversion, and Christ Himself had sanctioned their use when he struck Paul to the earth and blinded him on the road to Damascus. Fear and pain prepared the minds of wayward men for teaching. Furthermore, terror was an essential function of secular government; justified by Old Testament rulers, Christian princes could, and should, employ it to correct men and restrain them from sin. Through faithful rulers, the Church gained a useful device for its teaching mission: persecution as a work of love.[73]

Just as the Fathers employed the arts to symbolize aggression in theological disputes, so they used them to ritualize social divisions. The Fathers equated the holy simplicity of the Apostles with lowly status. They described the Apostle's mud-caked feet and the work-hardened hands. They invented ascetic practices of self-abasement by which they themselves experienced meanness of life. The Fathers were pulled in this direction by their emotional dependence, epitomized in humility and obedience; but they were pulled in quite a different way by their aggressive impulses. It was evident to them that not all could be leaders in the conflict, spiritual masters, and physicians. Like love and knowledge, likeness to God was always proportionate to the capacity of the individual person. Victory through mortification of the flesh and compunction of soul was open to all, but only those disciplined in the arts were qualified to achieve dominance in theological conflict. Teachers stood above "the unskilled commons," and health, or sickness, descended from them to the others, as though from the head to the lower members of the body.[74] The minds of those who had not imbibed of the good arts, Augustine observed, were stunted by hunger.[75]

In fact, the number of the inwardly famished was large. Slaves would have to be included—such as the slave girl with twins at her breast, and the four pairs of male and female slaves inventoried by Ausonius among gifts exchanged at a fashionable wedding.[76] (Augustine refers to the miraculous infusion of literacy into "a barbarian Christian slave" after three days of prayer.) [77] The lower social orders would also figure, represented by the crowds of feasting, drunken peasants who crowded into

St. Felix's basilica complex at Nola—"rusticity neither void of faith nor taught to read." Paulinus of Nola had paintings of sacred history executed "in varied colors" to divert them from their revels and to edify them. Paulinus clearly regarded pictures as books of the unlearned, though he had explanatory inscriptions placed over each painting so that peasants who could decipher them could be drawn all the more strongly away from their food and wine.[78]

Finally, the incentives for studying the arts were not fully open to women, including even Monica, the mother "to whose merit," Augustine wrote, "is due everything in my life (*omne quod vivo*)."[79] The ritualized distinction between wise and simple is most striking when applied to members of the same social order; for it illustrates particularly well the kind of dominance that the Fathers believed was accessible through the arts. At least in great families, boys and girls could have the same tutors during early childhood. Occasionally, tutors remained in families over many years, teaching boys and girls in different generations.[80] Boys and girls alike endured intimidation and beatings at school.[81] Women of exalted station could assemble coteries of distinguished scholars and encourage their studies.[82]

However, professional careers were not open to women, and such advanced training as men received to prepare them for lives in politics and teaching was considered superfluous for women. When Ausonius recalled his deceased male relatives, he remembered among other things their skills in the arts and their public dignities. When he characterized his female relatives, he mentioned their distinguished pedigrees, beauty, virtue, careful upbringing of children, and skill in spinning wool.[83] Augustine's mother belonged to a more modest social order than did Ausonius's senatorial relatives, but this makes all the more instructive the contrast between her intellectual achievements and her son's career as a teacher of rhetoric and his additional skills in theology. Subject first to her parents, later to her husband, and finally to her sons, Monica lived in a social milieu in which wife-beating and alcoholism among women were endemic.[84] Her natural grasp of grammar preserved her from the learned barbarisms cultivated in Rome, but both her sons recognized that she occasionally used "vulgar and bad Latin." From the depths of her own mind, she would draw forth sentiments akin to those of Cicero, though, unfamiliar with philosophical schools and discourse, she lacked the words in which to express them. Smitten with insight, she was known to cry out ecstatically with such force that, "almost forgetting her sex, we could believe that some great man was sitting with us."[85]

The letters of Jerome illustrate that the education of women, even those in the highest levels of the Roman aristocracy, was not intended to convey them beyond a rudimentary level. Significantly, Jerome described in a letter to a female disciple, Eustochium, the dream in which he was taken up into heaven and flogged for being a Ciceronian. He denied the charge that he forbade girls' training in secular letters while, despite the promise made in his dream, he continued to read and cite secular literature himself. However, it is evident that he did, in fact, retain secular letters in the education of boys (and in his own thought and writing) but exclude them from the educational program for girls.[86]

It was right, he wrote to one noble mother who had dedicated her daughter to the religious life, that she provide her daughter with "an education appropriate to her birth."[87] Instruction should include chanting (for the sake of singing psalms), correct diction, reading and writing, memorization of the Scriptures (in Greek and in Latin), study of a few select commentaries on the Scriptures, and wool carding and spinning. Jerome referred to no mathematical arts. He specifically excluded formal training in music and worldly songs.[88] The daughter was to live virtually isolated in a rigorously controlled environment. Convinced that she could not live without her mother and terrified of separation from her, she was to live ascetically from the beginning, reducing her body to subjection by fasts and vigils, deliberately soiling her beauty with filth. Following a set daily routine of prayer and reading, lightened by recreational spinning, she should know nothing of the world but think that the whole human race was like herself.[89]

This letter indicates how women were to be prepared for the life of dependency that Jerome considered appropriate for them in the Church. He blushed to think of those who learned from women what to teach men,[90] and one of his sharpest jibes against Rufinus was that he chose to discuss "the doctrines of divine law amid the spindles and workbaskets of girls," where he sought and found admiration, rather than debating, as he ought, with "learned men." Rufinus had been able to manipulate the gullibility of female devotees in his effort to defame Jerome.[91] Not surprisingly, Jerome venomously jibed, for presumptuous and foolish women, following their own instincts, had often been patronesses of heresy.[92]

Jerome's letters concerning his disciples, Paula, Marcella, and Demetrias, all characterize an education tailored to the needs of a devotional routine made up of psalmody, prayer, and scriptural readings, broken only by diversions of spinning and sewing. Even when they actually withstood heresy, they delivered not their own opinions, but those of Jerome and others, thus admitting that what they taught they had learned from others. For they knew that St. Paul had said, "I suffer not a woman to teach," and they were unwilling to seem to inflict a wrong on the male sex by presuming to teach in their own right.[93]

Jerome insisted that knowledgeable criticism of artists could come only from other artists; only poets could deliver worthwhile criticism of poets, and philosophers of philosophers. Thus, the learned could despise the carping censures of the uneducated.[94] This rule of thumb carried over into the art of interpreting Scripture and, as we have seen, it limited dominance in spiritual warfare to those men to whom the full range of training in the liberal arts, and the rewards of victory in conflict, were open. It was they who could perform the violent ritual purification of the arts described in the metaphors of the captive woman and the spoils of the Egyptians.

This line of argument could have led to the view expressed by Cicero when he argued that the object of education in the arts was to form and perfect humanity.[95] But the Fathers did not believe that the goal of mental and physical discipline was to perfect humanity. The elect were called, not to correspond with some ideal of humanity, but to become gods. Discipline was a formative process by which they "passed over" beyond humanity into God, each according to his own capacity. This process might be enhanced by education. It was impossible without sanctification; and "sanctification is not transmitted, but infused."[96] Awareness that sanctification—the introjection of the Holy Spirit—came by God's action limited the confidence that the Fathers could place in human arts, including the art of scriptural interpretation. The sense of ultimate dependence upon God brought with it praise of holy simplicity, and of its paradigms—the illiterate fishermen who became Apostles. Such praise sounds incongruous in the mouths of theologians and rhetoricians. But the learned were aware of the irony in their position. They recognized that, in their search for ever greater participation in God, the would-be purifiers of the arts could be overtaken by their own ingenuity: "the unlearned rise up and seize heaven by force, and, behold, we with our doctrines are entangled in flesh and blood."[97]

Holiness and erudition were neither mutually exclusive nor identical; but holiness had the greater weight. Beyond self-doubt, therefore, the Fathers' adaptation of incentives for studying the arts established grounds for conflict within the Church. The first ground was that between the wise and the simple, carved out by the Fathers' own praise of the simplicity of divine wisdom infused into the laborers who were Christ's parents, the fishermen who followed Him, and the children about whom He said, "of such is the kingdom of heaven." The second ground for conflict lay among the wise, and the rationales for theological dispute were fully enacted during the patristic era. The third, and perhaps the most dangerous to the Church as an institution, was the ground for conflict between those who considered themselves wise and bishops whom they considered not simple, but ignorant, and, through ignorance, destructive of the Church. No doubt envy sharpened dispute at this level, making it particularly corrosive of administrative authority.[98] The history of the western Church during, and after, the age of the Fathers can be read as a continual enactment of these three kinds of tension.

To summarize: From the patristic era onward, western authors in the ascetic tradition expressed a profound ambivalence toward the arts, especially the literary ones. They insisted on the usefulness of the arts, but they also disparaged the arts as conduits of superstition, heresy, and pride. This ambivalence became a distinct trait in western culture. Its age-old features were summarized by Peter Damian, at a relatively late stage in its history. It taught an acknowledged hatred of the arts, and, pressed to extremes, it appeared to leave no incentives at all for studying them.

However, examining the formative moment of that ambivalence, we have been able to identify a number of qualifications. Ambivalence arose from the efforts of many individuals to integrate the segments of their lives before and after conversion, the early quest for erudition with the later quest for holiness. This task involved the emotions even more than the intellect. Thus, the incentives that pagan (or, later, secular) society had held out for studying the liberal arts were rejected in a very oblique way: they were rendered into symbols. Convinced that they were dealing with concealed truths, in Scripture and in the arts, the Fathers had no difficulty in transferring secular incentives that had inflamed them in early life—motives of friendship and dominance—into spiritual ones. Their work consisted of two stages, through which the incentives for studying the arts were legitimated with reference to the emotional life of men, and ritualized in the teaching and disciplinary orders of the Church.

Why did the Fathers' adaptation of incentives for the study of the liberal arts to the service of Christian doctrine endure? Several reasons can be mentioned. Christian doctrine was a comprehensive system of thought, relating processes of human knowledge to the universal order of nature. It was preserved in the ascetic and theological core of the Church. Its inner tensions and potential for self-criticism kept it from stagnation. It consciously expressed the need and the power of the mind to integrate apparently conflicting stages of life, and it exposed for continual study the emotional processes of rationalization, adaptation, and disguise that such integration required. And finally, it promised through signs and symbols release from slavery to doubt-ridden knowledge and to the anguish of mixed emotions; it foretold freedom in a world where one would know without error, rejoice without sorrow, and love without fear.

NOTES

1. On the ambivalence of early Christian apologists and theologians toward the liberal arts, see J. Pelikan, *The Emergence of the Catholic Tradition (100-600)*, vol. 2 in *The Christian Tradition* (Chicago, 1971), pp. 27-41. Concerning the same trait during a period just after the era treated in the present essay, see P. Riché, trans. John J. Contreni, *Education and Culture in the Barbarian West (sixth through eighth centuries)* (Columbia, S.C., 1976), especially pp. 79-99. On the curriculum in the patristic era, see H. M. Klinkenberg, "Der Verfall des Quadriviums in frühen Mittelalter," in J. Koch ed., *Artes Liberales. Von der antiken Bildung zur Wissenschaft des Mittelalters* (Leiden, 1959. *Studien und Texte zur Geistesgeschichte des Mittelalters*, Bd 5), especially pp. 18f.

In subsequent notes, these abbreviations will be used to indicate important serial publications of patristic texts: *CSEL* = *Corpus Scriptorum Ecclesiasticorum Latinorum; Corp. Christ., ser. lat.* = *Corpus Christianorum, series latina; MGH, Epp.* = *Monumenta Germaniae Historica, Epistolae; PL* = J. P. Migne, *Patrologiae Cursus Completus, series latina.*

I am indebted to Miss Mary E. Rall for a critical reading of this essay.

2. *De sancta simplicitate*, ch. 8. Paolo Brezzi ed., *De divina omnipotentia e altri opusculi* (Florence, 1943. *Edizione nationale dei classici del pensiero italiano*, 5), p. 196.

3. *De sancta simplicitate*, 5. Brezzi ed., p. 182.

4. *De sancta simplicitate*, 5. Brezzi ed., pp. 178-80.

5. *De sancta simplicitate*, 8. Brezzi ed., pp. 196-200.

6. *De sancta simplicitate*, 7. Brezzi ed., pp. 188-92.

7. *Rule of St. Benedict* prologue and ch. 28.

8. *De vera felicitate ac sapientia*, 5. *De perfectione monachorum*, 2. Brezzi ed., pp. 210, 348.

9. *Serm.*, 55. *PL* 144: 814.

10. *De vera felicitate ac sapientia*, prologue and ch. 1. Brezzi ed., p. 334.

11. Cf. *De vera felicitate ac sapientia*, 5. Brezzi ed., pp. 348-52.

12. *De perfectione monachorum*, ch. 21. *De vera felicitate ac sapientia*, 5. Brezzi ed., pp. 304, 348-52.

13. Ch. 8. The sentence in parenthesis occurs in *De vera felicitate ac sapientia*, 3. Brezzi ed., pp. 192-96, 344.

14. *Ep.* 49 (48) .20, *CSEL*, 54, p. 385.

15. *De fide*, 4.2.26. *CSEL*, 78, p. 165.

16. *Ep.* 84.3. *CSEL*, 55, p. 124.

17. *Ep.* 49.13. *CSEL*, 54, p. 370.

18. *Ep.* 49.13. *CSEL*, 54, pp. 370, 463.

19. *De doctrina Christiana*, 4.63. *CSEL*, 80, p. 134. No egalitarianism should be read into Augustine's famous statement that it would be "better for gram-

marians to censure us [because of loose syntax] than for the people not to understand." *Enarrationes in Psalmos 138*, 20. *Corp. Christ., ser. lat.*, 40, p. 2004.

20. *Ibid.*, 4.25-30, 44f. *CSEL*, 80, pp. 123f., 128f.

21. *Ibid.*, 3.29; 4.45, 144. *CSEL*, 80, pp. 87, 128f., 163.

22. *Ibid.*, 4.87, 164. *CSEL*, 80, pp. 141, 169.

23. On the distinction between the truth of propositions, which were found only in the Church, and processes of inference, which could be learned outside the Church, see Augustine, *De doctrina Christiana*, 2.120; *CSEL*, 80, p. 68.

24. *Confessions*, 1.13. *CSEL*, 33, p. 19.

25. *De beata vita*, 1.3. *Corp. Christ., ser. lat.*, 29, p. 66.

26. "Longinus," *On the Sublime*, W. Rhys Roberts ed. (Cambridge, 1935), ch. 44, pp. 154-58. Ammianus Marcellinus, *Histories*, 14.6.17-19. *Loeb Classics*, 1, pp. 44-46. Libanius, *Oration 18 (Funeral Oration on Julian)*, 158, 160, attributing a decline in the arts to the Christianizing policies of Constantius II. *Loeb Classics*, 1, pp. 382, 384.

27. *De magistro*, 1.1. *Corp. Christ., ser. lat.*, 29, p. 158; *De opere monachorum*, 17.20. *CSEL*, 41, pp. 564f.

28. *De musica*, 1.3.4. (Paris, 1947. *Bibliothèque augustinienne, Oeuvres de Saint Augustin*, première série, p. 7, t. 4), p. 30. See C. J. Perl, "Augustinus und die Musik" *Augustinus Magister*, 3 (Paris, 1955. *Etudes augustiniennes*), especially pp. 444, 452.

29. *De musica*, 1.5.10, p. 46.

30. *Ibid.*, 1.4.5-6, pp. 32-38.

31. *Ibid.*, 1.6.12, p. 52.

32. *Ibid.*, 2.7.14, pp. 122-24.

33. *Ibid.*, 1.13.28, p. 84.

34. *Ibid.*, 1.4.8, pp. 40-42.

35. *Ibid.*, 1.6.11, p. 48.

36. *Ibid.*, 1.4.5 and 1.6.11, pp. 34, 48.

37. *Ibid.*, 6.17.58, p. 476.

38. *Ibid.*, 6.11.29, p. 424.

39. Jerome, *ep.* 70.2. *CSEL*, 54, pp. 702f. Augustine, *De doctrina Christiana*, 2.144-47, 151f. *CSEL*, 80, pp. 75f., 78. On Augustine's educational goals, see, most recently C. P. Mayer, "Der gebildete Christ. Fundamente und Ziele christlicher Gelehrsamkeit nach dem hl. Augustinus," *Theologie und Philosophie*, 52 (1977), 53, pp. 272-79.

40. Below, note 57.

41. *Confessions*, 2.3. *CSEL*, 33, p. 32.

42. *Confessions*, 1.9; 1.12; 1.16. *CSEL*, 33, pp. 12-14, 17, 23.

43. *Confessions*, 2.3. *CSEL*, 33, pp. 32-35.

44. *Confessions*, 1.11; 9.13. *CSEL*, 33, pp. 16, 225f.

45. See *Ep.* 60.5. *CSEL*, 54, p. 553.

46. *Ep.* 14.11. *CSEL*, 54, p. 61.

47. *Ep.* 14.3. *CSEL*, 54, p. 48f.

48. *Ep.* 14.2-3. *CSEL*, 54, p. 47f. In this passage, Jerome reworked the classical topos of a father trying to keep his son from going to war. H. Hagendahl, *Latin Fathers and the Classics. A Study in the Apologists, Jerome and other Christian Writers* (Göteborg, 1958. *Studia Graeca et Latina Gothoburgensia*, 6), p. 104. See also *Ep.* 117.4. *CSEL*, 55, p. 427: "crudelitas ista pietas est."

49. *Carm.*, 10. *CSEL*, 30, pp. 24-39.

50. *Ep.* 3.1. *CSEL*, 54, p. 13.

51. *Epp.* 3.6; 22.17. *CSEL*, 54, pp. 18, 166.

52. *Tractatus in Evangelium Johannis*, 65.2; 90.2,3. *Corp. Christ., ser. lat.*, 36, pp. 492, 551ff. *Confessions*, 4.12. *CSEL*, 33, p. 78: Souls should be loved in God, where, though mutable, they are fixed and do not perish. *De doctrina Christiana*, 1.79. *CSEL*, 80, p. 28: to enjoy a man in the love of God is to enjoy God rather than the man.

53. W. Jaeger, trans. G. Highet, *Paideia: The Ideals of Greek Culture*, vol. 1 (Oxford, 1945), pp. xiiif. On the general use of corporal punishment in pedagogy, see S. F. Bonner, *Education in Ancient Rome* (Berkeley, 1977), pp. 143-45. This study also provides an admirable introduction to the content and methods of instruction. A modern example of savage beating as a pedagogical device accepted by teachers, parents, and children occurs in Nikos Kazantzakis's autobiography, *Report to Greco* (New York, 1965), ch. 5, pp. 48, 52f.

54. Eadmer, ed. R. W. Southern, *The Life of St. Anselm, Archbishop of Canterbury* (Oxford, 1962), 22, p. 37.

55. *Dialogous adversus Pelagianos*, 1.28. *PL*, 23:544. Julian the Apostate left a valuable testimony to the permanent effect that early training could have. When ridiculed by the Antiochenes for walking with eyes downcast, he attributed that trait to his tutor, Mardonius, who, he said, had trained him to walk to school with downcast eyes and who was chiefly responsible for the ascetic way of life that he followed in adulthood, "a terrible old man" for whom he felt deep affection. *Misopogon*, 351 A, 353 B. *To Sallust*, 241 C. *Letter to the Athenians*, 274 D. *Loeb Classics*, 2. pp. 456, 462f., 168, 258.

56. *Memoirs*, 1.5-6. in ed. J. F. Benton, *Self and Society in Medieval France. The Memoirs of Abbot Guibert of Nogent (1064?-ca.1125)* (New York, 1970), pp. 46-50. On Augustine, below note 58.

57. Lucian, *On the Parasite*, 13. *Loeb Classics*, 3, p. 263. On hatred of worldly wisdom in Peter Damian. See above, note 12.

58. *Confessions*, 1.9; 6.6; 6.14; 11.16. *CSEL*, 33, pp. 12-14, 122, 138, 293. Below note 63.

59. *De doctrina Christiana*, 2.16-22. *CSEL*, 80, p. 39.

60. *Ep.* 49.12-13. *CSEL*, 54, pp. 367-70.

61. *Ep.* 50.5 *CSEL*, 54, p. 393, quoting Juvenal. The same quotation occurs in *ep.* 57.12. *CSEL*, 54, p. 525.

62. *De doctrina Christiana*, 4.14. *CSEL*, 80, p. 121.

63. *Confessions*, 1.9. *CSEL*, 33, p. 14.

64. *Confessions*, 1.13; 4.2-3; 10.37. *CSEL*, 33, pp. 20, 64-68, 273f. On the parallel survival of Jerome's youthful dreams, see J.N.D. Kelley, *Jerome. His Life, Writings, and Controversies* (London, 1975), pp. 7f., 10, 15.

65. *De doctrina Christiana*, 4.148. *CSEL*, 80, p. 164.

66. *De doctrina Christiana*, 1.91-92; 2.146-147; 4.76-77; 4.139-140; 4.148; 4.151-155; 4.164-165. *CSEL*, 80, pp. 32, 76, 138, 161f., 164, 165f., 169.

67. Jerome, *ep.* 22.40, on Matt. 11:12. *CSEL*, 54, p. 208.

68. *Ep.* 117.2 *CSEL*, 55, p. 424. See *ep.* 117.4. *CSEL*, 55, p. 426: "I am a harsh doctor, wounding myself with my own knife." Jerome's list of the liberal arts, including medicine, occurs in *Dialogus contra Pelagianos*, 1.21. *PL*, 23: 537. Tertullian called medicine "the sister of philosophy" because it dealt with the nature of the soul by way of physical treatments. Tertullian, *de anima*, 2.6, in ed. J. H. Waszink, *De Anima, mit Einleitung Übersetzung und Kommentar* (Paris, 1933), p. 26.

69. *Confessions*, 2.2; 6.4; 7.20. *CSEL*, 33, pp. 31, 119f., 122, 166.

70. *Ep.* 22.30. *CSEL*, 54, pp. 190f. Above note 55.

71. Jerome, *epp.* 22.39; 108.31. *CSEL*, 54, p. 206. *CSEL*, 55, p. 349.

72. *Confessions*, 12.14. *CSEL*, 33, p. 321.

73. This position is set forth in Augustine's *ep.* 185, *De correctione Donatistarum*. A fuller discussion is in my book, *The Mimetic Tradition of Reform in the West*. (Princeton, N.J.: 1982), pp. 84-88.

74. Jerome, *Commentarius in Esaiam*, 1.1.5. *Corp. Christ., ser. lat.*, 73, p. 11.

75. *De beata vita*, 2.8. *Corp. Christ., ser. lat.*, 29, pp. 69f.

76. *Cento nuptialis*, 11. 63-66. *Loeb Classics*, vol. 1, p. 382.

77. *De doctrina Christiana*, prol. 8. *CSEL*, 80, pp. 4-5.

78. Paulinus of Nola, *Carmen*, 27, 11. 542-92. *CSEL*, 30, pp. 286-88. Cf. Gregory the Great, *Registrum*, 11.10. *MGH Epp.*, 2, pt. 3, pp. 270f.

79. *De beata vita*, 1.6. *Corp. Christ., ser. lat.*, 29, p. 68.

80. Julian the Apostate, *Misopogon*, 352 B. *Loeb Classics*, vol. 2, p. 460. Julian had the same tutor—a Scythian eunuch—as had his mother in her time.

81. Ausonius, *ep.* 22, 11. 33-34. *Loeb Classics*, vol. 2, p. 74.

82. E.g., the Empress Julia Domna. See Philostratus, *Life of Apollonius*, 1.3. *Loeb Classics*, vol. 1, p. 11. Glen W. Bowersock, *Greek Sophists in the Roman Empire* (Oxford, 1968), pp. 5, 12, 101-09, demonstrating the absence of major figures from Julia's "circle," which appears to have been inhabited by "minor practitioners" of philosophy and the arts.

83. *Parentalia*, 2, 5f., 9, 12, 16, and *passim*. *Loeb Classics*, vol. 1, pp. 60, 66f., 70f., 74f., and *passim*.

84. *Confessions*, 9.8-9. *CSEL*, 33, pp. 210-15.

85. *De beata vita*, 2.10; 2.16; 3.20. *De ordine*, 2.1.1; 2.17.45. *Corp. Christ., ser. lat.*, 29, pp. 71, 74, 76, 106, 131f.

86. Kelly, *Jerome. His Life, Writings, and Controversies*, pp. 273-75. Hagendahl, *Latin Fathers and the Classics*, pp. 325f. Jerome, *Apology*, 3.32. *PL*, 23: 502f.

87. *Ep.* 107.3. *CSEL*, 55, p. 293.

88. *Ep.* 107.4, 9, 10, 12. *CSEL*, 55, pp. 294f., 300f., 302f.

89. *Ep.* 107.4, 9, 11, 13. *CSEL*, 55, pp. 294f., 300, 302, 303-05.

90. *Ep.* 53.7. *CSEL*, 54, p. 453.

91. *Epp.* 50.5; 57.13. *CSEL*, 54, pp. 393f., 526.

92. *Epp.* 130.17; 133.4. *CSEL*, 56, pp. 197f., 247f.

93. See *ep.* 127.7, on Marcella, but also chs. 9-10, concerning her opposition to Origenism at Rome. *CSEL*, 56, pp. 151-53.

94. *Ep.* 66.9. *CSEL*, 54, p. 659.

95. *De re publica*, 1.17. *Pro archia*, 3.4.

96. Ambrose, *De fide*, 1. prol. 2. *CSEL*, 78, p. 5. On the concept of man's deification, see my book, *The Mimetic Tradition of Reform in the West*, pp. 28, 56, and passim.

97. Augustine, *Confessions*, 8.8. *CSEL*, 33, p. 186.

98. E.g., on ignorant bishops, Jerome, *ep.* 53.3, 6, 10; *ep.* 130.17. *CSEL*, 54, pp. 447f., 452, 463. *CSEL*, 56, p. 198. Jerome's own resentment is evident in *Commentarius in Ecclesiasten*, *PL*, 23: 1142, where the Father remarked that ignorant men were advanced in the Church while the learned were left in obscurity to suffer persecution, need, and hunger.

3 *Grammar*

Jeffrey F. Huntsman

The liberal arts illustrate the concept of a techne—a complete system based on a clearly established principle—on several different levels. The canon of the seven arts, with its division into the verbal and mathematical arts, presumably is such a complete system at the most general level. Cassiodorus, for example, in his introductory remarks to the discussion of the Human Readings *seems to identify the trivium as the useful arts and the quadrivium as theoretical sciences. A few paragraphs later he distinguishes the three liberal arts from the four theoretical sciences.*

At a less general level, the trivium and the quadrivium can themselves be viewed as complete systems. Although the organizing idea of the trivium is never made explicit, the principle (or beginning point) is clearly the word. Cassiodorus's definition of the trivium as the useful arts then suggests they can be understood as those verbal skills essential for an educated man: exact speaking and writing, persuasive expression, and clear thinking.

Each individual art is of course a techne. Although grammar was the last art to be treated systematically, the Latin encyclopedists viewed it as the foundation of the trivium. As such, grammar turned its attention to the analysis of certain technical aspects of the word—the principle of the trivium. Yet grammar was also closely associated with literature. For one thing, grammatical theory at the Alexandrian Library grew out of the study of past literature; for another, grammar in both Greek and Roman education included literary criticism—especially of poetry. A division of the art into grammatical theory and literary criticism is implicit in the Alexandrian grammar commonly ascribed to Dionysius of Thrax, the ultimate source for Roman and medieval grammar, and explicit in Quintilian. Nevertheless both these scholars devoted most of their attention to grammatical theory; and the discussions of the Latin encyclopedists, as well as the handbooks of Donatus and Priscian, were limited to the theoretical side.

Grammatical theory was itself a techne—at the most concrete level. Its first major topic, the word, began with a discussion of individual letters. While this approach reflected the practice of Greek and Roman education, it depended on a philosophical theory regarding principles (i.e., beginning points), as Plato's discussion in the Cratylus *of letters as the elements of words makes clear. The examination of words turned next to syllables, and generally also included pronunciation and orthography, etymology, and analogy. The eight parts of speech were a second major topic, with analyses of the vices and virtues of speech the third and final topic.*

D. L. W.

I. INTRODUCTION

From the springtime of his seventh year until the end of his fourteenth, "when the light of reason begins to shine," a boy should make grammar his chief object of study. This recommendation of a medieval treatise on education,[1] however unappealing it may seem to us today, forcefully highlights the central position grammar held in the medieval system of education. Its importance as a fundamental skill challenged (unsuccessfully) only by arithmetic, grammar was the gateway to the more advanced linguistic topics of rhetoric and logic and thus to the study of literature and the Scriptures. Grammar was thought to discipline the mind and the soul at the same time, honing the intellectual and spiritual abilities that the future cleric would need to read and speak with discernment. Of course, for all the prominence given grammar in the curriculum, it was but one part of the total sequence of study necessary to prepare a young man for a successful career either within the Church or abroad in the secular world. Whether lawyer or scholar, priest or layman, the properly educated man needed the knowledge slowly accumulated by humankind to thrive in this world and to prepare himself for the next.[2] This sum of human knowledge was taught during the Middle Ages through the system of the seven liberal arts.

The original pattern for education in the thousand-year period called the Middle Ages was set in the academies of classical Greece, where the male children of aristocratic families studied those subjects whose mastery would give them the knowledge of philosophers, if perhaps not their wisdom. In Roman times, Marcus Terentius Varro (116-27 B.C.) codified the slowly evolving liberal curriculum in his *Nine Books of Disciplines (Disciplinarum libri IX)*, a work which was to be of crucial influence on the scope and direction of medieval education.[3] Although apparently lost before the medieval period, the *Disciplines* was partially known through quotations by other writers and, more importantly, through the model it provided for subsequent and similar compendia like the *Marriage of Mercury and Philology* (*De nuptiis Mercurii et Philologiae*) of Martianus Minneius Felix Capella (fl. 410-39).[4] By the late Roman period, the number of subjects thought necessary to a liberal education had been reduced to seven—Varro's architecture and medicine had become technological subjects suitable for practical men but not for philosophers with higher goals. A half-century after Martianus, Anicius Manlius Severinus Boethius (ca.480-524) more rigorously formulated the scheme of the seven liberal arts, and it is essentially his organization that was to be followed throughout the Middle Ages.[5]

The seven arts that Martianus presented as equals fell naturally into two distinct classes in Boethius's treatment of the scheme, called the trivium and the quadrivium, after the number of disciplines in each. The quadrivium—arithmetic, geometry, astronomy, and music—covered subjects concerned with the acquisition of particular knowledge and its measurement. Pedagogically, the quadrivium was doubly useful: the abstractions of arithmetic provided students with the concepts and methods to prove and understand the fundamental regularity of creation, and they taught the soul to appreciate abstractions in general, those immaterial things that would lead it away from the world and the flesh toward divine contemplation.

The trivium—grammar, dialectic, and rhetoric—was concerned with the ordering of experience and the means of giving expression to this knowledge. Like the quadrivial subjects, those in the trivium also sharpened the mind and provided mechanisms for communicating understanding. Dialectic established a regular and coherent frame for thinking, while rhetoric presented models and methods of expression and ultimately of persuasion.[6] But the foundation discipline, the first road to all knowledge, was grammar. Grammar as a subject supplied the body of information about the forms of language and the ways those forms might be combined into meaningful constructions. Grammar as it was conceived then also included tools for explicating the enduring and significant records of civilization in language—literature, philosophy, and theology. In the schoolboys' mnemonic encapsulating the functions of the seven arts, grammar is given the first place:

> Gram loquitur; Dia vera docet; Rhet verba colorat;
> Mus canit; Ar numerat; Ge ponderat; Ast colit astra.

> ('Grammar speaks; dialectic teaches truth; rhetoric adorns words; music sings; arithmetic counts; geometry measures; astronomy studies stars.')

These subjects were essential and, to most thinking until the Age of Scholasticism,[7] sufficient for the ascension to the higher intellectual endeavors, which were the understanding of philosophy (especially sacred philosophy) and, through the reading of God's words in the Scriptures and God's works in the world at large, the understanding of theology, the highest of man's intellectual attainments. Without grammar, these higher sciences were thought inaccessible. In the iconography of the seven liberal arts, Grammar is often shown variously as the oldest figure, as in Capella's *Marriage,* or as the youngest, as in Alain de Lille's *Anticlaudianus,* where Grammar is a virginal but sustaining figure nursing a host of infant Arts. Despite the seeming contradictions among some of these iconographic representations, the essential point to be made is identical: whether shown as the oldest and hence most experienced, or the youngest, hence the most simple, distinctive, and most direct in her teaching, Grammar has a real primacy among her sisters.[8] Although grammar was at times during the Middle Ages unthroned as the preeminent art when dialectic or rhetoric gained the ascendency within the trivium, it never lost its most fundamental position as the basis of all liberal learning.[9]

Medieval grammar had its origins in three classical traditions: the philosophical tradition of Aristotle and the Stoics; the Alexandrian grammatical tradition of Dionysios Thrax and Apollonios Dyskolos; and the Latin grammatical tradition of Varro, Donatus, and Priscian.[10] The first two traditions differed most fundamentally on their responses to two related metaphysical questions. First, is the world fundamentally ordered and regular, or is it irregular and perhaps somewhat untidy in its particular structures? Second, is language structured according to convention (*nómo*) or nature (*phýsei*) ; in other words, does language present the order it imposes on reality or does it present reality itself? The philosophical tradition beginning with the Sophists and ending (for our purposes here) with the Stoics is focused on problems of natural philosophy and, more especially, on humanity's quest to understand nature in order to live a harmonious and therefore virtuous life. The Stoics felt that some similarities but not a rigid set of formal correspondences could be discovered among the natural structures of the world. Since language was the product of man's nature, it was, like man's other attributes, subject to anomalies inexplicable within any strict system of grammar. By contrast, the grammarians of Alexandria faced a different task, that of making sense of texts several centuries old and therefore riddled with forms of the language no longer used. The Alexandrians, lacking the Stoics' philosophical ideal and having a different practical purpose, attempted to discover as many regularities as they could, trying to explain unusual or archaic forms by analogy with better understood forms. Thus the prime motivation of the Alexandrians was their desire to explicate poetical texts, not to establish a grammar for its own sake.

Although no one after Protagoras (ca.480 B.C.-ca.350 B.C.) seemed to have held a position at either extreme, these Greek confrontations, usually called the "anomaly-analogy" and the "physis-nomos" controversies respectively, shaped Roman and thus medieval grammar in significant ways. In a strictly grammatical sphere, these controversies seem to have been of little concern, for linguistic regularities merely offered guidance in choosing the correct literary form.[11] Nevertheless, an empirical result of this concern with the "right" form was the production of a set of grammars whose formal arrangements were chiefly paradigmatic. In the long view then, it may be said that in general the judgments of the analogists prevailed, as the grammars of Aelius Donatus (fourth century) and Priscian (early sixth century) maintained the paradigmatic approach begun by the Alexandrians. Nevertheless, the Stoic influence continued to make itself felt in two ways. First, in a narrow grammatical sphere, the anomalists' attempts to find cogent counterexamples to the analogists' regularities forced grammarians' attention closer to the fine details of language and therefore encouraged a continual refinement of their work. Second, in a more philosophical sphere, Stoic doctrines became part of Neoplatonism, the dominant late classical philosophy before the Christianization of the Roman world and a profound influence on such important early medieval churchmen as John Scotus Erigena and Remigius of Auxerre, whose teachings did much to prepare the way for the general revival of intellectual endeavor in the twelfth century.

II. THE TWO BRANCHES: PEDAGOGICAL GRAMMAR AND SCHOLARLY GRAMMAR

Out of this composite classical tradition emerged two rather different ways of defining the grammarian's task. Although both of these approaches dealt with essentially the same materials and, at least before the twelfth century, used many of the same grammatical texts, they constituted two major sets of beliefs, differing in the importance assigned to particular aspects of grammar and in the areas to which grammatical learning might be applied. One set of beliefs, historically the older, addressed the practical needs of the teacher concerned with instilling in students a Latin that was at once grammatically proper and rhetorically effective. With isolated exceptions, Latin was the only language so studied and so taught. It held the place in the old Roman West that English now has in much of the world. Latin was the common language of business and commerce, science and industry, philosophy and literature, and, most importantly, of theology and religion.

Although other languages were certainly spoken within its compass (including constantly diverging dialects of the original Latin vernacular), the written Latin preserved in most of our records from the Middle Ages was considered to be THE language and consequently THE grammar must have been the grammar of Latin. As embodied in the pedagogical works of the late Roman period, the grammar was descriptive in spirit and, strongly oriented toward the simple, directly observable data of language, stressed the correct forms of past writing rather than speculating about what the potentials of the language might be. Naturally, this pedagogical grammar was not monolithic, especially when viewed across its history, but in general it can be said to focus more heavily on literary matters and was more closely associated with rhetoric within the trivium than with logic. This type of grammar was not an especially interesting or important intellectual discipline in its own right but was rather a tool for explicating existing texts and for guiding students in a very elementary way in the writing of new texts. This literary, pedagogical grammar originally centered on Donatus's simple teaching texts and on Priscian's more lengthy work, which used the Latin classics as examples of literary and grammatical excellence. Later, elaborate commentaries surrounded the grammatical text with explanatory materials—literally surrounded in many cases, for the manuscripts often had the original in the center of the page with the commentaries filling the margins on all sides. Some wholly integrated the original into the commentary, often without any clear indication of where the original text ended and the commentary began, or quoted only parts, implying that the writer assumed the reader's familiarity with the original work. The commentary came to be regarded as a specific genre in its own right and many of its examples should more properly be considered new works, at least according to modern criteria of originality in scholarly writing. Finally, toward the end of the twelfth century, there appeared a new type of intermediate-level teaching material, metrical grammars like the *Graecismus* of Eberhard of Béthune and the *Doctrinale* of Alexander of Villa-Dei.

In contrast to these grammars that were designed to meet the needs of teachers and pupils, the grammars of the second branch of medieval linguistics addressed the scholar's more abstract concern with understanding language itself. Here an attempt was made to go beyond the practical classification of the simple phonology, morphology, and syntax of a language (the observable properties and relations like inflections and word order) to investigations of particular details of language, especially its broader—perhaps universal—semantic and syntactic properties. Some of these particular treatises were extensions of the standard grammars' commentaries on orthography, prosody, and etymology, as well as their more central discussions of letters and syllables, word formation, and syntactic structures. In specific, developments during the Middle Ages gave syntax and lexicology the shapes we now expect to find, representing major advancements over the practices of the classical period. But of greater prominence, if not importance, were the works of a critical and imaginative nature which were oriented more toward a general theory of language than toward particular data and more closely associated with logic than with rhetoric. These philosophical grammars attempted to achieve a level of explanation that was not only adequate for all languages but ultimately applicable to the organization of the world in general. For this reason, one type of philosophical grammar was called speculative grammar (from Latin *speculum* 'mirror') ,[12] for it attempted to mirror the structure of the universe. While this scholastic tradition, which culminated in the work of the Northern European schoolmen known as the Modistae, was in the ascendancy throughout the thirteenth and into the fourteenth centuries, it ultimately waned, although its principles have been revived independently many times since by grammarians as different as the seventeenth-century Jansenists of Port Royal and our contemporary, Noam Chomsky. While the philosophical tradition dominated the typical medieval university of Northern Europe toward the end of the Middle Ages, the pedagogical tradition was the more pervasive and enduring; in a very real sense, it is alive today in both its original texts and in the vernacular grammars of many of the world's languages.

These two distinctively dissimilar medieval approaches to the grammarian's duty drew from essentially the same heritage of materials and methods, yet produced grammars that differed radically in their interests and in their degrees of achievement. The rather limited goals of the pedagogical grammars naturally precluded both great successes and great failures, while the philosophical grammars, which attempted more, were less able to meet their own high expectations. In the thousand years between Donatus and a speculative grammarian like Thomas of Erfurt, there were many changes in the scope and direction of linguistic enquiry as understandings about language altered and as new discoveries (or rediscoveries) in areas adjacent to grammar influenced development of the language science.

The rest of this essay will trace a historical map of these two major grammatical traditions from the end of the classical era through the beginning of the fourteenth century, when newer interests and radically different approaches set in motion the forces that would end the Middle Ages (see Figure 3-1) . In contemplating this history, we must remember that there is still much we do not know about medieval grammar and the way it developed.[13] Because of the way medieval teachers and schol-

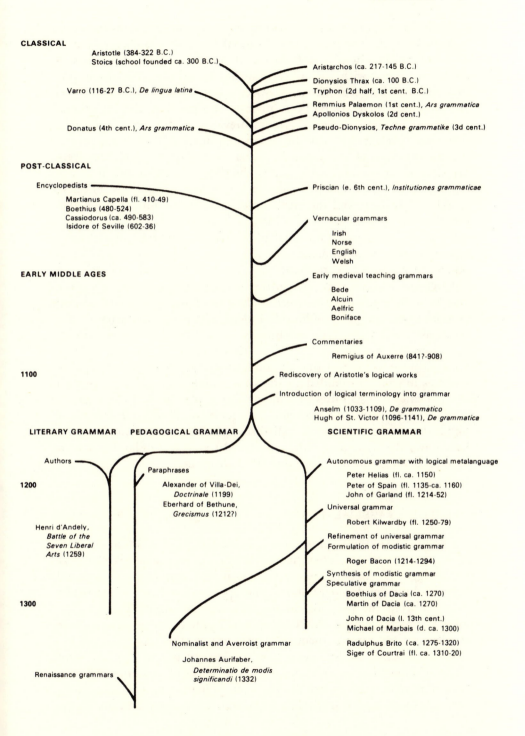

Fig. 3-1. Development of Medieval Grammar

ars often incorporated their own commentaries into earlier works, it is frequently difficult to separate an original text from its elaboration or its redaction. Further, the relations of grammar with the other arts in the trivium and with the other branches of science and philosophy that consider language in some aspect (particularly metaphysics and epistemology) have always been intricate and problematic. In contrast to our present term *language,* the medieval term *grammar* is too narrow, since it refers chiefly to the shapes and in some respects the etymological meanings of single words. Other aspects of our *language* were discussed by medieval scholars under the rubrics of *logic* (much of syntax and semantics) and of *rhetoric* (the affective and the effective aspects of discourse and the organization of syntactic units more elaborate than the sentence).

On the other hand, traditional philosophical enquiries into distinctions like those between matter and form, essence and attribute, act and potentiality, and being and significance, were not limited to philosophy but were central, though often inexplicit, concerns of medieval grammar as well, especially the more highly developed grammars labeled "speculative" or "philosophical." Indeed, the very similarity of the terms used in these several disciplines attested to the commonality of their interests and methods.[14] These similarities can be attributed in large measure to the fact that the underlying system of medieval grammar was in general founded on the same primary assumptions as most other medieval disciplines of enquiry and explanation. Not all grammarians were explicitly scientific, of course (although all the philosophical grammarians can be called so), but all shared some basic beliefs about the structure of the world and the most fundamental ways of approaching and understanding that structure.

III. THE CLASSICAL FOUNDATIONS OF MEDIEVAL GRAMMAR

The first period in the history of medieval grammar ends at the start of the twelfth century, when the reintroduction of crucial texts of Aristotle triggered a fresh interest in logical and empirical science and prompted the development of a second approach to language, radically different from the pedagogical tradition it challenged. The body of material taught during this first period is chiefly the product of the classical world; from a theoretical perspective, the linguistic innovations of the early Middle Ages were modest. In practical terms, most classical grammar was summarized by the works of Donatus and Priscian. Their grammars, virtually alone of their long tradition, not only were known to medieval scholars and teachers, but furnished the fundamental educational corpus which endured into the Renaissance. To the vast majority of schoolboys in Western Europe, Donatus and Priscian were all of grammar. After the founding of Constantinople in 330 as the center of the Byzantine Empire and the resulting severance of the original Roman Empire into the Latin-dominated West and the Greek-dominated East, Greek grammar became all but unknown to the students and teachers we are discussing here. Few Western European grammarians even knew Greek (Roger Bacon was a distinct exception) and fewer still had direct access to the primary texts of the classical period, even after the reopening of the West to the eastern Mediterranean and Arabic worlds after the eleventh century. Naturally, the Eastern Empire continued to use Greek,[15] and there were several important, although not extensive, contacts between the Byzantine world and the West. Overall, however, such occasional interrelations little increased the amount or altered the character of Western knowledge of Greek and the learned texts written in it. Nevertheless, Greek grammatical theories profoundly informed the study of grammar during the Middle Ages, even if only indirectly. Although it is true that for the early Middle Ages *classical grammar* meant virtually Donatus and Priscian alone, their works so thoroughly incorporated the essential beliefs of their precedessors, and thus in such large measure determined the scope of *grammar* for most medieval scholars, that an account of their sources presents perhaps the clearest way of delineating their most distinctive characteristics.

The development of classical theories of language was complicated in a variety of ways. First, perhaps more than in any other period of its history, grammar was less an independent discipline than an integral part of interlocking—and often conflicting—sets of philosophies. Since *philosophy* among the Greeks encompassed all human knowledge, even the practical Alexandrian grammars, whose primary function was to explicate ancient texts, were shaped by controversies about the nature of the world and hence the nature of human language. For this reason, differing grammars that conveyed much the same technical information about the particular language (Greek or Latin, specifically) were predicated upon rather different theoretical principles. As a result, while the same details given about one grammatical form or another might be found in each grammar, readers were required to make significantly different extrapolations about the nature of language and how it was to be investigated. For the schoolboy learning classical Latin, these differences would make little practical difference; for later readers like us whose interest is intellectual history, such differences are crucial. Second, early classical grammatical theory in general lacked a metalanguage which was clearly separated from the technical language that it inherited from the philosophies which gave it birth and from the logics with which it continued to be associated. As a result, a term like *logos* could have a variety of meanings from grammar ('sentence' or 'phrase'), from logic ('proposition'), or even from ordinary language ('speech,' 'reason,' 'meaning,' or 'argument'). Even today, our common grammatical phrase *part of speech* (*méros lógou*) reflects this confusion; it is better translated 'part of a sentence.' This kind of terminological vagueness or ambiguity continued to plague grammarians throughout the medieval period and into our own time; the definitions of *subject, predicate,* and *sentence* familiar to all of us from traditional teaching grammars are essentially weakened logical definitions stripped of their systemic force. Despite these failings, much progress was made, especially by the Greeks, in converting terms from other disciplines to specifically grammatical uses, and by the end of the classical period, grammarians had a well-developed, if incomplete, descriptive metalanguage, which was used throughout the Middle Ages. In short, the body of linguistic science bequeathed to the Latin Middle Ages was a remarkably unified grammatical tradition whose internal inconsistencies were largely insignificant when compared with its overall coherence.[16]

From the perspective of linguistic theory, perhaps the most interesting Latin grammarian was Marcus Terentius Varro. He was a prolific and much admired writer, important in the present context for his *Nine Books of the Disciplines* mentioned above and his grammar, *On the Latin Language (De lingua latina)*. Like many of his contemporaries, Varro was influenced by the doctrines of the Stoics, introduced to Romans about 168 B.C. by Crates of Mallos, ambassador from Pergamon.[17] The Stoics' ideas on language developed from those of the Sophists, Plato, and Aristotle and were more philosophical than scientific; that is, they looked for proof of their hypotheses to internal systematic consistencies and to logic, not to empirically verifiable information from outside the system. Central to the Stoics' linguistic doctrine is the belief that language was once regular but had become irregular as time passed because of man's linguistic innovations and perversions. Thus, unlike Plato and Aristotle, who taught that particular languages were essentially arbitrary conventions of mankind, the Stoics felt that originally there had been a necessary and logical connection between the things of the world and the things of language. Since the Stoics, like most grammarians before the late thirteenth century, took the *word* to be the fundamental unit of their theory of language, they were crucially interested in discovering the primary significance of individual words —the *etyma* which would provide unfailing guides to how the language *should* be understood. They believed that only when ultimate meanings were known could the system of language be unraveled. This interest in ultimate meanings—etymology—is one of the most long-lasting legacies of the Stoics to the European intellectual community; until the development of comparative linguistics in the late eighteenth and nineteenth centuries, grammarians continued to search for the same kind of ultimate meanings that interested the Stoics.

Despite the quality of his interesting and innovative analysis of language, Varro's approach to language was unaccountably not taken by his successors as the model for grammatical description, and the excellent reputation he enjoyed during the Middle Ages was not based on *De lingua latina,* which was wholly unknown to medieval scholars. Instead, the unified grammatical tradition of the Hellenistic Greeks furnished the pattern on which most medieval grammar was modeled. Based on the records we now have, Aristarchos (ca.217-145 B.C.), librarian and founder of the school at Alexandria, was probably the first significant grammarian in this tradition, which was to encompass Donatus, Priscian, and the majority of traditional pedagogical grammarians up until the present day. Unfortunately, we know little of Aristarchos's grammatical teachings from his own hand, but his judgments were incorporated and augmented by his pupil, Dionysios Thrax (ca. 100 B.C.), and perpetuated in a much later work, the *Techne grammatike.* The *Techne,* attributed to Dionysios but most likely a work dating from some four centuries after his period, is short, only twenty-five brief paragraphs, but of very considerable influence in the history of grammar. According to the *Techne,* the skill of grammar consisted of:

> the practical knowledge of the general usages of poets and prose writers. It has six parts: first, accurate reading (aloud) with due regard to the prosodies; second, explanation of the literary expressions in the works; third, the provision of notes on phraseology and subject matter; fourth, the discovery of etymologies; fifth, the working out of analogical regularities; sixth, the appreciation of literary composition, which is the noblest part of grammar.[18]

This statement from the introduction, which is perhaps the only part we have actually written by Dionysios Thrax himself, manifested the Alexandrians' chief concern with grammar as a tool for literary interpretation. The *Techne,* however, covered only the first and fifth parts, that is, the phonological values of the letters and the regularities, *paradigms,* of inflectional forms. Here we find the division of the sentence into eight parts of speech, probably attributable to Tryphon (second half, first century B.C.). This scheme, whose order of presentation reflected the logical importance of the parts, has remained one of the most enduring characteristics of European grammar.[19] The eight parts were noun, verb, participle, article, pronoun, preposition, adverb, and conjunction (*onoma, rhema, metoche, arthron, antonymia, prothesis, epir-rhema,* and *syndesmos*). For the most part, the *Techne's* definitions were formal. The noun was distinguished, not by what it meant, but by its having the distinctions (*parepomena*) of gender, type (primary or derived), form (simple or compound), number, and case. The verb had distinctions of mood, kind (active, middle, or passive), type, form, number, person, tense, and conjugation. Similar formal definitions were given for the participle, article, preposition, adverb, and pronoun (although the pronoun's chief characteristic, that it substituted for a noun, is more accurately described as syntactic). But for several of the parts of speech, the *Techne* also supplied correlative semantic definitions (for example, the verb showed action), and for the conjunction the definition was wholly semantic (it linked thoughts in a determined order and filled the gaps of speech).

A syntactic description of Greek and a model for syntactic description in subsequent grammars was supplied by another Alexandrian, Apollonios Dyskolos (second century). Of some twenty works ascribed to him, mostly on syntax, only four survive: particular treatises on the pronoun, the conjunction, and the adverb, and a more compendious work, *On Syntax (Peri syntaxeos)*, which treated the article, pronoun, verb, preposition, and adverb. Apollonios was a most careful scholar with a critical and historical turn of mind, and much of what we know about the development of grammar in the four centuries after the Stoics comes from his writings. His theoretical advances were limited, however, by the fact that his syntax was word-based. He assumed that the principles which distinguished the parts-of-speech scheme were sufficient for the further analysis of the sentence. Since he believed that the most important syntactic relations obtained only among the individual elements of the surface sentence, his syntax could not be fully developed, comprehensive, or consistent. Nevertheless, Apollonios engaged in a constant search for the principles of grammar, not the mere listing of examples of correct forms. Thus he aimed at a level of scientific adequacy that moved beyond simple observation to description and at times even explanation. He maintained clear distinctions between form and function, with the latter receiving more weight. Among the more important concepts he introduced into European grammar were the principles of concord and agreement (marking conventions which linked, for example, plural verbs with plural subjects) and the distinction between transitive and intransitive verbs (which allowed him to note a *syntactically* defined difference between subject and object, not a logical one). There are suggestions, for example, in his use of terms like *paralambanesthai* 'to be taken together,' that he was reaching towards an analysis of sentences based on hierarchically related constituents,[20] but these notions were never worked out. The work of Apollonios Dyskolos completed the general outline of the model of grammar still found today in traditional descriptions of Latin, Greek, and many modern languages, and it is altogether fitting that Priscian should have called him the *maximus auctor artis grammaticae,* 'the greatest authority on the art of grammar.'[21]

IV. THE BASIC TEXTS: DONATUS AND PRISCIAN

The several grammarians discussed so far might be called the founders of medieval grammar, for they first developed the terminology, elaborated the techniques, and established the salient questions for the centuries that were to follow. Although the works of these grammarians were not directly a part of the corpus of medieval grammar per se and most were not known even by name to medieval scholars, their views were perpetuated in their Late Latin successors. With Donatus and Priscian, however, we come to the two premedieval writers whose works survived intact and were widely used during the Middle Ages. Although written before the beginning of the medieval period, their enduring popularity throughout that era makes them central to any history of medieval grammar.

Aelius Donatus (fourth century) was the author of two of the most widely used schoolbooks of the entire medieval period, the *De partibus orationis ars minor* ('the lesser art, concerning the parts of grammar') and the *Ars grammatica* or *Ars major* ('the greater art').[22] From the perspective of grammatical theory, Donatus is hardly a significant figure, for he proposed no important new formulations, made no major alterations in the tradition he inherited, and offered few penetrating insights into either the structure of Latin in particular or the structure of human languages in general. As a practical grammarian, however, he was rivaled only by Priscian, and as a language pedagogue he was unsurpassed. Although the *Ars major* (except for Book III, the *Barbarismus*) was generally eclipsed by Priscian's *Institutiones grammaticae,* the *Ars minor* achieved an almost instant and extremely enduring fame. The praise offered this scholar and his work came first from his renowned pupil, Jerome, and began to die down only in the Renaissance. Besides the hundreds of manuscripts attesting to the widespread distribution of the *Ars minor,* there were numerous commentaries, elaborations, and paraphrases that helped promote at least the name of its author, if not his pure teachings. During the Middle Ages, the very name Donatus, in forms like *donat* and *donet,* became synonymous with *grammar* itself in a variety of vernacular languages including Irish, Welsh, French, English, and Provençal. Even after the Middle Ages gave way to the Renaissance, the grammar's influence continued to be felt. Luther and Rabelais learned from the Donatus, the first French-language book printed (1460) was a translation of the Donatus, and a reference in Cotsgrave's *Dictionarie of the French and English Tongues* (1611) indicates that the Donatus was then still in use in English schools.

The *Ars minor* consisted of an elementary treatise on the parts of speech cast in a question-and-answer form.

> How many parts of speech are there? Eight. What? Noun, pronoun, verb, adverb, participle, conjunction, preposition, interjection. *On the noun.* What is a noun? A part of speech with case signifying a person or a thing specifically or generally. How many attributes does a noun have? Six. What? Quality, comparison, gender, number, form, case.[23]

Here we can clearly see the basic organization already familiar from the *Techne*. The grammar was based on the division of a sentence into individual parts of speech; the parts of speech were defined by a mixture of semantic and formal features (a noun, for example, was said both to signify a person or thing and to show case) ; and finally the parts of speech were described by the number and type of their attributes (accidents). Because Latin had no article, the interjection was substituted (possibly by Remmius Palaemon in his *Ars grammaticae,* which apparently was a version of an Alexandrian grammar) in order to maintain the by-then traditional number of eight parts of speech. Donatus's grammar strongly resembles that in the *Techne*. To that work's set of nominal and adjectival characteristics, for example, Donatus added quality (common or proper) and comparison (positive, comparative, or superlative), while deleting type (primary or derived). His longer work, the *Ars major,* began with a discussion of *vox,* the substance of language, and proceeded through analyses of the values of the letters, syllables, stress, a number of points of rhetoric, and a treatment of the parts of speech more elaborate than that in the *Ars minor.*

If Donatus was the author of the most popular elementary teaching grammar of the Middle Ages, the more significant practical grammarian of the era was Priscian. Living in the first part of the sixth century, Priscian taught in Constantinople and based his *Institutiones grammaticae* on the writings of Apollonios Dyskolos, although his text also mentions Donatus and other writers. Thus the Alexandrians exerted a double influence on Roman, and hence on medieval grammar— directly through Palaemon's *Ars grammaticae* and less directly through Priscian's use of Apollonios. The *Institutiones grammaticae* comprised eighteen books, the first sixteen covering morphology and phonology (called the *Priscianus major*) and the last two covering syntax (the *Priscianus minor*).[24] In addition to the primary effects of the Alexandrians on his grammatical observations, Priscian shows a more general Alexandrian influence in his frequent use of classical authors, especially Vergil, to support his grammatical assertions. Hereafter many would know more of what they recognized of the classical texts from their grammar books, encyclopedias, and other compendia than they would from the primary texts. Like the *Artes major* and *minor*, the *Institutiones* survives in hundreds of manuscripts that, along with hundreds of different commentaries, attest to Priscian's profound and extensive influence throughout the Middle Ages.[25]

Despite the surface similarities of the *Institutiones* to the formal grammars of the Alexandrians, Priscian's approach was strongly semantic. For example, his definition of an *oratio* 'sentence' was that it consisted of a complete thought, with no consideration being given as to whether or not it was a syntactically complete entity. Like his predecessors, he kept the eight parts of speech, but his chief defining characteristics were semantic, not formal. The noun was distinguished principally by the fact that it indicated a substance and assigned a common or particular quality to every body or thing, not by its accidents of case, number, gender, and so forth. Similarly, a verb and an adverb were chiefly distinguished by their semantic qualities: the verb signified action or the condition of being acted upon and the adverb added its meaning to the verb. In this attempt to formulate a semantic grammar, there were many problems, including both internal contradictions and incorrect statements about the language. Despite his reliance on semantic criteria for his basic definitions, there was little mention of systematic semantics (semantics beyond the meanings of individual words) and his treatment of syntax was somewhat haphazard and occasionally confusing. In short, although it provided a wealth of information about the shapes and distribution of Latin words and suggested, by his frequent use of Greek examples, some principles of true etymology, his grammar did not penetrate particularly far into the more complex and interesting aspects of meaning-bearing linguistic elements and their functional combinations. As a result, Priscian's contribution to the history of grammar was not as profound as it might have been, however important he may have been to the history of education in the following centuries. This last distinction is a crucial one to mark, for the next five centuries—the time of the encyclopedists and the early commentators—would see only small advances in grammatical theory, even though the number and complexity of particular grammatical texts would continue to increase. In other words, though we find an enriching of the texture of grammars, especially teaching grammars, we find relatively few new

insights into the theory of language and the way it might have illumi-
nated either a particular language or the structure and operations of
human languages in general. Such advances would have to wait for a
renewed interest in the philosophical nature of grammar, with the
rediscovery of Aristotle's more technical texts and the new spirit of
scientific enquiry they sparked.

V. EARLY MEDIEVAL GRAMMAR: ENCYCLOPEDIAS AND COMMENTARIES

During the five centuries between the end of the Roman Empire and
the new awakening at the beginning of the twelfth century, the vitality
and breadth of learning, if not its quality, declined generally throughout Western Europe, even though the Eastern Empire, centered on the
still-thriving Byzantium (Constantinople), kept alive the spirit of enquiry that reached back to classical Greece. The effects of the decline
of the Roman Empire and the subsequent conquests by various Germanic peoples were real enough, but we now know that the "Dark
Ages" were not so uniformly dark as they were described by nineteenth-
century historians. Part of the reason for this apparent decline is that
scholarly efforts, instead of being concentrated in a few distinguished
centers, were diffused throughout most of Europe. It is true, however,
that everywhere except in the British Isles, where the Irish and Welsh
had escaped the worst fate of continental Europeans, there were fewer
and perhaps less-distinguished scholars than there were during the more
fertile periods of the Greek and Roman ascendancies. It is also true
that the character of learning in this period was different. It was a time
of conservation and even retrenchment, when scholars were painfully
conscious of what they perceived to be the difference between the golden
years of Greece and Rome and the poorer, more somber times they
lived in. Although there was a healthy state of learning in sixth- and
seventh-century Celtic Britain and a better-known flowering centered
on the court of Charlemagne, many scholars of these centuries were
more concerned with codifying and preserving the classical wisdom
than with extending it greatly (at least insofar as we may judge from
the surviving texts and the references of later scholars to the work of
their predecessors). Thus it is not surprising that we find few exciting
new characterizations of language and its study. Archetypically these
centuries were the time of the writers of compendia and encyclopedias.

Some of the important encyclopedists, particularly Martianus Capella, have already been mentioned because of their contributions to
the development of the seven liberal arts scheme. Boethius (ca.480-524)

also fits generally into this mold, although he was a far more original thinker and his influence was more profound than that of the others. In addition to the effect he had on medieval education in general, Boethius introduced the question of universals into grammatical studies.[26] While universals constituted more a philosophical than a linguistic problem at this time,[27] the question of universals involved both grammar and logic for two reasons. First, the grammatical use of terms like *substance* and *quality* implied that speakers did in fact recognize universals, such as those which allowed them to abstract the qualities signified by the words *man* and *red* from their experience with a series of men or a series of red objects. Second, grammar throughout the medieval period was thought to underlie at least the fundamentals of logic and thus constituted one of the tools needed to discover both meaning and truth. The complex intermixing of grammar and logic in this search for understanding is one of the most striking characteristics of the intellectual life of the Middle Ages, but to unravel it would require a more extended discussion than the present essay allows.

The last important encyclopedist of the postclassical period is Isidore, bishop of Seville (ca.570-636). Isidore's *Etymologiae sive origines,* like Martianus Capella's *Marriage of Mercury and Philology* and Cassiodorus's *Institutiones,* was a compendious schoolbook on the seven liberal arts and adjacent subjects.[28] But Isidore's real interest was grammar; over forty percent of the *Origines* was devoted to grammar and the other two subjects in the trivium occupied another thirty percent. Isidore's conception of grammar was limited. His text was largely taken, essentially unchanged, from Donatus, and his main interest clearly lay in the etymologies he sought to discover for the words of the Latin language. Isidore's etymologies must be approached from the anomalists' perspective; they designated the original senses words had before man's nature corrupted them.[29] Lacking any notion of true etymology (which must proceed in accordance with demonstrable linguistic facts and rules), Isidore manufactured histories for the words whose actual histories were unknown to him. He suggested, for example, that words were sometimes made up of reduced phrases, so that the etymology of *cadaver* was *CAro DAta VERmibus* 'flesh given to worms,' and even that words might derive their meanings from their opposites, so that *bellum* 'war' was derived from *bellus* 'beautiful' just because war was *not* beautiful. It is easy to laugh at such fantasies, but in fact many of his etymologies were correct or nearly so. His approach to etymology, although frequently wrongheaded and mostly unscientific by today's linguistic standards, was still a serious attempt to make the world rational in all its parts and easy for the learned man to comprehend. Whatever judgment might be made about the scientific accuracy of his work, the *Etymologiae* was of great influence on pedagogical writers throughout the medieval period and the hundreds of medieval manuscripts remaining attest to Isidore's authority long after other and better thinkers were forgotten.

In the centuries following the close of the Roman Empire, many commentaries accumulated around the works of Donatus, Priscian, Boethius, and other writers. The commentary was an extremely popular genre of scholarly writing throughout the Middle Ages and many so augment the original texts that they should be considered new works in the way that certain synthesizing examples of literary criticism today go well beyond an explication of the texts that precipitated their writing (see figure 3-1). Remigius of Auxerre (ca.841-908), for example, wrote many exegetical tracts, including commentaries on Donatus, Priscian, and Martianus, and was the founder of a school of exegesis that continued his kind of work for generations after his death.[30] Like the encyclopedias, the commentaries represented more importantly an impulse toward the preservation and explanation of earlier learning, leavened by a generally conservative inclination toward new knowledge. Overall, advances in grammar were modest and somewhat restrained. Interestingly, we find a number of significant departures from the Latin tradition in some of the teaching grammars written for speakers of particular languages (like those by Bede, Boniface, Alcuin, and Aelfric)[31] and in the vernacular grammars written by largely anonymous scholars among the Irish, Welsh, English, and Norse.[32] Of course, these departures were prompted by the differences between Latin and the other languages in question and should in most cases not be thought of as the independent discoveries of critical enquiry into the structure of language nor as a rejection of their Latin models. Rather, they are sensible reactions to the incongruities resulting from the application of the grammatical system developed for one language to the linguistic structures of another.[33] In any case, these various national and vernacular grammars represented divergences from the mainstream of grammatical history, not influences upon it.

VI. THE FLOWERING OF SCIENTIFIC GRAMMAR

By the end of the eleventh century, differences had developed between the patterns and goals of education in Southern and Northern Europe that were to have very significant consequences for the next three centuries of grammatical history. South of the Loire, in southern France, Italy, and Spain, the emphasis was on grammar combined with rhetoric and logic as a preparation for the study of civil and ecclesiastical law. The needs of the students for whom such grammars were prepared were very practical and, when combined with the *ars dictaminis,* which taught how to write letters and legal briefs, grammar had the rather practical and secular purposes of instructing the students in correct and effective Latin.[34] North of the Loire, in northern France, Flanders, Germany, Denmark, and (to a lesser extent) England, grammar was largely subordinated to logic. Rhetoric was not disregarded, but it was treated more as a post hoc adornment of speech and writing than as a set of guiding principles to effective and truthful reasoning. Whereas in the south the interests of law, business, and literature were dominant, in the north grammar and logic were supreme, dedicated to a serious and scholarly search for truth in the world, a more philosophical and, in some cases, more righteous enterprise. This partial disjunction does not represent a rejection of northern scholarship by the south; this possibility is belied by the serious consideration given those northern commentaries, verse grammars, and even speculative grammars that did penetrate southern France and Italy. Rather, the difference is more one of what might almost be called tone. As an accident of history, the northern universities were conservative, like the societies in which they were embedded, while the southern schools mirrored the expansive stirrings that were to expand into the Renaissance. Thus, although by 1100 there had been no extensive changes in the kinds of grammatical teaching offered to potential students anywhere in Europe, the way had been prepared for a split into approaches to and applications of grammar that were pedagogical and literary on the one hand and philosophical and scientific on the other.

The emergence of scientific grammar in the eleventh and twelfth centuries had little effect on the continued use of the original grammatical texts of earlier times, like those by Donatus and Priscian. In this parallel and more popular branch of the stream, Priscian reigned supreme during the twelfth century as the chief practical grammarian. During the thirteenth century a new genre emerged, the metrical grammar, whose verse form—it would be aesthetically inaccurate to call their jangling hexameters "poetry"—made it relatively easy to memorize. Particularly important are two intermediate-level texts written at the beginning of the thirteenth century. The first of these metrical paraphrases was the *Doctrinale puerorum* (1199), in 2645 hexameter lines, by Alexander of Villa-Dei in Normandy. The other was the *Graecismus* (1212?), in 4545 lines, by Eberhard of Béthune in Flanders.[35] Although their literary quality, as with most didactic verse, was negligible and their linguistic insight not great,[36] these grammatical poems were immensely popular, for they made the teaching and the learning of the simple facts of Latin easier than even the catechism-like, question-and-answer format of Donatus's *Ars minor*.

A final and minor division in the pedagogical stream of medieval grammar is the split that developed in France between literary study centered on the familiar doctrine of the seven liberal arts (as it evolved from the writings of Martianus Capella and Boethius) and literary study centered on particular authors. The more restrictive authors curriculum, like that promoted by Thierry of Chartres's *Heptateuchon* (1141),[37] contended for adherents with the arts curriculum, especially as it was promulgated in places like Paris, where the study of logic was considered to be of paramount importance. The conflict was allegorized in Henri d'Andely's *The Battle of the Seven Liberal Arts* (1259) where the forces of logic, aided by Aristotle and Boethius (among others), issue from Paris to do battle with the forces of Grammar, aided by Donatus, Priscian, and such classical authors as Vergil, Homer, and Ovid. Logic wins, but the author predicts that Grammar will triumph in thirty years because anyone who is not perfect in his parts of speech must be deemed the merest boy, unworthy of serious consideration.[38] Despite the fury of the verbal war that raged between centers of the arts approach (like Paris) and the authors approach (like Orléans), the debate seldom focused on matters of serious grammatical import and therefore has little relevance for the history of grammar.

While the pedagogical tradition continued in its own course, another approach to grammar was developing beside it. What caused this division of the grammatical stream into two branches was the rediscovery of several highly technical texts of Aristotle, particularly the writings on natural history contained in the *Metaphysics* and *De anima,* and the logical writings in the *Prior* and *Posterior Analytics, Topics,* and *Sophistics (Sophistici Elenchi)*. Known as the *Logica nova,* these last texts complemented the other parts of the *Organon* (the *Categories* and *On Interpretation*), which comprised the *Logica vetus*.[39] The reappearance of these works in the West reawakened an interest both in strict logic and in an empirical (as opposed to a philosophical) investigation of the world. Whereas before God's ways were generally thought to be difficult or even impossible to understand except through faith or revelation, the rediscovery of Aristotelian principles of scientific investigation offered the possibility that such an understanding could be arrived at rationally, through the exercise of man's powers of observation and reason. All science, in other words, must be founded on principles that were universal and immutable. Aristotle had to be interpreted carefully by devout Christians, of course, for he had been a pagan and some of his writings on natural history, taken literally, were in direct contradiction to Catholic dogma. Nevertheless, despite some formidable opposition to certain of Aristotle's doctrines, especially in Paris in the early years of the thirteenth century, the effects of the new science and logic spread rapidly throughout Europe.[40]

Aristotle's basic principles of nature and his methods of coming to an understanding of those principles (the categories) underlay all varieties of the medieval grammatical science, as they did all other sciences in the High Middle Ages. In the opening paragraphs of his *Grammatica speculativa,* the philosophical grammarian Thomas of Erfurt (fl. early fourteenth century) referred specifically to the beginning of Aristotle's *Physics:*

> *The rationale of the method.* In all science, understanding and knowledge derive from a recognition of its principles, as stated in I *Physicorum, Text Comment 1;* we therefore, wishing to know the science of grammar, insist that it is necessary first of all to know its principles which are the modes of signifying. But before we enquire into their particular features, we must first set forth some of their general features without which it is not possible to obtain the fullest understanding of them.[41]

The passage Thomas cites in Aristotle reads:

> In every field of inquiry that has to do with 'initiating principles' (*archê*) or 'determining factors' (*aition*) or elements (*stoicheion*) it is through acquaintance with these that we attain knowledge—or, at any rate, 'scientific knowledge' (*epistêmê*). For we can hardly be said to know a thing until we have become acquainted with its ultimate conditions (*aition*) and basic principles, and have analyzed it down to its elements. Clearly, then, in a scientific study of nature too, our first task will be to find out about its initiating principles.
>
> The natural path of investigation starts from what is more readily knowable and more evident *to us* although intrinsically more obscure, and proceeds toward what is more *self*-evident and intrinsically more intelligible; for it is one thing to be knowable to us and quite another to be intelligible objectively.[42]

Here we have the first of two central features of the Aristotelian explanation of causality: the discovery of essence through the analysis of its attributes.

The second central feature of the Aristotelian notion of causality comprises the four causes (*aitiai*) —material, formal, efficient, and final. The material cause (*hyle*) is the matter from which the object is created. The formal cause is the arrangement of the matter (*eidos* 'form'), the pattern of its occurrence (*paradeigma* 'model'), or its definition (*logos* 'meaning'). This last aspect of the formal cause is especially interesting in relation to grammar, for the stuff of which words are made is not actual matter, in the way bricks are made of clay, and thus an interpretation of its formal cause must be analogical. The efficient cause (identifiable with *archê* 'origin') is the initiating impulse, and the final cause (*telos*) is the goal or purpose for which the object was created. In most cases, we do not find grammarians writing overtly about the four causes, for they were the assumed basis of all science and therefore were seldom mentioned explicitly as part of any particular science. But the profound influence of Aristotle's doctrine can be traced through both types of medieval grammar, and its varying manifestations clearly characterize some of the major differences between the two approaches.[43]

For the Latin grammarians of both the pedagogical and philosophical schools, the material cause was relatively unimportant, since the essence of language was not considered to be found in the physical substance of moving air but in the arrangements of formal structures. Nevertheless, significant (if unsystematic) discussions of phonology are found throughout the many Latin orthographical treatises, and phonology was of major interest to the Welsh, Irish, and Icelandic grammarians writing about their own languages. Further, scholastic philosophers speculated about the production of speech sounds, especially in commentaries on Aristotle's *De anima,* and grammarians often took up similar questions in their commentaries.[44] Outside of these specialized works, however, the brief discussions that pass for phonology in most Latin grammars are rather superficial statements that say more about the writing system of the language than about the way it was spoken. Thus the material cause was not of great concern. Neither was the final cause given much treatment, since both schools assumed without significant comment that the chief purposes of language were to inform and to persuade, that is, to manifest a perfect expression (*perfecto*) of a complex mental concept by means of a proposition. On the formal and efficient causes, however, the two schools differed considerably.

In their investigation of the formal causes of language, the pedagogical grammars focused on a description of correct and efficient Latin; for them, grammar consisted chiefly of the association of a governing word with a governed word. Philosophical grammar, on the other hand, focused on the general categories of meaning. Concerning the efficient cause, the pedagogical grammars had little to say, although it is exactly this aspect that interested the philosophical grammars the most, for they were expressly concerned to track the correspondence of the attributes of reality with those of thinking and those of language.

From the perspective of grammar, the most important effects of the complex Aristotelian "revolution" appear to have been indirect and secondary, gained through the stimulation of new approaches to and a new reliance on logic and empirical science. Growing as well out of philosophical concerns with universals, logical questions were raised which must have affected grammatical thinking, even if obliquely. What was the relation of the parts of a whole to a whole, and what did this imply about the relation of the parts of speech or the parts of a particular sentence to the sentence as a unit? What were the characteristics of individuals in relation to the classes of individuals? What was the relation of substance to accidence, and how might one deal with problems of synonymy and homophony where, respectively, words with apparently the same substance had different accidents and others with apparently the same accidents had different substances? What was the relative scope of logical structures, and how did such structures correspond to grammatical constituents like phrases, clauses, and sentences? Was there any logical basis for grammatical processes like modification and qualification?

In a short time, a new logical terminology had penetrated the study of grammar as a result of attempts to deal with logical questions such as these and with more narrowly grammatical problems such as the distinction between the substantial and accidental signification of the verb. Both Anselm (1033-1109) and Hugh of St. Victor (1096-1141) were grammarians transitional to the new scientific period because, while they used Priscian as the source of their grammatical information, they asked different questions than had their predecessors.[45] Despite their attempts to maintain a separation between grammatical and logical uses of common terms, there was considerable interpenetration of the two fields in the works of these pivotal scholars.[46]

VII. PHILOSOPHICAL GRAMMAR

In the second half of the twelfth century, a partial synthesis between logic and grammar was achieved by scholars like Peter Helias (fl. ca.1150), the logician Peter of Spain (fl. 1135-ca.1160), and John of Garland (fl. 1214-52).[47] Henceforth in this branch of the stream, the grammarian was also to be a philosopher. As a thirteenth-century Modistic writer characterized the position: "It is not the grammarian but the philosopher who, carefully considering the specific nature of things, discovers grammar."[48] With this subsumption of grammar under philosophy, which replicated in a curious way its status among the early

Greeks like Plato and Aristotle, grammar in this view became an abstract thing like arithmetic, a universal construct that Robert Kilwardby (fl. 1200-50) compared to geometry; despite the superficial differences in individual entities, the systematic correspondences established the rightness of the general categories.[49] Thus grammar moved away from a concern with the individual forms of grammar—a concern that had been its earmark since the Alexandrians—toward an interest in general, even universal, structures. In this perspective, grammar was universal but discourse (words in order and agreement) was particular. This perspective was neither new nor unique to the Modistae, of course, but it was an indispensable axiom of their theory. Roger Bacon (1214-94), whose interest in Greek and Hebrew was in marked contrast to the exclusive concern of most grammarians with Latin, raised a specific and qualified objection, because he felt that a scientific treatment of just one language was impossible since certain problems of grammar were common to all languages while others were peculiar to just one or a few languages.[50] Thus, while he was himself part of the general movement toward a universal theory of grammar, he believed that grammarians must address themselves to more languages than only the one, Latin.

In the universities of Northern Europe,[51] the Modistae or speculative grammarians developed a form of grammar that showed a strong influence of contemporary logic in its use of terms and methods.[52] The superficial similarities between logical and Modistic terms not withstanding, however, these philosophical grammarians knew their job to be different from that of logicians. Logicians sought to establish the truth of propositions and the validity of manners of reasoning. They thus had to understand both the system of logic and the nature of reality. Grammarians sought to establish how and why propositions (and, more importantly, sets of propositions) were related, that is, grammatical (*congrua*).[53] Thus grammarians needed to understand only the congruent system of language. The studies of the speculative grammarians centered on the several manners or *modes* of language and thought (hence the name Modistae). In order to keep concepts (primarily the concern of logicians) distinct from the linguistic structures that manifest concepts, the Modistae modified the term *modi significandi,* which had been the common property of theologians, logicians, and grammarians.[54] The Modistae distinguished a variety of distinctively different grammatical entities whose understanding would reveal the modes of thinking and ultimately the modes of being. The basic three-fold division was Aristotelian in arrangement: things were represented by concepts which in turn were expressed by words. First, there was a level of actual existence, the *modus essendi* (see figure 3-2). Second, there was a level of mental existence, the *modus intelligendi.* Finally,

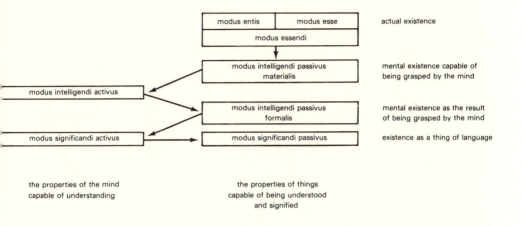

Fig. 3-2. Central Elements of Modistic Grammar

there was a level of existence as an entity of language, the *modus significandi.* (Mediating between these levels of potential or actual existence were the active modes of understanding and signifying, the *modus intelligendi activus* and the *modus significandi activus.*) It is important to note that the word *modus* here had its basic meaning 'way' or 'manner'; thus it refers to a process or relation, not a category of being. The *modus essendi* was the manner of existence; the *modi intelligendi* were manners of understanding; the *modi significandi* were manners of signifying. The same lexical entity (in a modern term, a *lexeme,* a unit of discrete meaning) could be realized by a variety of different *modi significandi.* Thus the lexeme **PAIN** might be realized as a noun (*dolor*), verb (*doleo*), participle (*dolens*), adverb (*dolenter*), or interjection (*heu*). Clearly the Modistae, like their immediate predecessors, showed little interest in the overt signals of language, the mere words that occupied the attention of Donatus and Priscian—these they thought grammatically trivial and thus of interest only to rhetoricians and literati. Instead, they concerned themselves with discovering the functional categories of language, its abstract forms and relations. This distinction they marked with the terms *consignificare,* which referred to language as a set of abstract forms and relations, and *significare,* which referred to language as a set of concrete forms, each of which signaled the relation between a word and what it signified. Thus the substance or material of speech, *vox,* might be manifested in either of two ways: consignified as a *pars orationis,* a part of speech (that is, a grammatical entity within the abstract system of universal grammar which derived its syntactic meaning from its collocation with other *partes orationis*), or signified as a *dictio,* a physical signal of a particular word in a particular language.[55] The modes of signifying showed how words functioned within grammar and how they signified or stood for the things of the world. In a curious way, then, the Modistae can be said to have replaced the etymologists' concern with the simple correspondence of words to things with a more sophisticated and refined version of the same quest. Isidore of Seville was really looking to understand *why* particular words stood for particular things; the Modistae wanted to know *how* language—any language—made words correspond directly to what is.

In sum, the Modistae's subject was the language of cognition, not the language of speaking. As Geoffrey Bursill-Hall characterized the situation, "the Modistae were teachers but teachers of grammar *not* of Latin."[56] Their subject was the language of thinking; thus the initiating impulse, the efficient cause, was what gave language its most interesting features. They fitted their theory with the facts of language, chiefly as presented to them in the grammars of their predecessors like Priscian, but looked beyond the surface configurations of these facts to their systematic semantic features. This interest in the abstract system of grammar over the particular forms of any language, though revived at various times since the fourteenth century, was not destined to enjoy a long period of prominence. One problem resulted from the growing complexity of the Modistic grammars, with their proliferation of distinctions and categories, which, nevertheless, could not hide the fact that the theory tended to confuse grammar and reality. Modistic theory did not, in fact, deal well with the compelling problems of the meaning of propositions and their signification. Another problem lay in the fact that the Modistae made their metatheory out of the language they were investigating, Latin; they attempted to explain all language using categories which had been discovered only in one. This flaw, which Roger Bacon anticipated more than a century before, was not necessarily insuperable, but, before the Modistae could revise their theories, broader and more profound changes in the culture at large radically altered the intellectual context of grammatical study. For one thing, both the Nominalists and the Averroists, like Johannes Aurifaber, objected to two absolutely fundamental aspects of the speculative theory, that there are such things as universals at all (including any universal principles of grammar) and that the notions of substance and accidence could properly be applied analogically to the nonphysical objects of language.[57] The Humanists, on the other hand, felt that the whole enterprise was wrongheaded, and they further objected to what they felt was the barbarity of the grammarians' Latinity. After a fairly brief period at the crest, Modistic grammar ebbed away, although its central concerns with universal structures of language were to be revived later, in seventeenth-century France among the grammarians of Port Royal, in seventeenth- and eighteenth-century England among the scholars interested in universal language schemes, and in contemporary America among the linguists and psychologists interested in the features of human communication common to all human languages. It is ironic that Modistic grammar, the form of medieval grammar that is of most interest from the perspective of linguistic theory, had perhaps the least effect on the vast sweep of grammatical history, but the records of civilization abound with such ironies.

VIII. CONCLUSION

In the preceding pages we have seen the science of language develop from its beginnings in a philosophical concern with the structure of the physical world to its high point in the Middle Ages, its return *as* a philosophical doctrine. The fundamental elements of the grammars bequeathed by the Middle Ages to the Renaissance were mostly developments of the classical, not the medieval, world. Except in lexicology (a somewhat separate domain that has not been discussed here), the major contributions of the medieval grammarians are not to be found in their treatment of the particular phonological and morphological facts of individual languages, even of Latin. Instead they reside in the grammars' syntactic descriptions and more strikingly in the theoretical questions they raised, even if sometimes indirectly, about the place and function of linguistic facts. Considering the turmoil left by the collapse of the Roman Empire, the Middle Ages in Western Europe would have achieved much if they had simply preserved what they did of Latin grammatical learning. That their work went well beyond mere preservation marks the intelligence, dedication, and perception of generations of scholars whose contributions to the history of our culture deserve further analysis and a wider acceptance than generally given. In our time we have witnessed a reawakening to the aesthetic values of medieval art, music, and architecture. It is time we recognized as well the achievements of the medieval intellectuals whose object of study was our language and mind.

NOTES

I am indebted to W. Keith Percival and Aldo D. Scaglione for their thorough and penetrating criticism of an earlier version of this essay. I of course am solely responsible for whatever blunders and infelicities remain.

1. Vatican Fondo Palatino, codex Latinus 1252; quoted from Lynn Thorndike, "Elementary and Secondary Education in the Middle Ages," *Speculum* 15 (1940), 405.

2. Although some girls received a modicum of schooling, intermediate and higher education was virtually entirely the privilege of males; obvious exceptions like the playwright Hroswitha of Gandersheim (10th century) and the poet Christine de Pisan (1363?-post 1429) only prove this general rule.

3. The *Disciplines* was partially reconstructed by Friedrich Ritschl, *Questiones Varronianae* (Bonn, 1845); repr. *Kleine philologische Schriften* (*Opuscula philologica*) 3.352-402 (Leipzig: Teubner, 1877).

4. Adolf Dick, ed. (Leipzig: Teubner, 1925; repr. 1969). Edited and translated by William Harris Stahl and Richard Johnson, with E. L. Burge, *Martianus Capella and the Seven Liberal Arts* (New York: Columbia University Press, 1971). The usage of Stahl and Johnson inverts the traditional order of names: *Philology and Mercury*.

5. For general studies on education in the ancient and medieval worlds, see the excellent commentary in the Stahl and Johnson edition of Martianus's *Marriage;* Paul Abelson, *The Seven Liberal Arts, A Study in Medieval Culture,* Teachers College Contributions to Education 11 (New York: Columbia University Press, 1906); Robert R. Bolgar, *The Classical Heritage and its Beneficiaries* (Cambridge: Cambridge University Press, 1954); Stanley F. Bonner, *Education in Ancient Rome: From the Elder Cato to the Younger Pliny* (Berkeley and Los Angeles: California University Press, 1977); Josef Koch, ed., *Artes liberales. Von der antiken Bildung zur Wissenschaften des Mittelalters,* Studien und Texte zur Geistesgeschichte des Mittelalters 5 (Leiden: Brill, 1959); and Friedmar Kühnert, *Allgemeinbildung und Fachbildung in der Antike,* Schriften der Sektion für Altertumswissenschaft, Deutsche Akademie der Wissenschaften 30 (Berlin: Akademie-Verlag, 1961).

6. On the character and function of dialectic and rhetoric in the Middle Ages, see the essays in this volume by Eleonore Stump and Martin Camargo.

7. On this matter, see the essay in this volume by Ralph McInery.

8. Marie-Terèse d'Alverny, "La Sagesse et ses sept filles: Recherches sur les allégories de la Philosophie et des Arts Libéraux du IXe au XIIe siècle," *Mélanges dédiés à la mémoire de Félix Grat* (Paris: Pecquer-Grat, 1946), 1.245-78.

9. There is an obvious tension, which persists today, between grammar as an elementary subject and its manifestations in so-called higher endeavors like literature and linguistic theory. To some, the very simple nature of introductory grammars seemed to diminish the stature of grammatical study so much as to turn scholars' serious attention away from language altogether. The Humanistic grammars of the early Renaissance, for example, show a studied reluctance to address themselves to general theories of language (the explicit

focus of their medieval predecessors, the speculative grammars). Part of this avoidance resulted from the Humanists' rejection of what they viewed as the medievals' overconcern with categorization and the barbarous Latinity of their tracts, but the force of the Humanists' reaction must also stem in part from their ambivalence toward the structure of language as a subject of intellectual enquiry. As a result, the Humanist grammars are characteristically manuals designed for incipient writers and other language users, not philosophical enquiries in the nature of language.

10. The matters sketched in these few paragraphs here will be discussed in greater detail below. Subsequent notes will refer to more specialized studies, but the following general histories of classical and medieval linguistics will always repay careful attention: Hans Arens, *Sprachwissenschaft: Der Gang ihrer Entwicklung von der Antike bis zur Gegenwart,* Orbis Academicus 1.6; 2nd edition, Freiburg and Munich: Alber, 1969 (repr. Frankfurt: Fischer and Athenäum, 1974); Geoffrey Bursill-Hall, "Toward a History of Linguistics in the Middle Ages, 1100-1450," *Studies in the History of Linguistics: Traditions and Paradigms,* ed. Dell Hymes (Bloomington: Indiana University Press, 1974), 77-92 and "The Middle Ages," *Current Trends in Linguistics 13: Historiography of Linguistics,* ed. Thomas Sebeok et al. (The Hague: Mouton, 1975), 1.179-230; Marie-Dominique Chenu, "Grammaire et théologie aux XIIe et XIIIe siècles," *Archives d'histoire doctrinale et littéraire du moyen âge* 10 (1936), 5-28; Francis P. Dinneen, S.J., *Introduction to General Linguistics* (New York: Holt, Rinehart, and Winston, 1967); Richard William Hunt, "The Introductions to the *Artes* in the Twelfth Century," *Studia Mediaevalia Raymundi Josephi Martin* (Bruges, 1948), 85-112 and "Studies on Priscian in the Eleventh and Twelfth Centuries," *Medieval and Renaissance Studies* 1 (1941), 194-231 and 2 (1943), 1-55, both repr. in *The History of Grammar in the Middle Ages,* ed. G. L. Bursill-Hall (Amsterdam: Benjamins, 1980); Norman Kretzmann, "History of Semantics," *Encyclopedia of Philosophy,* ed. P. Edwards (New York: Macmillan, 1967), 7.358-406; Rudolf Pfeiffer, *History of Classical Scholarship: From the Beginnings to the End of the Hellenistic Age* (Oxford: Clarendon, 1968); Robert Henry Robins, *Ancient and Mediaeval Grammatical Theory in Europe* (London: Bell, 1951; repr. Port Washington and London: Kennikat, 1971) and *A Short History of Linguistics* (London: Longmans; Bloomington: Indiana University Press, 1967; repr. 1970); John Edwin Sandys, *A History of Classical Scholarship,* three vols. (Cambridge: Cambridge University Press, 1903-06; repr. New York: Hafner, 1958); Aldo D. Scaglione, "The Historical Study of *Ars Grammatica:* A Bibliographic Survey," *Ars Grammatica,* Janua Linguarum ser. min. 77 (The Hague: Mouton, 1970), 11-43; Charles Thurot, *Notices et extraits de divers manuscrits latins pour servir à l'histoire des doctrines grammaticales au moyen âge* (Paris: Impr. impériale, 1868; repr. Frankfurt: Minerva, 1964); and Paolo Valesio, "The Art of Syntax and its History," *Lingua e stile* 9 (1974), 1-30. Despite its age, Thurot's indispensable study remains the best history of medieval grammar in all its diversity.

11. The influence of the anomaly-analogy controversy on the development of Hellenistic grammatical theory now appears to have been exaggerated. See Jean Collart, "Analogie et anomalie," *Entretiens sur l'antiquité classique* 9 (1962), 117-32; A. Dihle, "Analogie und Attizismus," *Hermes* 85 (1957), 170-205; Detlev Fehling, "Zwei Untersuchungen zur griechischen Sprachphilosophie," *Rheinisches Museum für Philologie* 108 (1965), 212-29; and especially

Jan Pinborg, "Classical Antiquity: Greece," *Current Trends in Linguistics* 13. *Historiography of Linguistics,* ed. Thomas Sebeok et al. (The Hague: Mouton, 1975), 1.69-126. See also the analysis of the conjectural relationship between the anomaly-analogy controversy and the Peripatetic-Stoic opposition that runs through Aldo D. Scaglione's *The Classical Theory of Composition from its Origins to the Present,* University of North Carolina Studies in Comparative Literature 53 (Chapter Hill: University of North Carolina Press, 1972).

12. The principle that language, and therefore grammar, must bear a direct, if not perfect, relation to reality is not at all the exclusive property of the speculative grammarians, of course. The belief that nothing may be thought of which does not exist first in reality is one of the major underpinnings of medieval theology, where it is perhaps most evident in the works of Thomas Aquinas.

13. Some of the problems are the simple ones posed by sheer bulk. There are extant today more than 4,000 European manuscript books containing approximately 7,000 grammatical tracts. Naturally this number records multiple copies of some works, but the list of different incipits (opening lines) and thus of presumably distinct works exceeds 2,500, of which only a small number has been edited. A comprehensive compilation of grammatical incipits may be found in Geoffrey Bursill-Hall, *A Census of Medieval Latin Grammatical Manuscripts,* Grammatica Speculativa 4 (Stuttgart: Frommann-Holzboog, 1981).

14. The terminological problem is complicated by the fact that scholastic Latin had a highly developed vocabulary for dealing with grammar. To choose a simple example, *vox* 'voice' does not mean the physical vibrations of the speaking apparatus but the substance or essence of speech, a concept that requires an understanding, not of anatomy as our sense of *voice* does, but of metaphysics. Thus key terms and concepts turn on distinctions no longer made or which now have very different implications.

An even more perplexing problem is posed by the difficulty we have in putting aside our comfortable and largely unconscious prejudices of mind, especially of the more subtle kinds that profoundly inform the ways we understand and explain the world. Today none of us, however religious, can ignore the deep feeling that the laws of physics are somehow of a different nature from those governing morality or justice. Even if we believe the immutable laws of physics to be ultimately grounded in the being of God, they seem to possess a lucid austerity, a profound clarity that even a direct moral law like "Thou shalt not kill" lacks. We also live in a skeptical age that questions the very parameters of enquiry. Thus the fundamental belief of the Modistae—stated variously, that modes of being govern modes of signifying, that the nature of ultimate reality is directly accessible through the facts of understanding, that language is precisely the thing that manifests both thought and reality, in other words, that what we say (or, more exactly, what we *can* say) corresponds precisely to what *is*—this fundamental Modistic belief would be truly impossible for any of us, however well we might come to appreciate it as an artifact of history.

15. Byzantine grammar remains relatively unstudied, although some recent work provides directions. See, for example, D. Donnet, "La place de la syntaxe dans les traités de grammaires grecques des origines au XIIe siècle," *L'Antiquité Classique* 36 (1967), 22-48 and *Le Traité* Peri syntaxeos logou *de*

Grégoire de Corinthe, Etudes de Philologie, d'Archéologie et d'Histoire anciennes publiées par l'Institut Historique Belge de Rome 10 (Brussels, 1967).

16. A third complexity of the history of classical theories of grammar arises from the fact that there was not (and still is not today) a generally accepted agreement as to the proper domain of the science of linguistics. For some grammarians, the only phenomena of language that rightly belonged to the discipline of grammar were the forms of individual words and the isolated phonetic values of the elements of the writing system. For others, the ambit of grammarians included all the shapes and meanings of language and most of its uses, notably literature and the stylistic arrangements governed by rhetorical principles. As a result of this lack of common ground, some grammarians who appeared to be talking about the same thing actually differed quite significantly because one of them wished to explain, or at least describe, certain linguistic phenomena that another explicitly excluded from the grammarian's area of responsibility. Associated with this problem is a fourth difficulty: linguists often disagreed as to the aspect of language that was the most basic—that is, the part of language whose structure should dictate the analytic procedures used throughout the grammar. Of course, there is actually no good reason to believe that the most useful principles for analyzing, say, phonological elements of language would also be the most useful for dealing with semantic features; nonetheless, the history of linguistics shows that most grammarians have tacitly assumed their science should be unified in this way and thus their judgments about the primes of language condition to a significant degree the structure of the entire grammar. (Again, contemporary linguistics mirrors these ancient controversies with the schoolroom traditionalists and the structuralists being mostly concerned with discovering and arranging taxonomically the surface manifestations of the phonological and grammatical units of language, with the generative syntacticians of Noam Chomsky's school being chiefly concerned with the syntactic functioning of grammatical categories and relations, and with the semanticists of several types being concerned with the ways languages signify meanings and how these are manifested in grammatical structures.) As we study this history, we must be aware that such conflicts were not always resolved. This need not seriously impede progress if we remember that many terms and the grammatical entities they label were local, that is, their referents might have differed—even though the term itself remained the same. In this sense, the historical continuity implied by the persistence of a common terminology is somewhat misleading. Nonetheless, the artifacts of language ultimately to be explained by the grammarian remained the same and, despite some differences dictated by varying theories of language, the problems they posed also remained reasonably constant.

17. Crates, anecdote has it, broke his leg in a ditch and decided, while waiting for his injury to heal, to give a course of lectures on Stoic philosophy. See also Karl Barwick, *Probleme der stoischen Sprachlehre und Rhetorik,* Abhandlungen der Sächsischen Akademie der Wissenschaften zu Leipzig, Phil. Hist. Klasse 49:3 (Berlin: Sächs. Ak. der Wiss., 1957).

Varro did not strictly follow the Stoics throughout *De lingua latina.* He was an eclectic, and influences of other philosophies abound, especially the atomistic physical theories of the Epicurean school. In particular, he chose to ignore the Stoic concern with the ultimate origins of language and focused instead on language as an attribute of contemporary humankind. He judged that language was essentially arbitrary insofar as it applied to things of the world, but that it had internal consistencies that made it amenable to philosophical analysis. Thus he avoided the potential extremes of both sides in the analogist-anomalist controversy in favor of an interesting and largely workable synthesis of the two views.

Probably Varro's most important contribution was his concept of *declinatio,* which allowed him to distinguish between inflection and derivation, that is, between the regular and productive processes like those that mark tense and plurality and the less common, more "irregular" processes by which nouns are formed from verbs, adjectives from nouns, and so forth. See Jean Collart, "Varron grammairien et l'enseignement grammatical dans l'antiquité romaine 1934-1963," *Lustrum* 9 (1964), 213-41 and Daniel J. Taylor, *Declinatio: A Study of the Linguistic Theory of M. Terentius Varro,* Amsterdam Studies in the Theory and History of Linguistic Science 3, Studies in the History of Linguistics 2 (Amsterdam: Benjamins, 1975). See also the faulty but stimulating essay by Luigi Romeo and Gaio E. Tiberio, "Historiography of Linguistics and Rome's Scholarship," *Language Sciences* 17 (October 1971), 23-44.

18. 18.2.30; quoted from Robins, *Short History,* p. 31. Ed. G. Uhlig, *Grammatici graeci* 1 (Leipzig: Teubner, 1883). See also V. Di Benedetto, "Dionisio il Trace e la *Techne* a lui attribuita," *Annali della Scuola Normale Superiore di Pisa* 27 (1958), 169-210 and 28 (1959), 87-118; R. H. Robins, "Dionysios Thrax and the Western Grammatical Tradition," *Transactions of the Philological Society* (1957), 67-106; and Antonio Traglia, "La sistemazione grammaticale di Dionisio Trace," *Studi Classici e Orientali, Università di Pisa* 5 (1956), 38-78.

19. See, for example, Ian Michael, *English Grammatical Categories and the Tradition to 1800* (Cambridge: Cambridge University Press, 1970) and Emma Vorlat, *The Development of English Grammatical Theory 1585-1737, with special reference to the theory of parts of speech* (Leuven: Leuven University Press, 1975).

20. See Robins, *Short History,* 37-38 and Pinborg, "Classical Antiquity," p. 120.

21. See Ruth Camerer, "Die Behandlung der Partikel *án* in den Schriften des Apolonios Dyskolos," *Hermes* 93 (1965), 168-204; E. A. Hahn, "Apollonius Dyscolus on Mood," *Transactions of the American Philological Association* 82 (1951), 29-48; and Fred W. Householder, "Introduction," *Syntactic Theory 1: Structuralist* (Harmondsworth, Middlesex: Penguin, 1972), 7-19.

22. "Donati de partibus orationis ars minor," ed. Heinrich Keil, *Grammatici latini* (Leipzig: Teubner, 1864), 4.254-66 and "Donati grammatici urbis Romanae ars grammatica," ed. H. Keil, *Grammatici latini* (Leipzig: Teubner, 1864), 4.367-402.

23. "Partes orationis quot sunt? Octo. Quae? Nomen pronomen verbum adverbium participium coniunctio praepositio interiectio. DE NOMINE. Nomen quid est? Pars orationis cum casu corpus aut rem proprie communiterve significans. Nomini quot accidunt? Sex. Quae? Qualitas comparatio genus numerus figura casus." *Ars minor,* 11.1-7.

24. *Prisciani institutionum grammaticarum libri XVIII, Grammatici latini* 2-3, ed. Martin Hertz (Leipzig: Teubner, 1855-58).

25. Margaret Gibson, "Priscian's 'Institutiones Grammaticae': A Handlist of Manuscripts," *Scriptorium* 26 (1972), 105-24 and Marinà Passalacqua, *I codici di Prisciano* (Rome: Edizioni di Storia e Letteratura, 1978).

26. See Willy Krogmann, "Universalität und Particularität des Mittelalters im Spiegel der Sprache," *Orbis* 15 (1966), 7-34.

27. Today the term *universals* in linguistics signals a concern with the structures and operations common to all human languages, such as processes of modification and subordination, the set of phonetic features from which each language draws its particular inventory, the realizations of semantico-syntactic categories like Agent and Benefactor, and so forth. See *Universals of Language,* ed. Joseph H. Greenberg (2nd ed., Cambridge: MIT Press, 1966) and *Universals of Human Language,* ed. J. H. Greenberg et al., four vols. (Stanford: Stanford University Press, 1978).

28. Isidorus Hispanelsis, Bishop of Seville, *Etymologiarum sive Originum libri XX,* ed. W. D. Lindsay, 2 vols. (Oxford: Oxford University Press, 1911). Flavius Magnus Aurelius Cassiodorus Senator (ca.490-ca.583), *Institutiones divinarum et saeculorum litterarum,* ed. R. A. B. Mynors (Oxford: Oxford University Press, 1937); *Introduction to Divine and Human Knowledge,* Records of Civilization 40, trans. Leslie W. Jones (New York: Columbia University Press, 1946).

29. Roswitha Klinck, *Die lateinische Etymologie des Mittelalters* (Munich: Fink, 1969).

30. See, for example, *In artem Donati minorem commentum,* ed. W. Fox, S. J. (Leipzig: Teubner, 1902) and *Commentum in Martianum Capellam,* ed. Cora E. Lutz, 2 vols. (Leiden: Brill, 1962-65). See also C. Lutz, "The Commentary of Remigius of Auxerre on Martianus Capella," *Medieval Studies* 19 (1957), 137-56 and "Remigius' Ideas on the Classification of the Seven Liberal Arts," *Traditio* 12 (1959), 63-86.

31. Alcuin (735-804), *Grammatica,* ed. J.-P. Migne, *Patrologia Latina* 101 (1863), cols. 849-902. Bede (673-735), *De octo partibus orationis,* ed. J.-P. Migne, *Pat. Lat.* 90 (1863), cols. 613-32. Aelfric (ca.955-1020), *Grammatica,* ed. J. Zupitza, *Aelfrics Grammatik und Glossar* (Berlin: Weidmann, 1880; repr. with an introduction by H. Gneuss, 1966). Boniface (ca.675-755), "Ars grammatica," ed. Angelo Mai, *Classicorum auctorum e Vaticanis codicibus editorum* 7 (1835), 475-548.

32. Among the important vernacular grammars are the *Auraicept na nÉces* ('primer for poets,' Irish, ca.650-950), ed. George Calder (Edinburgh: Grant, 1917); the *Gramadegau'r Penceirddiaid* ('grammar of the chief poets,' Welsh, ca.1250-1570), ed. G. J. Williams and E. J. Jones (Cardiff: Wales University Press, 1934); Uc Faidit, *Donatz Proensals* ('Provençal Donatus,' Provençal, ca.1240), ed. John Henry Marshall (London: Oxford University Press, 1969); Johan Barton, *Donait françois* ('French Donatus,' French, 1409), ed. Edmond Stengel, "Die ältesten Anleitungsschriften," *Zeitschrift für neufranzösischen Sprache und Literatur* 1 (1878), 25-40; and *The First Grammatical Treatise* (Icelandic, 1125-75?), ed. Hreinn Benediktsson (Reykjavik: Institute of Nordic Linguistics, 1972). For further details, see Jeffrey F. Huntsman, "Medieval Vernacular Grammars," forthcoming.

33. For some examples of the accommodation made in adapting Latin grammar to vernacular languages, see Maartje Draak, "Construe Marks in Hiberno-Latin Manuscripts," *Mededelingen der Koninklijke Nederlandse Academie van Wetenschappen, Afd. Letterkunde,* NS 20:11 (1957), 1-22 and "The Higher Teaching of Latin Grammar in Ireland During the Ninth Century," *Mededelingen der Koninklijke Nederlandse Akademie van Wetenschappen, Afd. Letterkunde,* NS 30:4 (1967), 1-38; see also Jeffrey F. Huntsman, "On the

Linguistic Understanding of the Early Celtic Grammarians," *Studia Celtica* (in press).

34. For more detailed discussions of this geographical disjunction, see the references cited in note 40 below, as well as the general histories listed in note 10 above. See also Jan Pinborg, *Die Entwicklung der Sprachtheorie im Mittelalter* (Münster: Aschendorff, 1967), 39ff.

35. *Das Doctrinale des Alexander de Villa-Dei*, Monumenta Germaniae Paedagogica 12, ed. Dietrich Reichling (Berlin: Hoffmann, 1893; repr. New York: Garland, 1974). *Graecismus*, Corpus grammaticorum medii aevi 1, ed. Johann Wrobel (Breslau: Koebner, 1887). Full and equal assessment of these two important works is hampered by the poor quality of Wrobel's edition; Reichling's, on the other hand, is "a model of the genre" (A. Scaglione, *Ars Grammatica*, p. 18).

36. The *Doctrinale*, it has been argued, is notably successful in its treatment of syntax. Cf. Remigio Sabbadini, "Dei methodi nell'insegnamento della sintassi latina: Considerazioni didattiche e storiche," *Rivista di Filologia* 30 (1902), 304-14 and Reichling's edition.

37. The *Heptateuchon* remains unedited. See A. Clerval, "L'Enseignement des arts libéraux à Chartres et à Paris dans la première moitié du 12e siècle d'après l'Heptateuchon de Thierry de Chartres," *Congrès scientifique international des catholiques tenu à Paris du 8 au 13 avril 1888*, 277-308.

38. *Two Medieval Satires on the University of Paris: La Bataille des Sept Arts of Henri d'Andeli, and the Morale Scholarium of John of Garland*, Memoirs of the University of California 4:1, ed. Louis J. Paetow (Berkeley: California University Press, 1914).

39. Cf. the essay in this volume by Eleonore Stump and the references cited in note 43 below.

40. For general treatments of medieval intellectual life, see Marcia Colish, *The Mirror of Language: A Study in the Medieval Theory of Knowledge* (New Haven: Yale University Press, 1968); Ernst R. Curtius, *European Literature and the Latin Middle Ages* (London: Routledge and Kegan Paul, 1953) and "The Medieval Basis of Western Thought," *Gesammelte Aufsätze zur romantischen Philologie* (1960), 28-39; David Knowles, *The Evolution of Medieval Thought* (London: Longmans, 1962); Louis J. Paetow, *The Arts Course at Medieval Universities with Special Reference to Grammar and Rhetoric*, University of Illinois Studies 3:7 (Urbana: University of Illinois, 1910); and Lynn Thorndike, "Elementary and Secondary Education in the Middle Ages," *Speculum* 15 (1940), 400-08.

41. *Grammatica speculativa*, ed. Geoffrey Bursill-Hall (London: Longmans, 1972), p. 135.

42. *Natural Science* <Bk. I, ch. I; Bekker 184a 10-19>, trans. Philip Wheelwright (enlarged ed., New York: Odyssey, 1951), p. 3.

43. Ingemar Düring, "The Impact of Aristotle's Scientific Ideas in the Middle Ages," *Archiv für Geschichte der Philosophie* 50 (1968), 115-33; Martin Grabmann, *Bearbeitungen und Auslegungen der aristotelischen Logik aus der Zeit von Peter Abelard bis Petrus Hispanus*, Abhandlungen der Preussischen Akademie der Wissenschaften, Phil. Hist. Klasse 5 (Berlin: Pr. Ak. der Wiss., 1937), "Ungedruckte lateinische Kommentare zur aristotelischen Topik aus dem 13ten Jahrhundert," *Arkiv für Kulturgeschichte* 28 (1938), 210-32; and R. A. Markus, "The Impact of Aristotle on Medieval Thought," *Blackfriars* 42 (1961), 96-102.

44. For a Latin treatise devoted exclusively to phonology, see Robert Grosseteste's "De generatione sonorum," *Die philosophischen Werke des Robert Grosseteste,* Beiträge zur Geschichte der Philosophie des Mittelalters. Texte und Untersuchungen 9, ed. Ludwig Baur (Münster: Aschendorff, 1912), 7-10, and the discussion by Karl Reichl, "*Tractatus de grammatic": Eine fälschlich Robert Grosseteste zugeschriebene spekultive Grammatik,* Veröffentlichungen des Grabmann-Institut NF 28 (Munich, Paderborn, Vienna: Schöningh, 1976).

45. *De grammatico,* Publications in Medieval Studies 18, ed. Desmond Paul Henry (Notre Dame: Notre Dame University Press, 1964). See also the review of Henry's edition by Aldo D. Scaglione in *Romance Philology* 19 (1966), 483-86 (repr., *Ars Grammatica,* 140-44) and Marcia Colish, "Eleventh Century Grammar in the Thought of St Anselm," *Actes* 4 (1969), 785-95. *Hugonis de Sancto Victore opera propaedeutica Practica geometriae, De grammatica, Epitome Dindimi in philosophiam,* Publications in Medieval Studies 20, ed. Roger Baron (Notre Dame: Notre Dame University Press, 1966).

46. See Richard William Hunt, "Studies on Priscian in the Eleventh and Twelfth Centuries," *Mediaeval and Renaissance Studies* 1-2 (1941-43, 1950), 194-231, 1-55 and cf. Louis G. Kelly, "*Modus Significandi:* An Interdisciplinary Concept," *Historiographia Linguistica* 6 (1979), 159-80.

47. See Karin Margareta Fredborg, "The Dependency of Petrus Helias' *Summa super Priscianum* on William of Conches' *Glose super Priscianum,"* *Cahiers de l'Institut du Moyen-Âge Grec et Latin* 11 (1973), 1-57. Peter of Spain (Petrus Hispanus, ca.1205-77), *Summulae logicales,* ed. Innocentius Bochenski (Rome: Marietti, 1947); *The Summulae Logicales of Peter of Spain,* Publications in Medieval Studies 8, trans. Joseph P. Mullally (Notre Dame: Notre Dame University Press, 1945); Richard William Hunt, "The *Summa* of Petrus Hispanus on *Priscianus Minor,"* *Historiographia Linguistica* 2 (1975), 1-23. John of Garland (fl. 1214-52), *The* Parisiana Poetria *of John of Garland,* ed. and trans. Traugott Lawler (New Haven: Yale University Press, 1974); for incipits of Garland's many unedited grammatical works, see Geoffrey Bursill-Hall, "Johannes de Garlandia—Forgotten Grammarian and the Manuscript Tradition," *Historiographia Linguistica* 3 (1976), 155-77.

48. "Summa super Priscianam"; Thurot, *Notices et Extraits,* p. 124; quoted from Robins, *Short History,* p. 76.

49. Robins, *Short History,* p. 77. Kilwardby's *Sophismata* remains unedited; see S. Harrison Thomson, "Robert Kilwardby's Commentaries *In Priscianum* and *In Barbarismum Donati,"* *New Scholasticism* 12 (1938), 52-65. Cf. "The Commentary on Priscianus major ascribed to Robert Kilwardby. Selected Texts," ed. Karin Margareta Fredborg, Niels Jørgen Green-Pedersen, Launge Nielsen, and Jan Pinborg, *Cahiers de l'Institut du Moyen-Age Grec et Latin* 15 (Copenhagen, 1975).

50. *Summa Grammaticae, Opera hactenus inedita Rogeri Baconi* 15, ed. R. Steele (Oxford: Clarendon, 1940).

51. Despite the general geographical division between dominance of the literary grammars in Southern Europe and the philosophical grammars in Northern Europe, the Modistic grammars were at least known to scholars in the South. The *Regule* of Magister Philippus of Florence (14th century), for example, makes clear reference to Modistic ideas (W. Keith Percival, "The Interpenetration of Grammar and Rhetoric in Fourteenth-Century Italy," paper presented at the conference *Grammar and Rhetoric in the Trivium,* Vancouver, B.C., 1978). See also Percival's "The Grammatical Tradition and the

Rise of the Vernaculars," *Current Trends in Linguistics* 13. *Historiography of Linguistics,* ed. Thomas Sebeok et al. (The Hague: Mouton, 1975), 1.231-75 and Jan Pinborg's introduction to Siger of Courtrai's *Summa* (note 53 below), where he mentions (p. xviii) Gentilis da Cingoli, who helped introduce Modistic doctrines into Italy.

52. Geoffrey Bursill-Hall, "Aspects of Modistic Grammar," *17th Annual Round Table, Monograph Series on Languages and Linguistics* 19 (1966), 133-48 and *Speculative Grammars of the Middle Ages: The Doctrine of* partes orationis *of the Modistae,* Approaches to Semiotics 11 (The Hague: Mouton, 1971); Martin Grabmann, "Die Entwicklung der mittelalterlichen Sprachlogik (Tractatus de modis significandi)," *Philosophisches Jahrbuch der Görres-Gessellschaft* 35 (1922), 121-35, 199-214; Jan Pinborg, *Die Entwicklung der Sprachtheorie im Mittelalter,* Beiträge zur Geschichte der Philosophie und Theologie des Mittelalters 42:2; Copenhagen: Frost-Hansen (Münster: Aschendorff, 1967), *Logik und Semantik im Mittelalter: Ein Uberblick,* Problemata 10; Stuttgart: Frommann-Holzboog, 1972; Heinrich Roos, "Martinus de Dacia und seine Schrift 'De modis significandi,' " *Classica et Mediaevalia* 8 (1946), 87-115; James Rodney Shay, *Grammar of the Mind: An Investigation of Medieval Speculative Grammar* (unpublished dissertation, University of California —Berkeley, 1977); Louis G. Kelly, "*Modus Significandi:* An Interdisciplinary Concept," *Historiographa Linguistica* 6 (1979), 159-80; and John Trentmann, "Speculative Grammar and Transformational Grammar: A Comparison of Philosophical Presuppositions," *History of Linguistic Thought and Contemporary Linguistics,* ed. Herman Parrett (Berlin: de Gruyter, 1976), 279-301. For texts of speculative grammarians see John of Dacia, *Summa Grammatica,* Corpus Philosophorum Danicorum Medii Aevi 1, ed. Alfred Otto (Copenhagen: Gad, 1955); Martin of Dacia, *De modis significandi,* Corpus Philosophorum Danicorum Medii Aevi 2, ed. Heinrich Roos (Copenhagen: Gad, 1961); Boethius of Dacia, *Questiones super librum Topicorum,* Corpus Philosophorum Danicorum Medii Aevi 2, ed. Niels Jørgen Green-Pedersen and Jan Pinborg (Copenhagen: Gad, 1976); Michael of Marbais, *Summa modorum significandi,* edition in progress by Timothy J. Coleman, Pontifical Institute, Toronto; Radulphus Brito, edition in progress by Heinz W. Enders and Jan Pinborg, Grammatica Speculativa 3 (Stuttgart: Frommann-Holzboog); Siger of Courtrai (Sigerus de Cortraco), *Summa modorum significandi sophismata,* Amsterdam Studies in the Theory and History of Linguistic Science 3, Studies in the History of Linguistics 14, ed. Jan Pinborg (Amsterdam: Benjamins, 1977); Thomas of Erfurt, *Grammatica speculativa,* ed. and trans. Geoffrey Bursill-Hall (London: Longmans, 1972); Pseudo-Albertus Magnus, *Quaestiones Alberti de modis significandi,* Amsterdam Studies in the Theory and History of Linguistic Science 3, Studies in the History of Linguistics 15, ed. Louis G. Kelly (Amsterdam: Benjamins, 1977); and the several short texts of a variety of grammarians in the *Cahiers de l'Institut du Moyen-Âge Grec et Latin* (Copenhagen, 1969-).

53. This emphasis on congruity, that is, the function of every part of speech in grammatical constructions, underscores the medieval focus on the systematicity of grammar (grammar and semantics) as against the classical focus on morphology. The parts of grammar described by the morphology were necessary, of course, but their classification was governed by the requirements of the *congruitas* of the semantico-syntactic constructions being described. See,

for example, Siger of Courtrai, *Summa*, 46-47 and Pinborg's introduction, xxi-xxii.

54. See Kelly, *"Modus Significandi."*

55. See Thurot, *Notices et Extraits*, 155-56 and Bursill-Hall *Speculative Grammars*, 54-55.

56. "Toward a History," p. 87.

57. See Pinborg, *Entwicklung*, 166-92 and 214-304.

SELECTED BIBLIOGRAPHY ON MEDIEVAL GRAMMAR

Bursill-Hall, Geoffrey Leslie. *Speculative Grammars of the Middle Ages: The Doctrine of* partes orationis *of the Modistae*, Approaches to Semiotics 11 (The Hague: Mouton, 1971).

———. "Toward a History of Linguistics in the Middle Ages, 1100-1450." *Studies in the History of Linguistics: Traditions and Paradigms*, ed. Dell Hymes (Bloomington: Indiana University Press, 1974), 77-92.

———. "The Middle Ages," *Current Trends in Linguistics* 13. *Historiography of Linguistics*, ed. Thomas A. Sebeok et al. (The Hague: Mouton, 1975), 1.179-230.

Hunt, Richard William. *The History of Grammar in the Middle Ages, Collected Papers*, ed. G. L. Bursill-Hall (Amsterdam: Benjamins, 1980).

Koerner, E. F. Konrad, Hans Josef Niederehe, and Robert Henry Robins, eds. *Studies in Medieval Linguistic Thought, Historiographia Linguistica* 7:1-2.1-321 (Amsterdam: Benjamins, 1980).

Kretzmann, Norman. "History of Semantics," *Encyclopedia of Philosophy*, ed. Paul Edwards (New York: Macmillan, 1967), 7.358-406.

Murphy, James J., comp. *Medieval Rhetoric: A Select Bibliography* (Toronto: Toronto University Press, 1971).

Percival, W. Keith. "The Grammatical Tradition and the Rise of the Vernaculars," *Current Trends in Linguistics* 13. *Historiography of Linguistics*, ed. Thomas A. Sebeok et al. (The Hague: Mouton, 1975), 1.231-75.

Pinborg, Jan. *Die Entwicklung der Sprachtheorie im Mittelalter*, Beiträge zur Geschichte der Philosophie und Theologie des Mittelalters 42:2 (Copenhagen: Frost-Hansen; Munster: Aschendorff, 1967).

Robins, Robert Henry. *Ancient and Medieval Grammatical Theory in Europe* (London: Ball, 1951).

———. *A Short History of Linguistics* (London: Longmans; Bloomington: Indiana University Press, 1967; repr. 1970).

Scaglione, Aldo Domenico. "The Historical Study of *Ars Grammatica*: A Bibliographic Survey," *Ars grammatica*, Janua Linguarum ser. min. 77 (The Hague: Mouton, 1970), 11-43.

Thurot, Charles. *Notices et extraits de divers manuscrits latins pour servir à l'histoire des doctrines grammaticales au moyen âge* (Paris: Impr. impériale, 1868; repr. Frankfurt: Minerva, 1964).

Valesio, Paolo. "The Art of Syntax and Its History," *Lingua e stile* 9 (1974), 1-30.

4 Rhetoric

Martin Camargo

Rhetoric, like the other arts of the trivium, took the word as its general principle. Its place within the complete system of the verbal arts was defined by the concern for correct expression (or, alternatively, persuasion). Basing his analysis on educational practice, Quintilian identified rhetorical theory and the study of literature as the two most basic divisions of the art. Nevertheless (as in the case of grammar), Quintilian concentrated on the technical side of the art—which became the almost exclusive concern of the Latin encyclopedists.

Traditionally, rhetorical theory was organized around five basic topics: arrangement, delivery, invention, style, and memory. Quaestio (the speech situation) can perhaps be viewed as another distinct topic, though of a different order. It differentiated the general question (which is independent of considerations of time, place, and person) from the limited question; the latter in turn was divided into the judicial, the political, and the ceremonial. Martianus Capella considered quaestio before turning to the five canonical topics; thus it may perhaps be viewed as the specific beginning point for rhetoric.

The canon of five standard topics reflected the historical development of the art. Rhetoric originated, according to Aristotle, at Syracuse early in the fifth century, with arrangement and delivery as its essential core. Aristotle himself added invention. Hermagoras then incorporated these three topics into what was presumably a complete system, rounding off the canon with style and memory.

Each of the five divisions of rhetoric was itself an art, or techne. Invention, at least through the first century A.D., was always the preeminent topic; Cicero's treatise by this name (De inventione) was the chief source of medieval rhetoric. Arrangement was often discussed both in the general treatments of all five topics and also as a separate art. Its quality as a techne is clearly evident in the analysis of the parts of a speech: introduction, preliminary statement and analysis of the theme, argument or proof, and peroration.

After the time of Quintilian, writers increasingly concentrated on style—a topic that included diction and composition, the virtues of language, and the characteristics of the grand, medium, and plain styles. Given this concern with style rather than content, it is not surprising to find these later writers emphasizing embellishment (one of the virtues of language). D. L. W.

The complexity of medieval rhetoric makes it difficult to summarize or even at times to identify. A good index of that complexity is the fact that the learned scholars who have studied the subject in depth have frequently reached seemingly incompatible conclusions. Charles Baldwin, for example, stresses the inheritance of the Second Sophistic in arguing that medieval rhetoric is almost exclusively concerned with stylistic ornament; while John Ward, to name one among several who share this view, sees instead an overriding concern with the sources and methods of argument. Richard McKeon insists on the fundamental diversity of medieval rhetoric, tracing three distinct but interrelated lines of development; whereas James J. Murphy, while distinguishing not three but four medieval rhetorical traditions, detects a kind of unity in the pragmatic and preceptive nature of all the treatises belonging to those traditions.[1] A survey of this length can neither match the breadth and detail of these basic studies, nor do justice to the abundance of new information that has appeared since the publication of Murphy's landmark synthesis seven years ago. Its goal will be to trace the broad outlines of the two processes that by any account are fundamental to a history of rhetoric in the Middle Ages: the preservation and adaptation of classical, "Ciceronian" rhetoric and the parallel evolution of a Christian rhetoric.

I. CICERONIAN RHETORIC IN THE MIDDLE AGES

A. The Sources of Medieval Rhetoric

For the Middle Ages, rhetoric was synonymous with the works of Marcus Tullius Cicero (106-43 B.C.). By Augustine's time, Cicero's early *De inventione* was well established as the chief authority on the subject. Nor did the broader, more philosophical works of Cicero's maturity ever rival in popularity the narrower, more technical *De inventione*. The *De oratore*, for example, was not widely read until the fifteenth century.[2] In the course of the Middle Ages, the anonymous *Rhetorica ad Herennium,* ascribed to Cicero from the time of St. Jerome through the first half of the fifteenth century, joined the *De inventione* as a standard text.[3] Besides the pseudo-Ciceronian *Ad Herennium,* however, the only text to rival the *De inventione*'s medieval popularity was Boethius's *De topicis differentiis,* IV.[4] The *De inventione* and *Ad Herennium* were to medieval rhetoric what Donatus and Priscian were to grammar. They were copied,[5] commented and glossed,[6] excerpted, summarized, even translated,[7] and studied more or less continuously, providing the chief unifying strand in the history about to be traced.

The *De inventione* so closely defined rhetoric for the Middle Ages that it was called simply *De rhetorica,* until its neglect of style, spotlighted by the late medieval popularity of the more complete *Ad Herennium,* earned it the traditional and more accurate title.[8] The first seven chapters of book I provide an overview of rhetoric that is probably the best single guide to the medieval conception of the art. Here Cicero first stresses the necessary connection between eloquence and philosophy/ethics (I.i-iv). He next classifies rhetoric as a branch of political science, identifies its function as speaking persuasively, its end as persuasion by speech, and its material as three types of subjects: epideictic, concerned with praising or blaming an individual person; deliberative, which involves the expression of an opinion in a political debate; and judicial or forensic, the prosecution or defense of a case in a court of law (I.v). He then distinguishes general questions, which are the province of philosophers, from special cases, which involve specific individuals and are alone the proper object of the orator's attention (I.vi). Finally, he lists the five parts of rhetoric: *inventio,* the discovery of valid or at least plausible arguments; *dispositio,* the effective arrangement of the arguments so discovered; *elocutio,* the fitting of proper language to the invented matter; *memoria,* the firm mental grasp of both matter and words; and *pronuntiatio,* delivery suited to both matter and words (I.vii). Cicero concludes chapter vii, and the introductory segment, by announcing his intention to limit his discussion to the materials and the parts of rhetoric, beginning with *inventio,* which "is the most important of all the divisions, and above all is used in every kind of pleading."[9]

Cicero did not carry through his plan to treat all five parts of rhetoric. The bulk of the treatise is concerned with *status* theory, whereby the type of case is discovered, and topics (*loci*) or sources of arguments to be used in pleading each type of case. Cicero specifies four different *status* or issues (*constitutiones*): dispute about fact, dispute about definition, dispute about the nature of the act, and dispute about jurisdiction or procedure (I.viii). After subdividing and illustrating the four *constitutiones,* he takes up *dispositio* (arrangement) and discusses the six parts of an oration: *exordium* (introduction), *narratio* (statement of facts), *partitio* (division), *confirmatio* (proof), *reprehensio* (refutation), *conclusio* (conclusion) (I.xiv). But the last three parts draw their materials from the topics or sources of argument. So most of the subsequent discussion (I.xxiv-lix) should again be classified under *inventio*. Book II sets out to show which arguments or combinations of arguments are appropriate for each of the four types of issue in each of the three types of oratory. This task is accomplished far more thoroughly for judicial or forensic (II.iv-li) than for deliberative and epideictic oratory (li-lix).

The *De inventione*, in short, is a partial handbook of forensic oratory. Aside from the brief general introduction and occasional nods in the direction of epideictic and deliberative oratory, its contents are directly relevant only to the pleading of cases in a Roman court of law.[10] Yet this work served to define rhetoric for nearly a millennium after the courts, and hence the type of orator for whom Cicero wrote, had passed out of existence. Its forensic emphasis, even more than the failure to cover *elocutio, memoria,* and *pronuntiatio,* should have prevented the *De inventione* from becoming a major source during the Middle Ages.

What was omitted by the *De inventione* or "rhetorica vetus" (old rhetoric), in any case, could easily be supplied from the "rhetorica nova" (new rhetoric) or *Rhetorica ad Herennium*. The *Ad Herennium* covers invention and arrangement in much the same fashion as the *De inventione,* with which it is nearly contemporary. Though it also treats delivery (III.xi-xv) and memory (III.xvi-xxiv), it complemented the *De inventione* above all by virtue of the long discussion of *elocutio* in the fourth and final book. Its division of style into three levels (IV.viii-x) —grand (*gravis*), middle (*mediocris*), and simple (*adtenuata*) —was extremely influential during the Middle Ages,[11] as was the discussion of stylistic faults (IV.x-xii). Most of book IV, however, has to do with the means of lending distinction (*dignitas*) to style by rendering it ornate. This is accomplished through two kinds of figures (*exornationes*): figures of diction and figures of thought (IV.xiii). The figures of diction are forty-five in number, of which ten form a special class called "tropes," while there are nineteen figures of thought. Each of these figures is named, defined, and then illustrated: a format that became standard for all subsequent catalogues of the figures. The popularity of *Ad Herennium,* IV caused *elocutio* to become synonymous with figurative ornamentation and had a great deal to do with the frequent reduction of *rhetorica* to *elocutio* that Charles Baldwin considered the defining characteristic of medieval rhetoric.[12]

For the early Middle Ages, however, the *De inventione* was the supreme authority. The *Ad Herennium* may not have joined it as a standard text until the ninth century; but from the mid eleventh century on, the "new rhetoric" posed a serious challenge to the supremacy of the "old rhetoric."[13] Baldwin's thesis that medieval rhetoric is dominated by the inheritance of the Second Sophistic, characterized by cultivation of epideictic oratory to the exclusion of the other types, therefore needs modification. At least until the mid-eleventh century, the dominant strain in rhetoric was technical rather than sophistical,[14] forensic rather than epideictic, and inventional rather than stylistic.

Conspicuous by their widespread neglect during the Middle Ages are those classical treatises that take a more philosophical approach to rhetoric, considering it in conjunction with questions of truth and morals rather than simply as a set of technical precepts. Aristotle's *Rhetoric,* the best example of a work that joins philosophy to precept, had very little impact on the medieval conception of rhetoric. For most of the Middle Ages it was unknown, and even when it was recovered and translated (twice) into Latin during the thirteenth century, its influence remained small and was confined to the universities of Northern Europe. Though William of Moerbeke's translation (ca. 1270) survives in more than one hundred manuscripts, all evidence suggests that it was associated not with rhetoric and the arts of discourse but rather with ethics and political science.[15]

Quintilian's treatise on the education of a perfect orator, the *Institutio oratoria* (ca. A.D. 94) fared somewhat better. The complete text ceased to be available throughout most of Europe by the ninth century; but the "mutilated text" and the excerpts gathered in *florilegia* (anthologies) had a considerable vogue among twelfth-century writers like John of Salisbury. Quintilian's ideas on education were especially popular in the French cathedral schools of this period. But he is almost never cited from the ninth until the twelfth century, and he is all but ignored during the thirteenth and fourteenth centuries. Not until the fifteenth century, with the recovery of the full text, does the *Institutio oratoria* again play a major role in the study of rhetoric.[16]

B. The De inventione *and the Intellectualization of Rhetoric*

The odds would seem to have been against the survival of classical rhetoric in any form after the fall of the Roman Empire and the disappearance of the civic life to which Ciceronian rhetoric owed its creation and without which it lost its relevance. As government became increasingly absolutist, there were few occasions for public debate of political policy. And the scope of the panegyric progressively narrowed, in Western Europe at least,[17] to the formulas of hagiography. But if deliberative and epideictic oratory were restricted, judicial oratory was effectively eliminated as a practical pursuit. When the Roman courts passed entirely out of existence, the Roman *orator* ceased to exist, and the technical manuals composed to define and pass on his craft relinquished their utility.

Yet it was precisely this oral, forensic type of rhetoric—the subject of the *De inventione*—that was dominant from late antiquity until the twelfth century.[18] The separation of rhetorical precepts from real life concerns, however, had its roots not in the Middle Ages but in late antiquity. The demise of the *orator*, and the degeneration of classical rhetoric from art to artifice, was virtually complete before the medieval period began. Under the empire, the law courts had become the province of specialists and political democracy had declined steadily. Though rhetoric remained the cornerstone of Roman education, by the fourth century its practice consisted of little more than panegyric and the declamation of the schools. It was a rhetoric of display, with little or no vital connection to civic life. For all practical purposes, the rhetorician displaced the orator; *artificiosa eloquentia* was the province of neither the philosopher nor the politician but rather the schoolmaster. The textbooks written for the late Roman schools of declamation by the third- and fourth-century Minor Latin Rhetoricians show the direction rhetoric would take during the Middle Ages.[19]

The loss of rhetoric's political function had two important, and reciprocally related, consequences for the history of medieval rhetoric: the steady decline of rhetoric's prestige among the arts of the trivium and an increasing tendency to reduce rhetoric to an abstraction. By the seventh century, rhetoric had been replaced by the more practical study of grammar as the dominant member of the trivium.[20] But the most serious threat came not from grammar but dialectic, the art which Ciceronian rhetoric, reduced to inventional theory and cut off from its judicial context, most resembles. In fact, the strength of the bond between rhetorical theory and judicial oratory may have forestalled any attempts to apply that theory to current needs and actually encouraged the development of dialectic as a study of discourse more suited to the conditions of medieval life.[21]

One need not wait until the eleventh century and the triumph of dialectic in the schools of Northern Europe to observe the threat posed to rhetoric by its sister science. Aristotle, at the beginning of his *Rhetoric*, had discussed the similarities between the two arts in some detail and concluded that rhetoric is a branch of dialectic. But Aristotle's work was not an important source of rhetorical doctrine during the Middle Ages and was rarely cited directly on this point.[22] The text that defined the relationship between the two sciences of constructing arguments was Boethius's *De topicis differentiis* (before 523).

In the fourth and final book of this very influential work, Boethius sets out to distinguish rhetoric from dialectic and, in particular, rhetorical topics from the dialectical topics that are the subject of the first three books. He distinguishes rhetoric from dialectic in terms of matter, use, and end (IV.1205c-1206D). The matter of rhetoric is the hypothesis, which is tied to circumstances, while that of dialectic is the thesis or general question, which is not. Dialectic sometimes uses circumstances, but always subordinates them to a thesis, while rhetoric, when it uses theses, always subordinates them to hypotheses. In terms of method, the disciplines differ in two ways: dialectic employs questions and answers, while rhetoric employs continuous discourse, and the rhetorician uses incomplete syllogisms (enthymemes), while the dialectician uses complete syllogisms. Finally, the end of dialectic is to refute a single opponent, while the end of rhetoric is to persuade a judge or some third party other than the opponent. The distinction based on matter is apparently the crucial one, for when Boethius comes to distinguish rhetorical from dialectical topics (IV.1215A-1216D), he finds they differ above all in that rhetorical topics can only be applied to specific questions or hypotheses, whereas dialectical topics can be applied both to hypotheses and to general questions or theses. In short, dialectic subsumes rhetoric as the general subsumes the particular.[23]

This view ran counter to that of the *De inventione,* which held that rhetoric is an art or science (*ars*) rather than a skill (*disciplina* or *facultas*) and that its subject matter is politics, not argumentation (I.v.6-7). Both the Ciceronian and the Boethian views occur throughout the Middle Ages. Among the encyclopedists, for example, Cassiodorus associates rhetoric with civil questions and regards it as a science (II.ii.1), while Martianus Capella subordinates it to dialectic (336-37) and considers it a skill (438). Alcuin (*Disputatio de rhetorica et de virtutibus,* 3) in the late eighth century, Rabanus Maurus (*De institutione clericorum,* III.19) in the ninth, Honorius Augustodunensis (*De animae exsilio et patria,* III) in the twelfth, and Brunetto Latini (*Trésor,* III) in the thirteenth century all follow Cicero in linking rhetoric to politics and ethics. Isidore, the third great encyclopedist, notes that rhetoric shares with dialectic the use of the syllogism (II.ix.3), but he also connects it with law (II.x) and decides that on the whole it has most in common with grammar (II.i.2). The ninth-century commentators of Martianus Capella naturally make rhetoric a division of dialectic,[24] as do the Scholastics who by the late twelfth century had made *De topicis differentiis,* IV a standard authority for the study of rhetoric at the universities of Northern Europe.[25] Other writers, notably Hugh of St. Victor, John of Salisbury, William of Conches, Aquinas, and Bonaventure, also detach rhetoric from politics, but devise more complex taxonomies in which dialectic is distinguished from logic, of which it, along with rhetoric, is a species.[26]

No longer capable of doing the job for which it was designed, increasingly intellectualized, in danger of losing its autonomy to dialectic (and, as we shall see, to grammar as well), grounded in principles antithetical to the prevailing Christian world view,[27] Ciceronian rhetoric was nonetheless transmitted to the Middle Ages and even enjoyed periods of considerable popularity. Why? The habitual "mind set" of the Church Fathers, most of whom were trained in Roman schools whose curricula were still dominated by rhetoric, was certainly a factor in this remarkable survival. St. Augustine provides the best example. The *Confessions* documented the inner struggle that accompanied his decision to cut short a brilliant secular career as a rhetorician in order to take up the Christian ministry; while near the end of his life, in the *De doctrina christiana* (finished in 427), he formulated what became the definitive Christian apologia for the study of pagan rhetoric. Just as the Israelites took with them the gold and other valuables of the Egyptians, leaving behind what was base or useless, he reasoned, so too the Christian should not spurn such pagan learning as can be shown to have value for the performing of God's work (II.xl). Selectively and judiciously employed, pagan rhetoric can be useful in helping Christians to understand the truth expressed, often darkly, in Scripture and to deepen through preaching the faith of others in that truth. In response to the objection that rhetoric is the tool of sophists and miscreants, he asked, "While the faculty of eloquence, which is of great value in urging either evil or justice, is in itself indifferent, why should it not be obtained for the uses of the good in the service of truth if the evil usurp it for the winning of perverse and vain causes in defense of iniquity and error?"[28] Though the pragmatic thrust of his argument was at best dimly understood before the Carolingian period, its basic logic was transmitted to the early Middle Ages through Cassiodorus's *Institutiones divinarum et saecularium litterarum* (see especially I. xxviii.3-4) and was instrumental in justifying the preservation of a rhetoric that had to all appearances lost its relevance.

Cassiodorus's encyclopedia (after 551) was important in yet another way. Following the pattern established by the *De nuptiis Philologiae et Mercurii* of Martianus Capella (fl. 410-439), and influencing in turn Isidore of Seville's *Origines* or *Etymologiae* (612-620), it helped enshrine rhetoric as one of the seven basic divisions of secular knowledge. These compilations presented the essentials of rhetoric in a schematic, easily memorized form that could serve either as an introduction to or a substitute for more advanced study. Later medieval encyclopedias, for example, those of Thierry of Chartres (*Heptateuchon*) in the twelfth century and Brunetto Latini (*Trésor*) and Vincent of Beauvais (*Speculum doctrinale*) in the thirteenth, also treat rhetoric; but the most influential were the three written between the fifth and seventh centuries.

Martianus Capella's *Marriage of Philology and Mercury* is both the earliest and the most unusual of the major encyclopedias. The first two books are devoted to the marriage of the god Mercury to the maiden

Philology, whose attendants, the Liberal Arts, introduce themselves in the remaining seven books. Stripped of the allegory, Martianus's work is a fairly extensive but entirely unoriginal summary of the seven liberal arts. The chief sources for the discussion of rhetoric (book V) are the *De inventione*, supplemented by references to Cicero's *Orator* and *De oratore*, and, for the figures, the fourth-century *Liber de figuris sententiarum et elocutionis* of Aquila Romanus.[29] The *De nuptiis* was popular throughout the Middle Ages, but especially during the Carolingian period, when it was the subject of several commentaries.[30]

The rhetorical part of Cassiodorus's *Institutiones divinarum et saecularium litterarum* is considerably shorter than that of Martianus, a fact that helps explain its great popularity as an introductory text.[31] Though he cites Cicero directly on occasion, Cassiodorus takes most of his material from the compendium of the minor Latin rhetorician Fortunatianus.[32] The first Christian encyclopedist, Cassiodorus helps guarantee the survival of rhetoric and the other liberal arts that constitute secular learning by incorporating them into the monastic discipline, not for their own sake but as aids to understanding Scripture (I.xxvii). But rhetoric, as Cassiodorus depicts it, has clearly lost its practical relevance. He says, for example, that rhetoric differs from dialectic primarily in its copiousness and eloquence (II.iii.2), but he never discusses *elocutio* in his chapter on rhetoric (II.ii), which is almost entirely devoted to *inventio*. The influence of Cassiodorus on later writers thus contributes to the intellectualizing tendency in medieval rhetoric.

One writer influenced by Cassiodorus was Isidore of Seville, whose *Etymologiae* was the most popular of the medieval encyclopedias. Isidore attempts to gather together all human knowledge, of which the liberal arts are an important part. In covering rhetoric (II.i-xxi), Isidore relies chiefly on Cassiodorus for the fifteen chapters on invention and on Donatus for the final six chapters on style.[33] Though interesting for its apparent awareness of the connection between rhetoric and the law (II.x), and though fuller than Cassiodorus by virtue of its material on style, the discussion of rhetoric in the *Etymologies* typifies the schematic and abstract form in which Ciceronian rhetoric was conveyed in the Middle Ages.

If the weight of authority, embodied in the encyclopedias, is the factor most directly responsible for the preservation of rhetoric during the early Middle Ages, and if the prevailing tendency up to at least the mid-eleventh century is to move rhetoric away from the practical and toward the theoretical, there are nonetheless signs of a more vital continuity of the classical tradition. An awareness, if only occasional and partial, of the original scope and purpose of Ciceronian rhetoric is particularly evident in Italy, where rhetoric finally regained a measure of its practical utility in the prosperous and stable municipalities of the eleventh to fourteenth centuries.[34] Despite its eccentricities, an early work like Anselm of Besate's *Rhetorimachia* (1046-48) indicates the rebirth of the full Ciceronian rhetoric in Italy.[35] In France, signs of a renewed rhetoric first appear during the "Carolingian Renaissance" of the eighth and ninth centuries. Rabanus Maurus's *De institutione clericorum* (819) is an important precursor of the pragmatism that would produce the arts of poetry, letter writing, and preaching in the twelfth and thirteenth centuries, and Alcuin's *Disputatio de rhetorica et de virtutibus* (end of eighth or beginning of ninth century), though neither very original nor very influential, attempts to reforge the old bond between rhetoric and ethics/politics and suggests ways in which rhetoric is relevant to contemporary, secular needs.[36] As we learn more about the uses to which rhetoric was put during the Middle Ages, we may in fact discover that it was better understood and of more practical value than it now seems to have been.[37]

C. The Rhetorica ad Herennium: *Rhetoric as Style*

Among the developments in rhetoric that can be traced to the Carolingian period, none was more immediately significant than the elevation of the *Rhetorica ad Herennium* to the status of a standard text.[38] It is appropriate that the *Ad Herennium* should have begun its long climb to an authority equal and finally, by the mid-twelfth century, superior to that of the *De inventione* during a period best known for the study of grammar. For rhetoric and grammar overlap in the area of style; and for all practical purposes, style was synonymous with the figures from the time of the third- and fourth-century Minor Latin Rhetoricians (see note 19). Grammar had intruded in this department of rhetoric as early as the fourth century. The third and final book of Donatus's *Ars maior* deals with metaplasms (the adding, deleting, or transposing of one or more letters in a word, for the sake of metrical ornament), schemes (or figures), and tropes, all of which are faults in prose but are permitted in poetry.[39] This short book, which circulated separately as the *Barbarismus,* joined the *Ad Herennium,* IV in shaping the medieval doctrine of the figures. Its authority was so great that it was named along with Boethius's *De topicis differentiis,* IV as one of the two chief textbooks for the study of rhetoric in the Northern European universities of the later Middle Ages. The distinction Donatus tried to make between grammatical and rhetorical *colores* or *figurae* did not stand the test of time.[40] In the seventh century Isidore drew his material on rhetorical figures (*Etymol.,* II.xxi) from Donatus, while of the twelfth- and thirteenth-century grammarians who composed the arts of poetry, only the earliest, Matthew of Vendôme, did not draw exclusively on the *Ad Herennium* for the figures.[41] It is the prominence of the figures and the partnership between grammar and rhetoric, especially evident after the Carolingian period, that led Baldwin to over-emphasize the "sophistic" quality of medieval rhetoric.

A good indication of the *Ad Herennium*'s growing importance and the resulting emphasis on *elocutio* is the appearance of rhetorical treatises devoted exclusively to the figures. The earliest medieval treatise on the figures, Bede's *De schematibus et tropiis* (700 or 701), belongs to the grammatical tradition. Bede, like Augustine, sought to demonstrate the primacy of sacred over secular eloquence. To illustrate seventeen schemes and thirteen tropes (several of which are further subdivided), he accordingly took from Scripture all but three of his examples, many of them previously used by Cassiodorus for the same purpose. But the order, the selection, and often the definitions themselves are those of Donatus. Nor does Bede ever indicate that his treatise should be associated with anything but the *ars grammatica*.[42] The collections of figures that appeared with increasing frequency after the Carolingian period, by contrast, were modeled on book IV of the *Ad Herennium* and were perceived by their authors as belonging to the *ars rhetorica*. Onulf of Speyer's *Colores rhetorici* (ca.1050) and Marbod of Rennes's (d. 1125) *De ornamentis verborum*[43] typify the increasing identification of rhetoric with stylistic ornament that accompanied the rising popularity of the *Ad Herennium*.

The figures, of course, continued to concern the grammarians; this is evident in the important textbooks that shaped late medieval instruction in grammar. Alexander of Villa-Dei's *Doctrinale* (1199), which replaced Priscian in the curriculum as the standard advanced grammar text, treats 80 figures (lines 2341-2645) and Evrard of Béthune's only slightly less popular *Graecismus* (1212) covers 103 figures (I-III).[44] It is therefore no surprise that a group of grammarians was responsible for devising, also in the late twelfth and early thirteenth centuries, a pragmatic adaptation of the *Ad Herennium*'s treatment of style.

Beginning with the *Ars versificatoria* (before 1175) of Matthew of Vendôme and ending with the *Laborintus* (before 1280) of Eberhard the German, there appeared a new sort of treatise offering instruction in the composition of verse. In all, six of these *artes poetriae* survive. Geoffrey of Vinsauf wrote the most popular of the six, his hexameter *Poetria Nova,* between 1208 and 1213, and followed it soon after with his prose *Documentum de modo et arte dictandi et versificandi,* extant in both a long and short version. Gervase of Melkley's *Ars versificaria* was composed after 1213, but before 1216; and the most ambitious of the six works, John of Garland's *De arte prosayca, metrica, et rithmica* or *Poetria Parisiana,* was probably written about 1220 and subsequently revised by its author.[45]

The authors of the arts of poetry were grammarians rather than rhetoricians and designed their works for use by their students, part of whose grammar studies consisted of composition exercises. Nevertheless, the treatises have long been tied to rhetoric, largely because of their extensive debt to the *Ad Herennium.* To avoid this misrepresentation, Murphy coined the term "preceptive grammar" to describe the *artes poetriae.* If the preceptive grammarians consciously emulated a specific author, it was not Cicero but their other chief source, Horace, whose *Ars poetica*—the *poetria vetus* or "old poetics"—Geoffrey set out deliberately to replace with his own "new poetics."

The works of Matthew and Eberhard are clearly more elementary than the others, aimed at beginning students of versification who are working with set topics assigned by their teachers. Accordingly, they stress imitation of other poets and embellishment, chiefly through figurative language, of preformed materials. Though he shares their emphasis on *elocutio,* Geoffrey differs from these pure grammarians in appealing to a more advanced student by covering as well what could be called *inventio* and *dispositio.*[46] John of Garland resembles Geoffrey in his broader, more "rhetorical" range, and even covers prose composition (i.e., letter writing) in addition to versifying.[47] But, without drawing a sharper boundary between the two arts than was recognized in medieval practice, it is probably more accurate to assign even these comparatively advanced textbooks to the *ars grammatica,* the traditional context for the study of poetry and poetics, than to the *ars rhetorica.*[48]

D. Pragmatism: *The* Ars dictaminis

The second half of the eleventh century initiated the highpoint of medieval interest in rhetoric. From this period date both the first selective application of Ciceronian precepts to practical, contemporary needs and the first in an unprecedented series of new commentaries and glosses on the *De inventione* and *Rhetorica ad Herennium* (see note 6). Yet at the same time, dialectic began to dominate the trivium, initiating the eventual triumph of scholasticism in the schools of Northern Europe. This third process has been particularly difficult to reconcile with the second. How does one explain the widespread study of classical rhetoric that reached its peak in Northern Europe from around 1080 to 1225, at a time when works like Hugh of St. Victor's *Didascalicon* (ca.1127) and John of Salisbury's *Metalogicus* (1159) were redefining the arts in such a way that rhetoric's very autonomy was threatened?[49]

One way of resolving the paradox is to redefine what at first seem three distinct traditions in twelfth-century rhetoric—pragmatism, classicism, and scholasticism—as aspects of a single historical phenomenon analyzed by R. W. Southern in his now classic essay "Medieval Humanism."[50] What seems generally to have characterized the twelfth and thirteenth centuries was a renewed faith in an order within nature and in man's ability to discern and describe that order. A natural consequence of this new attitude was an eagerness to examine one's own experience within the world and to reexamine all previous attempts at analyzing and describing that experience. The same impulse was responsible for renewed attention to the meaning of rhetoric, as it was defined in the standard sources; for more careful scrutiny of rhetoric's proper place and function within the whole of human knowledge; and for the analysis of areas of experience that had not as yet been reduced to systems. This "humanistic" impulse undermined the authority of the seven liberal arts and made evident the irrelevance of forensic rhetoric, as a coherent discipline, to contemporary needs. At northern universities like Paris and Oxford, the result was the reduction of rhetoric to a branch of logic.[51] At those schools with a strong tradition of grammar studies, on the other hand, the same challenge to the established view of classical rhetoric made possible a new, more practical synthesis in the *ars poetriae*. The thirteenth century was thus a lowpoint for classical rhetoric as theory, but a highpoint for its practical use.

In subject matter the most appropriate and in technique the most successful medieval adaptation of classical rhetoric was the *ars dictaminis* or science of letter writing.[52] The *ars dictaminis* grew up in response to an increasingly complex political and social situation that necessitated an ever greater quantity and variety of official correspondence. Collections of models for letters and documents had been kept by both lay and ecclesiastical secretaries since at least Carolingian times, but by the end of the eleventh century the inadequacy of these crude formularies and the need for a systematic, generative method had become clear. The earliest surviving treatise designed to satisfy this need is Alberic's *Dictaminum radii,* composed at Monte Cassino in 1087.[53]

From classical rhetoric, in particular the *Ad Herennium,* the *ars dictaminis* borrowed mostly principles of style and arrangement. The standard treatise, whose shape was permanently fixed by about 1140, transformed the six parts of a spoken oration (see section I.A above) into the five parts of a letter: the *salutatio* (greeting) , *captatio benevolentiae* (securing of goodwill; also called *exordium* or *proverbium*) , *narratio* (statement of facts) , *petitio* (request) , and *conclusio.* The need to observe decorum within an extensive social and political hierarchy—the main reason for the creation of the *ars dictaminis*—is reflected in the disproportionate attention the treatises usually pay to the *salutatio* by comparison with the other four parts.[54]

The typical dictaminal treatise consists of a relatively brief theoretical section (the *ars*) and a more or less extensive collection of models (*dictamina*) suited to various situations and social levels. The theoretical section usually begins with general definitions, before treating in turn each part of the letter (illustrated, especially in the case of the *salutatio,* with numerous examples), and often includes sections on prose rhythm (*cursus*),[55] privileges and other legal documents, and vices to be avoided in letter writing.[56] The formulary is frequently organized according to the social status of the correspondents (lay or ecclesiastical; superior, middling, inferior) as well as subject. Together the two parts form a *summa dictaminis,* a complete manual of the theory and practice of the art. Those who used such works, however, seldom respected their integrity. The practical nature of the models encouraged frequent excerpting and adaptation, and the preceptive introduction might circulate independently, often in abridged form. As a result, it can be difficult to establish the text of a popular manual like Bernard of Meung's *Flores dictaminum.*[57]

Scholars have for some time found it convenient to divide the history of the *ars dictaminis* into three main periods: an Italian phase, lasting from the late eleventh through the mid-twelfth century and centered around Bologna; a French phase, spanning the second half of the twelfth century and involving chiefly the schools of the Loire valley (Tours, Orléans, Meung); and a second Italian phase that saw the source of new doctrine shift back to Bologna around 1200.[58] For at least two reasons, this schema is misleading. Though the first treatises to spell out the rules of *dictamen* appeared in Italy during the late eleventh and early twelfth centuries, the practices they describe had long been observed not only in Italy, but also in France and Germany. The standard view encourages the false impression that the *ars dictaminis* was suddenly "invented" by a specific person at a specific time and place.[59] A second problem is that the "new" treatises produced in France during the latter half of the twelfth century are generally reworkings of earlier Italian manuals, like Bernard of Bologna's *Summa dictaminum.*[60] As regards the transmission of dictaminal doctrine through specific texts, therefore, it is more accurate to distinguish two phases. By the late twelfth century the influence of writers like Adalbert of Samaria, Hugh of Bologna, Henricus Francigena, and Bernard of Bologna extended into France, Germany, and England. Then, early in the thirteenth century, a new set of Italian teachers—men like Boncompagno, Bene of Florence, and Guido Faba—began to produce the manuals that would shape the subsequent history of the *ars dictaminis*.[61]

The thirteenth-century Italian *dictatores,* moreover, actually saw themselves as opposing their predecessors, especially the French. The controversy apparently had its source in the different circumstances under which *dictamen* was taught in the two countries. Like the *artes poetriae,* the *artes dictaminis* were associated with the cathedral schools in the north. This was significant in that the French centers of dictaminal instruction, especially Orléans, were known for their cultivation of the classical poets or *auctores* in connection with the teaching of grammar.[62] Whereas in Italy *dictamen* was linked to rhetorical and legal studies, and became, at Bologna, part of the regular university curriculum, in France the *ars grammatica* continued to exert the stronger influence.[63] The result, in the opinion of their adversaries, was that the French *dictatores* espoused a "pagan" style characterized by frequent quotations from the *auctores,* unusual vocabulary, and highly figurative language. The Italians sought to simplify the language of *dictamen,* to replace the pagan *stilus supremus* with the Christian *sermo humilis.*[64] Bene of Florence narrowed the dispute even further, condemning the French writers for using "imaginary dactyls and spondees" to describe the *cursus.* Due in large part to the strong tradition of grammatical studies within which they wrote, the French teachers borrowed terms of quantity from their study of classical, metrical cadences to describe what were actually rhythmical cadences and should accordingly, said Bene, be discussed in terms of stress.[65] There is evidence, however, that the disagreement about *cursus* involved not only the terminology but also the precepts.[66]

The *ars dictaminis* reached its peak in Italy during the first half of the thirteenth century. At Bologna, *dictamen* was studied as a separate discipline with its own faculty (a distinction it never attained elsewhere), while in southern Italy Thomas of Capua wrote his influential *Summa dictaminis* and Peter of Vinea his much-imitated *Epistolae.* But by mid-century the creative period seems to have ended. The *dictatores* remained a vital part of Italian civic life; but the teaching of *dictamen* was increasingly based on sterile collections of models. Lawrence of Aquilegia's very popular *Practica sive usus dictaminis* (ca.1300), whose user simply assembled a letter from sets of options arranged in series of vertical tables,[67] clearly illustrates the movement away from precept toward pure imitation. Insofar as it was sustained, the creative impulse manifested itself in the more practical notarial art. A work like the *Summa artis notarie* of Rolandinus Passagerius (d. 1300) more immediately suited the needs of the growing class of jurists than anything the teachers of *dictamen* produced.

II. CHRISTIAN RHETORIC

A. St. Augustine and His Influence

Though nearly eight centuries elapsed before the edifice was completed, St. Augustine laid the foundation for a practical Christian rhetoric when he completed the *De doctrina christiana* in 427. The importance of his achievement is difficult to exaggerate: not only did he settle the debate about whether it was proper for a Christian to use pagan learning, but he also devised a set of general principles from which a rhetoric of preaching was later constructed.[68] Among the most important tenets of the Christian eloquence Augustine envisioned in *De doctrina,* IV are the following: eloquence is learned by imitation of the eloquent rather than by precept; wisdom, which is equivalent to the understanding of Scripture, is more valuable and more persuasive than artificial eloquence; Scripture and the writings of the Church Fathers are not artless, as the pagans allege, but have a distinctive eloquence of their own; though delight and persuasion (the effects of the middle and high styles, respectively) are sometimes desirable, teaching, for which the clear and simple low style is best suited, is all that is necessary for the Christian orator; prayer rather than skill is finally the key to effective preaching; the needs and aptitudes of the audience should determine one's choice of style; and the speaker's example, his way of living, is more persuasive than his skill in speaking.

Within these guidelines, Augustine showed how Ciceronian rhetoric could be useful to the Christian preacher. His argument that Christians should not refuse to employ in the service of truth the potent weapon that their enemies used to spread falsehood was influential in preserving pagan rhetoric in the early medieval period. But his precepts regarding the active, practical application of rhetoric to Christian ends seem to have been ignored through most of the Middle Ages. Rabanus Maurus in the ninth century was the first to call attention to the pragmatic side of Augustine's seminal work, and Alain of Lille's *Summa de arte praedicatoria,* written at the end of the twelfth century, was the first attempt since Augustine's to develop a theory of preaching.

It is not difficult to explain the delayed emergence of a practical Christian rhetoric. Indeed, many of the reasons are evident in Augustine's own precepts. Christian homiletics, with their emphasis on external authority—the Bible, the speaker's *ethos,* divine grace—rather than the persuasive power of the speaker's language or performance, their antiformalist striving for conversational simplicity, and their general distrust of artifice, are characteristically counterrhetorical. The preacher is only an instrument through whom God speaks: conversion is something that takes place between God and the individual, not through human agency. Any study of technique is at best pointless (because true eloquence comes from God), at worst dangerous (because it smacks of pride). The preacher's proper study is the Bible; God will supply him with the words he needs to communicate the truth he finds there. It is no surprise, then, that the Church should have devoted so much energy to providing tools for the interpretation of Scripture and allowed the power of the message, rather than that of the medium, to carry the burden of persuasion. If Augustine discusses artificial style, he gives no advice on how to achieve it and warns against cultivating it to excess or for its own sake. About structure he says nothing at all.

The suspicion of artifice and the indifference to composition that characterize Augustine's "metarhetoric" are especially evident in the next important statement about preaching, Gregory the Great's *Cura pastoralis* (591). Gregory emphasizes the importance of preaching and the necessity of adapting one's approach to the specific audience addressed, but his overriding concern is with the content rather than the form of the sermon. If anything, the widespread use of the *Cura pastoralis* as a handbook reduced the influence rhetoric might otherwise have had on preaching.[69]

More sympathetic toward technique, though influenced by Gregory, is Rabanus Maurus's *De institutione clericorum* (819). Book III brings together from a variety of sources material relevant to the priest's duty as a speaker. Rabanus devotes a chapter to the value of rhetoric to the preacher (III.19) and concludes the book with thirteen chapters in which he applies rhetoric to preaching (III.27-39). Virtually all of this material is taken directly from *De doctrina christiana*, IV, with significant excerpts from Cassiodorus and Gregory; but the treatise is nonetheless important as an early instance of the pragmatism that produced the *artes dictandi* and *poetriae* in the twelfth century and would produce the *ars praedicandi* in the thirteenth.[70]

Rabanus's precedent was slow to be followed, however; the next treatise on preaching did not appear for another 250 years. Nor is Guibert of Nogent's *Liber quo ordine sermo fieri debeat* (ca.1084) a true rhetoric of preaching. The general discussion of preaching emphasizes such familiar points as the moral obligation to preach, the source in God of both content and delivery, the superiority of truth and simplicity over eloquence (the ideal preacher should thus be sincere and humble), and the need to adjust the sermon to the aptitude of the congregation.[71] Guibert's most original contribution is to point out the relevance of the four levels of scriptural interpretation—the literal, the allegorical, the tropological or moral, and the anagogical—to the preacher's task. Though this innovation probably sprang from the peculiar circumstances of Guibert's own treatise, which was written as a preface to his extensive *Commentary on Genesis,* the use of the four levels, with special attention to the tropological as the most useful for preachers, became a constant feature of later preaching manuals.[72]

Honorius Augustodunensis (d. 1136) also wrote a handbook for preachers (*Speculum ecclesiae*) ;[73] but it was not until the very end of the twelfth century that the first attempt to create a systematic rhetoric of preaching since Augustine was undertaken. Strongly influenced by Gregory's *Cura pastoralis,* Alain of Lille's *Summa de arte praedicatoria* (1199?) stresses the authority of Scripture and the speaker's *ethos* rather than arrangement, ornament, or delivery. But Alain foreshadows the systematic *artes* that would spring up almost immediately in his use of division as a mode of exposition and in his analytical spirit.[74]

B. *The* Ars praedicandi

Where Alain, and all of the other writers on preaching from St. Augustine onward, differ from the thirteenth-century *ars praedicandi* or science of preaching is in the attention to *materia* or subject matter to the virtual exclusion of form. With the very first true *ars praedicandi* that survives, Alexander of Ashby's *De modo praedicandi* (ca.1200), the shift to consideration of the sermon's structure and even its style is apparent. The practice on which the theory of the *ars praedicandi* was based, in fact, was almost certainly well established by the time the first treatises were written; and the theory itself arrived by 1220 at the shape it was to retain for centuries to come.[75]

Since the contents of the *artes praedicandi,* perhaps even more than the *artes dictaminis,* tend to uniformity, it is not necessary to describe individual treatises.[76] The sermon is divided into four parts, possibly based on the parts of an argument as outlined in the *Rhetorica ad Herennium:*[77] *thema*—a passage from the Bible that is the main subject of the sermon; *prothema* (often a sermon in miniature) —a second biblical text, related to the theme, but serving mainly as a transition to an invocation of divine aid through prayer; *divisio*—the breakdown of the *thema* into its constituent parts; *distinctio*—subdivisions introduced in the course of developing the *divisiones* of the *thema.* Any given *thema* has several *divisiones,* each of which is taken up in turn, with its *distinctiones.* Having described this format, the typical *ars praedicandi* goes on to treat the modes of amplifying the last two parts.[78] The number of these modes varies, but is most often eight. Separate treatises devoted solely to amplification were not uncommon, especially from the mid-thirteenth century on, and works designed to supply materials for amplification form an important part of the ancillary literature or "homiletic apparatus" that grew up around the *ars praedicandi*. This topical system of *amplificatio,* which served as a principle of both *inventio* and *dispositio,* links the *ars praedicandi* to the inventional theory that is the chief legacy of ancient rhetoric.[79]

Particularly when the ancillary literature is taken into account, the *ars praedicandi* resembles the *ars dictaminis* in the disproportionate space given to illustrative examples as opposed to theoretical precepts. Collections of sermons, often quite large, were themselves important pedagogical resources.[80] Unlike the *dictatores,* however, the authors of the *artes praedicandi* held fast to the rejection of ornate style in favor of unadorned truth.[81] Here again, Alain of Lille supplies an instructive precedent. When he personified Rhetoric in the *Anticlaudianus* (III. 2-3), he adopted the typical late medieval attitude of equating it with *ornatus* or highly figurative style. But when he came to apply rhetoric to the practical activity of the preacher, he pointedly spurned empty eloquence and embraced clarity and simplicity (*Summa de arte praedicatoria,* I).

A final word should be said about the reason why what has been called "the first major new oratorical plan to be proposed in the Western world since about 125 B.C., when Hellenistic rhetoricians developed the sequence made familiar by Cicero and the Pseudo-Cicero,"[82] should have sprung so suddenly into existence around 1200. Until recently, the consensus view was that the *ars praedicandi* originated in the thirteenth-century universities dominated by the dialecticians. But Murphy has challenged this view on the grounds that the dates and contents of the earliest treatises now known—those of Alexander of Ashby and Thomas Chobham—argue against university origins. He thinks that the formative stage of the movement should rather be associated with the intellectual milieu of the late twelfth-century schools and that it was only in its mature stage that the *ars praedicandi* came to be associated with the universities.[83] Either way, the *ars praedicandi* is, like the *ars poetriae* and the *ars dictaminis,* a product of what Southern defines as "medieval humanism." Its appearance, despite the centuries-old resistance to "artificial" preaching, can be attributed to the widespread faith in the existence of order in nature, the primacy of human reason, and the intelligibility of the universe that equally characterizes the twelfth and thirteenth centuries and that sets this period apart from the rest of the Middle Ages.

III. CONCLUSION

The decision to end this history with the thirteenth century is based primarily on developments that take place in Italy shortly thereafter.

Fourteenth-century figures like Petrarch provide the first unmistakeable signs that a full recovery of the original meaning and function of classical rhetoric is under way. To cite a single, significant example, the debate over the relationship between wisdom and eloquence or philosophy and rhetoric, which has for the Middle Ages its *locus classicus* in the opening of the *De inventione,* began to be restored to its classical context by the fourteenth-century Italian humanists. Though such figures as Alcuin, John of Salisbury, Abelard, Bonaventure, and Aquinas had addressed this important topic, the intellectualization of rhetoric that resulted from the loss of its political function prevented them from recognizing the true grounds of the opposition: the orator's need to sacrifice precision in order to achieve the intelligibility necessary for persuasion.[84] The subordination of rhetoric to dialectic that accompanied this same intellectualization and was epitomized in the medieval popularity of Boethius's *De topicis differentiis,* IV also began to reverse itself in the fourteenth century, until by the fifteenth century the hierarchy was inverted and dialectic was subordinated to rhetoric on the basis of political utility.[85]

The reemergence of genuine classical rhetoric occurred gradually and was slow in spreading to the rest of Europe. Even in Italy, medieval rhetoric endured long after 1300. The *ars dictaminis,* in particular, continued to be cultivated, and, though increasingly schematized and overshadowed by the *ars notaria* and the study of law, was an important precursor of humanism.[86] Though the last *ars poetriae* was composed before 1280, the flow of *artes praedicandi* continued unabated through the fourteenth century. It may therefore be more precise to date the transition as Murphy does, in the fifteenth century, when interest in Cicero's *De oratore* revived and the full text of Quintilian's *Institutio oratoria* was recovered.[87] The point is simply that, by 1300, all the developments that characterize medieval rhetoric had either reached maturity or already expired.

NOTES

1. Charles Sears Baldwin, *Medieval Rhetoric and Poetic (to 1400)* (New York, 1928; rpt. Gloucester, Mass., 1959) ; John O. Ward, "From Antiquity to the Renaissance: Glosses and Commentaries on Cicero's *Rhetorica*," in *Medieval Eloquence: Studies in the Theory and Practice of Medieval Rhetoric* [hereafter ME], ed. James J. Murphy (Berkeley and Los Angeles, 1978) , 25-67 (this outstanding article is based on Ward's unpublished, two-volume dissertation, "Artificiosa Eloquentia in the Middle Ages," Diss. Toronto, 1972) ; Richard McKeon, "Rhetoric in the Middle Ages," *Speculum,* 17 (1942) , 1-32

(rpt., with alterations, in *Critics and Criticism, Ancient and Modern,* ed. R. S. Crane [Chicago and London, 1952], 260-96) ; James J. Murphy, *Rhetoric in the Middle Ages* [hereafter RMA] (Berkeley and Los Angeles, 1974) . For McKeon's three traditions, see note 26 below; Murphy's four types of medieval rhetoric are the classical Ciceronian variety and the arts of poetry, letter writing, and preaching.

2. Murphy, RMA, 109.

3. Cicero, *De inventione, De optimo genere oratorum, Topica,* ed. and trans. H. M. Hubbell (Cambridge, Mass.: Loeb Classical Library, 1949) ; [Pseudo-Cicero], *Ad C. Herennium de ratione dicendi (Rhetorica ad Herennium),* ed. and trans. Harry Caplan (Cambridge, Mass.: Loeb Classical Library, 1954) . Caplan's edition is especially valuable for its extensive introduction. On Cicero's importance for medieval rhetoric, see Murphy, RMA, 106-23.

4. Ward, ME, 54.

5. Susan Gallick, "Medieval Rhetorical Arts in England and the Manuscript Traditions," *Manuscripta,* 18 (1974) , 67-95.

6. Victorinus's commentary on the *De inventione* was the most authoritative, especially before original commentaries displaced it in the twelfth century. Ed. Karl Halm, *Rhetores latini minores* (Leipzig, 1863; rpt. Frankfurt, 1964) , 153-304. Also important, though fragmentary, was another fourth-century commentary, by Grillius: Josef Martin, *Grillius. Ein Beitrag zur Geschichte der Rhetorik,* Studien zur Geschichte und Kultur des Altertums, 14, 2-3 (Paderborn, 1927) ; excerpts in Halm, 596-606. The first full-scale commentary on the *Ad Herennium* appeared in the second half of the eleventh century, and it was not until a century later that glosses and commentaries on the "new rhetoric" began to outnumber those on the "old." For the period 1080-1225, John Ward identifies eighteen different commentaries on the two treatises. The glossing of Cicero fell off dramatically during the last three quarters of the thirteenth century, but was resumed with even greater vigor in the fourteenth. For the commentaries, see Ward's essay in ME and Murphy, RMA, 116-22. On specific commentaries, see Mary Dickey, "Some Commentaries on the *De inventione* and *Ad Herennium* of the Eleventh and Early Twelfth Centuries," *Mediaeval and Renaissance Studies,* 6 (1968) , 1-41; Harry Caplan, "A Medieval Commentary on the *Rhetorica ad Herennium,*" in *Of Eloquence: Studies in Ancient and Mediaeval Rhetoric,* ed. Anne King and Helen North (Ithaca, N.Y., 1970) , 247-70; and three essays by Karin M. Fredborg: "The Commentary of Thierry of Chartres on Cicero's *De inventione,*" *Cashiers de l'Institut du moyen-âge grec et latin, Université de Copenhague,* 7 (1971) , 1-36; "Petrus Helias on Rhetoric," *ibid.,* 13 (1974) , 31-41; and "The Commentaries on Cicero's *De inventione* and *Rhetorica ad Herennium* by William of Champeaux," *ibid.,* 17 (1976) , 1-39.

7. Murphy, RMA, 112-16.

8. *Ibid.,* 109.

9. Trans. Hubbell, 21.

10. Murphy, RMA, 15.

11. See Franz Quadlbauer, *Die antike Theorie der Genera dicendi im lateinischen Mittelalter,* Österreichische Akademie der Wissenschaften, Philosophisch-Historische Klasse, *Sitzungsberichte,* 241, Band 2, Abhandlung (Vienna, 1962) .

12. See, e.g., *Medieval Rhetoric,* 142-44, 172-81.

13. See *ibid.*, 89-90; J. R. E. Bliese, "The Study of Rhetoric in the Twelfth Century," *Quarterly Journal of Speech*, 63 (1977), 364-83; Gallick (note 5); and Murphy, RMA, 109.

14. For this distinction, see George Kennedy, *Classical Rhetoric and Its Christian and Secular Tradition from Ancient to Modern Times* (Chapel Hill, N.C., 1980), 18-40.

15. Murphy, RMA, 90-101; Ward, ME, 55-56.

16. Murphy, RMA, 123-30; Priscilla S. Boskoff, "Quintilian in the Late Middle Ages," *Speculum*, 27 (1952), 71-78.

17. Panegyric proved more durable in the Byzantine Empire. For a very recent, very brief sketch of Greek rhetoric in the Middle Ages, see Kennedy, 161-72.

18. Medieval scholars were not unaware that changing circumstances had robbed classical rhetoric of its practical utility. Wibaldus of Stavelot, writing in the mid-twelfth century, pointed to the gap between classical rhetoric and medieval needs and attributed it to the difference between the Roman law courts and contemporary courts, both lay and ecclesiastical. Trans. Gerard Ellspermann, in *Readings in Medieval Rhetoric* [hereafter RMR], ed. Joseph M. Miller, Michael H. Prosser, Thomas W. Benson (Bloomington, Ind., 1973), 212. For medieval awareness of rhetoric's legal connections, see also Kennedy, 183ff.

19. Kennedy, 105. These textbooks are collected and edited by Karl Halm (note 6). One of them, the *Ars rhetorica* of Julius Victor, even has a chapter on letters (Halm, 447-48), thus anticipating the most significant medieval adaptation of classical rhetoric. The *rhetores minores* were used only sporadically during the Middle Ages, but interest in them revived in the Renaissance. Ward, ME, 53-54.

20. Baldwin, 90-91; Nancy S. Struever, *The Language of History in the Renaissance* (Princeton, N.J., 1970), 33-34.

21. Kennedy, 183. Cf. Ward, ME, 41-42.

22. The most notable exception is Giles of Rome (d. 1316), in his commentary on Aristotle's *Rhetoric* and in his *De differentia rhetoricae, ethicae et politicae*. See Murphy, RMA, 97-99.

23. Trans. Eleonore Stump, *Boethius's De topicis differentiis* (Ithaca, N.Y., 1978), 79-95. An excellent study of this work's significance for medieval rhetoric is Michael Leff, "Boethius' *De differentiis topicis*, Book IV," in ME, 3-24.

24. Cora Lutz, "Remigius' Ideas on the Classification of the Seven Liberal Arts," *Traditio*, 12 (1956), 70, 76.

25. Murphy, RMA, 68-71; Leff, 4.

26. See especially McKeon, 279-80, 285-86. McKeon feels that the connection between dialectic and rhetoric (the "tradition of Logic") is sufficiently important to constitute, along with the traditions of rhetoricians and of philosophers and theologians, one of the three directions rhetoric followed during the Middle Ages (*ibid.*, 263). Murphy, who is more interested in practical application than philosophical speculation, reaches the opposite conclusion. He probably has McKeon in mind when he observes that "some students of medieval rhetoric have assumed that the third part of the trivium—logic—had a greater influence on rhetoric than was actually the case. In point of fact there was a very close relation between grammar and Ciceronian rhetoric at almost every stage of medieval culture. . . . Medieval logic, on the other hand, had

very little influence on communication theory in the middle ages except for the university *disputatio* and some aspects of the 'university-style' sermon." *Medieval Rhetoric: A Select Bibliography* (Toronto, 1971), 42; cf. RMA, 363.

27. Ward, ME, 27.

28. Saint Augustine, *On Christian Doctrine*, trans. D. W. Robertson, Jr. (New York: Library of Liberal Arts, 1958), 118-19. His argument skirts a philosophical stumbling block of great magnitude—the assumption, fundamental to inventional rhetoric, that language defines truth. The *De inventione*'s undisputed authority in the field of rhetoric therefore worked against the practical implementation of Augustine's program. It is perhaps not coincidental that this implementation began at about the same time that style-centered rhetoric, represented by the *Rhetorica ad Herennium,* challenged the supremacy of *inventio.* Augustine may, in fact, have been partly responsible for the late medieval tendency to equate rhetoric with style. For the influence of rhetoric on the early Christian Fathers, see also Robert Dick Sider, *Ancient Rhetoric and the Art of Tertullian* (Oxford, 1971).

29. Ed. Halm, 22-37.

30. For an edition of book V, see Halm, 449-92; for a translation, see William Harris Stahl and Richard Johnson with E. L. Burge, *Martianus Capella and the Seven Liberal Arts,* Records of Civilization: Sources and Studies, 84, vol. 2 (New York, 1977), 155-214. The ninth-century commentaries have been published by Cora E. Lutz: Dunchad, *Glossae in Martianum* (Lancaster, Pa., 1944); John Scot Eriugena, *Annotationes in Marcianum* (Cambridge, Mass., 1939); Remigius of Auxerre, *Commentum in Martianum Capellam,* 2 vols. (Leiden, 1962, 1965).

31. Ward, ME, 54 note 73. For the section on rhetoric, see Halm (ed.), 493-504 and Leslie Webber Jones (trans.), *An Introduction to Divine and Human Readings by Cassiodorus Senator,* Records of Civilization: Sources and Studies, 40 (New York, 1946), 148-58.

32. Ed. Halm, 81-134.

33. Halm prints the rhetoric section on pp. 505-22; the first fifteen chapters are translated by Dorothy V. Cerino in RMR, 80-95.

34. Kennedy, 173-74, 187. Cf. Murphy, RMA, 110-11; Ward, ME, 44-45.

35. Murphy, RMA, 86n.; Kennedy, 185.

36. Ed. and trans. Wilbur S. Howell, *The Rhetoric of Alcuin and Charlemagne* (Princeton, N.J., 1941). Also see Luitpold Wallach, *Alcuin and Charlemagne: Studies in Carolingian History and Literature,* Cornell Studies in Classical Philology, 32 (Ithaca, N.Y., 1959), 29-96. If Alcuin and Rabanus encouraged the practical study of rhetoric, the ninth-century commentators of Martianus Capella confirmed the opposite attitude. The efforts of writers like Dunchad (Martin of Laon), John the Scot, and Remigius of Auxerre contributed to the philosophical systems of twelfth-century writers like Hugh of St. Victor, in which rhetoric became part of logic.

37. John Ward suggests that despite the prevalence of intellectual and political absolutism antithetical to the philosophy behind classical rhetoric, there were sporadic instances throughout the Middle Ages when rhetoric assumed some of its original function. These periodic "crises of communication," together with a continuing need to handle "situations that required persuasion at a non-technical level," helped ensure the preservation of classical rhetoric in a culture with which it was, strictly speaking, incompatible. ME, 64-66.

38. Baldwin, 90.

39. Ed. Heinrich Keil, *Grammatici latini*, vol. 4 (Leipzig, 1864; rpt. Hildesheim, 1961), 392-402.

40. Martianus Capella, for example, equivocates: Minerva names tropes, metaplasms, schemes, and figures as subjects proper to Grammar, but does not permit Grammar to discuss them. The implication is that grammarians treat these subjects at a more elementary level than do rhetoricians. *De nuptiis,* III.326.

41. Murphy, RMA, 32-37, 182-93; Edmond Faral, *Les arts poétiques du xiie et du xiiie siècle,* Bibliothèque de l'école des hautes études, 238 (Paris, 1924), 48-54.

42. Ed. Halm, 607-18; trans. Gussie Hecht Tannenhaus, in RMR, 97-122. See Murphy, RMA, 78-79.

43. Ed. Wilhelm Wattenbach, "Magister Onulf von Speier," *Sitzungsberichte der königlich preussischen Akademie der Wissenschaften zu Berlin,* 1894, pt. 1, 369-86 and J. P. Migne, *Patrologia Latina* [hereafter PL], 171 (Paris, 1854), 1687-92.

44. On the contents of these treatises, see Murphy, RMA, 146-52. Also see his discussion (182-91) of the complex relationship between the grammatical and rhetorical figures.

45. Except for the longer version of the *Documentum,* all six works have been printed and five have been translated in full. The standard source is Faral (note 41), which has a full introduction and texts of Matthew of Vendôme, Geoffrey of Vinsauf (*Poetria Nova* and shorter *Documentum*), and Eberhard. Matthew of Vendôme is partially translated by Ernest Gallo, "Matthew of Vendôme: Introductory Treatise on the Art of Poetry," *Proceedings of the American Philosophical Society,* 118 (1974), 51-92. Roger Parr is now preparing a complete translation. The *Poetria Nova* has been translated three times: by Margaret F. Nims, *Poetria Nova of Geoffrey of Vinsauf* (Toronto, 1967); by Jane Baltzell Kopp, in *Three Medieval Rhetorical Arts,* ed. James J. Murphy (Berkeley and Los Angeles, 1971), 32-108; and by Ernest Gallo, *The Poetria Nova and Its Sources in Early Rhetorical Doctrine* (The Hague and Paris, 1971); the *Documentum* once: *Geoffrey of Vinsauf, Documentum de modo et arte dictandi et versificandi* (Milwaukee, 1968).

For John of Garland, see Traugott Lawler (ed. and trans.), *The Parisiana Poetria of John of Garland,* Yale Studies in English, 182 (New Haven, Conn., 1974); for Gervase, Hans-Jürgen Gräbener (ed.), *Gervais von Melkley: Ars Poetica,* Forschungen zur romanischen Philologie, 17 (Münster, 1965) and Catherine Yodice Giles, "Gervais of Melkley's Treatise on the Art of Versifying and the Method of Composing in Prose: Translation and Commentary," Diss., Rutgers, 1973; and for Eberhard, Evelyn Carlson, "The *Laborintus* of Eberhard Rendered into English with Introduction and Notes," M.A. Thesis, Cornell, 1930. Murphy provides a good overview of this oft-discussed branch of medieval rhetoric: RMA, 161-82.

46. Douglas Kelly, "The Scope of the Treatment of Composition in the Twelfth- and Thirteenth-Century Arts of Poetry," *Speculum,* 41 (1966), 261-78.

47. Gervase also adds to the end of his treatise a brief discussion of letter writing (Gräbener [ed.], 216-29); but from a rhetorical standpoint the scope of his work is narrower than that of Geoffrey's or John's.

48. On the medieval distinction between rhetoric and poetic, see especially O. B. Hardison, Jr., "Medieval Literary Criticism: General Introduction," in

Classical and Medieval Literary Criticism, ed. Alex Preminger, O. B. Hardison, Jr., Kevin Kerrane (New York, 1974), 263-98. Medieval poetry is typically "rhetorical," in the sophistic sense, and this may explain the common confusion Hardison attacks. See, for example, Erich Auerbach, *Literary Language and its Public in Late Latin Antiquity and in the Middle Ages,* trans. Ralph Manheim (London, 1965), 192-200.

49. Ward, ME, 38-39, 57.

50. R. W. Southern, "Medieval Humanism," in *Medieval Humanism and Other Studies* (Oxford, 1970), 29-60.

51. Murphy repeatedly asserts that in the northern universities rhetoric was at best a bridge between grammar and dialectic. See RMA, 94-95, 105, 109-11, 175, 239.

52. For an earlier generation of scholars, medieval rhetoric was synonymous with *dictamen.* A typical example is Charles Haskins' statement that "Ancient rhetoric was concerned with oratory, mediaeval rhetoric chiefly with letter-writing." *The Renaissance of the Twelfth Century* (Cambridge, Mass., 1927; rpt. Cleveland, 1957), 138. Cf. Paul Abelson, *The Seven Liberal Arts: A Study in Mediaeval Culture* (New York, 1965), 60. The bibliography of the *ars dictaminis* is immense and rapidly growing. Murphy, RMA, 194-268 is probably the best general study but should be supplemented by Hans Martin Schaller's survey in "Die Kanzlei Kaiser Friedrichs II. Ihr Personal und ihr Sprachstil," pt. 2, *Archiv für Diplomatik, Schriftgeschichte, Siegel- und Wappenkunde,* 4 (1958), 264-89. Louis J. Paetow, *The Arts Course at Medieval Universities with Special Reference to Grammar and Rhetoric* (Champaign, Ill., 1910) and Baldwin's *Medieval Rhetoric and Poetic* contain discussions of *dictamen* which, though by now dated, include information not readily accessible elsewhere. For the earlier Italian manuals see also Charles H. Haskins, "The Early *Artes Dictandi* in Italy," in *Studies in Mediaeval Culture* (Oxford, 1929), 170-92 and Franz-Josef Schmale, "Die Bologneser Schule der *Ars dictandi,*" *Deutsches Archiv für Erforschung des Mittelalters,* 13 (1957), 16-34; for the French period, Noel Valois, *De arte scribendi epistolas apud gallicos medii aevi scriptores rhetoresve* (Paris, 1880) and Jean de Ghellinck, *L'Essor de la littérature latine au douzième siècle* (Louvain, 1946), vol. 2, 54-68; for the thirteenth-century Italians, Augusto Gaudenzi, "Sulla cronologia delle opere dei dettatori bolognesi da Buoncompagno a Bene di Lucca," *Bullettino dell'Istituto storico italiano,* 14 (1895), 85-174 and Giuseppe Vecchi, *Il magistero delle "Artes" Latine a Bologna nel medioevo,* Publicazioni della Facoltà di Magistero, Università di Bologna, 2 (Bologna, 1958); and for the later teaching in Italy, Helene Wieruszowski, *Politics and Culture in Medieval Spain and Italy,* Storia e letteratura, Raccolta di studi e testi, 121 (Rome, 1971), pt. II, essays 1-5, 7, 8, 10 and James R. Banker, "The *Ars Dictaminis* and Rhetorical Textbooks at the Bolognese University in the Fourteenth Century," *Medievalia et Humanistica,* n.s. 5 (1974), 153-68. The standard collection of texts is still Ludwig Rockinger, *Briefsteller und Formelbücher des eilften bis vierzehnten Jahrhunderts,* 2 vols., Quellen und Erörterungen zur bayerischen und deutschen Geschichte, 9 (Munich, 1863, 1864; rpt. New York, 1961). The best introduction to medieval letter writing in general is Giles Constable, *Letters and Letter-Collections,* Typologie des sources du moyen âge occidental, 17 (Turnhout, 1976).

53. Established by Rockinger and defended most recently by Murphy, the view that Alberic was the "father" of the *ars dictaminis* has been challenged

by Schmale ("Bologneser Schule") and others. About two-thirds of the *Dicta-minum radii* concerns figures, and only III.5-6 can be construed as dealing directly with letters. The work is translated by Joseph M. Miller, in RMR, 132-61. On the origins of the *ars dictaminis*, see I. S. Robinson, "The *Colores Rhetorici* in the Investiture Contest," *Traditio*, 32 (1976), 209-38; Heinz-Jürgen Beyer, "Die Frühphase der *Ars dictandi*," *Studi Medievali*, ser. 3, 18 (1977), 585-609; Vincenzo Licitra, "Il mito di Alberico di Montecassino inizia-tore dell'*Ars dictaminis*," *ibid.*, 1175-93; and especially William D. Patt, "The Early *Ars dictaminis* as Response to a Changing Society," *Viator*, 9 (1978), 133-55.

54. See Carol Dana Lanham, *Salutatio Formulas in Latin Letters to 1200: Syntax, Style, and Theory*, Münchener Beiträge zur Mediävistik und Renais-sance-Forschung, 22 (Munich, 1975) and Giles Constable, "The Structure of Medieval Society According to the *Dictatores* of the Twelfth Century," in *Law, Church, and Society: Essays in Honor of Stephan Kuttner*, ed. Kenneth Pen-nington and Robert Somerville (Philadelphia, 1977), 253-67.

55. The *cursus* has a sizeable bibliography of its own. Until recently the best historical study was Mathieu G. Nicolau, *L'Origine du "cursus" rythmique et les débuts de l'accent d'intensité en latin*, Collection d'études latines, 5 (Paris, 1930); but this has been superseded in important respects by Tore Janson, *Prose Rhythm in Medieval Latin from the 9th to the 13th Century*, Studia Latina Stockholmiensia, 20 (Stockholm, 1975). The *cursus* seems to have de-veloped independently for over a century before it became an important part of dictaminal doctrine in the late twelfth century. The traditional view is that the *cursus* was first introduced into the Papal Chancery by John of Gaeta, who may have studied under Alberic at Monte Cassino and who served as papal chancellor from 1089 until 1118, when he became Pope Gelasius II. But Janson (pp. 35-59) has proven by statistical analysis of papal documents that the *cursus* was in continuous use in the Chancery from at least the mid-eleventh century. Increasingly employed in official documents and correspondence, it began to appear in treatises on *dictamen* around 1180. The *Forma dictandi* (ca.1180) formerly attributed to Albert of Morra, later Pope Gregory VIII (1187), is apparently the first attempt to formulate the rules of *cursus;* but the flexibility in its dating makes such priority difficult to establish. Bernard of Meung and Peter of Blois (?), both writing in the 1180s, also treat the *cursus* in their works. On the early history of the *cursus*, see also Ann Dalzell, "The *Forma dictandi* Attributed to Albert of Morra and Related Texts," *Mediaeval Studies*, 39 (1977), 440-65.

56. Many treatises also cover the figures. See especially Guido Faba, *Summa dictaminis*, ed. Augusto Gaudenzi, *Il Propugnatore*, n.s. 3 (1890), pt. 2, 356-70.

57. See Martin Camargo, "The English Manuscripts of Bernard of Meung's *Flores dictaminum*," *Viator*, 12 (1981), 197-219.

58. See, e.g., Schaller, 266ff.

59. For this problem, see the essay by Patt (note 53 above).

60. Richard Spence is preparing an edition of this work, which was the chief source for the early French *dictatores*. For its influence (and the text of a late, interpolated redaction), see Mirella Brini Savorelli, "Il *dictamen* di Bernardo Silvestre," *Rivista critica di storia della filosofia*, 20 (1965), 182-230. See also Charles Homer Haskins, "An Italian Master Bernard," in *Essays in History Presented to Reginald Lane Poole*, ed. H. W. C. Davis (Oxford, 1927), 211-26.

61. The influence of the later Italian writers was even more widespread than

that of the earlier ones. See, e.g., Charles Faulhaber, *Latin Rhetorical Theory in Thirteenth- and Fourteenth-Century Castile,* University of California Publications in Modern Philology, 103 (Berkeley and Los Angeles, 1972) .

62. Murphy, RMA, 226-39.

63. The English schools, which took their teaching methods and curricula from their French counterparts, reflected this connection with grammar.

64. See Schaller's descriptions of the Orléanese and Bolognese styles in "Die Kanzlei," 275, 282.

65. Nicolau, *L'Origine,* 149-50.

66. See the studies by Janson and Dalzell. Hostility toward the *stilus gallicus* is not confined to the Italians, but is also voiced, for example, by the Frenchman John of Limoges (Schaller, 278) . The title of John's treatise—*Libellus de dictamine et dictatorio syllogismorum* (late twelfth century) —suggests that he aligns himself with the logicians of Paris rather than the grammarians of Orléans.

67. Partial ed., Rockinger, 956-66. See also Murphy, RMA, 258-63.

68. Murphy, RMA, 286-92.

69. *Ibid.,* 292-97; Kennedy, 179-80.

70. Murphy, RMA, 82-87, 300.

71. Trans. Joseph M. Miller, in RMR, 163-81.

72. Harry Caplan, "The Four Senses of Scriptural Interpretation and the Mediaeval Theory of Preaching," *Speculum,* 4 (1929) , 282-90; rpt. in *Of Eloquence,* 93-104.

73. Ed. Migne, PL, 172, cols. 807-1108.

74. Murphy, RMA, 303-09; Kennedy, 191. Joseph M. Miller translates portions of the *Summa* in RMR, 229-39. For the full text, see PL, 210, cols. 111-98.

75. The best short history of the *ars praedicandi* is Murphy, RMA, 310-55. Five important essays on the science of preaching, originally published between 1925 and 1933, are conveniently gathered in Harry Caplan, *Of Eloquence* [hereafter OE] (see note 6 above) , 40-159. An excellent, brief introduction to the structure, methods, and goals of late medieval sermons is Etienne Gilson, "Michel Menot et la technique du sermon médiéval," *Revue d'histoire franciscaine,* 2 (1925) , 301-50. Also see Edwin C. Dargan, *A History of Preaching,* vol. 1 (New York, 1905; rpt. New York, 1968) and A. Lecoy de la Marche, *La Chaire française au moyen âge, spécialement au xiiie siècle,* 2e ed. (Paris, 1886) .

76. The sheer number of such treatises—over 300—precludes individual discussion in any case. See Harry Caplan, *Mediaeval Artes Praedicandi: A Hand-List* and *Mediaeval Artes Praedicandi: A Supplementary Hand-List,* Cornell Studies in Classical Philology, 24 and 25 (Ithaca, N.Y., 1934, 1936) ; Th.-M. Charland, O.P., *Artes Praedicandi: Contribution à l'histoire de la Rhétorique au moyen âge,* Publications de l'institut d'études médiévales d'Ottawa, 7 (Ottawa and Paris, 1936) .

77. So says Murphy, RMA, 316; but cf. Caplan, OE, 124. Even if Murphy is correct, the fit is not as good as that between the parts of an oration and those of a letter.

78. Most *artes praedicandi* recognize that there are other ways to construct a sermon besides the "thematic" method they recommend. See, e.g., Caplan, OE, 76-78, 123.

79. Murphy, RMA, 337, 342-43; Caplan, OE, 121-25.

80. The vast quantity of such materials can be gauged from Johannes B. Schneyer, *Repertorium der lateinischen Sermones des Mittelalters für die Zeit von 1150-1350,* Beiträge zur Geschichte der Philosophie und Theologie des Mittelalters, 43 (Münster Westfalen, 1969-present [pt. 9 publ. 1980; index to follow]).

81. Caplan, OE, 119-20. See, e.g., *Treatise on Preaching by Humbert of Romans,* trans. Dominican Students of the Province of St. Joseph (Westminster, Md., 1951; rpt. London, 1955), excerpt in RMR, 250.

82. Murphy, RMA, 332.

83. *Ibid.,* 325-26. For the opposing view, see, e.g., Caplan, OE, 44, 124, 140.

84. Jerrold E. Seigel, *Rhetoric and Philosophy in Renaissance Humanism: The Union of Eloquence and Wisdom, Petrarch to Valla* (Princeton, N.J., 1968), 173-99. On Victorinus's attempt to Christianize the debate, see Ward, ME, 43. Martianus Capella's allegorical marriage of Philology to Mercury was taken throughout the Middle Ages to signify the necessary joining of wisdom to eloquence. See Lutz (note 24 above), 84-86.

85. Leff, ME, 15-24. The renewed enthusiasm for commenting the *De inventione* and *Rhetorica ad Herennium* that began in Italy around 1290 (Ward, ME, 38-39) could also be seen as part of this same process.

86. Seigel, 200-25, and Paul O. Kristeller, "Humanism and Scholasticism in the Italian Renaissance," in *Studies in Renaissance Thought and Letters* (Rome, 1956), 553-83 (originally publ. in *Byzantion,* 17 [1944-45], 346-74).

87. Murphy, RMA, 357-62.

SELECT BIBLIOGRAPHY ON RHETORIC

Saint Augustine. *On Christian Doctrine.* Trans. D. W. Robertson, Jr. New York: Library of Liberal Arts, 1958.

Baldwin, Charles Sears. *Medieval Rhetoric and Poetic (to 1400).* New York, 1928; rpt. Gloucester, Mass., 1959.

Charland, Th.-M., O.P. *Artes Praedicandi: Contribution à l'histoire de la Rhétorique au moyen âge.* Publications de l'institut d'études médiévales d'Ottawa, 7. Ottawa and Paris, 1936.

Cicero. *De inventione, De optimo genere oratorum, Topica.* Ed. and trans. H. M. Hubbell. Cambridge, Mass.: Loeb Classical Library, 1949.

[Pseudo-Cicero]. *Ad C. Herennium de ratione dicendi (Rhetorica ad Herennium).* Ed. and trans. Harry Caplan. Cambridge, Mass.: Loeb Classical Library, 1954.

Curtius, Ernst Robert. *European Literature and the Latin Middle Ages.* Trans. Willard R. Trask. Princeton, N.J., 1953.

Faral, Edmond. *Les arts poétiques du xiie et du xiiie siècle.* Bibliothèque de l'école des hautes études, 238. Paris, 1924.

Halm, Karl. *Rhetores latini minores.* Leipzig, 1863; rpt. Frankfurt, 1964.

McKeon, Richard. "Rhetoric in the Middle Ages." *Speculum,* 17 (1942), 1-32. Rpt., with alterations, in *Critics and Criticism, Ancient and Modern,* ed. R. S. Crane (Chicago and London, 1952), 260-96.

Manitius, Max. *Geschichte der lateinischen Literatur des Mittelalters,* 3 vols. Munich, 1911-31.

Miller, Joseph M., Michael H. Prosser, Thomas W. Benson, eds. *Readings in Medieval Rhetoric.* Bloomington, Ind., 1973.

Murphy, James J. *Medieval Rhetoric: A Select Bibliography.* Toronto, 1971.

————, ed. *Three Medieval Rhetorical Arts.* Berkeley and Los Angeles, 1971.

————. *Rhetoric in the Middle Ages.* Berkeley and Los Angeles, 1974.

————, ed. *Medieval Eloquence: Studies in the Theory and Practice of Medieval Rhetoric.* Berkeley and Los Angeles, 1978.

Paetow, Louis J. *The Arts Course at Medieval Universities with Special Reference to Grammar and Rhetoric.* Champaign, Ill., 1910.

Reinsma, Luke. "The Middle Ages." *Historical Rhetoric: An Annotated Bibliography of Selected Sources in English,* ed. Winifred Bryan Horner (Boston, 1980), 43-108.

Rockinger, Ludwig. *Briefsteller und Formelbücher des eilften bis vierzehnten Jahrhunderts,* 2 vols. Quellen und Erörterungen zur bayerischen und deutschen Geschichte, 9. Munich, 1863, 1864; rpt. New York, 1961.

Stump, Eleonore. *Boethius's De topicis differentiis.* Ithaca, N.Y., 1978.

5 Dialectic

Eleonore Stump

While Aristotle acknowledged his forerunners in rhetoric, he claimed that "in the subject of reasoning we had nothing else of an earlier date to speak of at all." Aristotle perhaps intended this claim to apply only to dialectical and contentious argument. Yet since he was here contrasting reasoning to the established arts of rhetoric and medicine, it would seem legitimate to interpret this statement in a boader sense. And although Aristotle failed to acknowledge his debt to previous philosophers, he could nevertheless rightfully claim to have established logic as a systematic study—i.e., as a techne.

Aristotle made this claim in On Sophistical Refutations *(184b) — a treatise he began, as he had the* Topics, *by analysing the relations between the different modes of reasoning. He considered not only reasoning as a whole to be a techne, but each of its component parts as well. Thus the* Topics, *explicitly characterized as a techne, proposed to give a complete and systematic analysis of dialectical argument; the* Prior Analytics *of syllogistic reasoning; the* Posterior Analytics *of demonstrative reasoning in general; and* On Sophistical Refutations *of sophistical argument.*

These topics were adopted by Martianus Capella and Cassiodorus, whose approaches to logic, however, differed from that of Aristotle in several respects. For one thing, they both included discussions of the hypothetical syllogism—derived, although the exact affiliation is unclear, from the propositional logic of the Stoics. On the other hand, they omitted any consideration of modal logic. Discussed only briefly by Aristotle, modal logic had been developed by his successors and would again become an important branch of logic during the Middle Ages.

Cassiodorus, unlike Aristotle, treated definition as a distinct topic. His source would seem to be the treatise On Defintions, *written in the fourth century by Marius Victorinus. This attention to definition, together with St. Augustine's concern with the relation of word to thing, can perhaps be viewed as one root of the semantic orientation that characterized medieval logic.*

Most importantly, Martianus Capella and Cassiodorus differed from Aristotle in their overall approach to logic. Their orientation, in which the term clearly serves as the principle of the art, derived from the organization that Hellenistic scholars had imposed on Aristotle's logical treatises. These Hellenistic philosophers had placed the Categories *(dealing with the individual term) and* On Interpretation *(dealing with the proposition, which connects two terms) before the works devoted to the art of reasoning to form the* Organon. *Martianus and Cassiodorus adopted this organization, broadening their treatment of the first topic (i.e., the analysis of the individual term) to include an analysis of the five predicables based on the* Isagoge *of Porphyry. D. L. W.*

I. INTRODUCTION

The subject on which I was asked to write in this paper is dialectic in the eleventh to thirteenth centuries; but to do so, it is necessary to clarify the meaning of the word 'dialectic.' In the works of Boethius, whose influence on the concept and tradition of the liberal arts was enormous, dialectic was understood in a fairly technical and restricted way. Boethius's concept of dialectic, which builds on a long tradition stemming from Aristotle and Plato,[1] can be comprehended best by thinking of Socrates' method of arguing in many of the Platonic dialogues. Socrates in the dialogues discovers arguments (often apparently in the process of arguing) that he uses in oral disputation with some opponent in order to compel his opponent to agreement. His arguments proceed by question and answer, and their aim is to bring Socrates' opponent to believe as he does. So the arguments Socrates uses have to be readily believable if they are to achieve their purpose. This requirement distinguishes dialectical arguments from the sort of arguments used in geometry, for instance. Geometrical arguments are an example of what Boethius calls 'demonstrative arguments.' A demonstrative argument, such as a geometrical proof, begins (ultimately) with certain axioms, which are self-evidently true, and works by strict deductive steps from these self-evident truths to conclusions containing new information about the subject matter. Following Aristotle, Boethius thinks that the only arguments that produce *knowledge,* whose conclusions we are entitled to say we *know,* are demonstrative arguments, whose conclusions can be accepted with certainty because they cannot be wrong. But dialectical arguments too can arrive at the truth, and they are much more useful for persuading an opponent than demonstrative arguments, which are frequently too difficult and unwieldy for such a purpose. So, for Boethius, dialectic has to do with the discovery of arguments that are readily believable and that can be used to compel agreement from an opponent in disputation. Not all arguments that we readily believe are good arguments, however; we sometimes readily accept the conclusions of bad arguments. Hence, not all dialectical arguments are good, logically sound arguments. This is one of the most important respects in which dialectic differs from demonstration. Demonstrative arguments are always logically sound arguments; their conclusions produce knowledge and are certain. But Boethius does not, because of this difference, conceive of dialectic as an inferior attempt at what demonstration does well; he thinks of the two as different methods with different aims, and he sees them both as important techniques for argumentation. In his view, then, dialectic is one branch of logic; demonstration is another (and there are others as well, such as the study of sophistical arguments).

When we turn to the early Scholastic period, we find a different understanding of dialectic. One of the earliest complete Scholastic logic books still extant, that written by Garlandus Compotista in the first half of the eleventh century, is titled simply 'Dialectica.'² Abelard's major logic book, in the next century, is also titled just 'Dialectica.'³ These two logic books deal with the subject Boethius calls dialectic, but it is only one part of the material they cover; both "dialectic" books range over all the subjects that were then understood to constitute logic. In the beginning of the Scholastic period, then, 'dialectic' is equivalent simply to 'logic.'⁴ This broad sense of the word persists in the late Scholastic period; but slowly the old Boethian sense of the term also begins to reappear. By the thirteenth century, the narrow, technical sense of 'dialectic' is again in use. For example, in Peter of Spain's Tractatus,⁵ one of the standard logic texts from the thirteenth to the fifteenth centuries, dialectic is again thought of as just one specialized branch of logic that deals with readily believable arguments that are (in theory at least) useful for disputation.⁶

So what is discussed in this paper under the heading of dialectic depends on which sense of 'dialectic' is being employed, and for several reasons I intend to take the word in its narrower and more specialized sense. First of all, dialectic so understood is a much more manageable topic for a paper than would be the whole of logic even if one concentrated only on the eleventh, twelfth, and thirteenth centuries. Secondly, as will emerge in the course of this paper, dialectic is a particularly long-lived and fruitful branch of medieval logic. And thirdly, the long tradition of this particular part of logic, beginning with Plato and Aristotle and going in an unbroken stream right through the end of the Middle Ages will elucidate the special character of Scholastic logic by contrasting discussions of dialectic in this period with discussions of it in the rest of the tradition.

I am going to concentrate, then, on just one part of logic in the eleventh to the thirteenth centuries, the part that deals with what Boethius thought of as dialectic and that stems directly or indirectly from Boethius's own work on dialectic. But before I turn to dialectic itself, in order to facilitate its discussion I want to say something briefly about logic as a whole in the eleventh to thirteenth centuries.[7]

II. THE PLACE OF DIALECTIC IN THE LOGIC OF THE ELEVENTH TO THIRTEENTH CENTURIES

As far as we now know, the eleventh century was fairly barren in the field of logic. St. Anselm did some creative work in the philosophy of language, which was commonly considered part of logic by the medievals; but in general this period seems to have been devoted to a reworking of material in two of Aristotle's books, *Categories* and *De interpretatione,* and in Boethius's logical treatises, including those on dialectic.[8] These Aristotelian and Boethian treatises or their subject matter constitute what the scholastics called the *logica vetus,* the old logic. The subjects covered in the *logica vetus* comprise not only logic as we now think of it but also metaphysics and philosophy of language. For instance, though the last two chapters of Garlandus Compotista's logic book discuss categorical and hypothetical syllogisms, the first three chapters discuss such things as genus and species, substance and quality, and names and verbs.

The twelfth century saw a renewal of intellectual life in all areas, including logic. The remaining four Aristotelian treatises on logic—the *Prior* and *Posterior Analytics, Topics,* and *Sophistici elenchi*—became available, and they constituted the basis for the *logica nova,* the new logic. Roughly speaking, the *logica nova* is characterized by its interest in fallacies and sophistical reasoning, the sort of material found in the *Sophistici elenchi.* The best-known twelfth-century philosopher is undoubtedly Abelard; but his work was done in the first half of the twelfth century and was still concerned with *logica vetus,* though his work on philosophy of language and the ontological status of universals had a great influence on the course of medieval philosophy.

At least partly under the stimulus provided by the newly discovered Aristotelian treatises, there was also in the twelfth century the beginning of a new branch of medieval logic, the *logica moderna.* The *logica moderna,* also called terminist logic, is one of the two most original and creative contributions that the Scholastics made to logic (the other is their work on consequences or conditional inferences). The beginnings of the *logica moderna* can be seen in anonymous logic treatises from the second half of the twelfth century; the recently uncovered *Ars Meliduna, Tractatus Anagnini,* and *Dialectica Monacensis* are among the most important of these.[9] The movement dominated the first half of the thirteenth century, and it had its flowering in the logic books of thirteenth-century terminist logicians, such as Peter of Spain, William of Sherwood, and Lambert of Auxerre.

The *logica moderna* has two main areas of interest. One is the properties of terms, and the other is a peculiar group of words known as syncategorematic. Terms are words that are the subjects or predicates of sentences, and terminist logicians typically discussed four properties of terms: signification, copulation, appellation, and supposition. A term's signification is the meaning or definition of the term considered apart from the context of a sentence. The signification of 'man,' for example, is 'mortal rational animal.' The terminist concept of the property copulation is obscure and did not receive much discussion, but, in general, copulation is the property adjectives have in virtue of being predicated of some subject. In the sentence 'A man is white,' the adjective 'white' has the property of copulation in virtue of being joined to the subject 'man.' Appellation is the reference of a term to all presently existing things signified by that term; that is, the appellation of the term 'man' in the sentence 'Every man is white' is all presently existing men. Supposition is the property of terms that was of most interest, by far, to terminist logicians. The supposition of a term is the reference of that term in a particular context or on a particular occasion of use. For instance, in the sentence 'That man is white,' the term 'man' supposits for (refers to) some particular man, namely, the one who is being picked out as white. In the sentence 'Every man is an animal,' however, 'man' supposits for each individual of the species *man.* And in the sentence "In the preceding example, 'man' is the subject term," 'man' supposits for a linguistic entity, namely, the word 'man.' Terminists distinguished many subtle varieties of supposition, and they were intrigued by what happens to a logical inference when the supposition of a term changes. For example, the word 'man' in the sentence 'Every man is running' was said to have distributive supposition; that is, it refers to each and every individual man. Consequently, from that proposition it is possible to infer 'Socrates is running,' descending from the universal 'every man' to the individual 'Socrates.' Adding the word 'only' to the subject term, however, changes its supposition and makes a difference to the inferences that can be drawn. From the sentence 'Only every man is running' (that is, every man is running, and men are the only ones running), it is not legitimate to infer 'Only Socrates is running.'

The addition of the word 'only' changes the supposition of 'man' and prohibits the descent from 'every man' to 'Socrates.'

Syncategorematic words, the other main subject of interest for terminist logicians, can be characterized roughly as words that have a signification only in case they are combined with some term, that is, with a subject or a predicate. 'Every' and 'only' are both syncategorematic words; so are 'alone,' 'both,' 'no,' 'if,' and 'unless.' Terminists were interested in the signification and function of these words in sentences and in their influence on logical inferences. We have already seen one of the differences that the syncategorematic word 'only' can make to a logical inference in the case of the inference from 'Every man is running' to 'Socrates is running.'[10]

In the second half of the thirteenth century, medieval logic developed in a new direction. Scholastic logicians in the period began to concentrate heavily on Aristotle's *Analytics,* especially the *Posterior Analytics,* and epistemological questions became more important than they had been. Aristotle maintained that in order to have a body of knowledge about a topic (what the Scholastics called a science), one must have arguments whose premises are necessary and unchangeable and whose inferences are valid—in short, demonstrative arguments. Scholastics in the latter half of the thirteenth century became increasingly concerned with two questions: (1) What are the *ultimate* criteria (rather than the simple formal criteria) for the validity of inferences?; and (2) What sorts of things in the world can be the subjects of necessary and unchangeable premises? These questions spawned commentaries on Aristotle's logical works, including many historically significant commentaries on the *Prior Analytics,* such as that previously (and mistakenly) attributed to Duns Scotus. The result of such work was, first, a closer connection between metaphysics and logic, as can be seen for example in the work of Boethius of Dacia (who is best known for his contributions to speculative grammar), and, secondly, a movement away from Aristotelianism in logic. The distinction between demonstration and dialectic became blurred, and the syllogism began to lose its special status as the foundation of all logic.[11] Both these developments can be seen clearly by the early fourteenth century in works by Ockham and Burley.[12] These interests and concerns are not closely tied to the work of the *logica moderna,* and a blending of the new concerns with the *logica moderna* occurs only later, in the fourteenth and fifteenth centuries.[13]

Dialectic, as I will be discussing it in this paper, is a standard and important part of the *logica vetus;* and in the eleventh to thirteenth centuries, two treatises by Boethius—*De topicis differentiis*[14] and *In Ciceronis topica*[15]—were the main sources for Scholastic work on dialectic. As a part of the *logica vetus,* dialectic was generally treated in a chapter of its own in logic texts in this period. It was not a primary area of interest for logicians concerned with *logica moderna,* though even for these terminist logicians the study of dialectic continued to be a standard part of logic and the terminists' discussions are an important link in the medieval tradition of dialectic. But with the rediscovery of the last four treatises of Aristotle's *Organon* in the twelfth century, Aristotle's own book on dialectic, the *Topics,* was brought to light; and it eventually gave dialectic a new lease on life in medieval logic. Furthermore, the strong interest in the *Posterior Analytics* in the latter half of the thirteenth century stimulated discussion about the character of a science and the nature of demonstrative arguments and consequently provoked inquiry also into the nature of dialectical arguments and the criteria for distinguishing dialectic from demonstrative arguments. Interest in dialectic was widespread in this period,[16] and under its impetus the study of dialectic developed and changed until dialectic became absorbed into the theories of consequences or conditional inferences important in the fourteenth and fifteenth centuries.[17]

III. BOETHIUS'S UNDERSTANDING OF DIALECTIC

I have already said something about the origin of dialectic in the sort of arguing Socrates does in some of the Platonic dialogues. The Socratic style of arguing consists in asking an interlocutor questions in such a methodical and skillful way that he is eventually compelled to admit that the position he adopted at the beginning of the argument is untenable. This style of arguing was apparently very popular among Socrates' followers; and since it was plainly more pleasant to win, philosophers and rhetoricians of the age bent their ingenuity to devising means for making men skillful at Socratic disputation.[18] The ability to discover convincing arguments quickly was especially valued as the chief characteristic necessary for excellence in Socratic arguing, and the art of dialectic gradually became the art of discovering arguments. Aristotle's treatise *Topics* contains some discussion of the nature of dialectical disputation and some *ad hoc* rules for getting the better of one's opponent; but, by and large, it is devoted to a *method* for discovering arguments. Aristotle claims that he is the first one to have systematized the means for the discovery of arguments;[19] and he maintains that he is presenting an *art* of discovery. The notion of an art of discovery caught the imagination of the ancients. It flourished especially among Latin rhetoricians, who were concerned with the discovery of arguments for use in the presentation of cases in courts of law. Cicero, for example, wrote a treatise on the art of discovering arguments, and he was only one of a number of Latin rhetoricians to discuss the subject.[20] Boethius wrote a commentary on Cicero's treatise, and he also wrote his own treatise on dialectic; these are the treatises *In Ciceronis topica* and *De topicis differentiis* I mentioned earlier as part of the *logica vetus.* Both works of Boethius were extremely influential for Scholastic discussions of dialectic; and in order to understand the Scholastic treatments of the subject, it is essential to have a good grasp of Boethius's views first.

Boethius's *De topicis differentiis,* his definitive work on dialectic, is concerned almost exclusively with the discovery of arguments. As there is a method for judging or evaluating arguments (which is the practical side of what we now call logic), so, Boethius believes, there is also a method for finding arguments; and that method is for Boethius the heart of dialectic. The main instrument of the method is something called a Topic (in Latin, *locus*). 'Topic' is the standard English translation for the Greek *'topos'* (the Aristotelian counterpart of *'locus'*), which means, literally, a place or area; and a dialectical Topic was thought of, metaphorically, as a "place" from which a variety of arguments can be drawn. Topics are the main concern of Aristotle's treatise *Topics* and of the work on dialectic carried on by Greek commentators[21] and by Latin rhetoricians in the period between Aristotle and Boethius. In *De topicis differentiis,* Boethius is working with a complicated and ingenious variation on Aristotelian Topics. It is unlikely that Boethius's method is original; but, as far as I know, there is nothing like it in any of the materials extant from late antiquity, though that period of philosophy is still far from adequately researched.

Boethius recognizes two different sorts of things as Topics. First of all, he says, a Topic is a maximal proposition or principle. A maximal proposition he describes as a self-evidently true generalization. As examples he gives principles such as these: "Things whose definitions are different are themselves also different"; "Where the material is lacking, what is made from that material is also lacking"; and "The properties of opposites must themselves be opposites."[22] One of the functions of a maximal proposition is to support dialectical arguments; in the examples Boethius gives of arguments employing maximal propositions, the maximal propositions serve to guarantee the validity of a crucial inference in the argument. This function of a maximal proposition has to do with proving, rather than discovering, arguments. A maximal proposition helps in discovering arguments, because (loosely speaking) it is the principle that gives the argument its force; it is the generalization on which the rest of the argument depends. Once one has the appropriate maximal proposition for a particular issue, it is not hard to construct the argument or the general outline of the argument on that issue. For example, suppose the question at issue is whether an envious man is wise (one of Boethius's examples). Given the maximal proposition 'Things whose definitions are different are themselves also different,' an arguer has the heart of his argument; the rest of the argument will consist in giving the definitions of wise man and envious man and showing that the two are different.[23] The crucial step in this process of finding arguments is the discovery of the maximal proposition appropriate for a given issue. Boethius, who thinks he is following Aristotle, conceives of this step as a matter of culling a suitable maximal proposition from a very long list of maximal propositions that the arguer has memorized. Plainly, if this is all the method of discovery comes to, it is much too unwieldy to be useful. But the real instrument of Boethius's method of discovery is a second sort of Topic, which he calls a Differentia. The Differentiae can be thought of, roughly, as the headings under which maximal propositions can be grouped. Some maximal propositions are generalizations about definition, so *definition* (or *from definition*) is a Differentia; other maximal propositions are about opposites, so *opposites* (or *from opposites*) is a Differentia; and so on. Boethius gives a list of twenty-eight such Differentiae in the second book of *De topicis differentiis*, and he claims that the list is exhaustive, containing all the kinds of Differentiae possible for maximal propositions.

Differentiae are Boethius's main instruments for finding arguments; what they provide is actually a third term for arguments. Boethius says that all argument is basically syllogism (by which he means something looser and broader than a demonstrative Aristotelian syllogism).[24] There are two terms in a typical dialectical question and the same two terms occur in the conclusion of its corresponding syllogistic argument. An argument arises when the two terms of a question are joined to each other in virtue of their relations to a third term, which is thus an intermediate between the two terms of the conclusion. Boethius gives as an example the question whether man is a substance. The two terms in the question are 'man' and 'substance'; in order to have an argument proving one or the other side of this issue, we need to find a third term joining 'man' and 'substance.' 'Animal' is an example of such a third term for this case. It can be connected to the term 'man' by the premiss 'A man is an animal,' and it can be connected to the term 'substance' by the premiss 'An animal is a substance.' And so the third term 'animal' serves to connect 'man' and 'substance' in such a way that we can conclude 'A man is a substance.'[25]

In his treatise *In Ciceronis topica*, Boethius gives a detailed example to show how the Differentiae provide third terms for arguments.

> There is a question whether civil law is a useful body of knowledge. Here 'civil law' is the subject, 'useful body of knowledge' is the predicate. What is asked is whether the predicate can inhere in the subject. Therefore, I will not be able to call civil law itself to the argument, for it is a constituent of the question. So I consider what might be incorporated in it. I see that no definition is disjoined from what it defines, so that the appropriate definition cannot be disjoined from civil law. So I define civil law, and I say, "Civil law is equity established among those who are of the same state for the sake of preserving what is theirs". After this, I consider whether this definition can be joined to the remaining term 'useful body of knowledge', that is, whether equity established among those who are of the same state for the sake of preserving what is theirs *is* a useful body of knowledge. I see that the equity mentioned above is a useful body of knowledge. And so I conclude, "Therefore, civil law is a useful body of knowledge".[26]

In this example, the two terms of the question, 'civil law' and 'useful body of knowledge,' are joined by the third term, 'equity established among those who are of the same state for the sake of preserving what is theirs'; and this third term is the definition of 'civil law,' one of the two terms in the question. The Differentia *definition* is not itself the third term for the argument, but it is the genus or class of the phrase that is the third term.

A Differentia, then, aids in finding arguments because it provides third terms for arguments. It does not specify the particular third term to be used in an argument, but rather gives the genus of third terms appropriate for the argument. Boethius claims that his list of Differentiae is exhaustive, that it contains *the* twenty-eight genera of all possible third terms for arguments; and he means it to be memorized. When an arguer wants to find an argument on some issue, according to Boethius's method he mentally runs through his list of twenty-eight Differentiae and chooses one that looks appropriate for the question at hand. (The criteria for appropriateness Boethius leaves to the arguer's intuitions.) Using the appropriate Differentia, the arguer finds the particular third term needed for his argument and with that third term readily constructs his argument.

To see more clearly how his method works, we can look at one of Boethius's simplest examples in a little more detail. Suppose that what is at issue is whether or not a tree is an animal,[27] and we want to produce an argument that it is not. We run through the list of Differentiae and decide that the Differentia *definition* looks appropriate. We have two terms in the question, 'tree' and 'animal'; and since we have chosen the Differentia *definition,* we want as a third term the definition of one of the terms in the question. If we try the definition of 'animal,' namely, 'animate substance capable of perceiving' (the definition generally given in the Middle Ages) , we have the first premiss of our argument: (1) An animal is an animate substance capable of perceiving. We believe that trees are not capable of perceiving, and so we see that the definition of 'animal' does not fit 'tree.' That observation gives us our second premiss: (2) A tree is not an animate substance capable of perceiving. From these two premisses it is easy to derive the conclusion that a tree is not an animal. Since, as we have constructed it, this is a dialectical argument with indefinite premisses, we need a maximal proposition to validate the conclusion. Boethius gives a slightly complicated one for this argument: "That to which the definition of a genus does not belong is not a species of the genus defined."[28] In this example, the Differentia has helped find the argument, and the maximal proposition has helped to validate it.

Dialectic for Boethius is, then, the art of discovering dialectical arguments, arguments that are readily believable. The heart of a dialectical argument is a third term, which can be linked to each of the two terms in the question in such a way that those two terms can be linked to each other in the conclusion of the argument. Topics that are Differentiae are the genera of third terms, and hence they provide the kind of third term needed in the argument. Topics that are maximal propositions play no real role in Boethius's method of discovery, but they are required to validate the argument discovered.[29]

IV. DIALECTIC IN THE WORK OF GARLANDUS COMPOTISTA

Dialectic in the eleventh to thirteenth centuries, though it derives largely from Boethius's work on the Topics and is couched mainly in his terms, is very different from the method and theory of dialectic in Boethius. I want to illustrate and analyze those differences, in order to provide some understanding of theories of dialectic in this period, by concentrating on the views of just one man: Garlandus Compotista. His *Dialectica*, which may have been written before 1040,[30] is the earliest complete medieval logic text still extant, as far as we now know; and that fact gives it several advantages for my purposes. It is chronologically—and also, I think, philosophically—closer to Boethius than is any other scholastic work on dialectic, so that it is easier in this case than in the later works to see and understand the Scholastics' divergence from Boethius's views and their own contributions to dialectic. On the other hand, it stands at the beginning of the Scholastic tradition, and many of the controversies and doctrines of later Scholastic work on dialectic are prefigured in or derived from the philosophical tradition represented by Garlandus. With a good grasp of Garlandus's work, it is possible to give a comprehensible sketch of dialectic in the following century and a half.

In many respects, Garlandus's chapter on dialectic is plainly derivative from Boethius's *De topicis differentiis;* and in some places it appears to be no more than a paraphrase of that Boethian treatise. The language of Garlandus's chapter, the crucial definitions, the order of the material discussed, and many of the examples are very similar to the corresponding elements of Boethius's treatise. Following Boethius, Garlandus divides Topics into maximal propositions and Differentiae; and his definitions of these two sorts of Topic are just quotations from Boethius. The major part of Garlandus's discussion of Topics is devoted to listing the Differentiae with corresponding maximal propositions and examples of their use. The list of Topics, the groupings of the Topics in that list, and even a number of the examples are taken from Boethius's treatise.[31] All of this should give the impression that Garlandus's treatment of the Topics closely resembles Boethius's, and in many respects it does. The dissimilarities, however, are many and important.[32]

On Garlandus's theory of Topics, the Differentiae provide conditional propositions that are the basis for simple hypothetical syllogisms with categorical conclusions. The maximal propositions demonstrate the truth of the conditional premiss of the hypothetical syllogism, because the conditional proposition of the hypothetical syllogism is shown to be an instance covered by the maximal proposition. To see how the theory works, we can apply it in detail to one of Garlandus's examples in connection with the Topic *from the universal whole* (or genus). Suppose there is a question whether man is white. We can make an argument using the Topic *from the universal whole* if we take the genus of one of the terms in the question; and suppose we take the genus of *man*. Then, according to Garlandus, there are five modes or ways in which we can make an argument; suppose we take the first mode, which is "universally attributing something to the genus." The "something" to be attributed in this case ought plainly to be the predicate *white,* since we want 'white' as another term in the argument. So we will make a conditional proposition in this way:

(1) If every animal is white, man is also white.
To derive an affirmative answer to the question at issue, we assert the antecedent:
(2) Every animal is white.

And by *modus ponendo ponens* we derive the conclusion:

∴ (3) Man is white.

By consulting the mode again we find the appropriate maximal proposition (MP) for this argument:

> (MP) What is universally attributed to the genus is also attributed to the species.

And this maximal proposition proves the conditional premiss by a categorical argument:

	(i)	Animal is the genus of man.
MP	(ii)	What is universally attributed to the genus is also attributed to the species.
∴	(iii)	If whiteness is universally attributed to animal, it is also attributed to man—or, If every animal is white, man is also white.[33]

The most important parts of this theory are the use of the Differentia and the maximal proposition in connection with the conditional proposition, I think.[34] The rest of the apparatus in Garlandus's account seems to be just part of what Garlandus inherited from Boethius and preserved because it was part of his intellectual legacy from antiquity. What Garlandus himself is really interested in is the Topics' usefulness for the analysis of conditional propositions. The Differentia finds or provides a conditional premiss, and that conditional premiss is proved by the maximal proposition in a categorical argument that has the conditional as conclusion. Garlandus's overriding interest seems to be in hypothetical syllogisms. The chapter on hypothetical syllogisms in his book is more than five times as long as his chapter on categorical syllogisms and more than twice as long as the next longest chapter in the book; it alone accounts for fully one third of his whole logic text. The study of Topics is propaedeutic to the study of hypothetical syllogisms, according to Garlandus (86.18-20); and in his view, all the Topics are useful for hypothetical syllogisms. It seems to me that they are useful for hypothetical syllogisms and propaedeutic to their study on Garlandus's account because he sees them primarily as means for providing true conditionals (the function of the Differentiae) and for demonstrating the truth of a given conditional (the function of the maximal propositions). Garlandus's chapter on hypothetical syllogisms concerns itself almost exclusively with the forms of acceptable hypothetical syllogisms, that is, with the acceptable combinations of conditional and categorical propositions in a hypothetical argument. The maximal propositions enable the arguer to judge the truth or falsity of the conditional premisses in these hypothetical arguments, and the Differentiae are the means for finding true conditional premisses.

This interpretation of Garlandus's theory explains the otherwise bewildering inanity of some of Garlandus's examples. Surely there never was a philosopher seriously interested in the question whether man is white; and the argument Garlandus gives in answer to that question—"If every animal is white, man is white"—will yield the false conclusion (and Garlandus must have known it was false[35]) that man as a species is white.[36] The oddness of Garlandus's examples is mystifying until we see that he is not interested in this or that particular question or conclusion but in the forms of acceptable inferences. He is not interested in settling issues about man's whiteness; his concern is with all inferences[37] of the type "If every animal is _____, then man is _____," where the same expression is to fill both blanks. Given Garlandus's concern, it is not unlikely that he deliberately chooses apparently inane examples. The peculiarity of the predicate 'white' in the example here, for instance, serves something of the same purpose that would be served by filling the blanks with a variable: it focuses attention on the form of the inference and not on its particular content.

We can summarize Garlandus's theory of the Topics by saying that he is interested in them primarily as guarantors of the validity of inferences, and especially as warrants for the inference from the antecedent to the consequent in a conditional proposition, because he has a very strong interest in hypothetical syllogisms. The Topics retain something of their old heuristic function (insofar as the Differentiae help in the discovery of conditional premisses), but by and large their most important role for Garlandus falls within the realm of confirmation and evaluation, insofar as they demonstrate the truth of conditionals and the validity of inferences. And it should be perfectly plain that there is a vast difference between Garlandus's conception and use of the Topics and Boethius's. For Boethius, the main function of the Topics is discovery, and what they aid in discovering are third terms around which categorical arguments can be built. For Garlandus, the important function of the Topics is confirmation; and though they confirm all inferences on his view, he is especially interested in them insofar as they confirm enthymematic inferences in conditional propositions and so help determine the truth or falsity of premisses in hypothetical syllogisms.

V. DIALECTIC IN SCHOLASTIC PHILOSOPHY
AFTER GARLANDUS

It seems clear that the differences between Garlandus and Boethius are not all the result of Garlandus's own original work on the Topics. He frequently refers to the opinions of others, adjudicating in cases of apparently well-recognized controversies;[38] and he gives the impression that he is writing for an audience of students.[39] We know that the Topics were discussed in the Carolingian Renaissance,[40] but we do not know much about Garlandus's immediate predecessors. The references in Garlandus's chapter on Topics to other discussions of the subject and the considerable difference between Garlandus's theory of the Topics and Boethius's leave the impression that the Topics had received some serious attention from medieval thinkers immediately preceding Garlandus, though as yet we know too little about philosophy in this early period to say anything very definite about Garlandus's sources for his work on the Topics.

After Garlandus, in the period from the eleventh to the thirteenth centuries, there was a great deal of work on the Topics; and for my purposes here, I want simply to give a brief sketch of some of that material. Abelard devoted well over 200 pages to the subject in his *Dialectica*,[41] and he also wrote a commentary on Boethius's treatise *De topicis differentiis*,[42] but Abelard's treatment of the subject is voluminous enough and original enough that full treatment of it is better left to one side here. A number of other twelfth-century commentaries have very recently been uncovered.[43] As a result, we now know of fifteen commentaries on Boethius's *De topicis differentiis* from this century. In their major concerns, these (including Abelard's work) show many points of contact with Garlandus's theory of the Topics. Such similarities are not nearly enough to conclude that Garlandus was a direct or indirect source for any of the commentaries—he may or may not have been—but they do show at least that the tradition represented by Garlandus was influential for the authors of these commentaries.

There is also considerable attention to Topics among the anonymous twelfth-century logic treatises edited by De Rijk in *Logica Modernorum*. For example, the *Tractatus Anagnini, Introductiones Parisienses, Logica "Ut dicit," Logica "Cum sit nostra,"* and *Dialectica Monacensis* have chapters on the Topics; and the *Introductiones Montane minores* and *Abbreviatio Montana* discuss Topics in their chapters on hypothetical syllogisms. The theory of Topics in these treatises is yet to be thoroughly investigated, and it is not impossible that there are also important points of contact between the sort of account of Topics found in Garlandus and the accounts found in these treatises. There are certainly resemblances that can be discerned even on a superficial reading of the treatises. To take just one example, the discussion of the two definitions of a Topic—'the foundation of an argument' ('*sedes argumenti*') and 'that from which an appropriate argument for the question at issue is drawn' ('*id a quo conveniens trahitur argumentum*')—in *Dialectica Monacensis*[44] is very similar to the discussion of those definitions in Garlandus.[45] The two accounts differ in that Garlandus attributes the first definition (*'sedes argumenti'*) to both Differentia and maximal proposition, while *Dialectica Monacensis* attributes it only to maximal proposition; but Garlandus attributes it to Differentiae only in virtue of the connection Differentiae have to maximal propositions, which he says are the only Topics properly thought of as *sedes argumenti* in their own right.

In the thirteenth century, detailed work on the Topics can be found in the logic books of each of the three best-known terminist logicians, William of Sherwood, Peter of Spain, and Lambert of Auxerre. Peter's discussion appears more basic and less complicated than those of the other two, but otherwise it seems to be a representative terminist treatment of Topics. In his account, though there is still some talk of the role of Differentiae in discovery, it is rather perfunctory. The main function of both Differentiae and maximal propositions is to confirm arguments; and they work together to validate the inference in an enthymeme, rather than in a conditional proposition, as in Garlandus's account.

According to Peter, a Topical argument is theoretically an enthymeme, an incomplete syllogism missing a premiss,[46] and all enthymemes can be reduced to syllogisms by supplying the missing premiss.[47] But the validity of an enthymeme that is a Topical argument is also shown and confirmed by a Differentia and a maxim (*'maxima'* is Peter's abbreviated version of *'propositio maxima'*). In Peter's view, a Differentia is a relationship of a certain sort[48] (for example, the relationship of a definition to its *definitum*) and a maxim is a rule governing inferences dependent on that relationship (for example, 'What is predicated of a definition is predicated also of its *definitum'*).[49] Any Differentia may (and usually does) have more than one maxim corresponding to it; the Differentia *from definition,* for example, has three maxims besides the one just given. Together, a Differentia and a maxim confirm an enthymeme in this way. Take the enthymeme 'A mortal rational animal is running; therefore a man is running.' The relationship of the subject in the premiss to the subject in the conclusion is that of the Differentia *from definition;* that is, *mortal rational animal* is the definition of man, the *definitum.* The maxim quoted above gives us an inference rule for such a relationship; and the maxim, the statement of the relationship between *mortal rational animal* and *man,* and the enthymeme's premiss together entail the enthymeme's conclusion. Peter gives twenty-five Differentiae and fifty-seven maxims, which are meant to cover all the kinds of Topical enthymemes.[50]

With Peter of Spain's treatment, the Topics have virtually completed their slow metamorphosis from instruments for the discovery of arguments to instruments for the confirmation and evaluation of arguments.

In the latter half of the thirteenth century, interest in the Topics only intensified as Scholastics discussed the nature of knowledge and debated the character of arguments dependent on the Topics. And in the four-teenth century, the Topics formed one of the bases for and became absorbed into the flourishing study of consequences, or conditional in-ferences, one of the two most creative fields in medieval logic. Boethius passed on to posterity the culmination of antiquity's work on a sys-tematic method for the finding of arguments. Near the beginning of the Scholastic period, in Garlandus's treatise, we already find the Top-ics considerably shifted away from discovering and toward confirming arguments. In the early Scholastic period, Topics are an established part of the *logica vetus,* traditionally thought to be not much more than paraphrases of and embroidery on material taken over from Aristotle and Boethius. By the end of the Scholastic period, Topics are com-pletely transformed into instruments for confirming and evaluating arguments, and they are incorporated into some of the most original medieval work on logic. The Topics, then, are a rich stream of medi-eval logic. They have their origin in material that the medievals simply took over as part of their heritage from antiquity; and in the study of consequences, they branch into some of the most creative Scholastic work on logic. That the Topics should have undergone the changes they did is in part a sign of the difficulty and obscurity of the treatise that was the ultimate source for Scholastic discussion of the Topics, Boethius's *De topicis differentiis;* but it is also testimony to the inten-sity of Scholastic interest in the confirmatory and evaluative part of logic, an interest so strong and pursued with such ingenuity that it bent the long, ancient tradition of the art of discovery into a powerful tool for the evaluation of the foundations of all inferences.[51]

NOTES

1. See, for example, my book *Boethius's De topicis differentiis* (Ithaca, N.Y.: Cornell University Press, 1978), especially pp. 18-23; and J. D. G. Evans, *Aristotle's Concept of Dialectic* (Cambridge: Cambridge University Press, 1977).

2. *Garlandus Compotista. Dialectica,* ed. L. M. de Rijk (Assen: Van Gorcum, 1959).

3. *Petrus Abaelardus. Dialectica,* ed. L. M. de Rijk, 2nd ed. (Assen: Van Gorcum, 1970).

4. I do not mean to suggest that the broad sense of 'dialectic' is original to Garlandus; it can be found also in certain ancient authors, such as Cassiodorus.

As for Garlandus's own use of the term, there are interesting parallel passages in Garlandus's and Boethius's work that shed light on the signification of 'dialectic' in the eleventh century. Boethius makes this division of arguments:

> Of all arguments, some are readily believable and necessary, some readily believable and not necessary, some necessary but not readily believable, and some neither readily believable nor necessary. . . . The dialectician and the orator occupy themselves with . . . these two kinds of argument: those that are readily believable and necessary and those that are readily believable and not necessary. The . . . demonstrator . . . uses two kinds of argument: those that are readily believable and necessary, and those that are necessary and not readily believable. So it is clear in what respect the philosopher differs from the orator and the dialectician in their areas of inquiry, namely, for them it consists in ready believability and for him in truth (*Boethius's De topicis differentiis*, p. 41, PL 1180C, 1181D-1182A).

Garlandus, clearly echoing this passage, says, "Some arguments are readily believable and necessary, and these are the province of dialecticians. Others are readily believable and not necessary, and these pertain to orators. Others are necessary and not readily believable or necessary; sophists dispute with these" (Garlandus, p. 93.1-4). Garlandus limits dialectical arguments to those that are both readily believable and necessary, thus circumscribing the range of dialectic. But he shows that he does not understand the special function of dialectic, as an instrument for compelling agreement from an opponent in oral disputation, when he fails to recognize that dialectical arguments need be *only* readily believable. And by losing sight of dialectic's special and technical use, he in effect broadens the range of dialectic and adds to its respectability as well. For a detailed discussion of Garlandus's understanding of dialectic, see *Garlandus,* pp. XLIX-LII.

5. *Peter of Spain. Tractatus,* ed. L. M. de Rijk (Assen: Van Gorcum, 1972), pp. 1.4-9 and 90.22-24. There are still traces of the broad, early Scholastic use of 'dialectic' in Peter's work; cf. pp. 2.20, 2.22, 2.30, 3.2, and 3.6. Simon of Faversham's commentary on Peter of Spain's *Tractatus,* probably written in the 1270s, says explicitly that 'dialectic' has two meanings, which correspond to the broad and narrow senses I have been discussing here; see L. M. de Rijk, "On the Genuine Text of Peter of Spain's Summule logicales," II, *Vivarium,* 6 (1968), pp. 80-81.

6. The history of the signification of 'dialectic' in the Scholastic period is probably related to the rediscovery of Aristotle. As the last four books of the *Organon* were reintroduced, and especially as the *Posterior Analytics* (and the *Topics* as well, perhaps) was absorbed and understood, the signification of 'dialectic' seems to have returned, in part at least, to its old, technical sense. For a thorough and useful study of the history of dialectic, see Pierre Michaud-Quantin, *Etudes sur le vocabulaire philosophique du moyen-âge.* (Rome: Edizione dell' Ateneo, 1970), pp. 59-72; and an article by Michaud-Quantin and James A. Weisheipl, "Dialectics in the Middle Ages" in the *New Catholic Encyclopedia.*

7. For a more complete study of the field of medieval logic, see *The Cambridge History of Later Medieval Philosophy,* ed. N. Kretzmann, A. Kenny, J. Pinborg (Cambridge: Cambridge University Press, 1982) and its extensive bibliography.

8. Cf., for example, L. M. de Rijk, *Logica Modernorum* (Assen: Van Gorcum, 1962-1967), vol. I, pp. 14-15, and *Garlandus*, p. XLVI for a more detailed discussion of *logica vetus* itself and a list of the Boethian treatises included in the *logica vetus*.

9. See L. M. de Rijk, *Logica Modernorum*, vols. I and II.

10. This is a simplified account of supposition and syncategorematic words; for a more detailed discussion, see, for example, Norman Kretzmann, "Semantics, History of" in *The Encyclopedia of Philosophy*, ed., Paul Edwards (New York: Macmillan Publishing Co., 1967).

11. Cf. my paper "Topics: Their Development and Absorption into Theories of Consequences" in *The Cambridge History of Later Medieval Philosophy*.

12. Ockham, *Summa logicae*, in *Opera Philosophica et Theologica*, t. I, ed. Stephen Brown, Gedeon Gál, et al., Franciscan Institute, 1974; and Walter Burley, *De puritate artis logicae tractatus longior, with a Revised Edition of the Tractatus brevior*, ed. Philotheus Boehner, Franciscan Institute, 1955.

13. For fuller discussions of logic in this period, see Jan Pinborg, *Logik und Semantik in Mittelalter. Ein Ueberblick* (Stuttgart-Bad Cannstatt: Frommann-Holzboog, 1972), pp. 13-127; Norman Kretzmann, "Semantics, History of"; and L. M. de Rijk, *Logica Modernorum*.

14. An edition of this treatise can be found in the *Patrologia Latina*, ed. J.-P. Migne (Turnholt: Brepols, n.d.), vol. LXIV; for a translation, see my book *Boethius's De topicis differentiis*.

15. This treatise is edited in the *Patrologia Latina*, vol. LXIV and in *Ciceronis Opera*, ed. J. C. Orelli and G. Baiterus (Zurich: Fuesslini, 1833), vol. 5, pt. 1. References to this treatise will be given first to the Orelli edition and then in parentheses to the *Patrologia* edition.

16. See, for example, Jan Pinborg, *Logik und Semantik*, pp. 81-87.

17. See, for example, Otto Bird, "The Tradition of the Logical Topics: Aristotle to Ockham". *Journal of the History of Ideas*, 23 (1962), 307-23; and my paper "Topics: Their Development and Absorption into Theories of Consequences", *op. cit.*

18. For discussion of Socratic disputation, see, for example, Paul Moraux, "La Joute dialectique d'après le huitième livre des *Topiques*" in *Aristotle on Dialectic*, ed. G. E. L. Owen (Oxford: Clarendon Press, 1968), pp. 277-311; and Gilbert Ryle, "Dialectic in the Academy" in *Aristotle on Dialectic*, pp. 69-79.

19. Cf. *Sophistici Elenchi* 183b23-184a8; also *Topics* 100a18-24.

20. Cf., for example, the following: *Cornelii Taciti Dialogus de oratoribus*, ed. Maximum Lenchantin de Gubernatis, Corpus Scriptorum Latinorum Paravianum (Turin: G. B. Paravia, 1949), p. 31; Quintilian, *Institutio oratoria*, trans. H. E. Butler (London: Heinemann, 1921), V.x. 20ff., V.x. 100ff., V.xii. 15ff.; *Victorini explanationum in Ciceronis rhetoricam libri II*, in *Rhetores Latini minores*, ed. Charles Halm (Leipzig: Teubner, 1863), pp. 213ff.; *Martiani Capellae liber de arte rhetorica* in *Rhet. Lat. min.*, pp. 465ff.; *C. Chirii Fortunatiani artis rhetoricae libri III*, in *Rhet. Lat. min.*, pp. 105ff.; Cassiodorus, *Institutiones*, ed. R.A.B. Mynors (Oxford: Clarendon Press, 1937), pp. 125ff.

21. Cf. especially Alexander of Aphrodisias *In Aristotelis topicorum libros octo commentaria* in *Commentaria in Aristotelem Graeca* ed. Maximillian Wallies (Berlin: G. Reimer 1891), supp. vol. II, pt. ii.

22. Respectively, *De topicis differentiis* (hereafter *De top. diff.*) , 1185D2-3, 1189D2-3, and 1191D12-13.

23. Cf. *De top. diff.*, 1185C10-D3.

24. Cf. *De top. diff.*, 1184D7-1185A3.

25. Cf. *In Ciceronis Topica*, 279.11-24 (PL 1050C6-D7) , where Boethius gives this example as a demonstrative argument.

26. *In Ciceronis Topica*, 288.4-17 (PL 1059C6-D8) .

27. It is typical of Boethius's examples that they argue for conclusions about which no one (or no medieval Christian philosopher) is in any doubt. What Boethius wants to teach is a method for finding *arguments,* not conclusions to arguments; and perhaps his purpose and the efficacy of his method are under-scored if he teaches us how to argue for conclusions to which we already adhere with strong, commonsense conviction.

28. *De top. diff.*, 1187A6-B1.

29. This is a sketchy summary of Boethius's method. For a fuller treatment, see my book *Boethius's De topicis differentiis,* pp. 179-204.

30. *Garlandus*, p. XLIX.

31. Garlandus's chapter is unusual in its closeness to Boethius's treatise in three other, more technical respects. First, he discusses the Ciceronian Topics, from Book III of *De top. diff.*, as well as the Themistian Topics from Book II. Most Scholastic treatments of Topics (Abelard's treatment in his *Dialectica* is a notable exception) concentrate exclusively on the Themistian Topics. Sec-ondly, he considers seriously Boethius's claim that the Differentiae are specific differentiae of maximal propositions. And thirdly, he follows Boethius in at-tempting to show (p. 114.17-18) which Topics are useful for which syllogisms (*De top. diff.*, 1173C10-11 and 1195A13-1196A3) .

32. See my "Garlandus Compotista and Dialectic in the Eleventh and Twelfth Centuries," *History and Philosophy of Logic,* I (1980) , 1-18, for a full discussion of Garlandus's theory of Topics.

33. For other examples in which the conclusion is a conditional proposition, apparently meant to be proved in this same way, for example, see p. 107.17-33.

34. To see that the categorical argument proving the conditional proposition takes second place in Garlandus's theory to the hypothetical argument, we need only remember that Garlandus claims that only Differentiae and not maximal propositions provide arguments. If Garlandus were not thinking of arguments in this connection just as the hypothetical arguments that I have tried to show are provided by the Differentiae, he would not make this claim, because maxi-mal propositions provide the categorical arguments in which they are used, just as the Differentiae provide the hypothetical arguments.

35. For example, one of Boethius's standard examples is that Ethiopians are black; see, for example, *De top. diff.*, 1179A13.

36. It is possible to take the questions here as 'Is every animal white?' The argument then will be, basically, that not every animal is white because man is not white. In this case, the conclusion of the argument will not be false, but the peculiarity of the example is scarcely decreased.

37. For the ambiguous use of the Latin *"si"* ('if') to mark sometimes an in-ference and sometimes an implication, see, for example, Ivo Thomas, "Kil-wardby on Conversion," *Dominican Studies,* 6 (1953) , 68-71.

38. *Garlandus*, pp. 87.16ff., 88.10-21, and 88.28-36.

39. Cf., for example, *Garlandus*, pp. 89.4-9, 96.18ff., and 111.15-20.

40. Cf. *The Rhetoric of Alcuin and Charlemagne,* trans. Wilbur Samuel Howell (Princeton, N.J.: Princeton University Press, 1941) pp. 112ff. and 120ff.; and *Rabani Mauri, De institutione clericorum libri tres,* ed. Aloisius Knoepfler (Munich: J. J. Lentner, 1901), pp. 227-230; and see also *Isidori Hispalensis Episcopi Etymologiarum sive Originum, Libri XX,* ed. W. M. Lindsay (Oxford: Clarendon Press, 1911), Bk. II, xxx.

41. *Dialectica,* pp. 253-466. For a recent study of topics in Abelard's *Dialectica,* see my "Boethius's Theory of Topics and Its Place in Early Scholastic Logic," *Atti congresso internazionale di studi boeziana,* ed. Luca Obertello (Rome, 1981), pp. 249-262.

42. *Scritti di Logica,* ed. Mario dal Pra, 2nd ed. (Florence: La nuova Italia, 1969), pp. 205-330.

43. N. J. Green-Pedersen, "The Doctrine of 'maxima propositio' and 'locus differentia' in Commentaries from the 12th Century on Boethius' "Topics," " *Studia Mediewistyczne,* 18 (1977), 125-163. In what follows I am indebted to Dr. Green-Pedersen for my understanding of these commentaries, and I am grateful to him for calling this material to my attention. See also his articles "On the Interpretation of Aristotle's Topics in the Thirteenth Century," *Cahiers de l'Institut de Moyen-âge grec et latin,* 9 (1973), 1-46; "William of Champeaux on Boethius' Topics according to Orleans Bibl. Mun.266," *Cahiers,* 13 (1974), 13-30; "Discussions about the Status of the Loci Dialectici in Works from the Middle of the 13th Century," *Cahiers,* 20 (1977), 38-78.

44. *Logica Modernorum,* vol. II, pt. 2, p. 529.19-25.

45. *Garlandus,* pp. 100.28-30 and 101.17-31. For a study of topics in the logic treatises of the twelfth century, see "Topics and Formal Logic in the Twelfth Century" in my forthcoming book *Boethius's In Ciceronis Topica.*

46. See *Boethius's De topicis differentiis,* pp. 218-21.

47. See Peter of Spain's *Tractatus,* pp. 57-58.

48. The character of the relata, as well as the nature and ontological status of a Differentia, were the subject of dispute among Scholastics. Peter's views on the subject are not unambiguous, but he seems to understand a Differentia as a relationship between two terms; see *Tractatus,* p. 59.11-6 and p. 61.21-5.

49. *Tractatus,* p. 60.17-9.

50. The numbers depend on what is counted as *one* Differentia or *one* maxim. For example, I have counted all four varieties of opposites as one Topic *from opposites.*

51. I am indebted to my friend Norman Kretzmann for various helpful comments and suggestions and I am grateful to John Crossett (d. 1981), whose efforts on my behalf made this paper possible.

SELECT BIBLIOGRAPHY ON DIALECTIC

Otto Bird, "The Tradition of the Logical Topics: Aristotle to Ockham," *Journal of the History of Ideas,* 23, 1962, pp. 307-23.

N. Kretzmann, "Semantics, History of" in *The Encyclopedia of Philosophy.* New York: Macmillan Publishing Co., 1967.

N. Kretzmann, A. Kenny, J. Pinborg, eds. *The Cambridge History of Later Medieval Philosophy.* Cambridge: Cambridge University Press, 1982.

G. E. L. Owen, ed. *Aristotle on Dialectic.* Oxford: Clarendon Press, 1968.

Jan Pinborg. *Logik und Semantik im Mittelalter. Ein Ueberblick.* Stuttgart-Bad Cannstatt: Frommann-Holzboog, 1972.

L. M. de Rijk, ed. *Garlandus Compotista. Dialectica.* Assen; Van Gorcum, 1959.

———. *Logica Modernorum.* Assen: Van Gorcum, 1962-67, vols. I-II.

———, ed. *Petrus Abaelardus. Dialectica.* Assen: Van Gorcum, 1970, 2nd ed.

E. Stump. *Boethius's De topicis differentiis.* Ithaca, N.Y.: Cornell University Press, 1978.

———, "Garlandus Compotista and Dialectic in the Eleventh and Twelfth Centuries," *History and Philosophy of Logic,* I, 1980, pp. 1-18.

———, "Topics: Their Development and Absorption into Theories of Consequences" in the *Cambridge History of Later Medieval Philosophy.* Cambridge: Cambridge University Press, 1982.

6 *Arithmetic*

Michael Masi

The quadrivium, even more explicitly than the trivium, was viewed as a techne. Its principle was number, which could be conceived either as a distinct entity or as magnitude. Boethius, in the Proemium *of the* De arithmetica, *in fact took the contrast between magnitude and multitude (i.e., a collection of items) as the basis for his systematic analysis of the four mathematical arts.*

The art of arithmetic, according to Boethius, had separable multitude as its subject. Arithmetic (what we would call number theory) was distinguished from both computation and arithmology, or number mysticism. The Latin encyclopedists ignored computation and usually mentioned arithmology only in passing.

For reasons I have discussed in Chapter 1, the early Pythagorean approach to arithmetic persisted throughout the classical and medieval periods, though not without a growing sophistication. The first standard topic was number-in-itself, the second ratio (the reltion of two numbers), and the third proportion or mean (analogia in Greek, originally signifying the relation among three numbers). This sequence paralleled that of medieval logic—which moved from one term to two terms (the proposition) to three terms (the syllogism).

As words had their beginning in letters, so too did number have its principle, unity (which was not regarded as a number). Numbers were classified as odd or even, with further distinctions within the latter class. Prime and perfect numbers, plane and solid numbers were other subdivisions of this topic.

The theory of ratio was developed to clarify the way in which one number was contained within another. Since it assumed that numbers were rational, any remainder would be a whole number. Nicomachus held that the principle of ratio was equality. Although equality itself was not included within the few basic types of ratio that were identified, the multiple represented a kind of equality in that the lesser was contained within the greater without remainder. Ratios that had unity as a remainder were singled out as a special case. All other ratios made up a final category.

> *The theory of proportion was orignally limited to the analysis of the arithmetic, harmonic, and geometric means; A. O. Taylor, in his commentary on Plato's* Timaeus, *argued that these means grew out of the analysis of musical consonances. While several further means were later identified, these three remained the most basic. Later theorists argued that only the geometric means is a proportion in the strict sense (a:b::b:c), giving rise to further analysis of the relation among four numbers. D. L. W.*

A student of the history of mathematics becomes quickly aware of the fact that the term "arithmetic" had a significance in the context of the medieval liberal arts curriculum different from that understood in modern times. This difference, essentially the distinction between number theory and computational mathematics, was inherited from Greek mathematics and its recognition is important for the understanding of the role that arithmetic played in the medieval liberal arts curriculum. The medieval *arithmetica*, derived from the classical arithmetikē ($\alpha\rho\iota\theta\mu\eta\tau\iota\kappa\eta$) is a philosophical study of number, of the nature of unity, of equality, of ratio, and of proportion. In modern mathematics, this kind of number theory is studied by theorists and philosophers and is generally referred to as the philosophy of number. What we understand by arithmetic, that is the practical use of the four mathematical operations of addition, subtraction, multiplication, and division, was referred to in the Middle Ages as *computus* or algorism, which was the Greek practical mathematics, logistikē ($\lambda o\gamma\iota\sigma\tau\iota\kappa\eta$).[1]

So, depending on which definition of arithmetic the student of mathematical thought takes, the material that he undertakes to study in medieval mathematics will differ. A study of the history of computational mathematics and of the antecedents of modern algebra will take one to treatises on the abacus and finger computations, to the practical calculations of the merchants and bankers, and to the writings of two mathematicians who refined this computation, Gerbert and Fibonacci. A study of number theory will take the student to texts on philosophical writing, to the treatises of Boethius and Cassiodorus, derived from Nicomachus, and later to Bradwardine and Grosseteste. For one interested in the liberal arts, it is essential to begin with the number theories since their principles underlie the study of the various treatises read for the study of the disciplines of the quadrivium. The four disciplines of the second part of the liberal arts are essentially mathematical in character: arithmetic, music, geometry, and astronomy. Each of these studies is concerned with numbers. According to various discussions of arithmetic from the early medieval period when the curriculum of the liberal arts was beginning to take shape, arithmetic defined the nature of numbers; music gave expression to the relationship between numbers, and so music was considered an extension of mathematical studies. In music, numerical relations acquired an expression in sound. Geometry, which developed the metaphor of harmony given to the study of ratio in music, extended proportion and harmony (harmony is ratio and proportion expressed in musical terms) to two- and three-dimensional figures. In astronomy, the final discipline of the liberal arts curriculum, proportion, harmony, and geometry find their broadest application in the study of stars, planets, and their celestial relationships.

Before proceeding to further discussion of mathematics and the liberal arts, it would be well to digress for a caution and a distinction. Most discussions of number theory do not clearly differentiate between mystical number theory and philosophical number theory. This distinction is significant because an interpretation or understanding based on philosophical number theory carries much more intellectual weight. Philosophical number theorists do not interest themselves in magical, secret, or hidden meanings of number. They depend instead on reasonably intelligible numerical relationships. Mystical numbers, on the other hand, depend on meanings derived from scriptural or cabalistic sources, such as the 140,000 virgins whom St. John saw in his *Apocalypse* and who somehow are understood to signify the number of souls to be saved on the Last Day. Or again, the number forty is fraught with mystical meaning since the Hebrew nation spent forty years in the desert and Christ spent forty years in fasting and prayer. Forty is consequently taken to signify some kind of fulfillment.[2] Philosophical number theory, however, is based on combinations and relationships among numbers that are entirely comprehensible to the mind. Thus, for example, a perfect number is one whose dividends, if added together, are exactly equal to that number. Such a number is 6, which can be divided into 1, 2, and 3, and these add up to 6. Another perfect number is 28, whose dividends are 1, 2, 4, 7, and 14 and these add up to 28. Furthermore, there is only one perfect number in each rank or order of numbers, tens, hundreds, thousands, etc. These are 6, 28, 496, 8,128, etc. As we may see, there is nothing secret or mysterious in these orders; all are perfectly comprehensible to the intellect. In addition, medieval thinkers were deeply impressed by this obvious order in the nature of things, an order that can be determined only by careful calculations. As can be demonstrated, the order is consistent and always present. The same kind of rational and consistent orders may be seen in the other ratios and proportions of numbers. But there are some numbers adopted by both philosophical and mystical camps. The number ten, for example, is, along with its multiples, the cornerstone for mystical numerologists. For philosophical number theorists, ten is the tetrakis, the sum of the first four numbers in the natural series.

ARITHMETIC AND THE ORDER OF THE LIBERAL ARTS

The liberal arts system was, then, an orderly procedure for the study of philosophical numbers. Just how orderly this procedure was is worthy of some consideration. There is to be found among the surviving texts for the arts curriculum a variety in the order of study of the disciplines in the quadrivium. But there is an order widely known, from the introduction to the *De arithmetica* of Boethius, that seems for some time to have been generally accepted. Although few scholars have discussed the nature of the order of the disciplines in the quadrivium, the notion of a proper order—with arithmetic first—was indeed important. Notable collections of texts for the study of the liberal arts, such as the *Heptateuchon* by Thierry of Chartres (d. ca.1150) give us some notion of how the liberal disciplines were presented. The *Heptateuchon* is an anthology of texts by authorities such as Ptolemy, Aristotle,, Euclid, Isidore, Cassiodorus, Martianus Capella, and Boethius. Excerpts from the Boethian *De arithmetica* and *De musica* form a substantial part of the sections on these two disciplines. Martianus Capella, who wrote on all the liberal arts in his *De nuptiis Philologiae et Mercurii*, is also represented. Martianus placed music in the final position. It seems from iconographic and textual evidence that the Boethian order of arithmetic followed by music was more generally adopted in the schools.[3] It is important to be aware of order and its function in these disciplines since, clearly, some studies were seen as "prerequisites" for more advanced studies. The student was envisioned as moving up the ladder of studies until his work prepared him for philosophical speculation. The mathematical disciplines of the quadrivium culminated with the study of astronomy from which the truly wise man moved to the study of metaphysics. Such is the order that was outlined by Boethius in the *De arithmetica* and that is testified to textually until the Renaissance.

Numbers, then, are important for those who seek wisdom. Boethius emphasizes this idea strongly and, after he defines the four disciplines in the prologue to the *De arithmetica,* he adds: "It stands to reason that whoever puts these matters aside has lost the whole teaching of philosophy. This, therefore, is the quadrivium by which we must travel, by which we bring a superior mind from knowledge offered by the senses to the more certain things of the intellect."[4] In this prologue, Boethius coined the term *quadrivium*, which means "the four paths" or "four ways," and he paves these four ways with numbers. Then he goes on to insist on a particular order:

> Which of these disciplines, then, is the first to be learned but that one which holds the principal place and position of mother to the rest? It is arithmetic. It is prior to all not only because God the creator of the massive structure of the world considered this first discipline as the exemplar of His own thought, and established all things in accord with it; or that through numbers of an assigned order all things exhibiting the logic of their maker found concord; but arithmetic is said to be first for this reason also, because whatever things are prior in nature, it is to these underlying elements that the posterior elements can be referred.

Boethius goes on to establish the priority of arithmetic on logical grounds and explains that just as the term "man" includes the term "animal," so "animal" must come first; likewise, the other disciplines of the quadrivium include arithmetic, and hence arithmetic must come first. He concludes the prologue of the *De arithmetica* thus:

> From this it follows that the power of music logically precedes the course of the stars; and there is no doubt that arithmetic precedes astronomy since it is prior to music, which comes before astronomy. All the courses of the stars and all astronomic reasoning are established exclusively by the nature of numbers. Thus we connect rising with falling, thus we keep watch on the slowness and speed of wandering stars, thus we recognize the eclipses and multiplicities of lunar variations. Since, as it is obvious, the force of arithmetic is prior, we may now take up the beginning of our exposition.

The study of mathematics penetrated to philosophical and theological disciplines as well, and several scholars have shown the extent to which mathematics can be found in the works of Plato, Aristotle, and Aquinas. Philosophy was thoroughly permeated with the ideas of number from the time of the Greeks. Plato refers regularly to numbers for his proofs and illustrations. In the Middle Ages, all the major theological systems were thoroughly grounded in number. For example, the thinkers of Oxford and Cambridge (as Professor Pearl Kibre has shown) insisted on the importance of mathematics.[5] Robert Grosseteste wrote extensively on the topic.[6] Roger Bacon, citing Boethius's *De arithmetica* in his *Opus maius*, said that any one who knows the four mathematical sciences can make progress without undue labor and difficulty in acquiring knowledge of both human and divine sciences. Bacon, who followed and expanded the ideas of Boethius on mathematics, insisted that philosophy cannot be known without mathematics. For him, not only the other quadrivial disciplines, but even logic, rhetoric, or grammar were unknown without mathematics. The discipline of mathematics is so basic that it was founded when the race began and it has continued as the first among the arts.[7] Bacon emphasized, "And therefore in mathematics alone are there demonstrations of the most convincing kind through a necessary cause. And therefore here alone can a man arrive at the truth from the nature of this science."[8]

Other philosophers stressed that logic and the quadrivial disciplines should come before mathematics, but the importance of mathematics always emerges. Aquinas maintained, for example, that logic teaches a student method upon which he will always rely. Then one is ready for mathematical studies and after that one proceeds to physical and natural philosophy. This program of learning is culminated by moral studies and by a knowledge of theology.[9] Bacon went on to prove his theory that, in spite of what Aquinas had written, mathematical knowledge is in fact indispensible for advance in any discipline. To illustrate his point he made a survey of the important works by a number of learned men from the Middle Ages whose intellectual excellence was directly due to their knowledge of mathematics. Among those he cited were Grosseteste and Friar Adam Marsh.[10] But Bacon also emphasized that the practical mathematics be studied with the theoretical. Thus must be combined the practical and the theoretical so that the well-educated man may be ready for knowledge of the sublime and of practical affairs.[11]

A SUMMARY OF THE BOETHIAN TREATISE

The treatise of Boethius on arithmetic certainly played a central role in the study of medieval number theory. Either by itself or in combination with other practical or theoretical works, it is the most frequently cited work in connection with the study of numbers in the liberal arts curriculum. Other works may have replaced it in some localities, such as the arithmetic of Cassiodorus or Isidore, or, later in the fifteenth and sixteenth centuries, original Greek works became more commonly known. Yet a close examination of the Boethian *De arithmetica* does provide the modern student of the liberal arts curriculum with an insight into what the discipline of medieval arithmetic involved. I will, accordingly, present an outline of the work's contents and show its relevance to the other disciplines of the quadrivium.

The *De arithmetica* is divided into two books, containing, respectively, 32 and 54 chapters. It is an early work of Boethius, as evidenced by his dedicatory epistle to his father-in-law and master, Symmachus;

we may see that in later life, when he wrote the *De musica,* he changed some of his ideas regarding the classification of the disciplines. The *De arithmetica* is derived with little change from the treatise on arithmetic by Nicomachus; Boethius, as he explains in his preface, expanded some parts and shortened others. The work is essentially Pythagorean in character, frankly rudimentary in mathematical difficulty, and intended, both by Nicomachus originally and by Boethius, as an introductory text for beginners. The proemium, perhaps the best-known portion, elaborates in some detail the division of the quadrivium into those disciplines that deal with number in itself (arithmetic) or number in relations (music) ; and quantity, which may be studied at rest (geometry) and in motion (astronomy) . Each of these disciplines includes knowledge of the previous. None can be studied and certainly comprehended without knowledge of the previous. In effect, the *arithmetica* must come first since it treats of the very elements of mathematics. After it explains number in itself, numbers in relation to others, and numbers in quantity, arithmetic has established the grounds for the study of music and geometry. (The work does not approach astronomy.) It is, in fact, a theoretical arithmetic and as well a theoretical (or mathematical) music and a theoretical geometry. Chapters 1-20 of book I deal with arithmetic in the strict sense, that is with number in itself. This discussion of number in itself is largely a matter of defining terms, and this portion of the treatise corresponds most closely with other medieval treatises on arithmetic known in the Middle Ages—for example those of Cassiodorus and Isidore of Seville. The definition of number, the distinction between multitude and magnitude, the division of number into even and odd, and what this means in mathematical terms are matters all familiar to students of modern number theory. Boethius also defines and gives examples of an even times even number, that is, one that may be divided into even numbers down to two: $16 = 4 \times 4 = 2 \times 2 \times 2 \times 2$; and even times odd, which is one that breaks down into even and odd: $90 = 9 \times 10 = 3 \times 3 \times 2 \times 5$. Since the discussion is dominated by metaphysical principles, the section on arithmetic culminates with a discussion of perfect number, that is, the number all of whose dividends will, if added together, equal the same number.

With chapter 21 Boethius leaves the domain of arithmetic as such and, insofar as he discusses relations between numbers, begins the discourse on the mathematics of music. The five types of ratio between numbers are essential parts of any medieval or Renaissance music theory and such discussions may be found in a wide variety of treatises on music well into the sixteenth century. The types may be outlined as follows:

1. *Multiplex ratio.* This is the ratio between two numbers, one of which may be divided evenly into the other:

    a) duplex: 1:2, 2:4, 3:6.
    b) triplex: 1:3, 3:9, 4:12.
    c) quadruple: 1:4, 2:8, 3:12, et cetera.

2. *Superparticular.* These are ratios between numbers, one of which may be divided into the other with a remainder that is a fraction of the smaller number. These are also arranged into ranks:

    a) a sesquialter superparticular in which the remainder is one half of the smaller: 2:3, 4:6, 6:9, et cetera.
    b) a sesquitertian superparticular in which the remainder is one third of the smaller: 3:4, 6:8, 9:12, et cetera.
    c) a sesquiquartan superparticular in which the remainder is one fourth of the smaller: 4:5, 8:10, 12:15, et cetera.

These continue in the same manner with the sesquiquintus, sesquisextus, and so on.

3. *Superpartient.* This is a ratio in which the remainder of the numbers does not divide evenly into either of the two, such as 4:7, 5:9, 9:13, et cetera.

4. *Multiplex superparticular.* This is a ratio that combines the first and second types. 3:8 is 3:6 plus 3:2, which is a duplex multiple and a sesquialter superparticular.

5. *Multiplex superpartient.* This ratio is a combination of the first and third. 5:13 is 5:10 plus 5:3.

The descriptions of all these ratios are accompanied by tables that instruct the student in the derivation of entire series of such ratios, and so ends the first book. Book II begins the theoretical geometry, that is the definition of the point, the line, and various figures: triangle, square, quadrangle, pentangle, et cetera. Each of these figures is equated with a number of points, in the ancient Pythagorean belief which postulated that all things are made up of numbers. Thus, three points comprise a triangle, four a square, et cetera. The figured numbers are extended into solid geometric shapes as well. Thus four cubed is sixty-four, the figured number for a cube. This discussion occupies chapters 1-39 and is of relatively minor importance for later medieval mathematical studies. With chapter 40 Boethius begins his discussion of proportionality, which is of immense significance to medieval mathematicians such as Bradwardine and Grosseteste who begin their more elaborate discussions of proportions with his definitions. The section on proportions is also important to musical treatises. A ratio is a relationship between two numbers, such as 1:2 (an octave in music), or 2:3 (a fifth in music), and so on. A proportion is a ratio between ratios. Boethius is particularly concerned with medial proportions, that is, a ratio among three numbers: 1:2:4. These are classified in ten categories, the most important of which are the first three, since all the following are merely variations of these three. With their description, Boethius concludes his treatise. The medial proportions are called arithmetic, geometric, and harmonic. They may be defined as follows:

Arithmetic

In an arithmetic medial proportion, the middle term exceeds the smallest term by the same amount as the largest exceeds the middle, as in 2, 3, 4. The three exceeds two by a third of itself. The four exceeds three by a fourth of itself.

Geometric

In a geometric medial proportion, such as 4, 6, 9, the median surpasses the smallest by the same fraction of itself as the largest surpasses the median. Thus six surpasses four by a third of itself, and nine surpasses six by a third of itself.

Harmonic

In a harmonic medial proportion, as 2, 3, 6, the median term surpasses the smallest by half of itself and is surpassed in the largest by half of itself.

These are merely examples of the relationships that exist among the three numbers of medial proportions. Each has others as well, which Boethius is at pains to explicate. Boethius also proceeds to apply these proportions to various geometrical and musical concepts.

PRACTICAL ARITHMETIC

Such was the nature of the mathematics being studied in the schools and universities well into the High Middle Ages. It was a mathematics that prepared a student for the ultimate learning of philosophy and had little practical application. But there was at the same time a practical mathematics studied among merchants for the calculation of monetary transactions. For such calculations the abacus was commonly used, an instrument found in wide usage, in different forms, in East and West. The learning of this instrument was transmitted orally and the abacus proved itself capable of rather complex calculations in addition and subtraction as well as in multiplication and division. The abacus was far more sophisticated a means of making calculations than was finger counting, devised by some medieval mathematicians, since the columns of beads or stones were arranged in groups of five or ten; it thus overcame the cumbersome Roman numerals that made long multiplication impossible.

By the tenth century, the beginnings of change were perceptible, although it was some time before the new developments were widely accepted and used. In the late 900s we find the mathematical writings of Gerbert of Aurillac, who eventually became Pope Sylvester II and reigned until 1003. Gerbert's significance rests chiefly on his introduction into the West of Arabic and Hindu mathematics, mainly in the form of treatises in arithmetic, geometry, and astronomy. Gerbert's interests are decidedly away from number theory and are imbued with a strong sense of practical mathematics. He is known for the use and development of several astronomical instruments; but, most significant for the discipline of arithmetic, there has been attributed to him a treatise on the abacus, *Regula de abaco computi,* which contains instructions on a new and simpler way of representing calculations of the four arithmetic operations. But while the representation in columns with counters (called *apices*) was clearer, the mathematical operation was more complex. The historical importance of Gerbert's work is that his discussion of the abacus was one of the first definite indications that western mathematicians were beginning to think of mathematical operations in decimal terms.[12]

By the twelfth century, medieval mathematics began to change on several levels, both theoretical and practical. The most important Arabic work to enter the West on the Hindu-Arabic mathematics was al-Khwarizmi's *Treatise on the Calculation with the Hindu Numerals,* written circa 825, translated into Latin circa 1143. This treatise, whose mathematical concepts came to be called algorism (a corruption of the Arabic author's name), explained the basics of a system where place value was part of the numerical expression, as we first noted in the columns of Gerbert's abacus. But in al-Khwarizmi's treatise, the longer operations of multiplication and division were still clumsy and lengthy exercises. For example, to multiply 496×23, one would proceed in this fashion:[13]

$$496 \rightarrow (2 \times 4 = 8) \rightarrow \underline{8}496 \rightarrow (3 \times 4 = 12) \rightarrow$$
$$23 \qquad\qquad\qquad\qquad 23$$

$$\underline{9}296 \rightarrow (\text{shift multiplier}) \rightarrow 9296 \rightarrow (2 \times 9 = 18) \rightarrow$$
$$23 \qquad\qquad\qquad\qquad\qquad 23$$

$$\frac{11096}{23} \rightarrow (3 \times 9 = 27) \rightarrow \frac{11276}{23} \rightarrow \text{(shift multiplier)} \rightarrow$$

$$\frac{11276}{23} \rightarrow (2 \times 6 = 12) \rightarrow \frac{11396}{23} \rightarrow (3 \times 6 = 18) \rightarrow$$

$$\frac{11408}{23} \qquad 496 \times 23 = 11408.$$

Awkward though this method was, the text of al-Khwarizmi's work provided an inspiration to other mathematicians of a practical bent. Two of the better-known works that were inspired by this treatise were the *Carmen de Algorismo* of Alexander de Villa-Dei (ca.1240) and the *Algorismus Vulgaris* of Sacrobosco (John of Holywood). The second of these is of particular interest because, written about 1240, it was the first important text to introduce practical mathematics into the university curriculum. It combined the theoretical text of Boethius with the practical calculations of al-Khwarizmi and so united the two basic traditions into one elementary text. It must be admitted, however, that its basic tendency was for the instruction of the practical functions of arithmetic. It examines numeration, addition, subtraction, mediation, duplication, multiplication, division, progression, and extraction of both the square roots and cube roots of numbers. The work is rich in examples and diagrams. By 1291 this treatise had acquired a commentary by Peter of Decia and in this form it was found suitable for continued use in universities for centuries.[14]

ARITHMETIC, AESTHETICS, AND THEOLOGY

As the intellectual ferment of the Middle Ages heightened during the period of the twelfth to fourteenth centuries, we may see that the mathematical activity produced new works and more original thinkers. Theoretical and computational arithmetic achieved some integration and new advances were certainly made in practical calculations. But of equal importance was the spread of mathematical concepts into other areas of intellectual and aesthetic endeavor. In another essay of this collection, the reader may find illustrations of how music composition was affected by number theory. Architectural design was similarly affected. In fact, one may find the influence of numbers in literature and painting as well by the late medieval and Renaissance periods. The reason for the penetration of number theory into all the arts is simple to understand when one realizes that the curriculum of the liberal arts was the standard format for the education of most who produced serious works of art. Numbers were then at the basis of many medieval conceptions of the beautiful. According to the aesthetics of number theory, the parts of a work of art are determined in their size, proportions, and relationships in terms of numerical ratios. These proportions and ratios among the parts of a cathedral, for example, have nothing at all to do with the engineering aspects of the structure. Instead, they order the parts of the whole according to an abstract notion of intellectual beauty, one which speaks not to the senses which in all likelihood are not even able to perceive the ratios and proportions, but to the mind, which, on a close examination of the relationships between aisle and transept, width and height of nave, or sizes and distribution in a row of arches, is able to perceive a higher order and so arrive at an intellectual notion of the beautiful in that work.[15]

But the function of numerical order and proportion in cathedrals is more than a matter of aesthetics. The ratio of numbers is the philosopher's guide to the divine order in the nature of the universe and by transmitting these orders to the structure of the cathedral, the architect brought the design of his church into accord with the structure of the macrocosm and responded to the order of the numbers determined by the Divine Intellect. That the mathematical orders are established by divine intent is repeatedly referred to in the *De arithmetica* when Boethius, for example, asserts: "God, the founder of this perishable world, had His reasoning as its primary exemplar and in accord with this He created all things" (I,1). "This order of numbers is perfected by the great consideration and great constancy of divinity" (I,9). "This is a divine disposition, that is, that all the angles are tetragonal numbers" (I,21).

The most notable example of how a cathedral may embody number theory and how that building expresses the idea currently active in its intellectual milieu is the cathedral at Chartres.[16] Other structures may be more convincingly submitted to a rigorous mathematical analysis, but Chartres represents a particularly interesting case since the spirit of the new Platonism and a flowering school of mathematical studies there certainly had an effect on the design of the church. We know that the liberal arts certainly flourished there and they are depicted in the statuary surrounding the Virgin's Portal.

The cathedral school of Chartres nurtured a revival of Pythagorean and Platonic studies that, under the particular inspiration of the learned bishops Fulbert, Gosselin of Mussy, Robert le Breton, William, and culminating with John of Salisbury (1176-78), was particularly fruitful in terms of Christian theological writings. During the eleventh and twelfth centuries, the scholars of Chartres exhibited great enthusiasm for mathematical pursuits and produced commentaries on the treatises of the quadrivium that still stand out from the entire period of medieval philosophy. Foremost among these scholars were Thierry, his brother, Bernard, and their teacher, Gilbert de la Porrée. The *Hepta-teuchon,* already mentioned, is a well-known text to emerge from the hand of Thierry.

For the schoolmen of Chartres, mathematics was the link between God and the world, the intellectual key that unlocked the secrets of the universe.[17] Thierry extended mathematical studies beyond the Greek logical and ethical preoccupations reflected in Boethius to the realm of Christian theological inquiry. With the help of arithmetic and geometry he attempted to discern and explain the workings of God in all of Creation. One of the principles of Chartrian philosophers was that the world is created according to a model in the divine mind and there is a resemblance between the model and the created product. This resemblance is seen foremost in the system of mathematics that, with the help of ancients, learned men have devised. This is a notion tied closely to the doctrine of forms, as explained by Thierry and in accord with Boethian Platonism. The reality of created forms is achieved by a participation in certain divine forms and ideas.[18] For Thierry, this fact enables one to know the mind of God by the study of creation and in his treatise *De septem diebus,* on the creation of the world, Thierry proposes to expound the creation *secundum physicam* ("according to natural laws"). Since the world is an intelligible phenomenon, understanding of it will make more intelligible the Divine Mind.[19]

In addition to describing the Neoplatonic doctrine of the world as mirror of the divine mind, Thierry brought the study of arithmetic to an understanding of the Trinity. His study of the Trinity is, of course, strongly influenced by the Boethian writing on the subject and both works are essentially arithmetic in character; that is, they are concerned with the definition of terms—as is the first section of the *De arithmetica* —and not at all with the calculating of numbers. Unity, for example, is identical with the nature of the eternal divinity, and this by its intellectual priority. The nature of unity and the nature of intellectual priority are made clear in the opening sections of the *De arithmetica.* The next important concept is that of equality, especially as we understand it in numbers. There is a unity and an equality between the Father and the Son.[20] The Trinity, with its rich implications of mathematical possibilities, was obviously appealing for Thierry and he attempted to explain its nature in terms borrowed from the treatises of the quadrivium. The equality of the three persons is represented, according to Thierry, by the equilateral triangle. The square of the sides unfolds the ineffable relationship between the Father and the Son.[21]

Von Simson's musical analysis of Chartres cathedral in his book on Gothic architecture is certainly valid and demonstrates how a building may be described as "frozen music" in a way not intended by the person who first coined that impressionistic phrase. Yet von Simson's demonstration of musical proportionality can distract one from a fundamental tie to a basic mathematical proportionality. What the von Simson musical demonstration really comes to is an application of mathematical proportions to cathedral design. The building's basic ground plan, as he describes it (pp. 207-08), is the pentagon and from it are derived the proportions of the Golden Mean for the elaboration of other proportions of the building.[22] (The Golden Mean is a medial proportion found, for example, among the parts of a line divided into two sections when the length of the smaller part compared to the longer is in the same ratio as the longer compared to the two added together.) The relationship between the height of the shafts (13.85 m.) and the distance between the base of the shafts and the lower string course (5.35 m.) and the height of the piers (8.61 m.) is in that proportion.

The diagrams and descriptive comments in the sketchbook of Villard de Honnecourt (ca.1244) provide examples of geometrical and arithmetical proportionality that begin with the human figure and extend to a model of the perfect church. Villard was closely connected with Chartres and very possibly studied with one of the masters of the school. He was a theoretical architect imbued with the intellectual life of Chartres. Since Villard's comments and diagrams indicate a close relationship between the human form and a church structure, they make explicit the mathematician's search for the perfect natural model from which may be derived mathematical definitions for the ideal structure. Villard provides the plan for a Cistercian church designed *ad quadratum*, that is, one whose proportions are derived from the square, which is used to determine the dimensions of the entire structure.[23]

The proportions of Villard's Cistercian church correspond to the Boethian sequence of proportions. Nor were his discussions merely theoretical, since there is evidence that these plans were utilized by Cistercians in the construction of some of their churches. According to Villard's canons, the length of the cathedral's nave is in the ratio of 2:3 to the transept. This relationship may be considered in the ratio of a fifth in musical terms or a sesquialter in mathematical vocabulary. The ratio of 1:2 (duplex) or the octave occurs between the side aisle and the nave. We find the same relationship between the length and width of the transept and the interior elevation. The ratio of 4:3 of the nave to the choir is a sesquitertial relationship or a musical fourth. The 5:4 relationship of the side aisles taken as a unit and the nave is a third or a sesquiquartan. The crossing, liturgically and aesthetically the center of the church, is based on the 1:1 ratio of a unison, the mathematical unity, the most perfect of consonances, the foundation for all numerical ratio and musical harmony.

CREATIVE MATHEMATICAL THINKERS:
JORDANUS AND FIBONACCI

By the thirteenth century we may perceive the intrusion of those elements that we know made for great change in the history of mathematics. But it was the nature of medieval intellectual life to change slowly and several centuries were to pass before the new mathematical elements made their presence felt. We may see, for example, the appearance of Greek mathematical texts; works by Nicomachus and Euclid appear in new copies in their original language at this time. But their influence was slight since not many could read them and older texts were only gradually displaced.

The same is true for the works of inventive mathematicians, such as Jordanus Nemorarius and Fibonacci who were roughly contemporaries. Neither had a following and the only work of Nemorarius that achieved any popularity was not one of his more original writings. Fibonacci was not totally appreciated until modern times, when hardly any mathematician is unaware of his name.

Jordanus Nemorarius, who flourished around 1220, was more important for his works on mechanics than for his mathematical studies. The only composition that scholars all agree came from his hand, the *Elementa Jordani super demonstrationem ponderum*, is written in the form of postulates and theorems. This treatise and the *De ratione ponderis* show evidence of experimentation with weights and their movements that goes beyond the mere acceptance of Aristotelian authority on those matters. Although nothing in these works is contradictory to traditional Aristotelian teaching in the science of statistics, Jordanus drew from Archimedes more rigorous proofs and more rigid mathematical formats for their expression. His ideas of positional gravity and static movement had more influence in the Renaissance several centuries later than they did in the Middle Ages. During the sixteenth century, Jordanus's work enjoyed several editions and commentaries, such as Peter Apian's *Liber Jordani nemorarii . . . de ponderibus propositiones XIII et earundem demonstrationes* (Nuremberg, 1533), which helped to disseminate his ideas. Galileo, among others, was influenced by the physics of Jordanus as well as by Greek mechanical theorists. Indeed, in some cases, Jordanus proved himself more precise than the classical mathematicians.[24]

Jordanus's treatise *De numeris datis* covered mathematical problems in what we clearly recognize as algebraic methods and formulated the equivalent of an equation. Again in this work Jordanus shows his independence of Greek mathematics and a closer affinity to Arabic sources. Among other techniques, he used letters of the alphabet to represent unknowns. Much of his discussion is theoretical in the sense that nonapplied modern algebra is, not in the philosophical sense that we find in Boethius.

Jordanus's treatise *Arithmetica* is a work very close to the Boethian spirit, although entirely different in format and beyond it in originality. It is made up of 400 propositions in ten books, more in the model of the Euclidian geometry, but which cover much of the same material of the Boethian *De arithmetica*. It provides definitions for perfect number, even times even, even times odd, as well as for the five types of ratios and the proportions. By the sixteenth century, the *Arithmetica* of Jordanus was published together with the *De arithmetica* of Boethius and at the end of the volume a diagrammatic scheme comparing the two was included showing how both works covered the same ground.[25]

Leonardo of Pisa, better known as Fibonacci, is certainly one of the most outstanding mathematicians to emerge from the Middle Ages. He was, however, recognized by few during that period and it is only in recent centuries that his innovative genius has come to be fully appreciated. He did attract the attention of the Emperor Frederick Barbarossa, who invited Fibonacci to his court for a command performance of mathematical learning. The mathematical concept for which he is best known has come to be called the Fibonacci Series and this has been recognized as the first statement of a convergence of a sequence of ratios. This idea alone, even if Fibonacci had evolved no other mathematical concepts, would make him the most original and noteworthy mathematician of his times in the eyes of modern mathematicians.

The mathematical writings of Fibonacci are many and varied in scope. His works evince a continued interest in number theory, but his orientation is usually practical, not philosophical. He differs markedly from Boethius who is notable for his logical and abstract approach to mathematics and for whom mathematics was to be a preparation for philosophical study. Fibonacci's initial interest and ultimate concern with the practical matters of numbers must certainly have begun in a close acquaintance with his father's work—commerce and the transaction, of merchants who exchanged money and goods. Fibonacci was fascinated with the abacus as an instrument for solving problems and for understanding and developing mathematical concepts. It is an especially significant tool for his development since it was able to solve problems almost impossible to work out in the clumsy Roman numerals that most medieval mathematicians used and that are often seen in arithmetic treatises, even in those of the fourteenth century. Most merchants traditionally did their computations on the abacus and so avoided the use of numbers altogether in calculations, though they would write their results and keep their records in Roman numerals.

For Fibonacci the abacus provided an opportunity to see numbers differently, that is, in terms of tens and, in combination with his knowledge of Arabic mathematics, the abacus provided some incentive for original speculation. His best-known book, consequently, was entitled *Liber abbaci,* though it was much more than a study of that calculating instrument and, in fact, has more to do with the extension of ideas probably derived from the abacus than with its use.

Fibonacci became familiar with the mathematics of merchant exchange during his travels with trade ships that brought him to Arabic ports around the Mediterranean. He visited Constantinople, Egypt, Syria, Sicily, and Provence. In these Mediterranean coastal cities he garnered mathematical learning from scholars of all nationalities. In 1202 he wrote his *Liber abbaci* in order to work out original solutions to problems inspired by interchange with mathematicians he had met. One traditional problem he confronted was to determine the approximate square root for some figure that is not susceptible of a precise square root. We may use, to demonstrate his method, the number 18. To find its square root, take the nearest perfect square in it, which is 16, and extract its root, which is 4. To this add a fraction: the numerator will be the difference between the original number, 18, and its nearest perfect square, 16, in this case 2. The denominator will be twice the square root already extracted (that is 4), which makes eight. The answer for the approximate square root of 18 is 4¼. (A pocket calculator enables us to discover that 4.25 squared is 18.0625; a more precise square root of 18 is 4.2426.)

One may consider this a theoretical problem and not typical of the solutions Fibonacci discussed. More commonly his ideas center on practical applications in such problems as the calculating of interest, of finding how much silver and copper are needed in an alloy to produce money with a specified proportion of such metal per pound, and examples of how objects may be distributed among a variable number of recipients. But the most striking of all Fibonacci's expositions is one susceptible of extensive theoretical application, yet it is one he approached from an apparently applied point of view. In an inconspicuous section from chapter XII of the *Liber abbaci* he poses the problem:

A certain man put a pair of rabbits in a place surrounded by a wall. How many pairs of rabbits can be produced from that pair in a year if it is supposed that every month each pair begets a new pair which from the second month become productive?

To find the number of pairs that would be produced by the end of 12 months, Leonardo proceeds a month at a time: the first month and the second month, 1 pair, since any given pair is not productive until the second month; by the third month there are two pairs (a new pair plus the original parents) then 5, 8, 13, 21, 34, 55, 89, 144, 233, and 377. The twelfth number in the series yields the final total—377 pairs. This recursive number sequence has since been discovered in many numbered series occurring naturally, in the spirals of seed patterns in sunflower heads, in the leaf buds on a stem, on cones, on daisy florets, and in other places.

Fibonacci has also written on some important concepts in geometry that he derived from Euclidian treatises. Among these is an extension of the Pythagorean theorem to solid geometry. While the *Liber abbaci* is his most significant work, some of the other treatises deal with interesting and innovative concepts as well. The more notable of these other ideas are presented by Sarton in modern algebraic formulation.[26] Fibonacci has, for example, found three squares:

$$X_1^2, X_2^2, X_3^2$$

and a number y (*congruum*) such that:

$$X_1^2 - y = X_2^2 \text{ and } X_1^2 - y = X_3^2.$$

Yet, though Fibonacci was interested in theoretical as well as practical mathematics and in Arabic numbers, he was not the founder of a school of commercial mathematics. He was a highly original thinker but a loner; only now is he recognized as having been truly an individual creator in the history of Western mathematics.[27] Modern scholars have noted his range of choice in finding solutions to mathematical problems as well as his knowledge of sources and a profound understanding of the nature of mathematics. On occasion he shows himself to have developed a particular technique or special procedure for which he supplies no specific name but which demonstrates itself to be well suited to the particular problem at hand. In the solution of many problems he shows himself well versed in algebraic methods, which he ascertained from careful and extensive study of Arabic texts (which he read only in Latin). Algebraic methods he referred to as *regulae rectae* and for the Arabic term for the unknown, *shai'* (thing), he used the Latin equivalent, *res*. But he never made use of any operational symbol or notation such as we know in modern algebra. When several unknowns were to be used, he employed the terms *radix, res,* and *pars.* For the X^2 he used the term *quadratus;* for X^3, *cubus;* and for X^4, *census de censu.* His knowledge of Arabic mathematics seems to have been complete, and he was acquainted with all their methods and important examples.

Such, then, are the contours of medieval arithmetic. Though we have surveyed a long period, from the end of the Roman Empire to the beginning of the Renaissance, we find a relatively uniform mathematical tradition. Change came slowly and theoretical mathematics dominated the learning of the schools over practical mathematics. The text of Boethius was for many years the central document for the study of arithmetic. But many singular mathematicians began to emerge in the late Middle Ages, and they started to disentangle arithmetic from extrinsic aesthetic and religious connections and move toward a modern function of mathematics. It is to be hoped that both the philosophical as well as the innovative mathematical thinkers will be seen and evaluated in the proper cultural context.

NOTES

1. See Sir Thomas Heath, *A History of Greek Mathematics* (Oxford: Clarendon Press, 1921), I, 13-16. Nicomachus of Gerasa, *Introduction to Arithmetic,* trans. Martin Luther D'ooge, intro., Frank E. Robbins and L. C. Karpinski (New York: Macmillan, 1926), pp. 3-4. Plato, *Gorgias,* Sec. 415C; *Theatetus,* Sec. 145A, 198A.

2. On Augustine's use of number symbolism, see Vincent Foster Hooper, *Medieval Number Symbolism* (New York: Cooper Square Press, 1969), pp. 78-88.

3. For an examination of pictorial evidence of the order of the liberal arts, especially the quadrivium, see M. Masi, "Boethius and the Iconography of the Liberal Arts," *Latomus,* 33 (1974), 57-75. Examples of the *de institutione arithmetica* bound with the *De institutione musica* in the Boethian order may be seen in these manuscripts and may thus indicate the order in which they were studied: Cambridge University Library, MS Ii, III, 12, S. XI; Oxford, Balliol College, MS 386, S. X-XI; Trinity College, MS 17, S. XI; Vienna, Österreichische Nationalbibliothek, MS 55, S. X; MS 2269, S. XI. A manuscript at Prague, Universitni knihovna, MS 1717, S. IX, contains the *De institutione arithmetica, De institutione musica,* and *De geometria* in that order.

4. *De institutione arithmetica,* ed. G. Friedlein (Leipzig, 1866; reprinted, 1967). English trans. M. Masi (Amsterdam, Holland: Rodopi, 1983).

5. One may consult the following works on the penetration of number theory into philosophical thought: L. E. Dickson, *History of the Theory of Numbers* (Washington: Carnegie Institute, 1919): M. Cantor, *Mathematische Beiträge zum Kulturleben der Völker* (Halle, 1863; reprinted, Hildesheim, 1964); Francois Lassere, *The Birth of Mathematics in the Age of Plato* (Hutchinson of London, 1964); Jacob Klein, *Greek Mathematical Thought and the Origin of Algebra,* trans. Eva Brann (Cambridge: MIT Press, 1968); Pearl Kibre, "The Quadrivium in the Thirteenth Century Universities (with special reference to Paris)," *Actes du Quatrième Congrès International de Philosophie*

Médiévale: Arts Libéraux et Philosophie au Moyen Age (Montreal: J. Vrin, 1969), pp. 175-91.

6. A. C. Crombie, *Robert Grosseteste and the Origins of Experimental Science* (Oxford, 1953) and *Die Philosophischen Werke des Robert Grosseteste,* ed. Ludwig Baur (Munster, 1912).

7. See the translation of Bacon's *Opus maius* by R. B. Burke (Philadelphia: University of Pennsylvania Press, 1928), I, 242-47.

8. Burke, I, 118-20.

9. Burke, I, 124.

10. See Kibre, pp. 178-79; *St. Thomas Aquinas Philosophical Texts,* trans. Thomas Gilby (Oxford: Oxford University Press, 1951), pp. 10-11.

11. Burke I, 125-26.

12. See the article on Gerbert in the *Dictionary of Scientific Biography* (1972) by D. J. Struik; also Moritz Cantor, *Vorlesungen über Geschichte der Mathematik,* 3rd ed. I (Leipzig, 1907), 848-78.

13. Adapted from Michael S. Mahoney, "Mathematics" in David Lindberg, ed., *Science in the Middle Ages* (Chicago: University of Chicago Press, 1978), p. 151.

14. See Maximilian Curtze, ed. *Petri Philomeni de Decia in algorismum vulgarem Johannis de Sacrobosco commentarius* (Copenhagen, 1897) and Guy Beaujouan, "L'enseignement de l'arithmétique élémentaire à l'Université de Paris aux XIIIe et XIVe siècles," *Homenaje a Milles-Vallicrosa* (Barcelona, 1954), I, 93-124.

15. For a development of a mathematical aesthetic one may see various chapters in E. de Bruyne, *Etudes d'esthétique médiévale* (Bruges: De Tempal, 1946).

16. Many scholars have written on these relationships between number theory and the medieval cathedral, so these observations are hardly original with the present essay. See Otto von Simson, *The Gothic Cathedral* (Harper and Row, 1956); H. Beseler and H. Roggenkamp, *Die Michaelskirche in Hildesheim* (Berlin: G. Mann, 1956); Paul Frankl, *The Gothic: Literary Sources and Interpretations* (Princeton, N.J.: Princeton University Press, 1960).

17. See B. Haureau, *Notes et Extraits de Quelques Manuscripts Latin de la Bibliothèque Nationale* (Paris: J. Vrin, 1890), pp. 64ff.; W. Jansen, "Der Kommentar des Clarenbaldus von Arras zu Boethius *De Trinitate*," *Breslauer Studien zu historischen Theologie,* VIII (1926), 108-12; E. Gilson, *History of Christian Philosophy in the Middle Ages* (New York: Random House, 1955), pp. 139-63; 619-25.

18. J. M. Parent, *La Doctrine de la Création dans l'Ecole de Chartres* (Paris: J. Vrin, 1938), p. 90.

19. *Ibid.,* p. 93.

20. *Ibid.,* pp. 77-79.

21. See also John E. Murdoch, "Mathesis in philosophiam scholasticam introducta," *Arts Libéraux et Philosophie,* pp. 215-55. For a discussion of Boethian philosophy of number and theology, see M. Masi, "The Liberal Arts and Gerardus Ruffus' Commentary on the Boethian *De arithmetica*," *Sixteenth Century Journal,* X (1979), 23-41.

22. On the aesthetic application of the Golden Mean, see R. C. Archibald's appendix to Jay Hambidge, *Dynamic Symmetry: The Greek Vase* (New Haven: Yale University Press, 1920), pp. 152-57.

23. See von Simson, pp. 198-99; Villard's influence on cathedral design is also described in E. Panofsky, "Die Entwicklung der Proportionslehre also Abbild der Stilentwicklung," *Monschefte für Kunstwissenschaft,* 14 (1921), 188-219, reprinted in English as "The History of Human Proportions as a Reflection of the History of Styles," *Meaning in the Visual Arts* (New York: Doubleday and Company, 1955), pp. 55-107. See also H. R. Hanloser, *Villard de Honnecourt* (Vienna, 1953).

24. Cf. Edward Grant's article in the *Dictionary of Scientific Biography* (p. 175) where he shows that Jordanus's inclined plane theorem was more correct than that of Pappus of Alexandria.

25. Published by Jacques LeFèvre d'Etaples (Faber Stapulensis) in the *Epitome Boethii* (Paris, 1503). For secondary material on Jordanus, see E. A. Moody and M. Clagett, *The Medieval Science of Weights* (Madison: University of Wisconsin Press, 1952); O. Klein, "Who was Jordanus Nemorarius?" *Nuclear Physics,* 57 (1964), 345-50; Benjamin Ginsberg, "Duhem and Jordanus Nemorarius," *Isis,* 25 (1936), 341-62.

26. George Sarton, *Introduction to the History of Science* (Baltimore, Md., 1927), I, 612.

27. An extensive and fascinating scholarly literature has been devoted to the works of Fibonacci that demonstrates his inventiveness and extraordinary mathematical abilities. See, for example, the article "Fibonacci" by Kurt Vogel in *Dictionary of Scientific Biography,* VII (1971), pp. 604-13. The original extant works of Fibonacci are five: The *Liber abbaci* (1220, revised 1221); the *Practica geometriae* (1220/1221); *Flos* (1225). Important or useful secondary sources include: A. Agostini, "L'use delle lettere nel Liber Abaci di Leonardi Fibonacci," *Bollettino dell'Unione matematica italiana,* 3rd ser., 4 (1949), 282-87; K. Vogel, "Zur Geschichte der linearen Gleichungen mit mehreren Unbekannten," *Deutsche Mathematik,* 5 (1940), 217-40; F. Woepke, "Sur un essai de déterminer la nature de la racine d'une équation du troisième degré contenue dans un ouvrage de Léonard de Pise," *Journal de mathématiques pures et appliqués,* 19 (1954), 401-06; R. B. McClenon, "Leonardo of Pisa and His 'Liber Quadratorum,'" *American Mathematical Monthly,* 26 (1919), 1-8; E. Bortolotti, "Le Fonti arabe di Leonardo Pisano," *Memorie R. Accademia delle scienze dell'Istituto di Bologna,* fis. mat. cl. 7th ser., 8 (1929-30), 1-30; M. Dunton and R. E. Grimm, "Fibonacci on Egyptian Fractions," *Fibonacci Quarterly,* 4 (1966), 339-54. A popular but useful work on Fibonacci is Joseph Gies, *Leonard of Pisa and the New Mathematics of the Middle Ages* (New York: Crowell, 1969).

SELECT BIBLIOGRAPHY ON ARITHMETIC

Dickson, L. E. *History of the Theory of Numbers* (Washington: Carnegie Institute, 1919).

Gies, Joseph. *Leonard of Pisa and the New Mathematics of the Middle Ages* (New York: Crowell, 1969).

Gilson, E. *History of Christian Philosophy in the Middle Ages* (New York: Random House, 1955).

Heath, Thomas. *A History of Greek Mathematics* (Oxford: Clarendon Press, 1921).

Hooper, Vincent Foster. *Medieval Number Symbolism* (New York: Cooper Square Press, 1969).

Lassere, Francois. *The Birth of Mathematics in the Age of Plato* (Hutchinson of London, 1964).

Mahoney, Michael S. "Mathematics," *Science in the Middle Ages,* ed. David Lindberg (Chicago: University of Chicago Press, 1978).

Nicomachus of Gerasa. *Introduction to Arithmetic,* trans. Martin Luther D'ooge, intro., Frank E. Robbins and L. C. Karbinski (New York: Macmillan, 1926).

Sarton, George. *Introduction to the History of Science* (Baltimore, Md.: 1927).

Von Simson, Otto. *The Gothic Cathedral* (New York: Harper and Row, 1956).

7 *Music*

Theodore C. Karp

Music formed an essential part of early Greek education and was believed to play an important part in the formation of character. Although musical performance virtually disappeared from the curriculum in the fourth century B.C., *the tie between music and ethos was never forgotten. The Latin encyclopedists generally began their discussions of music by drawing attention to its power and its ability to soothe the spirit. Boethius's discussion of heavenly music, of paramount importance for medieval musical theory, as the following essay makes clear, seems to grow out of this concern with ethos.*

The approach in the liberal arts tradition, however, was primarily methematical. Music, like the other arts, was viewed as a complete system. Martianus Capella's analysis of music was extremely complex; yet his discussion—and this was generally true of the encyclopedists—was essentially restricted to harmonics and rhythm. Both harmonics and rhythm can be viewed as technai, and both were explained in terms of Pythagorean arithmetic.

Martianus Capella divided harmonics into seven parts. The first part discussed tones (soni), the principles of the art, which were (as Martianus noted) comparable to the point in geometry and the unit in arithmetic. The second part discussed the intervals of sound between a higher-pitched and a lower-pitched tone. Like the proposition in logic and ratio in arithmetic, interval expressed the relation between two of the basic elements of the art. Boethius defined music in terms of a multitude that refers to some other thing and exists only in relation to that thing. Thus the intervals between two tones would seem to be the essence of music.

The third and fourth parts of Martianus's harmonics discussed those series of notes that span the octave and the fourth. The third part analyzed octave systems, or modes. The "perfect system" of modes—achieved by varying the position of half-tones within the eight tones that make up an octave—represents a striking illustration of the Greek desire for complete and systematic analysis. Prior to the adoption of the octave as the basic interval (probably by the time of the early Pythagoreans), the tetrachord—a group of four tones in the span of a fourth—had served as the basic unit. The fourth part of the discussion of harmonics established the genera of tetrachords. The fifth part (tonoi), the sixth part (melodic modulation), and the seventh part (melodic composition) completed this analysis. These final sections examined the relationships between octave systems, tetrachords, and pentachords (five tones spanning a fifth).

Martianus adopted a similar pattern in his treatment of rhythm. Beginning with its principle, tempus *(the basic unit of time), he rather arbitrarily divided the discussion of rhythm into seven sections, for symmetry with his analysis of harmonics. D. L. W.*

The liberal arts, which provided the cornerstone for education during antiquity and the Middle Ages, are characterized by a certain approach to discovering the realities of the world. While recognizing the usefulness and pleasurability of the senses, men of antiquity and the Middle Ages deemed the senses far too prey to illusion to provide a reliable key to reality. The secure path to reality was sought instead through the abstract processes of the mind. This outlook changed gradually during the Renaissance. Modern man, while recognizing the fallibility of the senses, depends heavily upon them and upon the processes of observation. The senses are the keys to discovery and verification. This contrast in outlook has parallels in changed views regarding the nature of the various disciplines forming the liberal arts, and nowhere is the contrast sharper than in the realm of music. The connotations that the word *musica* held for medieval men differ markedly from modern connotations of the word, music. I shall first try to clarify the meaning that *musica* had in earlier times and then try to show that the resulting outlook affected the creation and perception of what modern man calls music.

MUSIC AS A LIBERAL ART IN ANTIQUITY

Obviously, the most immediate appeal of music is to the senses. The power of certain kinds of music to stir and to calm the passions was well known to the Greeks and was often illustrated both by supposedly historical anecdotes and myths. It was the ethical power of music to strengthen or weaken character that led Plato to treat music with such prominence and seriousness when considering the proper education for citizens of his ideal state. But when the philosophers sought to probe beyond the sensual appeal of music in an attempt to grasp its fundamental principles, they were led to consider the measurable aspects of music, especially its acoustic foundations. At this point they were not concerned with problems of musical creativity or of musical perform-ance. Nor were they occupied primarily with the effect of music on the listener. They wished rather to investigate what they felt to be the essence of music, to discover the physical laws underlying designs in sound.

This trend was reinforced by changes of musical style. By the fourth century B.C., the austere and stylized music that had held the interest of the educated aristocracy gave way to an art concerned with pleasing the crowd. Though performers were well paid, they occupied a lower social stratum than grammarians and rhetoricians, and the intelligentsia with-drew increasingly to a contemplation of inaudible abstrations. In late antiquity the educated felt that Plato could not have admired a music such as was familiar to them and thus assumed that his primary con-cern was with a harmonic science equivalent to that of astronomy. "Unheard music is better than heard," according to a late proverb.

TRANSMISSION OF GREEK THOUGHT TO THE EARLY MIDDLE AGES

Abstract speculation plays a major role in early medieval writing on music. In his *De institutione musica*, Boethius states:

> Anyone seeing a triangle or a square easily recognizes what he sees, but to know the nature of a square or triangle he must inquire of a mathematician.
>
> The same may be said of other matters of sense, especially of the judg-ment of the ear, whose power so apprehends sounds that it not only judges them and knows their differences, but is often delighted when the modes are sweet and well-ordered, and pained when disordered and incoherent ones offend the sense.
>
> From this it follows that, of the four mathematical disciplines, the others are concerned with the pursuit of truth, but music is related not only to speculation but to morality as well. Nothing is more characteristic of human nature than to be soothed by sweet modes and stirred up by their opposites. . . . From this may be discerned the truth of what Plato not idly said, that the soul of the universe is united by musical concord. For when, by means of what in ourselves is well and fitly ordered, we apprehend what in sounds is well and fitly combined, and take pleasure in it, we recognize that we ourselves are united by this likeness.[1]

Three points of importance emerge from this passage: 1) Boethius seems to take actual music as his ultimate point of departure; 2) he considers mere sense perception to be of a much lower order than theoretical understanding; and, 3) he finds that the order and rationale observable in music affords a mirror to the similar order and rationale of the entire universe.

Mathematical Aspects of Musical Tunings

Boethius's musical "mathematicians" sought particularly to understand why it was that certain tones sounded high and others low and what relationships existed among tones of different pitch. In practice, the physical relationship between tones was normally investigated by means of a monochord, an instrument consisting of a single string that was stretched over a long, resonating chamber. The instrument was provided with a movable bridge, a thin, upright wedge that the string would be made to touch. When shifted about, the bridge would either lengthen or shorten the vibrating segment of the string. The length of vibrating string required to produce one sound was measured and then compared to the length required to produce another. Various sets of mathematical ratios resulted. The discipline itself is supposed to have originated with Pythagoras. The Greeks quickly found that the octave —the sound normally occurring when men and boys sing the same melody, and represented nowadays by notes having the same letter name— was produced by a length ratio of 2:1, the lower sound requiring twice the length of the upper. Similarly, the fifth—the interval produced by the first main pitches of *Twinkle, twinkle little star*—is equivalent to a ratio of 3:2, while the fourth—the interval that opens *Reveille* and *La Marseillaise*—is equivalent to a ratio of 4:3. These intervals, which seem to have special significance in terms of human physiology, are thus representable using the numbers 1, 2, 3, and 4, the set constituting a tetractys having mystical significance for various Pythagoreans.

Naturally it was necessary to investigate the relationships of sounds that were closer together in the pitch spectrum. Theorists wished to ascertain the relationships existing between the various tones of different scales. (A scale represents an abstract of the main tones of a melody arranged from low to high, from high to low, or in both forms.) Or, since it was the mind rather than the sense of hearing that often was the ultimate arbiter in these matters, they sought to establish the relationships that ought to exist in a properly constructed scale. More than one way was known to establish such relationships and each method produced slightly different results. In each the arithmetical complexity rose rapidly from the very elementary levels mentioned in connection with the octave, fifth, and fourth.

To illustrate this increase in complexity, we may consider the tuning known as Pythagorean. In this tuning, the basic tones are derived by following a cycle of fifths (3/2) and reducing the results to the space of an octave. If, for example, we begin with the tone c and assign it the relative value of 1, then the tone f (a fifth below) will have the value of 2/3. The f an octave higher (a fourth above c) will thus have the value of 4/3 (2/3 × 2/1, the ratio of the octave). The tone g (a fifth above c) will have the value of 3/2, while d' (a fifth above g) will be 3/2 × 3/2. In order to bring this d' down an octave so that it will be close to the original c, we must divide the product, 9/4, by 2, thus arriving at the ratio 9/8. When we take the cycle one step further, we find that the tone a (a fifth above d, and thus 3/2 × 9/8) has the value of 27/16. Continuing in this fashion, we obtain a set of results that may be expressed as follows:

c	d	e	f	g	a	b	c'
1	9/8	81/64	4/3	3/2	27/16	243/128	2

Additional calculations are necessary if one wishes to know also how each of these tones relates to the neighboring tones. If, for example, the relationship between c-d is expressed by the ratio, 9/8, and the relationship between c-e is expressed by the ratio, 81/64, then the relationship between d-e is calculated by multiplying the larger number by the inversion of the smaller. Thus, 81/64 × 8/9 = 9/8, demonstrating that the relationship between d-e is the same as that between c-d. Indeed, the intervals, c-d, d-e, f-g, g-a, and a-b, are all whole tones and in this tuning system all have the ratio, 9/8. The intervals, e-f and b-c', on the other hand, are semitones, and, in this tuning system, have the ratio, 256/243.

In order to establish the relationships between whole tones and semitones within the Pythagorean system, still more complex calculations are required. When "subtracting" the latter from the former, we produce not another equal semitone, but one that is slightly larger. To be precise, 9/8 × 243/256 (the inversion of the semitone ratio) yields 2187/2048. This larger interval was known as the *semitonium majus* (or *apotome*) while the smaller one was known as the *semitonium minus* (*diesis* or *limma*). If, as a last step, we wish to establish the difference between these two interval sizes, we must multiply 2187/2048 by 243/256, and we shall obtain the result, 531441/524288, an interval known as the Pythagorean comma. Had we continued with our original cycle of fifths until we had assembled a set of 12 tones, we should have come to the tone, b sharp, which is very nearly equivalent to c', but which is distinguishable from c' by the very ratio of the Pythagorean comma. The difficulty inherent in each of the "natural" tuning systems lies in the fact that none produces a perfectly symmetrical, balanced, closed system; each has its own internal quirk.

Acoustic Calculations as an Abstract Discipline

Whether or not this acoustic discipline originated in a desire to investigate the art of music, it soon led the Greeks beyond that art to an abstract consideration of proportion in sounds. The ear's acuity in discerning the smallest possible differences in pitch was tested, and it apparently made little difference to the speculatively inclined whether or not the pitch ratios under consideration formed part of an artistic fabric. The fascination that the investigation of interval ratios held for such persons is mirrored in the common medieval definition that "music has to do with number as related to sounds." And it is in this way that Boethius is able to refer to music as one of the four "mathematical disciplines."

Various philosophers perceived different sets of relationships among these disciplines and placed them in different order depending upon the characteristic of each that was deemed most important.[2] One of the common orderings is expressed clearly by Cassiodorus, a near contemporary of Boethius, who writes that:

> Mathematical science is that science which considers abstract quantity. By abstract quantity we mean that quantity which we treat in a purely speculative way, separating it from its material and from its other accidents, such as evenness, oddness, and the like. It has these divisions: arithmetic, music, geometry, astronomy. Arithmetic is the discipline of absolute numerable quantity. Music is the discipline which treats of numbers in their relation to those things which are found in sounds. Geometry is the discipline of immobile magnitude and of forms. Astronomy is the discipline of the course of the heavenly bodies.[3]

Such was the place of music in the quadrivium.

It was only natural that within such a framework there was little concern for either spontaneous creativity or sensual receptivity. Persons such as St. Augustine declared that, after all, even a singing bird is musically creative. That which separates man, and more specifically the wise and educated man, from the lower animals is the power of reason. And to the extent that the medieval philosophers cultivated an aesthetic of music and articulated value judgments concerning musical beauty, they felt that such beauty was directly attributable to proportion and number. Taking their departure from a biblical passage in the *Wisdom of Solomon* that reads, "Thou hast ordered all things in measure and number and weight,"[4] philosophers from St. Augustine to John Scotus Erigena, Thierry of Chartres, Bernard of Clairvaux, and St. Thomas Aquinas concluded that a knowledge of proportion and number was essential to an understanding of God's universe and of the arts, and they incorporated such views into their theological and cosmological constructions.[5] Music had a place of honor within such systems because, by means of analogies, it could help demonstrate connecting links between things sensed, reason and speculation, and ultimately the divine.

Such modes of thinking are also to be found in the initial quotation drawn from Boethius. In that passage Boethius draws a parallel between musical concords or ratios and other concords, basing his remarks on Plato. To make his words concrete, we might say that if the vibration ratio of 2:1 produces an octave and the ratio of 3:2 a fifth, then objects exhibiting either of these ratios are in a sense musical. An echo of this concept survives even today when we say that we find certain proportions "harmonious." The philosophers of antiquity and the Middle Ages were not interested in music and music making as an isolated and idle pastime, but in music's role as part of an integrated and divinely ordered universe. The fact that analogies could be drawn in terms of numbers and proportions inherent in various aspects of human experience and existence was demonstration to them of this basic interrelatedness.

It is this kind of analogical expansion that determines the constitution of the Boethian musical universe. This is comprised of three parts: *musica mundana* (the harmony of the world), *musica humana* (the harmony of the body), and *musica instrumentalis*. The first of these comprised such matters as the movement of the heavenly bodies, the ordering and interrelationship between the elements, and the changing of the seasons. Many medieval philosophers indeed felt that the planets in their orbits emitted specific sounds, and several devoted efforts to deducing the actual sounds thus produced, that is, the music of the spheres. The fact that no such sounds are perceived by man was explained in terms of the imperfection of the senses and human insensitivity to any property that is constantly present. *Musica humana* is concerned with the binding together of body and soul as in a simultaneously sounding interval comprised of two sounds; it takes into consideration such other matters as bodily proportions, humors, the proportions of various virtues and strengths, etc. *Musica instrumentalis* originally referred to instrumental music and was perhaps intended to refer especially to those instruments—the monochord in particular—that were used for the measurement of interval ratios. However, no medieval division of *musica* could ignore the importance of ecclesiastical chant and endure, so that the concept of *musica instrumentalis* was soon widened to include all of sounding music, both vocal and instrumental.

Although the Boethian view of the constitution of music is echoed and re-echoed by later writers for centuries, it is by no means the only classification of music employed during the Middle Ages.[6] For example,

Regino of Prüm (active about the turn of the tenth century), proposes a division of music into two categories: natural and artificial. The composition of each of these categories is somewhat vague owing to the brevity of the earliest known version of his treatise. A late amplification provides clarification:

> Natural music is that which is made by no instruments nor by the touch of fingers, nor by any touch or instigation of man: it is modulated by nature alone under divine inspiration teaching the sweet modes, such as there is in the motion of the sky or in the human voice.[7]

In the minds of the philosophers, unheard "sounds" are sweeter than those that are heard. In the mystical writings of the pseudo-Dionysius, Dionysius the Areopagite, whose philosophies entered into the concepts underlying the construction of the Gothic cathedral, the material world is a reflection of divine harmony and beauty. There is a chain of being that comprises a celestial hierarchy and an ecclesiastical hierarchy, and the musician plays the essential role of receiving the hymns sung in heaven and transmitting these, making them audible to mortal man.

There are, to be sure, more practical views of music, such as those propounded by the Parisian theorist, Johannes de Grocheo (active ca.1300). He declares that contrary to the beliefs of earlier writers, including Boethius and the mid-thirteenth century theorist, Johannes de Garlandia, the heavenly bodies make no sound in their orbits. He asks somewhat scornfully whether anyone has ever heard a human constitution sounding. Grocheo proposes instead a division of music into three categories: ecclesiastical (Gregorian chant), measurable (polyphonic), and civil or vulgar (vernacular).[8] But the philosophical viewpoint exercised such a powerful influence on even the more practically inclined theorists that Grocheo's opinions seem to represent a minority viewpoint among even late writers dealing with the subject.

The prevalent philosophical view of the musical universe had natural consequences relating to the concept of the musician. In a slightly later passage Boethius declares:

> There are three classes concerned with the musical art. One class has to do with instruments, another invents songs, a third judges the work of instruments and the song. But that class which is dedicated to instruments and consumes there its entire efforts, as for example the players of the cithara and those who show their skill on the organ and other musical instruments, are separated from the intellect of musical science, since they are servants, as has been said, nor do they bear anything of reason, being destitute of speculation. The second class having to do with music is that of the poets, which is borne to song not so much by speculation and reason as by a certain natural instinct. Thus this class

is also to be separated from music. The third is that which assumes the skill of judging, so that it weighs rhythms and melodies and the whole of song. And seeing that the whole is founded in reason and speculation, this class is rightly reckoned as musical, and that man as a musician who possesses the faculty of judging, according to speculation or reason, appropriate and suitable to music, of modes and rhythms and of the classes of melodies and their mixtures. . . .[9]

Thus, according to the philosophers, it was not essential to be able either to play, sing, or compose in order to qualify as a musician! They fostered a division between the senses and the mind, and precedence was given to the mind. It is this precedence that permitted the Boethian concepts of *musica mundana* and *musica humana*.

Obviously the concepts and values described up to this point are those of a limited group. And it may be noted that many of the more prominent of the medieval speculative writers dealing with music were not primarily what we would call musicians but were concerned more with either statecraft, theology, or philosophy. This situation is by no means unique to the time but has various parallels of more recent date. For example, several important writers and philosophers of the nineteenth century, including Nietzsche, had decided views on music; even though these men were not necessarily musically sophisticated, their opinions helped shape the general trends of the time. And although the views of music within the liberal arts did not consistently govern musical creativity during the Middle Ages, it would have been difficult for the more learned composers to escape entirely the influence of such modes of thinking. In general, the individual disciplines were not as isolated as their modern counterparts tend to be. Many of the figures mentioned elsewhere in this book in connection with other liberal arts—Martianus Capella, Boethius, Cassiodorus, St. Augustine, Isidore of Seville, Alcuin, Rabanus Maurus, Remigius of Auxerre, Notker Labeo, Hermannus Contractus, Johannes de Garlandia,[10] Alain de Lille, and Johannes de Muris—provide important information concerning music and attitudes toward music of their times. (Hermannus Contractus has been credited with the composition of two of the lovely Marian antiphons, *Alma Redemptoris Mater,* and *Salve Regina,* both of great importance for their use in later music.)

Naturally, the more practically minded theorists display a different range of concerns in dealing with music. One of the most famous of these, Guido d'Arezzo (ca.990-1050) , remarks in his *Epistola de ignotu cantu* that he has departed from Boethius in certain respects since the latter's treatise "is useful to philosophers, but not to singers."[11] Furthermore, it is difficult to appreciate fully the dynamic that existed between sounding music and music theory in the early Middle Ages since the first sizable collection of music to survive dates only from the turn of the tenth century. Even then we do not obtain a balanced view of music inasmuch as the skills of writing and of musical notation were mastered only by those with access (whether direct or indirect) to church education. It is entirely understandable that the monks of the early Middle Ages had little interest in preserving or discussing the secular music of their time. Indeed, our first major manuscripts devoted to secular music date only from the middle of the thirteenth century, and the only theoretical treatment of such music that is known to survive is that of Johannes de Grocheo. Opinions concerning the relative richness of the secular musical culture before 1100 are based primarily on tantalizingly vague references in literary works and thus vary considerably among different scholars.

SELECTED ASPECTS OF MEDIEVAL MUSIC AND MUSIC THEORY

The major musical interests of the early Middle Ages revolved about the creation, organization, and preservation of music for the various rites of the Church, especially the Mass and the Office. The former, instituted by Christ on the occasion of the Last Supper, has as its climax the Eucharist, the thanksgiving for the sacrifice of Christ recalled through the transformation of consecrated bread and wine into the flesh and blood of the Savior. The opening portion of the Mass (the fore-Mass) centers about readings from Scripture. The Office, primarily a monastic rite, derives from the Jewish Prayer Hours and is concerned especially with the chanting of psalms. While the basic ground plan of each rite submits mainly to surface changes on a seasonal basis, many of the constituent parts change texts and music from day to day. Thus there is a very rich repertory of music consisting of unaccompanied melody that grew up over a period of centuries.

During the first millennium of Christianity, the variable texts underlying the main musical portions of the Mass were taken chiefly from the Book of Psalms. These could be performed by the same person or group of persons throughout. But the textual structure of the psalms also encouraged both responsorial performance—in which passages for a leader alternate with choral responses—and antiphonal performance—in which the two segments of each verse are divided between two halves of a chorus. Congregational participation was apparently important during the first centuries but gradually gave way to performance by trained choirs and gifted soloists.

Many details concerning the celebration of Mass were at first a matter of local custom rather than of uniform legislation, and there grew up in the West several related families of rite. Gradually, however, there arose a desire for uniformity of practice, which assumed great importance during the Carolingian period, fanned particularly by the political goals of Charlemagne. Other rites were either suppressed or restricted to specific locales.

Gregorian Chant

The music for the rite that was propagated throughout Europe is known as Gregorian chant—in honor of Pope Gregory I, who was thought by the Carolingians to have received the chant from the Holy Spirit, which appeared to him in the form of a dove. Although Gregory's role in the composition or codification of chant was accepted for the most part until the mid-twentieth century, it is now thought that the form of the chant known in the High Middle Ages took shape during the eighth century, and that it was heavily influenced by Frankish contributions.[12]

During the High Middle Ages (i.e., from the eleventh century on), the normal structure of the Mass was as follows. (The items in italics are those that were sung, the remainder being recited or spoken; the items prefaced by an asterisk have a fixed text, the others having texts that vary according to the specific feast being celebrated.)

> *Introit*
> *Kyrie
> *Gloria
> Collect
> Epistle
> *Gradual*
> *Alleluia* or *Tract*
> Gospel
> *Credo
> *Offertory*
> Secret
> Preface
> *Sanctus
> Canon
> *Agnus Dei
> *Communion*
> Post-Communion
> *Ite missa est* or *Benedicamus Domino*

It is quite possible that the main impulse toward the development of European musical notation was provided by the efforts toward the standardization of the chant melodies. Surviving evidence suggests that earlier singers permitted themselves a certain degree of freedom in the performance of chant while remaining within the bounds of an accepted formulaic framework. Oral transmission of chant was eminently practical under such conditions. But when relatively fixed norms were sought, means for establishing such norms and transmitting them from one place to another and from one generation to another were urgently needed. Although musical notation had existed previously—notably in Greece—earlier notation was known to few and the theorists and musicians of the Middle Ages began essentially afresh. This was no easy process and several different methods were attempted. And while the general principles of the method eventually adopted were observed throughout Western Europe, there were sharp graphic differences between the chant notations of various areas. Inasmuch as many chants were basically of formulaic construction and inasmuch as numerous chants often had more than one tone per syllable, the notation that was developed served mainly to indicate the shape of small note groups rather than the precise height of individual pitches. Thus our earliest surviving sources can be read only by comparison with later readings of the same or similar material. The notation was primarily of benefit to those already familiar with the melodies and the basic principles on which they were built.

Solmization

In the end this limited degree of notational fixity was not deemed sufficient. It is not surprising that questions of notation assume a prominent place in many theoretical discussions of music throughout the Middle Ages. Means had to be developed for fixing the relative pitches of melodies and for indicating rhythm. Nomenclature had to be developed. The present system of using the alphabet letters a-g to indicate the white keys of the modern piano was not the only one to be tried out during the ninth and tenth centuries. Means for reading music without the use of prior example or the monochord had to be found. To meet this need Guido d'Arezzo employed as a model *Ut queant laxis,* a hymn to St. John the Baptist in which each of the first six phrases began a step higher than the previous one. He abstracted the text syllables beginning these, obtaining the succession: *ut, re* (sonare), *mi* (ra), *fa* (muli), *sol* (ve), *la* (bii). The syllables are not sufficient to cover all of the tones within an octave, but by employing the hexachordal pattern successively on G, c, f, g, c′, f′, and g′, an interlocking system was formed that would account for the entire pitch spectrum necessary for the performance of chant. These solmization syllables remain the basis for traditional instruction in sight-singing to this day, although the guttural syllable, *ut,* is frequently replaced by the more open sound, *do,* and a seventh syllable has been added to complete the octave. The singers were aided in their memorization of the relative height of the various tones denoted by the syllables by associating these with various points on the palm and at finger joints of the open hand. Just as medieval man conceived of the universe as a closed and finite system, so did he conceive of a closed and finite musical pitch system.[13] Even though tones not accounted for by the Guidonian system were employed outside the realm of chant during the High and late Middle Ages, these were not accorded official theoretical recognition but were treated as *musica falsa* or *musica ficta.* This situation continues to be reflected in the fact that we have a complex system of sharps and flats, double-sharps and double-flats in order to refer to the customary twelve pitches of the octave by means of seven rather than twelve alphabet letters.

Intervals and Modes

Another subject of interest for the medieval theorist was the classification of intervals. As might be expected from previous discussion, this was first done in terms of ratios, and the ratios were frequently classified in the manner indicated in the chapter dealing with arithmetic. In addition, there was a need to declare which intervals were stylistically suitable for compositional use and which were not. Such questions became increasingly important with the rise of polyphony, and thus will be touched upon later.

A much broader problem that faced musical theorists of the Middle Ages concerned the classification of chants according to their basic substructures. Several chants, among them the Introit (the introductory chant of the Mass itself) and the Communion, were comprised of different sections, the first having an individual melody and a text chosen for the specific feast being celebrated. The other sections had for text either a psalm verse or the Lesser Doxology (Glory to the Father, the Son, and the Holy Spirit . . .) and were chanted to one of a group of common recitation formulae. The section with a freely composed melody was known as an antiphon, and the recitation formula, known as a psalm tone, was selected so as to accord as well as possible with the characteristics of the antiphon that were deemed most important. Not only does Gregorian chant employ greater tonal variety and subtlety than most music of the standard concert repertoire (cast either in the major or the minor mode), but the theorists wished also to take into account in their classification the interrelationship between the range of a chant and the tone on which it ends. Thus they established a set of eight church modes, the number quite probably being patterned after a similar Byzantine set (the *octoechos*) and originally having symbolic significance. The system of church modes furnished a reasonably adequate and practical classification for the majority of chants in existence by the ninth century, as well as a general guide for the composition of melodies that were later created in accordance with earlier practices. It did not, however, apply to the optional adjuncts to chant, such as tropes and sequences. Nor was the modal classification intended to apply to secular melodies with vernacular texts or to early polyphony. (Later theorists did, however, widen the framework of modal classification, and this vocabulary did provide the only terminology available for tonal analysis that was known until the late Renaissance.)

MEDIEVAL MUSIC AS VIEWED FROM THE PERSPECTIVE OF THE LIBERAL ARTS

While it is hazardous to claim that the views of *musica* fostered by the liberal arts were a decisive influence on the creative processes that produced the various medieval repertories of unaccompanied melody, it is important to acknowledge the effect that such views had on the explanation of this music. When, for example, an early eleventh-century theorist sought to establish the number of sounds that ought to be employed in a properly constructed melody, he did not write of a need for variety, or of the development of a musical line, or yet of a sense of general shape or climax. Instead, he justified a melody of eight pitches on the basis that the diapason (the octave) includes eight pitches and that he understood the citharas of the Greeks to have had eight strings. The justification for a melody of nine pitches arises from the conjoining of two fifths, while the support for a melody of ten pitches may be based on "the authority of David's psaltery, or because the triple diatessaron [fourth] is found at the tenth pitch."[14]

Early Polyphony

However important was the role of chant throughout the early and High Middle Ages, the distinctive feature of European music in general for the past nine centuries has been its increasing concentration on textures that involve a variety of simultaneously sounding tones. In order to achieve remarkable beauties in this manner, we have had to sacrifice in part the melodic subtleties achieved in much Near Eastern music and the rhythmic subtleties achieved in much African and Indian music. The roots of European polyphony cannot be ascertained with security. Our earliest records—dating from the end of the ninth century—already treat of polyphony as a going concern. Two kinds are described from the beginning. In one type, one or more added voices parallel a line of chant at the interval of a fourth, fifth, or octave. In the other, two voices begin at the unison. The newly added voice remains stationary while the voice consisting of a chant moves until the interval of a fourth is reached. Parallel motion then is employed through the body of the phrase until there is a cadence on the unison at the close. This early polyphony is known as organum, and this term is used for polyphony in diverse styles from the ninth to thirteenth centuries, the common factor being the use of chant for the founding voice.

In the tenth and eleventh centuries, the original emphasis on parallel motion gradually gave way to an increasing use of contrary motion between the chant-bearing voice and the newly created voice. And by the early twelfth century, the earlier one-to-one relationship between the numbers of tones in the two voices was being replaced by textures in which the newly created voice was more active than the one based on chant.

Throughout this period, and indeed throughout the Middle Ages, the points of stability and rest are achieved when the voices are at the interval of either the unison, octave, fifth, or fourth. In other words, the main underpinnings of the polyphony—the consonances—consist of pairs of tones related to one another in the proportions of 1:1, 2:1, 3:2, and 4:3. These intervals are of primary importance even in passages with a strong forward-moving thrust. It is difficult to determine the role exercised by mathematical speculation in the selection of these intervals as the main harmonic bases for this music. Probably this role was slight. However, the intervals that best satisfied the composers' artistic needs fit perfectly within the framework of abstractions provided by the philosophers. Undoubtedly this agreement was regarded as corroboration both of the soundness of the composers' artistic preferences and of the correctness of the philosophers' reasoning. The classification of consonances and the enlargement of this category of interval with the admission of the third and later the sixth was another of the major theoretical interests of later medieval theorists.

Parisian Polyphony of the Late Twelfth and Thirteenth Centuries

While there are huge gaps in our knowledge of the development of polyphony before 1150, we begin to have more satisfactory information from this time onward. It appears that France became the leader in this art, and that polyphony was practiced at a few major cathedrals by the late twelfth century. It was at this time that the first polyphonic repertory of major international importance arose, a repertory that was created at Notre Dame and certain neighboring churches in Paris and later was known as far away as Spain, Germany, and Scotland. Thanks to an anonymous treatise by an Englishman active about 1275, we know that there was a Master Leonin who created a great cycle of organa for two voices for the major feasts of the church year.[15] His successor, Perotin, was cited for a variety of contributions: 1) he created an independent repertoire of organa for three and four voices, employing the same liturgical bases as did Leonin; 2) he revised the work of Leonin, bringing it into greater conformity with newer styles; and 3) he wrote compositions known as conductus that adorned the liturgy without being a part of it.[16] A reference by Eudes de Sully to the performance of four-part organa on New Year's Day and St. Stephen's Day in 1198 and 1199 permits us to deduce that Perotin was probably at the peak of his career during the decade 1190-1200. We conclude, therefore, that Leonin was active a generation earlier, circa 1160-70, possibly even before the founding of Notre Dame in 1163. Tentative identification of the two great polyphonists has been made but not universally accepted.

The organa are settings of graduals, alleluias, and responsories. The first two groups comprise the most impressive chants for Mass and occur between readings from Scripture. The last group comprises equally impressive chants for the Office. All have long, flowing lines and alternate solo and choral portions. Only the solo portions are used as the substructure for the polyphony, while the choral portions continue to be sung as unaccompanied melody by the choir. The overall architecture of the settings thus consists of sections of polyphony alternating with sections of monophony.

Within the polyphony one finds two different styles of writing. In one, irregular arabesques in the newly composed voice weave above and below isolated notes of the chant, which are greatly prolonged and which change only at irregular intervals. This style is normally termed *organum purum*. In the other, the melody and rhythm of the newly composed voice are more tightly controlled and are set against notes of the chant that move at a deliberate pace, either steadily or in some simple rhythmic pattern. This style, known as discant, occurs frequently when there are many notes in the chant that are sung to a single syllable. A section of music in this style, or a similarly constructed brief composition, with all voices moving in measured rhythms, is known as a clausula. Several hundreds of these survive, both embedded in organa and in separate sections of various major manuscripts.

In the sections of *organum purum,* we find passages of flexible rhythm in the newly created voice. These we cannot interpret with security, although we hope to achieve an increasing degree of historical validity in our transcriptions. Side by side with these passages are others of more regular construction, and the passages in discant style are also fairly regular in construction. The balance between the flexible passages and those that were more regularly constituted tipped increasingly in favor of the latter. In fact, the organa were revised on different occasions by removing passages in *organum purum* style and replacing them with passages in discant style.[17]

After this drive toward stricter constructive principles in musical composition had reached a sufficient level, early thirteenth-century theorists began to create systems for the description and governance of rhythmic patterns. They turned naturally to the traditional vocabulary provided by metrics and envisaged a series of musical patterns which in their pure forms were either identical or roughly analogous to some of the most basic poetic meters: the trochee, iamb, dactyl, anapest, spondee, and tribrach. Some of their problems in terminology are relevant to present concerns.

Metrics provided musical theorists with a vocabulary for two time values, a long and a short. The former occupied two time segments to one for the latter. (I am avoiding the use of the word "beat," inasmuch as these time segments were apparently brief enough that three would fit within the space of time that would now be perceived as a beat.) But the composers used still other time values in their music. These were initially termed *ultra mensuram,* beyond measure. Notice, however, that note durations of three time segments or one-half time segment are not actually beyond the sense's power to measure. They are beyond measure only from the standpoint that they exceed the capacity of the earliest vocabulary and the system founded thereon. Such values were soon incorporated within the slightly enlarged system. The note duration occupying three time segments was also termed a "long." The number three quite naturally suggested the Trinity to the medieval theorists, and the Trinity was obviously to be equated with perfection, so that this note value was called a perfect long. As a result, the value occupying only two time segments was called an imperfect long. There was also a minority opinion that dissented from the trend by questioning whether any note value or note shape could be more perfect or less perfect than any other. While this form of speculation derived from already created music, it fed back into creative channels to the extent that until the late thirteenth century the only rhythms that we are able to document depend upon patterns that subdivide the basic time unit into threes.

The patterns encompassing groups of time units are of even greater interest for it is such patterns that furnish the strongest examples of the interpenetration of speculative thinking and artistic creativity during the High and late Middle Ages. Had these been governed by speculative processes from the beginning, one would expect to find a predominance of patterns encompassing three time units, particularly in music for religious services seeking to establish paths between mankind and God. Although such patterns may be found upon occasion, they are rare. Most patterns are built up in groups of twos. In the following brief excerpt from Perotin's *Viderunt omnes,* one can see how the composer is working in modules of four. Small ideas having four beats each are repeated in the same voice either unchanged or in slight variation, or they are handed back and forth from one voice to another. It is not necessary to know musical notation in order to verify this statement since it is possible merely to compare the visual patterns formed by the notation in order to ascertain the regularity. However, for the sake of greater clarity, the various ideas are labeled with letters and primes are added to indicate variations.

Passages such as these reflect especially the growing desire for balance and symmetry, which are artistic values and not merely servants of number speculation. The balance and symmetry are clearly perceivable by the senses. But interest in rhythmic formulae increased steadily and gradually took on compositional values that appealed more and more to the mind and that were less readily perceptible by the senses.

In discant sections one of the most commonly used rhythmic patterns in the tenor—the chant-bearing voice—is comprised of two balancing halves. One half consists of three tones of one beat each, followed by a beat of silence. The other consists of a tone lasting two beats, a tone of one beat, and one beat of silence. Either half may be used to begin the rhythmic progression. Since a pattern such as this rapidly uses up the melodic material of the borrowed chant, the composers resorted to repetition of the chant fragment in order to achieve the length desired for the section or composition. Each statement of the pattern obviously uses up five tones of the melody. If the number of tones in the chant fragment is a multiple of five, the repeat of the melody will coincide naturally with the beginning of a presentation of the rhythmic pattern. But if the melody has twenty-two notes or nineteen, or any other number not divisible by five, the composer must face a choice. He may alter the length of the melodic segment so that the number of tones becomes divisible by five, or he may momentarily drop the rhythmic pattern he

Fig. 7-1. Opening of Perotin's *Viderunt omnes*

has established so that the melodic and rhythmic repeats will coincide. But the composer may also decide to retain both the expected length of the chant fragment and the unaltered presence of a pervasive rhythmic pattern. In that event the melodic repeat will begin somewhere in the middle of the rhythmic pattern, and all of the rhythmic values associated with the first presentation of the melody will occur in changed position. This alternative was frequently adopted.

Example 2 shows a tenor voice part that achieves the desired length by the repetition of a chant melisma. In order to show the identity of the tones constituting the first and second statements of the melody, the two halves have been aligned one under the other. The full voice part consists of the top staff of each pair, followed by the bottom ones. This order is indicated by Roman numerals. When the example is read in the normal order, one will find that it consists of eight complete statements of a single rhythmic pattern, plus a partial statement. The several presentations of the pattern are marked by horizontal brackets and identified by alphabet letters. One may verify the consistency of the pattern by noting that the filled note heads, void note heads, and rests continually follow the same order. Since the second melody statement begins with note three of the rhythmic pattern E, the melodic repetition is disguised by appearing in new rhythmic form. While the interaction between the two forms of repetition will not be perceived by the untrained ear, while the primary appeal is not to the senses, the mathematical rigor is readily explainable. The appeal is to the intellect.

The regular use of small and large silences to define rhythmic patterns in the tenor—the chant-bearing voice—has important consequences. The foundation for the polyphony is lacking in continuity. A sense of onward flow must be built up through the interaction of the newly composed voice or voices with the one that is based on preexistent material. There arises the opportunity for a fascinating interplay between patterns of different kinds and lengths.[19] This is observable both in the genres of clausula and motet. The latter originated at the turn of the thirteenth century through the addition of text to the upper voice (or voices) of clausulae and went on to become the major musical form of that century. The texts of the earliest motets normally had some word or words related to the text of the chant that was employed in the tenor. By the 1210s new motets were being written in clausula style, employing sections of chant in the tenor voice and with all voices in measured rhythm.

The work chosen for discussion next reaches us in three forms: 1) as a clausula for three voices having no text other than the few words associated with the chant fragment; 2) as a motet for two voices having a sacred Latin text for the upper voice that expounds upon the few

Fig. 7-2. Structure of the Tenor of a Nostrum Clausula[18] (for the *Alleluya Pascha nostrum*)

words of the chant fragment; and 3) as a motet for three voices with separate, secular texts in the vernacular for each of the upper voices.[20] The number of beats in each of the structural subdivisions of the different voices is indicated by Arabic numerals. In part these subdivisions are articulated by the various rests that interrupt the rhythmic flow at numerous points. Following the first two tones of the tenor part (the lowest written), the rests subdivide the remainder into modules of three beats each. The structural organization of the upper voices is determined not only by punctuating rests, but also by the repetition of small tonal patterns. For example, in the middle voice, tones ten to thirteen are the same as five to eight. Similar parallelisms in the same voice may be found at the end of the first brace of staves. The uppermost voice is less regular.

During the late thirteenth century, there was a tendency for tenor patterns to be longer, and there was increasing differentiation between the rapid pace of the decorative upper voices and that of the stolid tenor. The latter began to move so slowly that it no longer functioned as a strong melodic force but mainly as a polyphonic support. Constructive principles became increasingly important in the motet.

Fig. 7·3. Structure of the Clausula *Flos filius eius*

Arithmetic Construction in an Early Fourteenth Century Motet

Our final example is taken from one of the more famous motets by Philippe de Vitry (1291-1361), musician, poet, stateman, and Bishop of Meaux. A friend of Petrarch and of the mathematician Gersonides,[21] Philippe de Vitry was also one of the most influential music theorists of his time. His motet *Garit Gallus / In nova fert / Neuma (quinti toni)*, is constructed as a complex palindrome. The central element of the structure is a rhythmic pattern of nine measures in the tenor. In the center of the pattern is a measure of rest. Flanking that on either side is a measure containing two tones having one beat each, and still further from the center is a measure comprising two tones having one and two beats respectively. Finally, at the outermost points of the pattern we find a single tone of three beats. There are three statements of this rhythmic pattern to each presentation of the tenor melody, and two statements of the melody to the entire piece. Looking at the piece as a whole, one finds that at either end of the tenor part there are tones totaling six breves in triple rhythm. Moving one segment closer to the center, one finds at either end tones and silences in duple meter totaling ten breves. The next segment closer to the center comprises tones and silences in triple meter that total fifteen breves. Succeeding steps closer to the center continue to alternate units of ten and fifteen until one arrives at the center itself, which consists of a unit of fifteen beats. In the part with the text, *In nova fert,* the first phrase (including the rest that terminates it), contains a total of fifteen breves. So does the last. The second and second from last phrases each contain seventeen breves, while the third and third from last comprise eight. The alternation between phrases of seventeen and eight breves continues until one reaches the central phrase, which consists of seventeen breves. Philippe de Vitry is working with consistent modules of twenty-five beats, whether these are constituted of fifteen plus ten or seventeen plus eight. The same module prevails in the uppermost voice. Here, in order to avoid a coincidence of structure in the two upper parts, Philippe employs flanking units of sixteen and fourteen breves at the beginning and end of the piece.

When Boethius refused to admit "poets" (i.e., composers) to the class of "musicians" since their creations were governed "not so much by speculation and reason as by a certain natural instinct," he could not have been thinking of works such as *Garit gallus*. Here we find a determined effort to bring the creative processes under the control of the speculative powers of the mind. The striking symmetries and the consistent use of the module, twenty-five, do not result from simple, natural balances, but from the foresight of an intellect that has left nothing to chance.[22]

Because of the overall numerical control of structure, there are many other numbers that are of importance on the detail level of the composition. A fascinating series of analogies may be drawn between the symbolic meanings of these numbers and those of the two texts. We cannot prove that Philippe de Vitry consciously brought into being each of the numbers present in the detail structure, but the nature of such analogical interpretation of their meaning is consistent with the explicative processes of medieval thought that were operative within the system of the liberal arts.

Within the field of the motet, the influence of number on structure continued to grow for another century. Sometimes the composers worked with modules of constant size. Sometimes they worked with modules that were treated proportionately, as described in the chapter on arithmetic. But while there were genres such as secular polyphony that were relatively free of numerical control, it was not until the mid-fifteenth century that controlled structures receded markedly in the face of the newer sensual appeals of the Renaissance.[23]

NOTES

1. Translation from Oliver Strunk, *Source Readings in Music History* (New York: W. W. Norton, 1950), p. 80.

2. Concerning various arrangements of the liberal arts, see Edward A. Lippman, "The Place of Music in the System of Liberal Arts," *Aspects of Medieval and Renaissance Music,* ed. by Jan LaRue (New York: W. W. Norton, 1966), pp. 545-59.

3. Translation from Strunk, *Source Readings,* p. 88.

4. *Liber Sapientiae,* 11:21.

5. An excellent introduction to this subject from the twin standpoints of music and architecture is provided in the chapter, "Measure and Light," in Otto von Simson, *The Gothic Cathedral* (New York: Harper and Row, 1956), pp. 21-58.

6. See Gerhard Pietzsch, *Die Klassifikation der Musik von Boethius bis Ugolino von Orvieto* (1929; repr. Darmstadt, Wissenschaftliche Buchgesellschaft, 1968).

7. Translation from Calvin M. Bower, "Natural and Artificial Music: the Origins and Development of an Aesthetic Concept," *Musica Disciplina,* 25 (1971), p. 21.

8. Ernst Rohloff, ed., *Der Musiktraktat des Johannes de Grocheo* (Leipzig: Gebrüder Reinecke, 1943), pp. 46-47; English translation by Albert Seay, *Johannes de Grocheo: Concerning Music,* 2nd ed. (Colorado Springs: Colorado College Music Press, 1974), pp. 10-12.

9. Translation from Strunk, *Source Readings,* p. 86.

10. The identity of Johannes de Garlandia, the grammarian, and Johannes de Garlandia, the music theorist, has been challenged by certain scholars.

11. Translation from Strunk, *Source Readings,* p. 125.

12. A general survey of Gregorian chant, together with related Ambrosian and Old Roman repertories is provided in Willi Apel, *Gregorian Chant* (Bloomington: Indiana University Press, 1958).

13. Concerning parallels between medieval views on music and astronomy, see Edward Lowinsky, "The Concept of Musical and Physical Space in the Renaissance," *Papers of the American Musicological Society for 1941* (1946), pp. 57-84. See further, F. Alberto Gallo, "Astronomy and Music in the Middle Ages: the *Liber Introductorius* by Michael Scot," *Musica Disciplina,* 27 (1973), pp. 5-9.

14. Translation from Strunk, *Source Readings,* p. 113. In this anthology the treatise is attributed to Odo of Cluny, but it has been demonstrated more recently that the treatise is of unknown, northern Italian provenance. It might

seem that adding together two fifths ought to produce ten pitches rather than nine; however a reduction is caused by the fact that there is one pitch that is common to both sets. Similarly, there are two common pitches among the three groups of fourths, reducing the potential of twelve pitches to ten.

15. Since the treatise is the fourth in the initial group of anonymous treatises published a century ago by Edmond de Coussemaker, its author has become known as Anonymous IV. A modern critical edition is provided by Fritz Reckow, *Der Musiktraktat des Anonymous IV*, Beihefte zum Archiv für Musikwissenschaft, 4-5 (Wiesbaden: Franz Steiner, 1967). An English translation, based primarily on the Coussemaker edition is provided in Luther Dittmer, *Anonymous IV*, Musical Theorists in Translation, 1 (Brooklyn, N.Y.: Institute of Mediaeval Music, 1959).

16. Unlike the organa, the conductus are based on newly written poetic texts and on tenor melodies that are normally created by the composer rather than being borrowed from chant.

17. There is a repertoire of more than four hundred alternative passages, known as substitute clausulae.

18. See the facsimile edition, Luther Dittmer, ed., *Firenze, Biblioteca Mediceo-Laurenziana Pluteo 29.1*, Publications of Mediaeval Musical Manuscripts, 10-11 (Brooklyn, N.Y.: Institute of Mediaeval Music, n.d.), folio 157v. The tenor serves for the last two of the three clausulae on *Nostrum* preserved in the MS.

19. Further examples of numerical constructions in music of the very late 12th and early 13th centuries are discussed by Ernest Sanders in his contribution to Frederick Sternfeld, ed., *Music from the Middle Ages to the Renaissance*, (London: Weidenfeld & Nicolson, 1973), pp. 113-24, *passim*.

20. The three versions are given together in Archibald Davison and Willi Apel, eds., *Historical Anthology of Music*, 1 (Cambridge: Harvard University Press, 1946, rev. ed., 1959), p. 27.

21. See Eric Werner, "The Mathematical Foundation of Philippe de Vitri's Ars Nova," *Journal of the American Musicological Society*, 9 (1956), pp. 128-32.

22. For additional examples of modular constructions employed by the same composer, see Ernest Sanders, "The Early Motets of Philippe de Vitry," *Journal of the American Musicological Society*, 28 (1975), 24-45.

23. Investigation of numerical control of musical structure in the late 15th and 16th centuries has barely begun and early results are still controversial. See M. van Crevel, ed., *Jacobus Obrecht, Opera Omnia, Missae, 7 (Maria zart)* (Amsterdam, 1964), Secret Structure, pp. LV-CXLVI.

BASIC BIBLIOGRAPHY OF MUSIC

General encyclopedia of music:

The New Grove Dictionary of Music and Musicians, ed. by Stanley Sadie, 20 vols. London: Macmillan, 1980. Contains numerous articles on medieval music incorporating original research by many outstanding authorities.

Bibliography:

Hughes, Andrew. *Medieval Music: The Sixth Liberal Art* (Toronto Medieval Bibliographies, 4). Toronto: University of Toronto Press, 1974. A selective, annotated bibliography of major research into medieval music.

Histories of medieval music in English:

Caldwell, John. *Medieval Music*. Bloomington: Indiana University Press, 1978.

Hoppin, Richard H. *Medieval Music*. New York: W. W. Norton, 1978. A fine, new study, taking a fresh look at many materials.

Music from the Middle Ages to the Renaissance, ed. by F. W. Sternfeld. New York: Praeger, 1973. Individual chapters are contributed by various distinguished scholars.

The New Oxford History of Music: Vol. II, *Early Medieval Music up to 1300*, edited by Dom Anselm Hughes. London: Oxford University Press, 1954. Vol. III, *Ars Nova and the Renaissance, 1300-1540*, edited by Dom Anselm Hughes and Gerald Abraham. London: Oxford University Press, 1960. Individual chapters are written by various eminent scholars; these volumes are particularly strong with respect to English music of the late Middle Ages.

Reese, Gustave. *Music in the Middle Ages*. New York: W. W. Norton, 1940. For decades the most influential history of medieval music in English, this basic reference tool is in course of being reissued in a greatly expanded and entirely rewritten form, with the participation of Edward Roesner.

Medieval aesthetic of music:

Bruyne, Edgar de. *Etudes d'esthétique médiévale*, 3 vols. Bruges: University of Ghent, 1946. A one-volume abridgement, translated by Eileen B. Hennessy, appeared under the title, *The Esthetics of the Middle Ages* (New York, 1969).

Anthologies of medieval music:

Davison, Archibald T. and Willi Apel, editors. *Historical Anthology of Music*. Cambridge: Harvard University Press, 1946. Numerous later editions have occasional changes in contents.

Medieval Music (The Oxford Anthology of Music), ed. by W. Thomas Marrocco and Nicholas Sandon. Oxford: Oxford University Press, 1977. A fresh selection of works representing a wide variety of the major medieval genres.

(Note: There are various series of recordings issued for each of the above anthologies.)

Discography:

Coover, James B., with Richard Colvig. *Medieval and Renaissance Music on Long-playing Records*. Detroit, 1973. Provides excellent indexing of records up to 1973.

8 Geometry

Lon R. Shelby

Boethius identified geometry as the science of immovable magnitude. Cassiodorus adopted this definition, adding "and of figures"; he identified its divisions as "plane figures, numerable magnitude, rational and irrational magnitudes, and solid figures." This analysis exactly reflects the major divisions of Euclid's Elements *(which presumably was known to Cassiodorus in a translation by Boethius) : Books I-VI, plane geometry; Books VII-IX, arithmetic; Book X, irrationals; Books XI-XIII, solid geometry.*

Greek geometry represented the axiomatic-deductive system (and thus a techne) in its purest form. In Euclid's Elements *the definitions, postulates, and axioms (or "common notions" in Euclid's terminology) stated the principles of the system. While the postulates and axioms served as principles for the art as a whole, each major division began with definitions appropriate to its particular subject.*

The proposition, the essential building block of the Elements, *can itself be viewed as a techne. Sir Thomas Health, in his* History of Greek Mathematics *(Vol. I, pp. 370-71), listed the six parts contained in the most complete form of a proposition: the enunciation (of the problem) ; the setting-out (of the given data) ; the specification (which repeats the problem in terms of the given data) ; the construction; the proof; and the conclusion (which reverts to the enunciation). (This analysis recalls the organization of a speech in the art of rhetoric.)*

Each division is also a techne; and perhaps the most interesting of these is plane geometry. The essential core of the art, it was the earliest form of geometry to develop. Its similarity to the art of arithmetic is striking, with Books I and II of the Elements *corresponding to the arithmetical topics of number-in-itself and ratio.*

The geometrical analogue to number is figure. While the point serves as the principle of geometry, similar to letters in grammar, unity in arithmetic, and tones in music, length can be taken as the principle of figure. Two lines either intersect in an angle (the basis for the analysis of triangles) or are parallel (the basis for the analysis of parallelograms).

The geometrical analogue to ratio is equivalence between different figures; here too equality is the key to the analysis. Plato viewed the equivalence of areas as the defining characteristic of geometry:

> When one has learned this [the theory of numbers], there follows what is called by the highly ridiculous name geometria [literally: land measurement], but which really consists in making clear, by reference to plane figures, the likeness of numbers that are not alike by nature. (Epinomis 990D)

Book I in Euclid considered equivalence in its application to triangles and parallelograms. It concluded with a proof for the Pythagorean theorem, a proof that was necessary to establish the equivalence of squares and rectangles, the subject of Book II.

Regular geometrical figures seem to be analogues to the perfect numbers of arithmetic. The most perfect figure, the circle, was the subject of Books III and IV in Euclid, who concluded his discussion of plane geometry with an analysis of proportion based on Eudoxus's theory. D. L. W.

During the first half of the twelfth century many Western scholars were busily translating, transmitting, and organizing the learned books that were coming to Europe from medieval Arabic scholarship, or from the Greco-Roman scholarship of the ancient world. One of the most important of these Western scholars was Hugh of St. Victor, a prominent theologian who wrote and taught at the Abbey of St. Victor in Paris. Hugh concerned himself with the study of the liberal arts as a preparation for the study of theology, and to this end he wrote the *Didascalicon,* a handbook to guide his monastic students through their readings in the liberal arts.[1] He also wrote more specialized books on the liberal arts; one of these was a small treatise which he entitled *Practica geometriae,* or "The Practice of Geometry." Since this was an introductory manual, Hugh began with basic definitions of the subject:

> The entire discipline of geometry is either theoretical, that is, speculative, or practical, that is, active. The theoretical is that which investigates spaces and distances of rational dimensions only by speculative reasoning; the practical is that which is done by means of certain instruments, and which makes judgments by proportionally joining together one thing with another.[2]

Hugh's real interest was in practical geometry, and in order to develop his explanation of this art, he divided it into *altimetria, planimetria,* and *cosmimetria.*

> *Altimetria* is that which investigates heights and depths. . . . It is called *planimetria* when one seeks to find the extent of a plane. *Cosmimetria* however takes its meaning from the word cosmos. Cosmos in Greek means the world; hence *cosmimetria* is the measurement of the world, that is to say, it concerns the measurement of circumference, as in the motion of a heavenly sphere and of other heavenly circles, or in the globe of the earth and many other things which nature has placed in the round.[3]

In short, Hugh's *Practica geometriae* was a textbook on surveying, both terrestrial and celestial. Hugh's distinction between theoretical and practical geometry became widely accepted as an appropriate definition of this liberal art, and his tripartite division of practical geometry became a standard framework for later treatises on this subject. Thus "practical geometry," as defined in the medieval handbooks written after Hugh, meant surveying and metrology, that is, the measurement of surfaces and volumes.

It might have been otherwise had medieval scholars followed the suggestions of Dominicus Gundissalinus, a twelfth-century Spanish philosopher and translator who borrowed directly from Arabic learning in developing his schematization of knowledge, which he called *De divisione philosophiae,* or *On the Divisions of Philosophy*.[4] Within his elaborate scheme mathematics was divided into seven arts, one of which was geometry. He further divided each of these arts into its theoretical and practical aspects. Regarding geometry, Dominicus followed Hugh of St. Victor by defining practical geometry in terms of altimetry, planimetry, and cosmimetry. But Dominicus gave considerably broader scope to the application of geometry in the world of work:

> The artificer of practice is he who uses [geometry] in working. There are two kinds of these, namely, surveyors and craftsmen. Surveyors are those who measure the height and depth and plane surface of the earth. Craftsmen are those who exert themselves by working in the constructive or mechanical arts—such as the carpenter in wood, the smith in iron, the mason in clay and stones, and likewise every artificer of the mechanical arts—according to practical geometry.[5]

Following the leads of Hugh of St. Victor and Dominicus Gundissalinus, we may assert that geometry took three forms of expression in the culture of the High Middle Ages.[6] One was theoretical, or mathematical, geometry. This was a subject of study in centers of higher learning that offered courses in all of the seven liberal arts. The second was practical geometry, and this was both a subject of study in educational institutions, as well as a technique for surveying surfaces and measuring volumes commonly used in the everyday world. The third was what I have called constructive geometry, and it was the type of geometry used by medieval craftsmen in working the particular materials of their crafts.[7] Constructive geometry was not a subject of study in formal educational institutions, nor did the scholastics write treatises on it. What we know about it has to be reconstructed from the work of the craftsmen themselves, and from a few booklets written by craftsmen at the end of the Middle Ages.

I. CLASSICAL AND EARLY MEDIEVAL GEOMETRY

Ancient Greek mathematics was the ultimate source of medieval geometry, and the textual fountainhead was Euclid's *Elements*.[8] Euclid wrote his famous treatise in Alexandria, Egypt, during the first half of the third century B.C. Although there were excellent Greek geometers before and after Euclid, none of them wrote books that rivaled the influence of the *Elements*. The only other Greek mathematician who came close was Archimedes, who lived in Syracuse, Sicily, late in the third century B.C. Archimedes wrote specialized treatises on geometry that did not attempt to compete with the comprehensive character of Euclid's *Elements*.[9] The geometrical treatises of neither Euclid nor Archimedes were translated into Latin during the heyday of the Roman Empire, when so much of Roman education and culture depended upon Greek culture. An educated Roman who was serious enough about geometry to have studied Euclid and Archimedes would have been able to read them in Greek anyway. But as the political, economic, and cultural strength of the Roman Empire declined during the fourth and fifth centuries A.D., fewer educated Romans in the West could read Greek.[10] Consequently, around A.D. 500 when the self-appointed translator and transmitter of Greek culture and learning, Anicius Manlius Boethius, set himself the monumental task of translating into Latin the major classics of Greek learning, he included Euclid's *Elements* among the list of works to be translated. Apparently he began a translation, or at least an abbreviated version of the geometrical books in the *Elements*. In some medieval manuscripts dealing with geometry, there survive fragments of an *Ars geometriae* which may have been written by Boethius, and which does contain some Euclidean propositions, but without Euclid's proofs.[11] Nevertheless, even if this is a Boethian fragment of Euclid, it is a far cry from the comprehensive treatise on geometry that Euclid wrote. Thus with the collapse of the Roman Empire in the West and the subsequent cultural distress in the centuries that followed, direct knowledge of the geometrical treatises of Euclid and Archimedes disappeared from the world of Latin scholarship.[12]

But a commitment to the study of geometry lingered on. Knowledge of geometry had been firmly stipulated in classical culture as a necessity for the truly educated person; it was one of the *artes liberales,* the knowledge of which identified one as a cultured, educated, and free person.[13] This viewpoint was enshrined in the fifth century A.D. by another Latin transmitter of Greek learning, Martianus Capella, who published a compendium on the seven liberal arts that he called *The Marriage of Mercury and Philology.* Martianus was widely read in the early Middle Ages, and his inclusion of geometry in the canon of the seven liberal arts at least assured lip service to the study of geometry in early medieval clerical and monastic education.

But there was precious little mathematical geometry in Martianus's treatise. Indeed, most of the section on geometry was devoted to descriptive geography, that is, to literary descriptions of the various regions of the known world. This had been a subject of considerable interest to Greek scholars, who had developed an extensive literature on the description and measurement of the earth. The Greek word for earth was *gē.* Geography (Gk. *geōgraphia*) meant literally earth describing; geometry (*geōmetria*) meant literally earth measuring. The latter could be of two types. One was land surveying, used, for example, in measuring fields and laying out towns. The other was what we now call geodesy (again from a Greek word, *geōdaisia*), that is, determining and measuring the shape and size of the earth. Geodesy was a regular part of Greek geography, and Martianus followed this tradition by first presenting arguments that the earth was spherical, then giving a brief description of its dimensions before moving on to the main portion of his text on "geometry"—a descriptive geography of the known world. He concluded with a few pages devoted to the mathematical subject that geometry had become through the works of Euclid, Archimedes, and other Greek mathematicians.[14] Thus, Martianus's *Marriage of Mercury and Philology* provided for early medieval scholars more information on classical geography than it did on geometry.

Unfortunately, Martianus overlooked the strongest tradition in Roman culture that had dealt with geometry, namely, that of the Roman *agrimensores,* or land surveyors. Roman scholars had never shown much aptitude for the pure mathematics of the Greek tradition. Whatever advances were made in mathematics during the time of the Roman Empire were made by Greek authors, or at least by authors writing in Greek. But the Romans were keenly interested in applied mathematics in the form of surveying and metrology, or what Hugh of St. Victor later called practical geometry. With the commitment of the Romans to extensive building of superb roads and aqueducts, and to carefully laid-out fortified camps, colonial towns, and major urban centers, there was a constant need for the application of practical geometry. The result was the development of a class of professional surveyors, the *agrimensores*.[15]

Beginning in the first century A.D., some surveyors wrote manuals explaining the technical procedures used in their profession. These small books, or fragments of them, were eventually collected together in what has come to be called the *Corpus agrimensorum*.[16] While this collection was probably made around A.D. 450, the earliest copies survive in manuscripts dating from the sixth and ninth centuries. Although the texts are fragmentary, one can readily determine the general character of the practical geometry used by the *agrimensores*. It was, in effect, applied mathematics: the surveyors faced specific problems of measurement that required geometrical and arithmetical calculations. In the agrimensorial manuals these problems were stated concretely, and the calculations required to solve the problems were set forth dogmatically. That is to say, one was told how to solve the problems by going through certain mathematical steps; but there was no attempt to prove that the solution was mathematically correct. One was simply told to do it that way to get the correct answer. The applied or practical geometry of the *agrimensores* was thus substantively different from the mathematical geometry of Euclid and Archimedes. In the geometry of these Greek mathematicians there was an obligation to prove, through mathematical reasoning, the correctness of a proposed solution to a problem.

The geometry that passed from the ancient world into early medieval Latin culture was the practical geometry of the *agrimensores,* as well as summary accounts of geometry in the handbooks of authors like Martianus Capella. Even if their geometrical treatises had survived in Latin translations, Euclid and Archimedes would have been quite beyond the mathematical capabilities of even the most learned Latin scholars of the early Middle Ages. Indeed, it is evident that these scholars had sufficient difficulty just mastering the practical geometry of the *agrimensores*. Perhaps the first scholar to do so with any degree of success was the famous polymath of the tenth century, Gerbert of Reims, who eventually became Pope Sylvester II. He compiled a *Geometria* which contained excerpts and ideas from the *Ars geometriae* attributed to Boethius, as well as extensive material on surveying taken from the manuals of the *agrimensores*.[17] Basically the same sources were used by an anonymous later contemporary of Gerbert who compiled a *Geometria* and ascribed it Boethius; hence this unknown compiler has been labeled the Pseudo-Boethius.[18]

The utilization of the agrimensorial tracts by Gerbert and the Pseudo-Boethius, as well as the numerous copies of these tracts that were being made in the tenth and eleventh centuries, raises the question, what was the reason for this interest in the *agrimensores?* Was it a practical need to master the skills taught by the *agrimensores,* in order to carry out surveying tasks required at this time? This practical need may have played some part in the interest shown in these treatises. On the other hand, the primary reason for this interest may have been that the *agrimensores* provided a major part of the "art of geometry" within the traditional seven liberal arts of monastic and clerical education. Without a real Euclid being available in Latin, these scholars were doing their best to put together a geometry from the Boethian/Euclidean fragments and from the traditions of the Roman *agrimensores.*[19]

II. PRACTICAL GEOMETRY

We can now return to Hugh of St. Victor. When Hugh wrote his *Practica geometriae* in the first half of the twelfth century, Euclid was still not available in the West, though soon he would be. Hugh was a monastic theologian and a teacher of monks. He was not in any sense a surveyor, nor was he primarily writing the *Practica geometriae* for surveyors to use in the actual world of work. He was writing for monastic students and others who were studying the seven liberal arts in preparation for their more advanced studies in theology. Thus Hugh's textbook fitted within a centuries' long tradition of virtually identifying the art of geometry with the practical geometry of surveying and metrology.

But even after the full text of Euclid's *Elements* returned to the West during the twelfth century, practical geometry continued to be studied as a part of the quadrivium in higher studies. Furthermore, Latin scholars continued to write on the subject, as evidenced by several *Practica geometriae* composed after Hugh wrote his work.[20] It is interesting to note that—even though Euclidean geometry had been reintroduced into Western culture—these practical geometries generally continued the mathematical character of the agrimensorial treatises. That is, they formulated specific problems and provided specific solutions to those problems in didactic or dogmatic fashion. Mathematical calculations were involved in this practical geometry, but there was little inclination or sense of need to demonstrate mathematically that those solutions were correct. Euclidean definitions, postulates, or theorems might be drawn upon; but the Euclidean proof or demonstration generally played little or no part in these treatises.

In the increasingly complex society of twelfth-century Europe, there was a growing need for the technical skills of surveying embodied within the agrimensorial treatises and practical geometries written by Latin scholars. The growth of towns with their tightly compacted real estate called for accurate means of surveying and setting off property lines. Commercial activities within these towns generated the necessity for accurate measurement of the volume and weight of goods. While the better-educated merchants and craftsmen might have acquired enough Latin to read the *agrimensores* or the practical geometries written by scholars, there were many who needed access to this information but who could not read the Latin treatises. By the thirteenth century this had produced sufficient pressure to induce authors to compose these manuals in the vernacular languages. One such was a French *Pratike de geometrie,* dating from circa 1275.

The anonymous author began his short book with this prefatory statement:

> We shall commence a work on the practice of geometry, which we shall divide in three parts. In the first part we shall teach how to find the measurement of plane surfaces; in the second, how to find the measure of heights and depths and of large measures; in the third, how to find the details of geometry and astronomy appropriate to the preceding parts.[21]

One recognizes immediately the customary tripartite division of practical geometry into planimetry, altimetry, and cosmimetry—which shows the influence of Hugh of St. Victor's *Practica geometriae* even on this vernacular text of a century later. However, the author did not follow his three-part division very well, as may be ascertained from a brief review of the contents of the treatise.

First there was a short description of how to use the astrolabe in calculating the length of a straight line, for example, the distance across a woods or river, or the height of a tree or steeple. Next came an explanation of how to find the area of various geometrical figures—the circle, square, pentagon, hexagon, heptagon, and a number of different triangles. This was followed by exercises in finding "surpluses," that is, the difference between the areas of a circle and of a square which inscribes it. The author then turned to some practical surveying problems, such as how to find the number of house lots within a round city. The last of the geometrical problems concerned the measurement of volumes of various containers, such as the hogshead and tun.

It is obvious from this outline that this vernacular "Practice of Geometry" remained largely within the traditions of the *agrimensores* and the Latin *Practica geometriae.* With the exception of the tunmaker, the author scarcely bothered with the application of practical geometry to crafts concerned with mechanical and constructive arts.

III. THEORETICAL GEOMETRY

Let us resume the history of theoretical geometry in medieval culture. The story takes up around the middle of the twelfth century, when Euclid's *Elements* again became available in the West. This occurred during what has come to be called the "Renaissance of the Twelfth Century," when European scholars were greedily soaking up every scrap of ancient Greek and of medieval Arabic learning that they could get their hands on. Many of the classical texts of Greek philosophy, science, medicine, and mathematics had been translated into Arabic during the early Middle Ages, when Arabic learning far surpassed that of contemporary Latin learning. By the beginning of the twelfth century there were many contacts between Latin and Arabic scholarship—in Syria, Sicily, southern Italy, and, most importantly, in Moslem Spain. Some western scholars learned Arabic so that they were able to translate into Latin the classical Greek treatises which had previously been translated into Arabic. They also translated Arabic commentaries on the classical texts, as well as original works of Arabic scholarship.[22] It was through this transmission process that a full text of Euclid's *Elements* again became available in the West. Indeed, so great was the interest in Euclid that during the twelfth and thirteenth centuries several translations, versions, and editions were made.[23]

The famous English scholar and translator, Adelard of Bath, completed his first translation from Arabic sometime before 1150. While other versions were based on one or the other of Adelard's translations, or else were made directly from an Arabic text, at least one translation of the thirteenth century was made from a Greek text.[24] The textual history of these various translations and editions is quite complicated; suffice it here to say that by the latter part of the twelfth century a Latin Euclid was available for anyone who was determined to get a copy.

Now that the complete text of Euclid's *Elements* was finally available, what impact did this have on the study of theoretical geometry? This question is not easy to answer. Certainly geometry maintained its formal role in the curriculum of higher education. As the universities emerged out of the cathedral schools during the twelfth century, the traditional seven liberal arts continued to provide the curricular framework for the baccalaureate degree.[25] These arts were placed in two groups, the trivium, consisting of grammar, rhetoric, and logic; and the quadrivium, consisting of arithmetic, geometry, music, and astronomy. But of these arts, logic was assuming an increasingly dominant role as the best preparation for studying the philosophical and scientific works of Aristotle.

And it was Aristotle's writings that were rapidly becoming the real core of both the bachelor of arts and master of arts degrees.

University statutes of the thirteenth and fourteenth centuries show the domination of Artistotelian studies in the arts degree; nevertheless, these statutes reveal that geometry was hanging on as a small part of the total curriculum. At Oxford University in the fourteenth century, arts students were required to hear lectures on the first six books of Euclid's *Elements* for at least five weeks during their program of study.[26] But certainly geometry was not a major part of the arts curriculum; it occupied about the same space as mathematics in the general education requirements of American undergraduate education today.

There are other analogies between what was happening in the medieval university and what has happened in the twentieth-century American university. Just as the specialized studies of the undergraduate major field have crowded general education courses into a corner of the university curriculum, so did the major subject in the medieval arts degree—namely, the philosophical and scientific writings of Aristotle—encroach upon the time available for the traditional seven liberal arts, with the exception of logic. Taken in the broadest perspective then, theoretical geometry never played a truly important role in higher education in the Middle Ages. If we equate Euclid's *Elements* with theoretical geometry, it was not even available until the second half of the twelfth century, and the clean sweep of the university curriculum that Aristotle made in the thirteenth century never really gave Euclid a chance. Without doubt, most medieval professors and their students preferred Aristotle's books on *Ethics, Physics,* and *Metaphysics* over Euclid's *Elements.*

On the other hand, there were some scholars who seriously concerned themselves with theoretical geometry beyond teaching it in introductory lectures to undergraduates. Their activities took three forms. One was that of providing Latin editions of the classical works of Greek mathematicians. In geometry this meant Euclid first and foremost. The numerous different Latin versions of the *Elements* indicate the continuing interest of scholars in providing a variety of translations of Euclid from both Arabic and Greek texts.

In particular I may cite here the thirteenth-century version by Campanus of Novara, which was even more widely used in the later Middle Ages than the translations of Adelard of Bath.[27] Professor John Murdoch of Harvard has studied closely the versions of Euclid based upon the translations of Adelard and Campanus. He has drawn some interesting conclusions about the character of these medieval Latin translations. Even when ostensibly just translating a classical text, medieval scholars could turn the text to serve a particular purpose. We have seen how geometry, as one of the seven liberal arts, had long been considered a preparation for higher studies. In the development of the early university curricula, the trivium and quadrivium became subordinated to the study of Aristotle's philosophical and scientific works. Professor Murdoch's analysis shows that the translators of Euclid used every opportunity to direct the mathematical content of the *Elements* toward broader philosophical problems, particularly the logic of philosophical argument.[28] In short, theoretical geometry was not allowed to stand alone as a subject worth pursuing for its own sake; rather, it was utilized, wherever possible, as a way into the philosophical and theological problems that really intrigued medieval professors and their students.

Euclid's *Elements* was not the only source of theoretical geometry in the High Middle Ages; Archimedes' treatises were also translated in the twelfth century from Arabic versions, and then in the thirteenth century from the original Greek.[29] As pointed out earlier, Archimedes had not written a comprehensive treatise like Euclid but rather had developed special problems in both plane and solid geometry. Thus his works were of interest only to more mathematically advanced scholars; but the number of surviving Latin Archimedean texts shows that there was a continuing group of geometers who concerned themselves with the advanced problems that Archimedes posed.

A second type of scholarly activity by medieval geometers was that of providing commentaries on Euclidean or Archimedean texts. This, of course, was a standard form of intellectual exercise by the Schoolmen: to "gloss the text" of a famous literary, biblical, theological, or legal treatise was not merely to provide a commentary to aid students in understanding difficult texts; it was a way of advancing the "state of the art" in that particular discipline to which the text pertained. But since these medieval Latin commentaries on Euclid have not been edited, published, or closely studied, I shall not comment on the character of the geometry that was developed in these commentaries.[30]

Yet a third way by which medieval geometers advanced the state of the art of theoretical geometry was to apply Euclidean and Archimedean geometry to practical or theoretical problems that interested them. At the head of the list of such scholars was Leonardo Fibonacci of Pisa, who was certainly one of the most outstanding of medieval mathematicians. Born around 1170, Leonardo was the son of an Italian merchant who made it possible for Leonardo to visit commercial centers in Algeria, Egypt, Syria, Byzantium, and Sicily.[31] While learning about the merchant's trade, Leonardo acquired all of the applied and theoretical mathematics that he could from merchants and scholars alike.

Upon returning to Pisa, Leonardo wrote a number of mathematical treatises designed to teach calculations required in everyday affairs, as well as to advance the state of the art in mathematics. One of these books he entitled *Practica geometriae*. While he did include some practical surveying problems, this book is scarcely like the other *Practica geometriae* that I mentioned earlier. In the first place Leonardo provided proofs for the solutions of many of the problems that he stated. In effect, he combined the theoretical geometry of Euclid with the traditional surveying and measurement problems of the *agrimensores* and the medieval *Practica geometriae*. But he did not confine himself to those traditional problems, for he took up theoretical geometry problems that were quite beyond the mathematical level of the practical geometries. These he labeled "geometrical subtleties," and they concerned geometrical figures like the pentagon and decagon.[32] Yet he did not simply compile another version of Euclid's *Elements,* or a commentary on that book in the tradition of the university Schoolmen. He knew and understood Euclid, and he even cited and borrowed from Euclid; but he wrote an independent treatise, based on his own mathematical interests and capabilities that he had developed in contacts with his fellow Italian merchants and scholars, as well as those from Moslem and Byzantine cultures.

However, Leonardo paid a price for his geometrical subtleties, for only the simpler portions of his treatise seem to have had much direct influence during the later Middle Ages. His more complex mathematics was beyond the interests of merchants. Furthermore, since his geometry was not set within the framework of those philosophical and mathematical problems which interested university scholars, his *Practica geometriae* did not carry much influence in later medieval scholastic thought.

It is interesting to compare the influence of another major medieval mathematician and geometer, Jordanus de Nemore, who did work within Scholastic interests in the science of mechanics.[33] Because Jordanus directed his mathematical abilities toward areas of intellectual concern to the Schoolmen, rather than to the more workaday problems of merchants, his treatises were much more widely copied in the book-producing world of the Scholastics. In medieval mechanics Euclidean and Archimedean geometry was widely used to express in mathematical terms those mechanical problems relating to weights, levers, balances, inclines, declines, and so forth. These problems could be represented by geometrical figures that could be analyzed and manipulated by means of mathematical or theoretical geometry. Jordanus is most famous for his books on mechanics; but it was natural for him to write a treatise on theoretical geometry, which he entitled *Liber de triangulis.*[34] In this work he dealt with pure geometrical problems concerning lines, angles, triangles, quadrangles, and circles. In developing his proofs, Jordanus borrowed from Latin translations of Arabic geometrical treatises that had been based on previous Greek works, although he felt free to disagree with these authorities if he did not approve of the proofs that they had developed. Sometimes he developed his own proofs. Jordanus had advancd beyond the point of translating, editing, or commenting upon received texts; he had an independent mathematical mind which he set to the Scholastic tasks that interested him.

While Jordanus utilized mathematical geometry to solve problems in mechanics, geometry also played a critical role in other areas of scientific interest to the Scholastics. This was particularly true in optics; after all, Euclid himself had written a treatise on *Optics* that became available in Latin in the Middle Ages. The science of optics really got underway in the Latin West in the thirteenth century with the work of two famous English scholars, Robert Grosseteste and Roger Bacon.[35] Besides dealing with abstract problems of reflection and refraction, they tried to explain in optical terms the phenomenon of the rainbow. What is of interest to our present story is that Grosseteste and Bacon, and the continental scholars who followed them in working on these problems, perceived mathematical geometry as a fundamental technique for the investigation of natural phenomena.

Grosseteste formulated this position explicitly, as can be seen in the following quotations from two of his scientific treatises.

> The usefulness of considering lines, angles and figures is the greatest because it is impossible to undertand natural philosophy without these. They are efficacious throughout the universe as a whole and its parts, and in related properties, as in rectilinear and circular motion. . . . For all causes of natural effects have to be expressed by means of lines, angles and figures, for otherwise it would be impossible to have knowledge of the reason (*propter quid*) concerning them.

> Hence these rules and principles and fundamentals having been given by the power of geometry, the careful observer of natural things can give the causes of all natural effects by this method. And it will be impossible otherwise, as is already clear in respect of the universal, since every natural action is varied in strength and weakness through variation of lines, angles and figures. But in respect of the particular this is even clearer, first in natural action upon matter and later upon the senses, so that the truth of geometry is quite plain.[36]

In summary regarding theoretical geometry in late medieval Scholastic thought, it is probably fair to say that the greatest advances were not made in geometry itself. While several medieval geometers showed that they had fully mastered Euclidean and Archimedean geometry and were able to develop some purely geometrical problems independently of Euclid and Archimedes, still there was no significant advance beyond the limits set in the treatises of these classical Greek mathematicians. On the other hand, medieval Scholastics did become quite sophisticated in applying the methods and the content of Greek geometry to the scientific problems that interested them. In so doing, some of them advanced beyond ancient Greek scientific thought in applying mathematical techniques to the solving of scientific problems dealing with the natural world. In combining mathematical with empirical modes of investigation, these medieval Scholastics previewed, and in some ways prepared the way for, the Scientific Revolution of the seventeenth century.[37] Although modern scholarship has firmly established this point, it is not sufficiently recognized by many who still look upon the Middle Ages as an Age of Faith, with virtually no scientific accomplishments. We now know that some of the Schoolmen devoted considerable effort to sophisticated scientific inquiry and that geometry often played a major role in their inquiries.

IV. CONSTRUCTIVE GEOMETRY

The third type of geometry that played a significant role in medieval culture was the constructive geometry of the craftsmen. While many different crafts used this geometry, it was the masons who were most closely identified with having developed it, so I shall illustrate this type by specifically discussing the geometry of the masons. The masons themselves proclaimed that their craft was founded on the art of geometry. The thirteenth-century craftsman, Villard de Honnecourt, introduced his famous *Sketchbook* with these words:

> Villard de Honnecourt greets you and bids all those who work with the devices found in this book to pray for his soul and to remember him. For in this book one will find good advice concerning the proper technique of masonry and the devices of carpentry. You will also find the technique of drawing—the forms—just as the art of geometry requires and teaches it.[38]

Around 1400 an anonymous author compiled a historical introduction to a set of customs and regulations pertaining to the mason's craft in England. The author began with a review of the seven liberal arts, but he quickly singled out geometry for special consideration. "Marvel you not that I said that all science lives only by the science of geometry. For there is no artifice nor handicraft that is wrought by man's hand but it is wrought by geometry."[39] The author proceeded to say "that among all the crafts of the world of man's craft, masonry has the most notability and most part of this science of geometry."[40] He then turned to the origins of masonry and recounted a delightful story. It seems that

Euclid had been a clerk of Abraham during the latter's sojourn in Egypt. Indeed, it was Abraham who had taught the science of geometry to Euclid, who had in turn taught it to the Egyptians: "And they took their sons to Euclid to govern them at his own will, and he taught to them the craft of masonry and gave it the name of geometry. . . . "[41]

What was the nature of this geometry that had come to be so closely identified with the masons' craft? It can be observed in Villard's *Sketchbook*, although this has to be parsed out with the most careful analysis, for neither the sketches nor the verbal comments in the *Sketchbook* are self-explanatory. It is easier to turn to other booklets written at the end of the Middle Ages by several German craftsmen—mostly master masons —who explained in quite clear detail the nature of this geometry and how it functioned within the masons' craft. Mathes Roriczer, a master mason from Regensburg, and Hanns Schmuttermayer, a silversmith from Nürnberg, each wrote small pamphlets in which the masons' use of geometry was clearly illustrated in certain design problems.[42] But the essence of that geometry is even more clearly revealed in another booklet which Roriczer wrote, and which later came to be called the *Geometria Deutsch,* "Geometry in German." From this booklet we learn that the constructive geometry of the masons was virtually a non-mathematical geometry. The problems in this short booklet are mostly constructional problems—how to construct a right angle, a pentagon, a heptagon, or an octagon. The instructions for so doing are straightforward, but there is no effort to demonstrate the correctness of the procedure. This is also true of other simple geometrical problems that Roriczer presented—how to find the length of the circumference of a circle; how to find the center of a circle with only part of the circumference known; how to construct a square and a triangle that have the same areas. It is not surprising that there was no effort at Euclidean demonstrations of mathematical correctness; we have seen that this was a characteristic of many of the medieval *Practica geometriae.* What is interesting is that not only were there no mathematical proofs; there were no mathematical calculations in the *Geometria Deutsch!* This can readily be seen in Roriczer's solution to the problem of finding the length of the circumference of a circle:

> If anyone wishes to make a circular line straight, so that the straight line and the circular line are the same length, then make three circles next to one another, and divide [the diameter of] the first circle into seven equal parts, with the letters designated *h a b c d e f g.* Then as far as it is from *h* to *a,* set a point behind [h], and mark an *i* there. Then as far as it is from *i* to *k,* equally as long in its circularity is the circular line of one of the three [circles] which stand next to each other, as the figure stands made hereafter.[43] [See figure 8.1.]

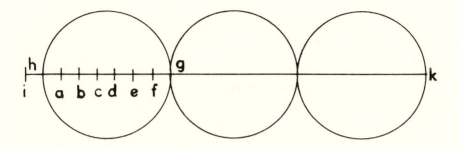

Fig. 8-1. Roriczer's Solution for the Length of the Circumference

The language of Roriczer's formula suggests that he was hardly thinking of this as a mathematical problem. He seems to have been visualizing certain geometrical forms—a circle and a straight line—and asking himself, "How do you make a straight line that is as long as a circle is round?" This mental "set," it seems to me, differs importantly from the geometer's question, "Given the diameter, how do you find the circumference of a circle?"

We can observe this mental set of the *Geometria Deutsch* in the design books by Roriczer and Schmuttermayer and in a somewhat later book of "Instructions" written by a Heidelberg master mason, Lorenz Lechler. Roriczer and Schmuttermayer were concerned with the same problems, the design of pinnacles and small gables. Their technique was to take simple geometrical forms and manipulate these with their basic geometrical instruments—compass, square, and straightedge. In these particular design problems the fundamental geometrical figure was the square, which they rotated, inscribed, halved, and otherwise manipulated in a long series of carefully prescribed steps. The end result was to produce a grid of straight lines, curves, and points that provided a geometrical framework for the architectural elements that they were designing. Once this framework was constructed, it was relatively easy to fill in the architectural details.[44]

But these geometrical grids or frameworks were not used simply for architectural elements like pinnacles and small gables. Lorenz Lechler's "Instructions" shows how the masons used constructive geometry for setting out the overall plan of the building, as well as the geometrical frame for the elevations and cross sections.[45] These larger building components were set out in much the same way as were the smaller architectural details: basic geometrical figures were manipulated through a prescribed series of steps to produce the desired geometrical frame. It is important to note that these prescribed steps were essentially arbitrary; they were not mathematically logical or necessary. Roriczer and Lechler were saying, in effect, if you want to design a pinnacle, or if you want to determine the basic form and dimensions of a church choir, then follow these steps that I have prescribed for you. In short, the constructive geometry of the masons was not a deductive, logical, mathematical line of reasoning from axioms, postulates, and theorems in Euclidean fashion. Nor was it a set of mathematical calculations designed to solve geometrical and arithmetical problems, as in the practical geometry of the *agrimensores* and the medieval practical geometers. Rather, it was the physical manipulation of certain geometrical figures that allowed the masons to construct geometrical frames for the architectural design and construction of buildings.

To conclude my remarks: It should be evident from this survey that the word geometry had many meanings in the Middle Ages. Every society has certain words that acquire rich cultural overtones; for example, in our present American society the word "psychology" has accumulated this kind of richness. Such words carry so much cultural freight that one cannot hope to understand a given society without understanding the significance of these words in the society's culture. But one can seldom provide a single sufficiently comprehensive definition of such words; one must seek the particular meaning of the word within a particular context. So it is with the word geometry in the Middle Ages. It simply will not do to suppose that Gerbert of Reims, Hugh of St. Victor, Leonardo Fibonacci, and Mathes Roriczer had quite the same thing in mind when they used the word geometry. I have tried to clarify at least three major meanings of this word in terms of practical geometry, theoretical geometry, and constructive geometry. Even these definitions do not suffice to sound out all the historical meanings of this term, but perhaps they will do as a beginning to help one appreciate the broad significance of geometry in medieval culture.

NOTES

1. For the Latin text, see the *Patrologia Latina* 176: 741-838. For an English translation, see *The Didascalicon of Hugh of St. Victor*, trans. Jerome Taylor, Records of Civilization Sources and Studies, 64 (New York: Columbia University Press, 1961).

2. Roger Baron, ed., *Hugonis de Sancto Victore Opera Propaedeutica: Practica geometriae, De grammatica, Epitome Dindimi in philosophiam,* Publications in Medieval Studies, 20 (Notre Dame: University of Notre Dame Press, 1966), p. 16. (My translation.)

3. Ibid., p. 17. (My translation.)

4. For the place of Hugh of St. Victor and Dominicus Gundissalinus in the medieval development of the classification of the sciences, see the wide-ranging article by James A. Weisheipl, "Classification of the Sciences in Medieval Thought," *Mediaeval Studies,* 27 (1965), 54-90; and the shorter chapter by the same author on "The Nature, Scope, and Classification of the Sciences," in *Science in the Middle Ages,* ed. David C. Lindberg (Chicago: University of Chicago Press, 1978), pp. 461-82.

5. Dominicus Gundissalinus, *De divisione philosophiae,* ed. Ludwig Baur, Beiträge zur Geschichte der Philosophie des Mittelalters, Bd. 4, Heft 2-3 (Münster i. W.: Aschendorff, 1903), p. 109. (My translation.)

6. Although medieval geometry has usually received at least some attention in the general histories of mathematics and in more specialized histories of geometry, a full-scale history of medieval geometry remains to be written. Significant advances were made in this direction in the late nineteenth century, and these were effectively summarized in two articles by Paul Tannery, "La géométrie au xie siècle," *Mémoires scientifiques,* ed. J. L. Heiberg et al. (Toulouse: Gauthier-Villars, 1922), 5:79-102 [rpt. from *Revue générale internationale, scientifique, littéraire et artistique,* 15 (1897), 343-57]; and "Histoire des sciences: Géométrie," *Mémoires scientifiques,* 10: 37-59 [rpt. from *Revue de synthèse historique,* 2 (1901), 283-99]. But the task was not completed at that time. Interest in medieval geometry diminished after World War I and did not revive until after World War II, when Marshall Clagett, John Murdoch, Guy Beaujouan, Roger Baron, and H. L. L. Busard undertook further specialized studies. As yet no one has attempted a full-scale history of geometry in medieval culture. For a useful brief survey of medieval mathematics that provides a balanced account of both geometry and arithmetic, see Michael S. Mahoney, "Mathematics," in *Science in the Middle Ages,* ed. David C. Lindberg (Chicago: University of Chicago Press, 1978), pp. 145-78.

7. Lon R. Shelby, "The Geometrical Knowledge of Medieval Master Masons," *Speculum,* 47 (1972), 409-10.

8. For the Greek text and a Latin translation see J. L. Heiberg, ed., *Euclidis Elementa,* 5 vols. (Leipzig: B. G. Teubner, 1883-88); and now *Euclidis Elementa,* vol. 1, *Libri I-IV cum appendicibus,* post J. L. Heiberg, ed. E. S. Stamatis (Leipzig: B. G. Teubner, 1969). For the English edition, see *The Thirteen Books of Euclid's Elements,* Translated from the Text of Heiberg with Introduction and Commentary by Thomas L. Heath, 3 vols., 2nd ed. (Cambridge: At the University Press, 1926).

9. *Archimedis opera omnia cum commentariis Eutocii,* ed. J. L. Heiberg, 3 vols. (Leipzig: B. G. Teubner, 1880-81); *The Works of Archimedes,* Edited in Modern Notation with Introductory Chapters by T. L. Heath (Cambridge: At the University Press, 1897).

10. H. I. Marrou, *A History of Education in Antiquity,* trans. George Lamb (New York: Sheed and Ward, 1956), p. 262.

11. For discussion of this complex textual problem, see Nicolaus Bubnov, ed., *Gerberti postea Silvestris II papae opera mathematica* (Berlin, 1899; rpt. Hildesheim: Georg Olms, 1963), pp. 161-79; B. L. Ullman, "Geometry in the

Mediaeval Quadrivium," *Studi di bibliografia e di storia in onore di Tammaro de Marinis* (Verona: Stampera Valdonega, 1964), 4: 270-71; and Menso Folkerts, ed., *"Boethius" Geometrie II: Ein mathematisches Lehrbuch des Mittelalters,* Boethius: Texte und Abhandlungen zur Geschichte der exakten Wissenschaften, 9 (Wiesbaden: Franz Steiner Verlag, 1970), pp. 69-82.

12. The loss of Greek mathematics was paralleled by the loss of direct knowledge of other Greek sciences; see William H. Stahl, *Roman Science: Origins, Development, and Influence to the Later Middle Ages* (Madison: University of Wisconsin Press, 1962), pp. 259-60, where he chastises Roman Latin civilization for not having produced a more genuine interest in Greek mathematics and science, with the result that only watered down and inept summaries were passed on to early medieval Latin civilization.

13. Marrou, *Education in Antiquity,* pp. 175-79.

14. For the Latin text of the portion of Book VI, *De geometria,* which deals with Euclidean geometry, see *Martianus Capella,* ed. Francis Eyssenhardt (Leipzig: B. G. Teubner, 1966), pp. 246-54. The work has recently been translated in *Martianus Capella and the Seven Liberal Arts,* Vol. 2, *The Marriage of Philology and Mercury,* trans. W. H. Stahl, Richard Johnson, and E. L. Burge, Records of Civilization: Sources and Studies, 84 (New York: Columbia University Press, 1977), pp. 264-72. For a summary and analysis of the book on geometry in Martianus, see Vol. 1, *The Quadrivium of Martianus Capella: Latin Traditions in the Mathematical Sciences 50 B.C.-A.D. 1250* by W. H. Stahl (New York: Columbia University Press, 1971), pp. 125-48.

15. See Moritz Cantor, *Die Römischen Agrimensoren und ihre Stellung in der Geschichte der Feldmesskunst: Eine historisch-mathematische Untersuchung* (Leipzig: B. G. Teubner, 1875); and more recently, O. A. W. Dilke, *The Roman Land Surveyors: An Introduction to the Agrimensores* (Newton Abbot: David and Charles, 1971), for historical surveys of the *agrimensores* in classical times.

16. See F. Blume, K. Lachmann, and A. Rudorff, eds., *Die Schriften der Römischen Feldmesser,* 2 vols. (Berlin: Georg Reimer, 1852), for the edition of the *Corpus agrimensorum.*

17. Gerbert's *Geometria* was edited in Bubnov, *Gerberti . . . opera mathematica,* pp. 48-97.

18. Edited in Folkerts, *"Boethius" Geometrie II,* pp. 109-71.

19. Ullmann, "Geometry in the Mediaeval Quadrivium," pp. 266, 285.

20. For a brief overview of these works, see Mahoney, "Mathematics," pp. 155-157. For editions of the works, see Maximilian Curtze, "Practica Geometriae. Ein anonymer Tractat aus dem Ende des zwölften Jahrhunderts," *Monatshefte für Mathematik und Physik,* 8 (1897), 193-224; idem, "Die 'Practica Geometriae' des Leonardo Mainardo aus Cremona," Part 2 of *Urkunden zur Geschichte der Mathematik im Mittelalter und der Renaissance,* in *Abhandlungen zur Geschichte der mathematischen Wissenschaften,* 13 (1902), 335-434; idem, " 'De Inquisicione Capacitatis Figurarum'. Anonyme Abhandlung aus dem fünfzehnten Jahrhundert," *Abhandlungen zur Geschichte der Mathematik,* 8 (1898), 29-68; Paul Tannery, "Le Traité du Quadrant de Maître Robert Anglès (Montpelier, xiiie siècle). Texte latine et ancienne traduction grecque," *Mémoires scientifiques,* 5: 118-97 (rpt. from *Notices et Extraits des Manuscrits de la Bibliothèque Nationale,* 35, pt. 2 (1897), 561-640); H. L. L. Busard, "The Practica Geometriae of Dominicus de Clavisio," *Archive for History of Exact Sciences,* 2 (1962-66), 520-75; and Stephen K. Victor, ed., *Practical Geometry in the High Middle Ages: Artis cuiuslibet consummatio and the*

Pratike de geometrie, Memoirs of the American Philosophical Society, 134 (Philadelphia: American Philosophical Society, 1979).

21. Charles Henry, "Sur les deux plus anciens traités français d'algorisme et de géométrie," *Bulletino di bibliografia e di storia delle scienze matematiche e fisiche,* 15 (1882), 49-70.

22. Still fundamental for the study of these translators are the several articles published by Haskins early in this century and reprinted, with some additional chapters, in Charles H. Haskins, *Studies in the History of Medieval Science* (Cambridge: Harvard University Press, 1924).

23. Mahoney, "Mathematics," p. 152, suggests that, indeed, the multiplicity of versions "stood in the path of the assimilation of Greek geometry in the twelfth and thirteenth centuries." For analyses of these various translations, see H. Weissenborn, "Die Übersetzung des Euklid aus dem Arabischen in das Lateinische durch Adelard von Bath nach zwei Handschriften der Kgl. Bibliothek in Erfurt," *Zeitschrift für Mathematik und Physik, Supplement zur historischen-literarischen Abtheilung,* 25 (1880), 143-66; Marshall Clagett, "The Medieval Latin Translations from the Arabic of the *Elements* of Euclid, with Special Emphasis on the Versions of Adelard of Bath," *Isis,* 44 (1953), 16-42; John E. Murdoch, "The Medieval Euclid: Salient Aspects of the Translations of the *Elements* by Adelard of Bath and Campanus of Novara," *Revue de synthèse,* 89 (1968), 67-94; and H. L. L. Busard, "The Translation of the *Elements* of Euclid from the Arabic into Latin by Hermann of Carinthia (?)," *Janus,* 54 (1968), 1-8.

24. John E. Murdoch, "Euclides Graeco-Latinus: A Hitherto Unknown Medieval Latin Translation of the *Elements* Made Directly from the Greek," *Harvard Studies in Classical Philology,* 71 (1966), 249-302.

25. The papers of two other symposia on the liberal arts in the Middle Ages have been published in Josef Koch, *Artes Liberales von der Antiken Bildung zur Wissenschaft des Mittelalters,* Studien und Texte zur Geistesgeschichte des Mittelalters, 5 (Leiden: E. J. Brill, 1959); and *Arts libéraux et philosophie au moyen âge,* Actes du quatrième congrès international de philosophie médiévale, 1967 (Montreal: Institut d'études médiévales, 1969). For the present subject the papers in the latter book by Philippe Delhaye (pp. 161-73), Pearl Kibre (pp. 175-91), and James A. Weisheipl (pp. 209-13) are particularly useful.

26. James A. Weisheipl, "Curriculum of the Faculty of Arts at Oxford in the Early Fourteenth Century," *Mediaeval Studies,* 26 (1946), 171.

27. Unfortunately, the medieval Latin translations of Euclid have not received a comprehensive edition like that which Marshall Clagett has provided in his monumental *Archimedes in the Middle Ages* (see note 29 for bibliographic reference). The translation of Euclid by Campanus was published in Basel in 1558 but has received no modern edition. For medieval MSS of the versions of Adelard, Campanus, and Gerard of Cremona, see Murdoch, "The Medieval Euclid," p. 70, note 9. On the other hand, one other medieval version of Euclid has been published by H. L. L. Busard in "The Translation of the *Elements* of Euclid from the Arabic into Latin by Hermann of Carinthia (?)," *Janus,* 54 (1968), 9-140.

28. Murdoch, "The Medieval Euclid," pp. 80-86.

29. Marshall Clagett, *Archimedes in the Middle Ages,* vol. 1, *The Arabo-Latin Tradition* (Madison: University of Wisconsin Press, 1964); Vol. 2, *The Translations from the Greek by William of Moerbeke,* Memoirs of the American Philosophical Society, 117 (Philadelphia: American Philosophical Society, 1976).

30. See the list of manuscripts of some of these commentaries and paraphrases in Clagett, "Medieval Translations of Euclid," p. 29, note 31.

31. For a handy biography and bibliographical guide, see the article by Kurt Vogel on Leonardo Fibonacci in the *Dictionary of Scientific Biography,* ed. Charles Gillespie (New York: Charles Scribner's Sons, 1971), 4: 604-13.

32. *Scritti di Leonardo Pisano, matematico del secolo decimoterzo,* ed. Baldassarre Boncompagni, vol. 2, *Leonardi Pisani Practica Geometriae ed Opuscoli* (Rome: Tipografia delle scienze matematiche e fisiche, 1862), 207ff.

33. See Edward Grant's article on Jordanus de Nemore in the *Dictionary of Scientific Biography,* 7: 171-79.

34. Edited by Maximilian Curtze, *Jordani Nemorarii Geometria vel de triangulis libri IV,* Mitteilungen des Coppernicus-Vereins für Wissenschaft und Kunst, 6 (Thorn: E. Laubeck, 1887); portions of this work have been reedited and translated by Clagett, *Archimedes in the Middle Ages,* 1: 572-75, 662-63, 672-77.

35. See the article on Grosseteste by A. C. Crombie in the *Dictionary of Scientific Biography,* 5: 548-54; and the one on Bacon by Crombie and J. D. North, 1: 377-85.

36. Passages from Grosseteste's *De lineis, angulis et figuris* and *De natura locorum* translated in A. C. Crombie, *Robert Grosseteste and the Origins of Experimental Science 1100-1700* (Oxford: At the Clarendon Press, 1953), p. 110.

37. The classic presentation of this thesis is in A. C. Crombie, *Augustine to Galileo,* 2nd ed. (London: Mercury Books, 1961), 2: 103-19.

38. H. R. Hahnloser, ed., *Villard de Honnecourt: Kritische Gesamtausgabe des Bauhüttenbuches ms. fr. 19093 der Pariser Nationalbibliothek,* 2nd ed. (Graz: Akademische Druck- und Verlagsanstalt, 1972), p. 11. (My translation.)

39. Douglas Knoop, G. P. Jones, and Douglas Hamer, eds., *The Two Earliest Masonic MSS. The Regius MS (B.M. Bibl. Reg. 17 A1); The Cooke MS (B.M. Add. MS 23198),* Publications of the University of Manchester, 259 (Manchester: Manchester University Press, 1938), p. 73. (Spelling and punctuation modernized.)

40. *Ibid.,* p. 75. (Spelling and punctuation modernized.)

41. *Ibid.,* p. 97. (Spelling and punctuation modernized.)

42. For the latest edition of these booklets, see *Gothic Design Techniques: The Fifteenth-Century Design Booklets of Mathes Roriczer and Hanns Schmuttermayer,* Edited, Translated, and Introduced by Lon R. Shelby (Carbondale: Southern Illinois University Press, 1977).

43. *Ibid.,* p. 121.

44. This can readily be seen from the illustrations that Roriczer and Schmuttermayer provided for their booklets: Shelby, *Gothic Design Techniques,* plates I-III.

45. Lechler's booklet was printed in an uncritical edition, with transliterated text, by August Reichensperger, *Vermischte Schriften über christliche Kunst* (Leipzig: T. O. Weigel, 1856), pp. 133-55; Reichensperger based his edition on the late sixteenth-century copy by Jacob Feucht, now preserved in Cologne, Historisches Archiv, Hs. Wf. 276*. Recently another late sixteenth-century copy has appeared and is now kept in the Heidelberg Universitätsbibliothek, under the signature Hs. 3858. I am presently preparing a critical edition and translation of Lechler's booklet.

BIBLIOGRAPHY ON GEOMETRY

Arts libéraux et philosophie au moyen âge. "Actes du quatrième congrès international de philosophie médiévale, 1967" Montreal: Institut d'études médiévales, 1969.

Clagett, Marshall. *Archimedes in the Middle Ages.* Vol. 1: Madison: University of Wisconsin Press, 1964. Vol. 2: Philadelphia: American Philosophical Society, 1976.

————. "The Medieval Latin Translations from the Arabic of the *Elements* of Euclid, with Special Emphasis on the Versions of Adelard of Bath," *Isis,* 44 (1953), 16-42.

Dilke, O. A. W. *The Roman Land Surveyors: An Introduction to the Agrimensores.* Newton Abbot: David & Charles, 1971.

Haskins, C. H. *Studies in the History of Mediaeval Science.* Cambridge: Harvard University Press, 1924.

Heath, Thomas L. *The Thirteen Books of Euclid's Elements,* 2nd ed. rev. Cambridge: At the University Press, 1926. 3 vols.

Lindberg, David C., ed. *Science in the Middle Ages.* Chicago: University of Chicago Press, 1978. See especially Michael S. Mahoney, "Mathematics," pp. 145-78.

Murdoch, John E. "The Medieval Euclid: Salient Aspects of the Translations of the *Elements* by Adelard of Bath and Campanus of Novara," *Revue de Synthèse,* 89 (1968), 67-94.

Stahl, W. H. *Roman Science: Origins, Development and Influence to the Later Middle Ages.* Madison: University of Wisconsin Press, 1962.

Tannery, Paul. "La Géométrie au xie siècle," *Revue générale internationale, scientifique, littéraire, et artistique,* 15 (1897), 343-57. [Rpt. in *Mémoires scientifique,* vol. 5, ed. J. L. Heiberg. Paris: Gauthier-Villars, 1922.]

————. "Histoire des sciences: Géométrie," *Revue de synthèse historique,* 2 (1901), 283-99: [Rpt. in *Mémoires scientifiques,* Vol. 10, ed. J. L. Heiberg et al. Paris: Gauthier-Villars, 1930.]

Ullman, B. L. "Geometry in the Mediaeval Quadrivium," *Studi di bibliografia e di storica in onore di Tammaro de Marinis.* Verona: Stampera Valdonega, 1964. Vol. IV, pp. 263-85.

Weisheipl, James A. "Classification of the Sciences in Medieval Thought," *Medieval Studies,* 27 (1965), 54-90.

9 *Astronomy*

Claudia Kren

Astronomy, according to Boethius, is the science of movable magnitude. To understand its place in medieval thought, it is necessary to view it from a perspective broader than that of the Latin encyclopedists. Basic to this understanding is the distinction between descriptive and theoretical astronomy. The latter, which analyzed planetary motion, was itself marked by a fundamental tension between physical and mathematical explanation.

Classical astronomy was dominated by the mathematical approach, culminating in Ptolemy's Almagest. *While Cassiodorus apparently based his analysis of the essential topics of astronomy upon Ptolemy, he did little more than cite various chapter headings, with brief definitions. Ptolemy's mathematical astronomy was far too complex to be understood during the early Middle Ages, when astronomy was primarily descriptive.*

This distinction between theoretical and descriptive astronomy can be traced back to two treatises by Eudoxus. On Motion, *which is no longer extant, was the first analysis of heavenly motion to be based on Plato's assumption that planets move in circular paths at a constant velocity. His* Phaenomena, *in contrast, was purely descriptive. The latter treatise served as the source for Aratus's poem, the most popular work in astronomy during antiquity.*

While the principle of mathematical astronomy presumably was the circle, both theoretical and descriptive astronomy took the celestial sphere as their beginning point. This concept goes back to the early Pythagoreans—who, despite their emphasis on celestial harmony, were keen observers of the heavens.

The most satisfactory account of astronomy in the Latin encyclopedist tradition, and the basic source for medieval scholars until the recovery of Greek astronomy, was that of Martianus Capella. Following a brief consideration of the five elements of the geocentric universe, his discussion turned to the standard topics of classical astronomy.

The first topic identified the ten celestial circles. These included the five parallel (or horizontal) circles: the arctic and antarctic cir-

cles, the two tropics, and the celestial equator; the colures (two longitudinal circles dividing the heavens into four equal sections) ; the oblique circles of the Zodiac and Milky Way; and a final circle, the horizon.

The second topic described the sphere of the fixed stars, identifying the constellations and their risings and settings. The final topic focused on the planets, including—as was customary in ancient and medieval astronomy—the sun and the moon. The discussion began with a general consideration of planetary motion, notable for the inclusion of Heraclides' heliocentric theory of the motions of Venus and Mercury. Following an analysis of the distances between the planets (a topic found only in Martianus) , it concluded with a consideration of the individual orbits of each planet. D. L. W.

It is not remarkable that the study of celestial objects, astronomy, should be among the oldest of the sciences. Our primitive forebears, bemused by the spectacle of the night sky and the life-giving splendor of our star, the sun, regarded celestial bodies as divinities requiring respectful attention. The regular periodic motions of celestial bodies, especially the sun and moon, came to control the rhythms of social life and to provide the basis of calendars, hours of the day and night, and other features of human time in the earliest civilizations. Above all, the complexity underlying the superficial regularity of celestial motions early excited intellectual curiosity and awe, a perennial challenge to explain and to understand the universe.

THE ANCIENT LEGACY

The astronomical thought of the Middle Ages, along with so many other aspects of medieval culture, was indebted to conceptions that originated in classical Greece. There, during the fifth century B.C., a cosmology that was to dominate the European mind until well into the Renaissance first appeared among the Pythagoreans, whose sketch of a spherical universe was fashioned into a cosmos by Plato (fourth century B.C.) . Plato's universe, described in the *Timaeus,* was the construction of his Demiurge, a creative force who formed this cosmos according to the mathematical relationships Plato regarded so highly. This symmetrical world was bounded by a sphere containing the fixed stars, with an immobile earth at its center. Below the stars traveled the other celestial bodies: the sun, moon, and the five planets that can be seen with the unaided eye (see figure 9-1) . The starry sphere rotated from

I I. Syſtema Platonis, aut Platonicorum.

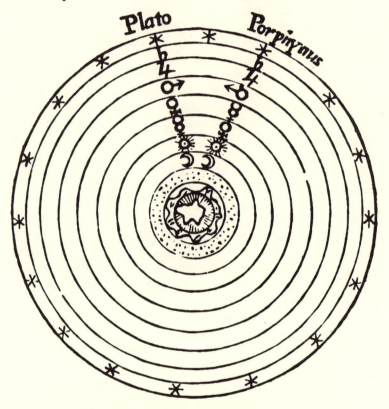

Non deſunt tamē rationes & authoritates,quibus pro-
babile fieri poiſet Eudoxum, Calippum & Ariſtotelem
ſecutos fuiſſe ſyſtema Pythagoræ , de quibus ſuo loco .
Interim falſum eſt,quod ait *Clauius* in ſphæra , ſolum eſ-
ſe Authorem libelli de Mundo ad Alexādrum, qui Mer-
curium ſub Ioue ac ſupra Venerem ponat. Demum Plato concedit in Timæo , Terram verti circa ſuum cen-
trum,quod negat Ariſtoteles.

Fig. 9-1. The Cosmological Scheme of Plato and the Neoplatonists. (From
Pedersen and Pihl, *Early Physics and Astronomy*. With permission of
Neale Watson Academic Publications, Inc.)

east to west every twenty-four hours (the diurnal motion), carrying with it the seven celestial bodies, which moved in the opposite direction, from west to east with individual motions of their own, in or near the inclined path of the ecliptic (the apparent orbit of the sun). The stars, planets, sun, and moon revolved about the central earth with a uniform speed most suited to their eternal, unalterable, and divine nature. Although there will be modifications and added complexities, Plato's model was to provide the outline of the universe for some 1,700 years after the writing of the *Timaeus*.

This beautiful and simple cosmos could not account for the observed irregularities in the motions of the sun, moon, and planets.[1] The planets particularly, the so-called erratic stars of the Middle Ages, presented great complexities to the observer's eye, most unlike the uniform circular motion with which they were assumed to make their way around the earth. As tradition has it, Plato challenged his students to construct mathematical schemes or models that could account for celestial irregularities, always presupposing uniform circular motion around a central earth. The challenge to "save the appearances," to devise an astronomical model that would accord sense with impression, was ably met by Eudoxus of Cnidos,[2] who designed an ingenious system employing concentric spheres, a set for each celestial body. In the Eudoxian scheme, the fixed stars retained their one sphere; the sun and moon had three spheres apiece; while the more complex apparent motion of the five planets required four spheres each (see figure 9-2). The location of the axes, the speeds and direction of motion of the individual spheres in a given set were arranged so that the resultant motion of the planet, attached to the innermost sphere of its set, reproduced the observed irregularities; the entire system of encased concentrics required twenty-seven spheres. Eudoxus may not have been the only pupil of Plato to attempt an astronomical model. A scheme in which Mercury and Venus (planets nearer the sun than the earth and which never appear far from it) actually orbited the sun, while the sun and the other celestial bodies moved around the earth (see figure 9-3), has long been attributed to Heraclides of Pontus. We know little about Heraclides' astronomical ideas; although his heliocentric notions will be reported regularly throughout the medieval period, his views never entered the mainstream of medieval astronomical thought.

The model of Eudoxus, the first genuine mathematical scheme of the universe, though ingenious and admirable, was plagued with difficulties and in many cases failed to "save the appearances." Even the addition of further spheres by the astronomer Callipus could not repair its deficiencies. It might have faded into obscurity had it not been enthusiastically taken up by a better-known pupil of Plato—Aristotle.

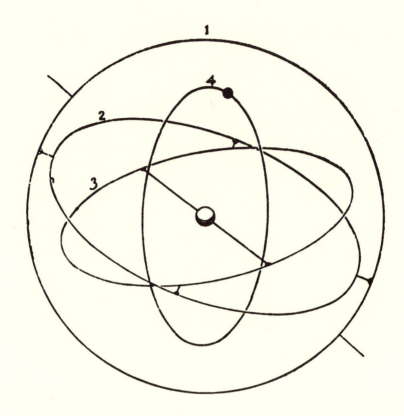

Fig. 9-2. The Planetary Model of Eudoxus. (From Pedersen and Pihl, *Early Physics and Astronomy*. With permission of Neale Watson Academic Publications, Inc.)

In his astronomical work, *On the Heavens,* and also in Book XII of his *Metaphysics,* Aristotle developed a physical theory of the celestial region in which the Eudoxian spheres fitted very well. The heavens were composed of a special material, the "first body" or aether—eternal and unchanging—whose only permitted motion was a uniform circling of an immobile earth. Eudoxus quite likely intended his concentric model to be only a mathematical design, but in Aristotle's adaptation, the Eudoxian spheres were transformed into a physical reality, an actual depiction of the heavens. To accomplish this, Aristotle was forced to add many more spheres to the Eudoxian model as improved by Callipus,

III. Syſtema Ægyptiorum, Vitruuij, Capellæ, Macrobij, Bedæ &c.

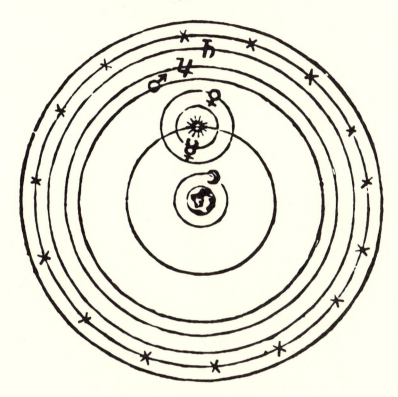

Fig. 9-3. The System of Heraclides of Pontus. (From Pedersen and Pihl, *Early Physics and Astronomy*. With permission of Neale Watson Academic Publications, Inc.)

ending with fifty-five spheres in all. This produced a cluttered celestial region which, while consistent with Aristotle's physical principles, betrayed the mathematical integrity of its source and was, above all, inadequate to account for the facts of observation.[3]

But the mathematical tradition was to reach its apogee in the second century A.D., during the Hellenistic period, with the astronomical system of the Alexandrian astonomer, Claudius Ptolemy. In his work, called the *Almagest*, a name given it by later Arabic admirers, Ptolemy retained the mandatory, uniform, circular motion with the earth as an unmoving center. However, each of the seven celestial bodies was treated as an isolated mathematical problem and their apparent motions were explained by the use of three mathematical devices; the eccentric, the epicycle, and the equant. The first two of these had previously been studied by the mathematician, Apollonius of Perga, and then

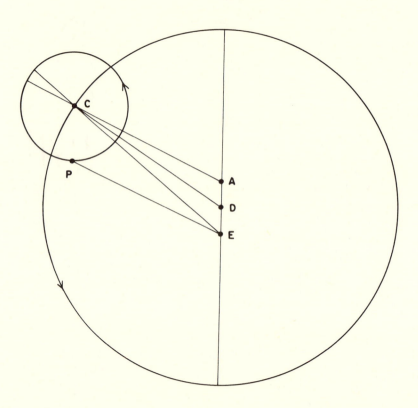

Fig. 9-4. Simplified Ptolemaic Scheme for the Planets (except Mercury). The large circle is the eccentric deferent (center at D), on which moves the small circle, the epicycle (center at C). The planet, P, is carried around the epicycle; the direction of motion of the epicycle and of the epicycle center on the eccentric is indicated by the arrows. The earth is at E; A is the equant center, the center of equal motion, while the eccentric center (D) is the center of equal distance. AD = DE.

utilized by Ptolemy's predecessor, the astronomer Hipparchus (second century B.C.) ; the equant was Ptolemy's own contribution. In the Ptolemaic system, the eccentric is the circular orbit of the celestial object, but, as the name implies, its center is not the earth. The epicycle is a small circle whose center in turn moves on the eccentric's circumference; the planet, for example, being carried around on the epicycle. The equant, which Ptolemy found necessary to introduce into his planetary models, is a point lying on the line joining the earth and the eccentric center, with the distance of earth to eccentric center equal to the distance of eccentric center to equant. The function of the equant is to serve as the center of uniform motion while the center of the eccentric is the locus of equal distance. Ptolemy used one or more of these devices in his various models; in the case of the planets, all three were necessary (see figure 9-4) .

The Ptolemaic scheme worked very well indeed; it did "save the appearances" in that it made the prediction of celestial position possible. However, this success was achieved at a high price. The devices of the *Almagest* violated several Aristotelian tenets as to the motion of the celestial substance; for example, that all celestial bodies must move uniformly equidistant from a physical earth. There was also a deeper conflict between the older system of Aristotle-Eudoxus and the mathematical presentation of Ptolemy, one which was deeply felt by the commentators and astronomers of the late Hellenistic age. Whatever its astronomical deficiencies, the earlier scheme had created a physically real and unified cosmos that Ptolemaic models, with each celestial body as a distinct problem in spherical trigonometry, could not provide. Faced with the agonizing confrontation of a material universe that was astronomically invalid on the one hand and a mathematical design that, although satisfying sense impression, was physically impossible on the other, late antiquity seized on a convenient compromise. The physicist, or natural philosopher, had as his purview the physical causes of celestial phenomena, while the task of the astronomer was to design hypotheses that need not be true so long as they were mathematically viable and "saved the appearances." Yet this assignment of disparate roles was not really satisfactory. Since the physicist supplied the causes for the motions that the astronomer's hypotheses were to explain, the astronomer's speculations were not completely free; his hypotheses were constrained by the presumed characteristics of the Aristotelian "first body."

Eventually, when the texts that underlie this conflict were again available, the Middle Ages would inherit this dilemma. But not for centuries; during a long period of decline, when neither the *Almagest* nor the relevant texts of Aristotle were directly known, medieval astronomical writers would confront an entirely different problem—to preserve and transmit the vague rudiments of a past glory.

LATE ANTIQUITY

The admirable achievements of Greek astronomy reached their highest point in the Hellenistic period, a triumph that was, however, shadowed by a perceptible decline of inventiveness in the Greek spirit. Technical subjects such as astronomy increasingly tended to be explicated in a popular type of treatise, the handbook or manual, in which complex ideas were excerpted and simplified. By no means were all of these compilations inferior; those of Geminus, Cleomedes, and Theon of Smyrna reveal a high level of astronomical expertise.[4] But it appears that familiarity with such technical epitomies was confined to a very small group; while astronomy remained a popular field of study in the schools of Hellenistic Greece, it was a work such as the *Phaenomena* of Aratus, a superficial and not very accurate compilation dealing with the constellations, that was more valued.

The decline in the cultivation of technical astronomy was exacerbated by the Roman inheritance of the Hellenistic world. The Roman spirit was not attracted to theoretical science; Romans had a marked penchant for the practical, for handbooks that supplied basic and concise information but omitted the intricacies of technical detail. While Roman education did include the mathematical quadrivium, this was primarily because Greek educational methods were fashionable. Aratus was repeatedly translated into Latin, while more informative materials remained unread. In Hellenistic Greece, the handbook or manual of epitomized astronomical information had been the lowest level of treatise available; in Rome, the handbook flourished. Roman neglect of technical science can be illustrated by the fate of the enormous and learned encyclopedia of Varro, a vast work that covered all the arts and also included architecture and medicine. It did not survive beyond the early centuries of the Common Era, while such works as the mythologically oriented *Astronomicon* of Hyginus, Vitruvius's *On Architecture*, and above all, the monumental *Natural History* of Pliny were to be respected as authoritative for centuries. Due to the decline in late Greek cultivation of technical science and the Roman indifference to this heritage, the early Middle Ages received, on a whole, a legacy of superficial and meager astronomical information, usually remote even from the Hellenistic handbook. The major works of Greek science, philosophy, and mathematics were to be unread for the most part in the first medieval centuries; they were transferred to the Arabs, both in the East and in Spain, to be conserved until their eventual return to Latin Europe.

When Christianity came to be the only vital force in a dying Roman world, leaders of the Christian community in the West faced serious decisions regarding pagan culture, including science and philosophy. A small but articulate minority was prepared to sever all connection with pagan learning. Fortunately, although Christian attitudes toward the classical heritage were long to remain ambivalent, the dominant attitude became one of compromise. While, for example, Tertullian would have jettisoned all Greek learning, the moderate views of Augustine prevailed. His rationale—to separate out what was inoffensive in the pagan legacy—was a powerful influence in the survival of the liberal arts as a program of study for Christian youth. Indeed, his view of these disciplines as an indispensible introduction for the journey of the human soul toward the true wisdom of Scripture will be echoed repeatedly throughout the early Middle Ages. Augustine himself apparently intended to write treatises on each of the arts; he compiled several lists of the subjects to be included among them, although astronomy was omitted from his last list. One can speculate that this omission may well reflect the fear of astronomical studies shared by many of the Christian elite due to the close ties between astronomy and its pseudoscience sister, astrology. As had astronomy, astrology reached a peak of technical perfection in Hellenistic Greece; Ptolemy was also the author of a major astrological work, the *Tetrabiblos*. Popular astrology, especially the casting of horoscopes, had a tremendous appeal in imperial Rome. From the quack of the street and circus to the pet astrological expert close to the throne, astrological influences were widespread indeed. One can understand Christian suspicion of an area of study that was based on the belief that individual destiny was fatalistically determined by the stars rather than by the will of God.

In addition to its association with astrology, the study of the heavens was a sensitive area where the fathers of the church might well believe that they could speak with considerable authority. However, church fathers such as Ambrose and Augustine managed to reconcile their rudimentary knowledge of the Greek universe with the doctrines of *Genesis*. Even the waters over the firmament, mentioned in the first chapter of *Genesis*, provided no real difficulty. Mentioned repeatedly by Christian authors during the early medieval period, these celestial waters were usually considered as transparent, cold, crystalline, or even allegorical. Thus, despite association with a dubious superstition and the need for compliance with scriptural doctrine, astronomy received Christian approbation as a suitable area of study and concern.

EARLY MIDDLE AGES

Thus astronomy is found among the quadrivium subjects in the discussions of such important Christian authors as Cassiodorus and Isidore of Seville. Cassiodorus's *On Sacred and Profane Letters,* written for the guidance of his scholar-monks at Vivarium, displays a very limited knowledge of Greek astronomical thought, although what he includes is factual and clear. He describes the Greek spherical cosmos in fragmentary fashion; the motion of the planets is to be calculated by adding or subtracting corrections, a pathetic remnant of Ptolemaic procedures. Cassiodorus refers to Ptolemy by name, but the great Alexandrian is a mere memory. Whether or not Boethius completed a handbook on astronomy remains unknown. Apparently, he did intend to write on all the mathematical disciplines; there is a letter of Cassiodorus addressed to Boethius stating that the latter had made the astronomy of Ptolemy available to the Italians. And centuries later, there are also the letters of Gerbert that allude to an astronomical work, perhaps by Boethius, located at the northern Italian monastery at Bobbio.[5]

Isidore, bishop of Seville during the seventh century, is another example of the Christian accommodation to classical learning. Isidore treats astronomy in his *On the Nature of Things* as well as in his better-known and exhaustive encyclopedia, the *Etymologies.* As was true of Cassiodorus, his familiarity with Greek astronomy is meager. In the *Etymologies,* Isidore reports that astronomy was invented by the Egyptians, among whom Ptolemy, king of Egypt, was paramount. In common with other early medieval compilers and commentators, Isidore becomes confused when his sources are complex or possibly unreliable. Thus, in *On the Nature of Things,* the Spanish encyclopedist appears to transfer celestial circles such as the equator and the tropics to a flat earth, but this is surely due to the inadequacy of his sources or his own inaccurate copying; there is no reason to assume that Isidore believed the earth was flat.

Limited as it was, the astronomical information in Cassiodorus and Isidore became a valued part of the Latin encyclopedic tradition. The inclusion of astronomy, even at a primitive level, in works by Christian authors of unimpeachable respectability must have furthered the acceptance of the discipline in a curriculum of secular studies under church patronage. Even in the late sixth century, classical learning was by no means entirely acceptable in the higher circles of church opinion as a letter from Isidore's contemporary, Pope Gregory I, rebuking a bishop in Gaul for teaching secular subjects, reveals.[6]

The fund of astronomical information drawn on by early medieval authors was generally remote from ancient sources. But there is one notable exception; the first two-thirds of Plato's *Timaeus* was translated into Latin and supplied with an extensive commentary by the fourth-century Neoplatonist, Chalcidius. The *Timaeus,* a difficult work containing strange notions on a variety of subjects, had long been a focus of commentary. The belief that it must contain the secrets of nature undoubtedly ensured that of all Plato's dialogues it would have been made available to the early Middle Ages. Chalcidius's commentary on the work, illustrated with complicated diagrams, is the most technical of the early medieval treatments of astronomy. This is not surprising; in 1849, T. H. Martin established that Chalcidius had copied portions of the astronomical manual of Theon of Smyrna, although in the style of medieval commentators, Chalcidius never mentions his source. Thus, as Chalcidius had copied one of the best of the Greek handbooks, written close to the time of Ptolemy, it is not remarkable that his commentary reveals considerable expertise. Chalcidius describes what purports to be the heliocentric notion of Heraclides. The account is garbled, with Chalcidius attributing epicycles to both Heraclides and Plato, a temporal confusion not unknown among early medieval writers; however, he is the only author of this period who actually mentions Heraclides by name.

The medieval heirs of the epitomizing tendency of Hellenistic popular science, which the Romans had found so much to their liking, were the Latin encyclopedist, Martianus Capella, and the commentator, Macrobius, both of the fifth century. Astronomy appears in Book VIII of Martianus's *Marriage of Philology and Mercury;* as are her companion bridesmaids, she is an awesome authority in her specialty. She has flown through the entire heaven, but will limit her discussion to phenomena observed in the Northern Hemisphere; she knows the marvels of astronomical knowledge accumulated by Egyptian priests, among whom she has spent 40,000 years. Book VIII, however, is on the whole an excellent guide to Greek astronomical thought, reflecting the professional nature of its source, the lost encyclopedia of Varro. Although the shortest of the quadrivium discourses in the *Marriage,* it is certainly the best. Martianus has his personification of astronomy provide a clear statement of the purported heliocentric motion of Mercury and Venus, and thus Book VIII of the *Marriage* became the primary transmitter of this notion in the Middle Ages. In summary, where astronomy limits herself to elementary material, she speaks very well; where she ventures into more complex areas, her displays of erudition fail to inspire confidence. But Book VIII provided the early medieval period with a satisfactory astronomical handbook, and, as W. H. Stahl, the editor of the *Marriage*, suggests, Ptolemy, who is among the wedding guests, would have joined in the applause following her speech.

Martianus was used as a school text during the fifth and sixth centuries in North Africa and Southern Europe. The work was especially popular during the Carolingian period, when the *Marriage* was the subject of several commentaries. Even after the end of millenium, when Greek astronomical thought was filtering back into Western Europe, Martianus retained his authority. The work was still read at Chartres, even though the Neoplatonism of Chartrain scholars naturally drew them to the *Timaeus*. Book VIII continued to be excerpted in the later Middle Ages, appearing disguised as the so-called *Book of Hipparchus*, although Martianus had no connection with Ptolemy's predecessor. Copernicus also, in the sixteenth century, mentioned Martianus Capella as one of those in the past who had suggested heliocentric orbits for Mercury and Venus.

Rivaling Book VIII of the *Marriage* in force of authority and in popularity was Macrobius's *Commentary on the Dream of Scipio*, based on a small work by Cicero. While it is not possible to identify Macrobius with certainty, he was a Neoplatonist, and his commentary was to become, next to that of Chalcidius, a major source of Neoplatonic thought in the medieval period. However, almost half of the *Commentary* deals with astronomy, and this section was often bound separately. It circulated widely and was obviously of great interest to medieval readers to judge by the many marginal glosses and notations in the manuscripts of the work. Macrobius's astronomical information came directly from Greek material; his primary source was the lost commentary on the *Timaeus* by the Neoplatonist, Porphyry (third century A.D.). Like the work of other derivative authors, Macrobius's astronomical account reveals occasional inconsistencies and confusions. An example is his attempt to arrive at an order for the planets, counting out from the earth. Traditionally, the difficulty, actually not solvable in either the Middle Ages or antiquity, concerned only the positions of the planets Mercury and Venus, whose orbits are within that of the earth; there was never disagreement as to the relative positions of the other celestial bodies. In the *Almagest*, Ptolemy had placed Mercury and Venus below the sun, but Macrobius apparently preferred the Platonic order in which these planets are located above the sun. His discussion of this subject is so ambiguous that he has been associated with Chalcidius and Martianus Capella as a transmitter of the Heraclidean system. However, in another passage of the *Commentary*, it is evident that, as a Neoplatonist, Macrobius favored positioning above the sun all five planets visible to the unaided eye.

Throughout the medieval period, the *Commentary on the Dream of Scipio* commanded the same level of high esteem as did the encyclopedia of Martianus; both continue to be mentioned as astronomical authorities for centuries, even after the return of Greek astronomy to the Latin West.

Encyclopedists such as Isidore of Seville or Martianus Capella and commentators on classical works such as Chalcidius and Macrobius preserved a certain amount of simple, descriptive, astronomical information. Oddly enough, during the seventh and eighth centuries, a theological crisis necessitated the revival of a somewhat higher level of technical astronomy. The issue arose from the pressing need to calculate the date of Easter. Originally, Easter had been associated with the Hebrew festival of Passover, but early in the Christian era those who wished to dissociate Easter from the Jewish holiday found that to determine the day on which Easter would fall in any given year, an adjustment had to be made between the Julian calendar in use in Rome, based on the apparent motion of the sun, and the Hebrew calendar, which was lunar. As the length of the Julian year and that of the month (the "year" of the moon) were not commensurable, calculation of the Easter date in a given year meant use of a scheme of intercalation based on some definite cycle. By the fourth century, the church had decided on a nineteen-year cycle containing 235 lunations or appearances of the moon. However, it was difficult to arrive at complete uniformity among all Christians, and the problem remained as to just how a series of Easter dates was to be calculated. There was, however, an understandably strong motivation to achieve uniformity in the date of Easter throughout all of Christendom. This demanded more astronomical expertise, especially in regard to the motion of the moon, than could be found in the handbook authors. In fact, the Easter problem created a genre of astronomical writing, the *computus,* that was to retain a permanent niche in medieval astronomical literature. *Computi* were usually small treatises, often anonymous, that included directions for the calculation of Easter tables, tables of the moon's motion used to assist calculation, and the dates of coming Easters. They originated in Spain but by the eighth century had spread throughout continental Europe and to England and Ireland. Undoubtedly the most influential eighth-century *computus* was that of the learned Northumbrian monk, Bede. Northumbria, in northern England, had experienced an Easter dating crisis and had been brought into conformity with Rome, but Bede found that his students were still confused as to methods and procedures. Thus he composed the long computistical treatise, *On the Reckoning of Time,* for their use. While intended for Bede's students at his monastery at Jarrow, the reputation of his *computus* spread to the schools of Carolingian France as well as to other educational centers where it served as a model for subsequent *computi*. The tradition was a persistent one; even in the late Middle Ages, it is not uncommon to find a *computus* among the texts to be read by university students.

CAROLINGIAN AND OTTONIAN REVIVALS; CHARTRES

On the continent, the educational reforms brought about by Alcuin of York's arrival in Carolingian France in the latter part of the eighth century revived the teaching of the liberal arts at the Palace School and inspired efforts elsewhere in the Frankish realm. Alcuin, despite some suspicion of secular learning, explicitly favored what was by now a traditional attitude of Christian teachers: the study of the arts would not only enable Christian youth to surpass the heretics but was a beneficial preparation for the understanding of Scripture. Astronomical studies were part of this program; Alcuin himself wrote a *computus* among the texts he composed for instruction at the Palace School, and perhaps at Tours, where he spent his last years. His famous pupil, Rabanus Maurus, abbot of the German monastery at Fulda where the cultivation of learning begun with Alcuin was to continue, wrote an astronomical work in imitation of Isidore and, like Alcuin, composed a computistical treatise. At about this time also, Helperic of Auxerre produced his own *computus*. Helperic's work, Bede's *On the Reckoning of Time*, and the *computus* of John of Gerland, written in the eleventh century, were to be the most influential medieval treatises in this genre.

The cultural revival in Carolingian Frankland brought to France several Irish scholars who were especially attracted to the *Marriage* of Martianus Capella. During the ninth century, Dunchad of the Irish colony at Laon, the better-known John Scotus Erigena, as well as Remigius of Auxerre, all wrote commentaries on Martianus that faithfully endorsed the heliocentric motion of Mercury and Venus mentioned in their source. Remigius's commentary, based on those of Dunchad and Erigena, was far more extensive and influential than those of his predecessors. He was one of a small group of scholars, often linked by personal ties, who kept alive the study of astronomy and the other arts under difficult circumstances at such centers as Auxerre and Rheims. At the latter cathedral school, the great bishop, Hincmar, teacher of the computist Helperic of Auxerre, had established a program of secular studies, and Remigius taught the astronomy of Martianus and Macrobius at both Rheims and Auxerre.

Despite the political turmoil following the dissolution of the Carolingian empire and the devastation resulting from Viking and Magyar invasions, the revival begun in Frankish lands spread to German Lotharingia. Under Cluniac inspiration, church reformers such as John of Gorze led the rejuvenation of education in monastic and cathedral schools in the dioceses of Metz, Gorze, and Liège. The cathedral school at Liège became famous for its instruction in the quadrivium; there scholars such as Notker of Liège stressed mathematical and astronomical studies. Astronomy was of considerable interest in other German foundations. A student of Notker, Heriger, as abbot of Lobbes, supervised a library containing many astronomical texts and also wrote computistical treatises, while to the south, at St. Gall, still famous today for its collection of manuscripts, Notker Labeo taught astronomy using a celestial globe he had constructed. Notker Labeo also wrote a *computus* based on Bede as had so many of this group of scholars.

The tenth century marked the beginning of European contact with the superior scientific culture of Moslem Spain. John of Gorze had spent three years at Cordova, perhaps in contact with Arabic materials. It is probable that the first Latin European treatise on the astrolabe was written during the late tenth century by Llobet of Barcelona in Catalan Spain. Llobet's work, derived from Moslem sources, obviously spread to German Reichenau, where Herman the Lame wrote an early treatise on the astrolabe similar to that of Llobet. There were evidently Arabic materials at Reichenau; Herman, who knew no Arabic, likewise composed treatises on two instruments of Islamic origin—a type of quadrant and a portable sundial.[7] The astrolabe was familiar to Lotharingian scholars, as mention of the instrument in a letter of Radolf of Liège to a friend at Cologne clearly attests. There were connections between Lorraine and German lands to the south; for example, Berno, a master at Reichenau, had previously been abbot of Prüm, a Lotharingian foundation. Lotharingian astronomers enjoyed a high reputation during the eleventh century, and many were encouraged to emigrate to England under royal patronage. In the last decade of the century, the astrolabe could be found in England, introduced by Walcher of Malvern, himself a Lotharingian import.

The appearance of the astrolabe returned to Latin Europe its most important and best-known astronomical instrument. Originally Greek, the astrolabe had been in Moslem hands for centuries where it enjoyed the same esteem it was now to experience in Christian Europe. As one can see in figure 9-5, the astrolable consisted of three superimposed metal plates. The bottom one, with a graduated limb, was recessed so as to hold the middle plate on which was engraved a stereographic projection of the tropics and the celestial equator, as well as the horizon line, the hour-angle lines, and the lines of equal azimuth and equal altitude (the *almucantars*) for a particular geographical latitude. A

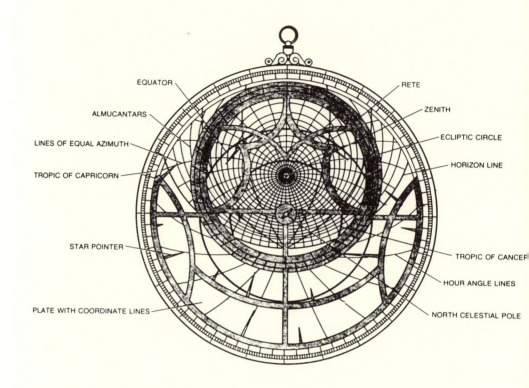

EQUATOR
RETE
ALMUCANTARS
ZENITH
LINES OF EQUAL AZIMUTH
ECLIPTIC CIRCLE
TROPIC OF CAPRICORN
HORIZON LINE
STAR POINTER
TROPIC OF CANCER
HOUR ANGLE LINES
PLATE WITH COORDINATE LINES
NORTH CELESTIAL POLE

Fig. 9-5. The Front of an Astrolabe. (From J. D. North, "The Astrolabe." Copyright © January, 1974 by *Scientific American*. All rights reserved.)

third or top plate (the *rete*) had a projection of the ecliptic and also the positions of a number of significant stars. As figure 9-5 reveals, as much of the *rete* as possible was cut away so as to make the underlying plate as visible as possible. All plates were fastened by a pin at the point designating the north celestial pole so that the *rete* could be rotated. The back of the astrolabe (figure 9-6) was provided with various useful scales and a pivoted sighting device. European astrolabes also had such a pointer on the front of the instrument. The astrolabe was used to determine celestial altitudes and to tell time; it could also be employed in surveying problems such as finding the depths of wells or the heights of objects. Above all, it served as a kind of computer as with it one could solve problems in spherical trigonometry of astronomical or astrological interest without recourse to calculation. During the Middle Ages, the most influential treatise on the instrument was that written in Arabic by Māshā' allāh and translated into Latin in the late thir-

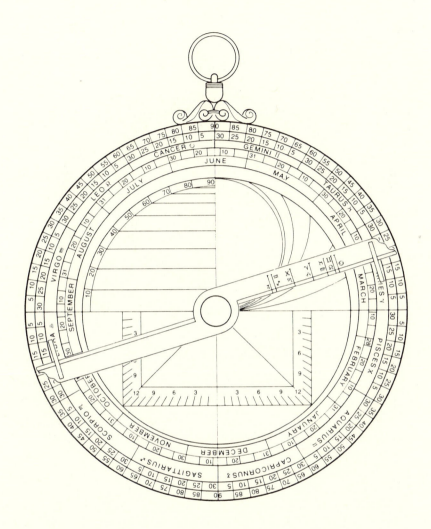

Fig. 9-6. The Back of an Astrolabe. (From J. D. North, "The Astrolabe." Copyright © January, 1974 by *Scientific American*. All rights reserved.)

teenth century. This work was the source of several late medieval astrolabe treatments, including that written in English for his son by Chaucer. The astrolabe retained its popularity in Europe well into the seventeenth century.

Early connections between Moslem Spain and Latin Europe are discernible also in the career of Gerbert of Aurillac, who became Pope Sylvester II around the turn of the millennium. As a young man Gerbert studied at the monastery of Santa Maria de Ripoll in Catalan Spain; there is evidence of literary contacts between Ripoll and Barcelona, and it seems likely that Gerbert was exposed to Arabic astronomical information during his student days. Before his ascension to the papacy, Gerbert taught at various schools, among them Rheims, where he was one of the few masters of his day capable of teaching all the liberal arts. Gerbert has left a legacy of letters that confirm his astronomical interests. He was familiar with the traditional authorities such as Pliny, Isidore, Martianus, and Macrobius, but his astronomical teaching transcended the information in these earlier authors. He wrote a work on the astrolabe and designed several astronomical instruments for teaching purposes. One of these devices combined sighting tubes with a celestial globe so as to enable his students to relate with greater precision the actual position of heavenly bodies to their location on the sphere.

During the twelfth century, just as the trickle of astronomical information coming into the Latin West from Arabic sources was to rise to a flood, interest in older Neoplatonic materials, the *Timaeus* and the *Commentary on Scipio's Dream of Macrobius,* was revived by a group of scholars and teachers at Chartres. As might be expected, the writing of commentaries and glosses on these works was a favorite literary activity of Chartrain masters. However, William of Conches, Thierry of Chartres, and Bernard Silvestris treated their Neoplatonic sources with a fresh outlook. Seemingly an outpost of the old astronomical learning at a time when Europe was undergoing a scientific revival, Chartrain scholars were not immune to new influences. They considered themselves moderns; to paraphrase slightly the famous statement of Thierry's brother, Bernard of Chartres, they did believe that they saw further than their predecessors even if they stood on the shoulders of giants. Chartrain authors attempted to explicate the Platonic cosmos of their sources in terms of natural causation; in their view, nature itself was to be exalted and placed in the realm of the divine. Sacred texts were subject to a natural exegesis; for example, Thierry of Chartres in his commentary on *Genesis* explained that the universe and its celestial bodies operated according to the laws of nature. Even the well-known waters above the firmament received a physical explanation. The main constituent of the celestial region is fire (an old Platonic view) that has vaporized the terrestrial waters and raised them above the heavens. Thierry also wrote an encyclopedia of the liberal arts that he explicitly links to the tradition of Varro, Pliny, and Martianus Capella. In this work, the *Heptateuchon,* Thierry compiled a reading list of some forty-five books, a complete curriculum of the arts; his texts for the study of astronomy were the old *Astronomicon* of Hyginus and some material he identified with the name of Ptolemy. The same attitude toward nature, and the same blend of the old with recent materials, can be found in the *Cosmographia* of Bernard Silvestris, a contemporary of Thierry. In Bernard's view, the cosmos is a grandiose production with the macrocosm of the heavens and the microcosm of man linked together by natural causes, even by an astrological determinism that Bernard found in the Hermetic tradition, but particularly in the newly translated work of the Arabic astrological author, Albumasar.[8]

TWELFTH-CENTURY RENAISSANCE AND AFTER

About the time that Chartrain scholars were engaged with older Neoplatonic sources, scientific works, long absent from Latin Europe were being restored, first in translation from Arabic and, somewhat later, directly from Greek. Among the twelfth-century translators from Arabic, Gerard of Cremona unquestionably did more to restore the Greek scientific heritage to the Latin West than any other individual; for example, he was responsible for the return of the *Almagest*. While in Moslem hands, Greek astronomy had been carefully studied and mastered, and Europe's translators—again Gerard of Cremona is prominent —found numerous works on technical astronomy of Arabic origin.[9] These translations provided a valuable bonus for the Latin West. During this time also, the long-absent works on natural science of Aristotle, including his *On the Heavens* and the *Metaphysics,* also returned to Latin Europe, accompanied, as part of the Arabic bonus, by the commentaries of the Spanish Moslem, Averroes. Later, in the thirteenth century, Aristotle's *On the Heavens* was translated from Greek by William of Moerbeke, who also translated the commentary on that work by the sixth-century Neoplatonist, Simplicius.

This restoration of the Greek heritage and the reception of Arabic materials roughly coincided with the birth of a new type of European educational institution, the university. During the early thirteenth century, faculties of arts at the new institutions developed rapidly, as a degree in arts was a mandatory gateway to the study of medicine, theology, or law. Although logic was always to be the dominant subject in the medieval arts curriculum, astronomy was among the requirements for the arts degree. At an elementary level, the most frequently used text was the *Sphere,* written in the early thirteenth century by John of Sacrobosco. While Sacrobosco's *Sphere* was by no means the only work of this type or with this title, it was always to be the most popular and was often a focus of commentary. As an elementary work that presented simple and clear information on the celestial sphere as well as the out-

demands? This was certainly attempted by several Arabic astronomers. Unfortunately, the more ingenious of these efforts did not reach Europe during the Middle Ages, although the Latin West did have a translation of the concentric system devised by the Spanish Moslem, Alpetragius (al-Biṭrūjī) ; however, this alternative was never a serious rival to Ptolemy.

So long as astronomical theory was dominated by the purported characteristics of a metaphysical entity—Aristotle's "first body," itself a hypothesis—the peculiar distinction between physical and mathematical astronomy was possibly the only resolution of the celestial dilemma confronting the Middle Ages. Eventually, after a period of slow erosion, this domination will vanish, and a fresh start will be made that will see the end of both the spheres of Aristotle and the epicycles and eccentrics of Ptolemy.

Our volume on the liberal arts during the Middle Ages has concluded with this survey of astronomy during the medieval period. One must stress here, as a final word, that throughout their long history, the liberal arts have always comprised an interconnected group of disciplines and have ever been considered preparatory for a definite and much desired end.

To the Greeks, who invented the body of studies called the liberal arts, they were an *enkuklos paideia,* an educational round or circle. Plato considered pursuit of the liberal arts as a necessary first step in his ideal system of education.

During the Middle Ages, the liberal arts, fixed at seven, still were an educational unity in the old Greek sense; their purpose now a preparation for the true understanding of divine Scripture.

Today, the conception of what constitutes a program of liberal arts has enormously enlarged with the inclusion of studies undreamed of by our ancient and medieval forebears. But our liberal arts programs still retain the ancient notion of an *enkuklos paideia*—do we not speak of a person trained in the arts as "well-rounded?" Today also, study of the liberal arts is still a preparation for a higher goal, a basic step toward the fulfillment of our human capacity.

NOTES, SOURCES, AND SUGGESTED READING

1. The apparent eastward motion of the celestial bodies is not uniform, nor do they appear always equidistant from the earth. Irregularities in the motion of the planets are especially evident; due to the optical illusion created by the

assumption that the earth is not in motion, the planets appear to stop at intervals and even go backward for a period.

2. Eudoxus described his astronomical model in a work, *On Speeds,* which is lost. However, Aristotle provided a summary account in Book VII of the *Metaphysics,* and it was also discussed by Simplicius in his commentary on Aristotle's *On the Heavens.* Eudoxus's associate, Callipus, tried to improve the model by adding one sphere to the sets of Mars, Venus, Mercury, plus two additional spheres to each set of the sun and the moon.

3. In his adaptation of the Eudoxian system, Aristotle suggested a mechanical linkage, with motion transferred from the sphere of the fixed stars downward through all the spheres. The extra spheres he added were to counteract those motions that were not to be transferred.

For Greek cosmology from the pre-Socratics through Heraclides of Pontus, T. H. Heath, *Aristarchus of Samos* (Oxford: Clarendon Press, 1959), is very valuable. Most histories of astronomy have chapters on Greek cosmology and Hellenistic astronomical thought. Excellent accounts can be found in J. L. E. Dreyer, *A History of Astronomy from Thales to Kepler* (New York: Dover Publications, 1953). Other histories of use are: G. Abetti, *The History of Astronomy* (New York: H. Schuman, 1952); D. R. Dicks, *Early Greek Astronomy* (Ithaca, N.Y.: Cornell University Press, 1970); A. Pannekoek, *A History of Astronomy* (New York: Interscience Publications, 1961); S. Toulmin, J. Goodfield, *The Fabric of the Heavens* (London: Hutchinson, 1961).

For an edition of the *Timaeus,* with extensive commentary, see F. M. Cornford, *Plato's Cosmology* (London: Routledge and Kegan Paul, 1952). There are English translations of Aristotle's works in the Loeb Classical Library and in the volumes published by Oxford under the general editorship of W. D. Ross. Heath and Dreyer (mentioned above) are very useful on the cosmological ideas of Plato and Aristotle. Also, for Aristotle's cosmology as presented in *On the Heavens,* see Friedrich Solmsen, *Aristotle's System of the Physical World* (Ithaca, N.Y.: Cornell University Press, 1960).

An English translation of the *Almagest* can be found in R. C. Taliaferro, *Great Books of the Western World,* XVI (Chicago: W. Benton, 1952). For helpful explanations of the details of Ptolemaic theory, see O. Neugebauer, *The Exact Sciences in Antiquity* (New York: Harper Torchbook, 1962), Appendix I; F. S. Benjamin, Jr. and G. J. Toomer, *Campanus of Novara and Medieval Planetary Theory* (Madison: University of Wisconsin Press, 1971), 39-56; O. Pedersen, *A Survey of the Almagest* (Odense: Odense University Press, 1974).

An account of the various attitudes toward conflicting astronomical theories in late antiquity can be found in S. Sambursky, *The Physical World of Late Antiquity* (London: Routledge and Kegan Paul, 1962).

4. Geminus (first century B.C.), *Introduction to the Phaemonena;* Cleomedes (possibly first century B.C. or first or second century A.D.), *On the Cyclic Motions of the Celestial Bodies;* Theon of Smyrna (second century A.D.), *A Manual of Mathematical Knowledge Useful for an Understanding of Plato.*

W. H. Stahl, *Roman Science* (Madison: University of Wisconsin Press, 1962) is indispensible for the Greek handbook tradition, Roman science, and attitudes toward learning, as well as for early medieval encyclopedists and commentators. On education in late antiquity and Christian attitudes toward pagan learning, see H. I. Marrou, *A History of Education in Antiquity,* G. Lamb, trans. (New York: Sheed and Ward, 1956). R. R. Bolgar, *The Classical*

Heritage and Its Beneficiaries (New York: Harper Torchbook, 1964) is also valuable.

The fortunes of Greek science and philosophy among the Arabs is the topic of two books by F. E. Peters: *Allah's Commonwealth* (New York: Simon and Schuster, 1973) and *Aristotle and the Arabs* (New York: New York University Press, 1968). For the transmission of Greek thought to the Islamic world, see D. L. O'Leary, *How Greek Science Passed to the Arabs* (London: Routledge and Kegan Paul, 1949).

Augustine's educational theories and his attitude toward the liberal arts are discussed in George Howie, *Educational Theory and Practice in St. Augustine* (London: Routledge and Kegan Paul, 1969). For early medieval education, see: Pierre Riché, *Education et culture dans l'occident barbare, VI—VIIIe siècles* (Paris, 1962).

The elaborate structure of Hellenistic astrology is thoroughly treated in A. Bouché-Leclercq, *L'Astrologie grecque* (Brussels: Culture et Civilisation, 1963). Ptolemy's *Tetrabiblos* can be found in the Loeb Classical Library; Frederick H. Cramer, *Astrology in Roman Law and Politics* (Philadelphia: American Philosophical Society, 1954) is an informative work on astrology in imperial Rome. For the attitude of the church fathers toward Greek astronomical thought, see Pierre Duhem, *Le Système du monde,* 10 vols. (Paris, 1913-59), vol. II, 393-501.

5. The evidence for an astronomical work by Boethius is discussed in W. H. Stahl, *Martianus Capella and the Seven Liberal Arts,* vol. I, *The Quadrivium of Martianus Capella* (New York: Columbia University Press, 1971), 173, note 6.

6. R. R. Bolgar, *The Classical Heritage,* 96.

As previously mentioned, there is an extensive discussion of early medieval encyclopedists and commentators in Stahl, *Roman Science.* Editions of Cassiodorus and Isidore of Seville are: L. W. Jones, ed., *An Introduction to Divine and Human Readings by Cassiodorus Senator* (New York: Columbia University Press, 1946) and E. Brehaut, ed., *An Encyclopedist of the Dark Ages* (New York: Columbia University Press, 1912). The definitive edition of the *Marriage of Philology and Mercury* of Martianus Capella, with extensive notes and discussion, is that due primarily to W. H. Stahl. Volume I of this edition, which analyzes the quadrivium books, has been mentioned above. Volume II is an edition of the *Marriage.* W. H. Stahl, Richard Johnson, trans., *Martianus Capella and the Seven Liberal Arts,* vol. II, *The Marriage of Philology and Mercury* (New York: Columbia University Press, 1977).

Stahl has also edited the *Commentary* of Macrobius, with a valuable introduction and notes. W. H. Stahl, trans., *Macrobius, Commentary on the Dream of Scipio* (New York: Columbia University Press, 1952).

A good treatment of the Easter problem, Easter cycles and tables, and *computi* can be found in the introductory section of C. W. Jones, ed., *Bedae Opera de temporibus* (Cambridge, Mass.: Mediaeval Academy of America, 1943). This volume also contains an edition of Bede's *On the Reckoning of Time,* but not in English translation. Robert R. Newton, *Medieval Chronicles and the Rotation of the Earth* (Baltimore: The Johns Hopkins University Press, 1972), 15-41, is also useful.

7. The quadrant described by Herman was the so-called old quadrant (fig. 9-7). A flat plate, one-quarter of a circle (hence the name), its curved edge graduated in degrees, the instrument was equipped with a pointer and

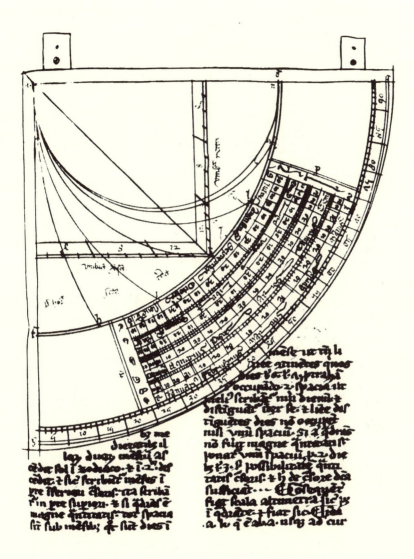

Fig. 9-7. The "Old" Quadrant with Cursor. (From Pedersen and Pihl, *Early Physics and Astronomy*. With permission of Neale Watson Academic Publications, Inc.)

sighting-holes. The "old" quadrant also had hour-lines engraved on one of its surfaces and had a "cursor" that indicated the position of the sun in the ecliptic; it could thus be used to tell time, a function it shared with the astrolabe. At the end of the thirteenth century, a more complex "new" quadrant was introduced by Profatius Judaeus. On this, see O. Pedersen and M. Pihl, *Early Physics and Astronomy* (New York: American Elsevier, 1974) , and J. M. Millás-Villicrosa, "La introducción del cuadrante con cursor en Europa," *Isis*, vol. 17 (1932) , 218-58.

Herman also described a small, cylindrical portable altitude sundial (called the chilinder due to its shape) , which was very popular during the Middle Ages.

8. Abū Ma'shar (787-886) , or Albumasar as he was known in the Latin West, was a Persian scholar whose *Introductiorium in astronomiam* became one of the main astrological sources of Latin Europe. It was translated by John of Spain in 1113 and later by Herman of Carinthia in 1140. For further information on Albumasar, see R. Lemay, *Abū Ma'shar and Latin Aristotelianism in the Twelfth Century* (Beirut, 1962) .

On Alcuin and the Carolingian period in general, Bolgar, *Classical Heritage*, is very useful. Luitpold Wallach, *Alcuin and Charlemagne: Studies in Carolingian History and Literature* (Ithaca, N.Y.: Cornell University Press, 1959) ; C. J. B. Gaskoin, *Alcuin: His Life and Work* (New York: Russell and Russell, 1966) are helpful. The three commentaries on the *Marriage* of Martianus Capella by Dunchad, John Scotus Erigena, and Remigius of Auxerre have been edited by Cora E. Lutz. *Dunchad, Glossae in Martianum* (Lancaster, Pa.: Publications of the American Philological Association, 1944) , No. XII; *Iohannis Scotti Annotationes in Marcianum* (Cambridge, Mass.: Mediaeval Academy of America, 1939) ; *Remigii Autissiodorensis Commentum in Martianum Capellam*, 2 vols. (Leiden: E. J. Brill, 1962, 1965) . No English translations, but the introductory material in these editions is useful.

For tenth-century developments, see Cora E. Lutz, *Schoolmasters of the Tenth Century* (Hamden, Conn.: Archon Books, 1977) ; Harriet Pratt Lattin, "Astronomy: Our Views and Theirs" and Luitpold Wallach, "Education and Culture in the Tenth Century," both in "Symposium on the Tenth Century," *Medievalia et Humanistica*, vol. 9 (1956) , 3-29.

On Lotharingian astronomy, the following are of value: Harriet Pratt Lattin, "The Eleventh Century Ms. Munich 14,436: Its Contribution to the History of Coordinates, of Logic, of German Studies in France," *Isis*, vol. 38 (1947/48) , 205-25; M. C. Wellborn, "Lotharingia as a Center of Arabic and Scientific Influence in the Eleventh Century," *Isis*, vol. 16 (1931) , 188-99; J. W. Thompson, "The Introduction of Arabic Science into Lorraine in the Tenth Century," *Isis*, vol. 12 (1929) , 184-92.

C. H. Haskins, *Studies in the History of Mediaeval Science* (Cambridge: Harvard University Press, 1927) , Chapter VI is very valuable on the subject of transmission of scientific ideas to Europe.

There is an extensive literature on the astrolabe. Of these materials, the following is a small selection: the excellent article by J. D. North, "The Astrolabe," *Scientific American*, vol. 230, no. 1 (January, 1974) , 96-106; O. Neugebauer, "The Early History of the Astrolabe," *Isis*, vol. 40 (1949) , 240-56; W. Hartner, *The Principle and Use of the Astrolabe, Oriens-Occidens* (Hildesheim, 1968) , 287-318; H. Michel, *Traité de l'astrolabe* (Paris: Gauthiers-Villars, 1947) . The second volume of R. T. Gunther, *The Astrolabes of the World*, 2 vols. (Oxford, 1932) contains descriptions and illustrations of many European astrolabes. On Chaucer, see R. T. Gunther, *Chaucer and Messahalla on the Astrolabe* in *Early Science in Oxford*, vol. V (Oxford, 1929) . For the transmission of the astrolabe to the Latin West: Harriet Pratt Lattin, "Lupitus

Barchinonensis," *Speculum,* vol. 7 (1932), 58-64; E. Poulle, "L'Astrolabe médiéval d'après des manuscrits de la Bibliothèque Nationale," *Bibliothèque de l'Ecole des Chartres,* vol. 112 (1964), 81-103. The letters of Gerbert as well as information on his career are in Harriet Pratt Lattin, *The Letters of Gerbert* (New York: Columbia University Press, 1961).

For the liberal arts, astronomy, and cosmology at Chartres, and the world view of Chartrain masters, see the following: A. Cherval, *Les Ecoles de Chartres au moyen âge du Ve au XIVe siècle* (Paris, 1895), and Cherval's article, "L'Enseignement des arts libéraux à Chartres et à Paris dans la première moitié du XIIe siècle d'après *l'Heptateuchon* de Thierry de Chartres," *Congrès Scientifique International des Catholiques,* vol. II (Paris, 1888); Haskins, *Studies,* 88-90; M.-D. Chenu, *Nature, Man and Society in the Twelfth Century* (Chicago: University of Chicago Press, 1968); Brian Stock, *Myth and Science in the Twelfth Century* (Princeton, N.J.: Princeton University Press, 1972); Tina Steifel, "The Heresy of Science: A Twelfth-Century Conceptual Revolution," *Isis,* vol. 68 (1977), 347-62.

9. The most important treatises comprising the "Arabic bonus" are the following: The astronomical tables of al-Khwārizmī (ninth century); the *Opus astronomicum* of al-Battānī or Albategnius (ca.850-929), a resume of Ptolemaic astronomy; the astronomical work of Ibn al-Haitham or Alhazen (ca.965-1039), who introduced the physical spheres of Ptolemy's *Planetary Hypotheses* to the Latin West, the Toledo Tables and the canons on these tables by al-Zargāli or Arzachel (ca.1029-ca.1087); the *Liber 30 differentiarum* by al-Farḡānī or Alfraganus (ca.800-ca.870); Thābit ibn Qurra's *On the Motion of the Eighth Sphere,* which introduced to the West the erroneous notion of the oscillation of the equinoctial points and the paraphrase of the *Almagest* by Jābir ibn Aflaḥ or Geber (fl. mid-twelfth century). The last four treatises the West owed to Gerard of Cremona.

10. Little would be gained by a list of late medieval astronomers; however, the following examples serve to illustrate this activity. During the thirteenth century, William of St. Cloud made astronomical observations at Paris, and Companus of Novara wrote an excellent *Theory of the Planets.* In the fourteenth century, John de Lineriis wrote astronomical tables and canons as well as a theory of the planets, while John de Muris made observations and constructed tables. During the early fourteenth century, the Alfonsine Tables, composed under the patronage of Alfonso X (the Wise) and based on Ptolemy, reached Paris. They were widely used along with the canons of John of Saxony.

A number of astronomers wrote on astronomical instruments. By way of example, Campanus, John de Lineriis, Petrus de Sancto Audomaro, Jean Fusoris, Richard of Wallingford, and probably Chaucer, wrote on the *equatorium,* a planetary computer. Of these authors, the English mathematician and astronomer, Richard of Wallingford, was one of the most significant. He invented astronomical instruments and also designed a mechanical clock. The contributions of some of these astronomers have been edited. For Campanus of Novara's *Theory of the Planets* and description of his *equatorium:* F. S. Benjamin, Jr., G. J. Toomer, *Campanus of Novara and Medieval Planetary Theory* (Madison, Wis.: University of Wisconsin Press, 1971); On "Chaucer's" *equatorium:* D. J. Price, *The Equatorie of the Planetis* (Cambridge: Cambridge University Press, 1955); on the work of Fusoris, E. Poulle, *Un Constructeur d'instruments astronomiques au XVe siècle, Jean Fusoris,* Bibliothèque de l'école pratique des hautes études, IVe sec., sciences historiques et philologiques, fasc. 218 (Paris, 1963); Richard of Wallingford's career and work are thoroughly treated in J. D. North, *Richard of Wallingford. An Edition of His Writings with Introductions, English Translation and Commentary,* 3 vols. (Oxford: Clarendon Press; New York: Oxford University Press, 1976); for Petrus de Sancto Audomaro, see O. Pedersen, "The Life and Work of Peter Nightingale," *Vistas in Astronomy,* 9, ed. A. Beer (Oxford: Pergamon Press, 1967).

11. The commentators, guided by Averroes, were especially distressed that motion on an epicycle or on an eccentric did not take place around a center that was the physical earth. Moreover, the natural and only motion of the celestial substance should be a circular one, but a planet's motion on its epicycle could be interpreted as both up and down relative to the earth. Again, Aristotle had denied the existence of a vacuum in the heavens (or anywhere else), but the motion of the epicycle around its eccentric would leave a void area as it moved. Or if this did not occur, the movement of the epicycle would cleave the substance of the heavens—again impossible according to Aristotle. However, the commentators were also very aware of the most serious fault of any concentric scheme; that it could not account for the observed fact that celestial bodies are not always the same distance from the earth.

Haskins, *Studies in Mediaeval Science* provides a valuable account of the transmission of both Greek and Arabic astronomical material to the Latin West. The *Almagest* had been translated from Greek in 1160, but the version most used in the Middle Ages was Gerard of Cremona's translation from Arabic, made in 1175. The commentaries on Aristotle by the Spanish Moslem, Ibn Rushd or Averroes (1126-1198), were translated into Latin early in the thirteenth century by Michael Scot.

The best study of the medieval university remains Hastings Rashdall, *The Universities of Europe in the Middle Ages,* F. M. Powicke, A. B. Emden, eds., 3 vols. (London, 1958). Gordon Leff, *Paris and Oxford Universities in the Thirteenth and Fourteenth Centuries* (New York: John Wiley and Sons, 1968); J. A. Weisheipl, O. P., "Curriculum of the Faculty of Arts at Oxford in the Early Fourteenth Century," *Medieval Studies,* vol. 26 (1964), 143-85; Philip Dehaye, "La Place des arts libéraux dans les programmes scolaires de XIIIe siècle;" Pearl Kibre, "The Quadrivium in the Thirteenth Century Universities," both in *Arts libéraux et philosophie au moyen âge, Actes du quatrième congrès international de philosophie médiévale* (Montreal, 1969); Josef Koch, ed., *Artes liberales von der antiken Bildung zur Wissenschaft des Mittelalters* (Leiden: E. J. Brill, 1959) are useful. For Sacrobosco: Lynn Thorndike, *The Sphere of Sacrobosco and Its Commentators* (Chicago: University of Chicago Press, 1949). On the "theory of the planets" genre, and the so-called Gerard version in particular, see: Olaf Pederson, "The *Theorica planetarum* Literature of the Middle Ages," *Classica et Mediaevalia,* vol. 23 (1962), 225-32; O. Pedersen, "The Decline and Fall of the *Theorica planetarum*," *Studia Copernicana, Science and History, Studies in Honor of Edward Rosen* (Warsaw: The Polish Academy of Sciences Press, 1978), 157-85.

The most exhaustive account of medieval astronomical thought remains Pierre Duhem, *Le Système du monde,* especially vols. II, III, IV. More recent materials are: Edward Grant, "Cosmology," 265-302 and Olaf Pedersen, "Astronomy," 303-37 in David C. Lindberg, ed., *Science in the Middle Ages* (Chicago: University of Chicago Press, 1978); also the section entitled,

"Astronomy, Astrology and Cosmology" in Edward Grant, ed., *A Source Book in Medieval Science* (Cambridge: Harvard University Press, 1974), 442-568.

Aspects of fourteenth century empiricism are discussed in E. A. Moody, "Empiricism and Metaphysics in Medieval Philosophy," in *Studies in Medieval Philosophy, Science and Logic, Collected Papers, 1933-1969* (Berkeley: University of California Press, 1975), 287-304. Some Moslem alternatives to Ptolemy are treated in E. S. Kennedy, "Late Medieval Planetary Theory," *Isis*, vol. 57 (1966), 365-78. The work of al-Biṭrūjī or Alpetragius (fl. 1185) was translated into Latin in 1217.

SELECTED BIBLIOGRAPHY ON ASTRONOMY

Benjamin, Francis S. and Toomer, G. L. *Campanus of Novara and Medieval Planetary Theory*. Madison, 1971.

Cramer, Frederick H. *Astrology in Roman Law and Politics*. Philadelphia, 1954.

Duhem, Pierre. *Le Système du monde*. 10 Vols. Paris, 1913-59. Especially vols. II, III, IV.

Grant, Edward, ed. *A Source Book in Medieval Science*. Cambridge, Mass., 1974; pp. 442-568.

———. "Cosmology," *Science in the Middle Ages*. David C. Lindberg, ed. Chicago, 1978; pp. 265, 302.

Heath, T. L. *Aristarchus of Samos*. Oxford, 1959.

Jones, C. W., ed. *Bedae Opera de temporibus*. Cambridge, Mass., 1943.

Kennedy, E. S. "Late Medieval Planetary Theory." *Isis*, vol. 57 (1966), 365-78.

Nasr, S. H. *Science and Civilization in Islam*. New York, 1968.

North, J. D. "The Astrolabe." *Scientific American*, vol. 230 (January, 1974), no. 1, 96-106.

Pedersen, O. "The *Theorica planetarum* Literature of the Middle Ages," *Classica et Mediaevalia*, vol. 23 (1962), 225-32.

———. "The Decline and Fall of the *Theorica planetarum*." *Studia Copernicana. Science and History. Studies in Honor of Edward Rosen*. Warsaw, 1978; pp. 157-85.

———. "Astronomy," *Science in the Middle Ages*. David C. Lindberg, ed. Chicago, 1978; pp. 303-37.

Stalh, W. H. trans. *Macrobius, Commentary on the Dream of Scipio*. New York, 1952.

———. *Roman Science*, Madison, 1962.

———. *Martianus Capella and the Seven Liberal Arts*. Vol. I, *The Quadrivium of Martianus Capella*. New York, 1971.

——— and Richard Johnson, trans. *Martianus Capella and the Seven Liberal Arts*. Vol. II. New York, 1977.

10 *Beyond the Liberal Arts*

Ralph McInerny

In the introductory chapter, surveying the relation between the liberal arts tradition and classical scholarship, I described the fundamental change that occurred in intellectual history in the course of the High Middle Ages. The revival of learning that has come to be called the "Twelfth-Century Renaissance" had generated a desire for knowledge beyond that provided by the few classical sources that were then available. The military resurgence of Europe made possible the recovery of Greek learning, which had been preserved in the Moslem world. At the same time, Western scholars were introduced to original Arabic philosophy and science. These developments in turn occasioned further changes in the intellectual world: Aristotelianism, Scholasticism, and the rise of universities.

The essays in this volume have shown the decisive role of these changes in the history of the various individual arts. The transformation of the intellectual world did not merely affect the arts individually, however; it also affected the status in the university curriculum of the seven liberal arts taken as a whole. In the introductory chapter I have sketched what is probably the customary interpretation of this change—the subordination of the art to the higher disciplines of philosophy and theology. In the following essay, Professor McInerny argues that this traditional view requires careful qualification. D. L. W.

"Non est consenescendum in artibus."[1]

Once upon a time—in the early Middle Ages, to be less inexact—the liberal arts tradition reigned supreme and education consisted or could consist largely in the pursuit of these arts for their own sake. Yeats said of Lady Ann Gregory that only God could love her for herself alone and not her yellow hair. In the godly times of which we speak, students loved a liberal art for herself alone and not for any ladder that might be plaited of her yellow hair and used for ascent or descent to other windows. This golden age was not to last. It was succeeded by another in which the arts, while not ignored, were pursued in interested ways, as stepping stones to other matters. The liberal arts became enslaved and were made subservient to allegedly higher disciplines. This sad story can be summed up by saying that the liberal arts tradition was replaced by Scholasticism.

That is the story. History, of course, is a good deal more complex, as I hope to show here. Nonetheless, it is well to start with an assumption that is widely made, even though no one would embrace it in the simplistic form I have given it. What can be accurately said is this: there was a time when the liberal arts were preeminent in education, and this was followed by a time when they were not preeminent but subsumed within a vision of knowledge wider in scope. This simple statement is historical. There is in it no suggestion of a fall from grace, as if scholars of the period following the preeminence of the liberal arts had weakened and succumbed to a temptation that those of the preceding age had manfully resisted. It may be well to set down at the very outset a sort of *syllabus errorum* on the topic assigned me.

1. There was a time when the liberal arts were studied for their own sake.
2. There was a time when the trivium and quadrivium were studied uniformly everywhere.
3. We need not worry too much about the difference between the monastic and cathedral liberal arts schools.
4. Scholasticism is something that can be opposed to the liberal arts tradition.

All of these propositions are false. As the terms *trivium* and *quadrivium* suggest (and the latter goes back to Boethius), the liberal arts were grouped in terms of a threefold way and a fourfold way—they were stepping stones, means to an end beyond themselves.[2] Prior to the thirteenth century, different schools could be distinguished not only in terms of an emphasis on the trivium to the virtual exclusion of the quadrivium, but, among those that emphasized the trivium, differences obtained because of an emphasis on dialectic in one place and on grammar in another. Further, the very character of grammar differed from school to school depending on whether study focused on grammarians or on the reading of classical texts.[3] The time when the liberal arts were preeminent in education was not a time when schooling was uniform.

The third and fourth errors will be seen to be such after we rephrase our task with greater sensitivity to historical fact.

Something happens between the twelfth and thirteenth centuries with respect to the organization of secular learning. In the twelfth century, the traditional liberal arts could still seem to provide sufficient categories to contain the full range of secular knowledge. In the thirteenth century this is no longer so. It is not so only because the arts school, formerly associated with the cathedral or monastery, has now become a faculty of the university, a faculty through which one must go if one would enter the faculty of theology or law or medicine. The great reason for the replacement of the liberal arts as an adequate division of secular learning is the flood of literature that comes in from the Arabic world. More simply, it is the introduction of the complete Aristotelian corpus, with the result that one of the divisions of philosophy that had been known all along is suddenly made concrete in a library of hitherto unknown works.[4]

The second chapter of the *De trinitate* of Boethius had acquainted the early Middle Ages with the Aristotelian division of theoretical philosophy into natural science, mathematics, and theology, but for all practical purposes this triad of speculative sciences enjoyed only a nominal existence. What was natural science other than that portion of the *Timaeus* that had been translated into Latin plus reflections generated by *Genesis?* Like the Stoic division of philosophy into physics, ethics, and logic, the Aristotelian division was known but for the most part as labels without the labeled. Only after the introduction of the whole Aristotle could it be asked whether the liberal arts provided an adequate division of secular knowledge.

This claim needs qualification, but let us seek initial support for it by comparing several reactions to the Boethian mention of the threefold division of speculative philosophy, that of Thomas Aquinas in the thirteenth century and those of Gilbert of la Porée and Thierry of Chartres in the twelfth. First the text of Boethius:

> Speculative Science may be divided into three kinds: Physics, Mathematics and Theology. Physics deals with motion and is not abstract or separable. . . . Mathematics does not deal with motion and is not abstract. . . . Theology does not deal with motion and is abstract and separable.[5]

Thomas began a commentary on this work that he did not complete; indeed it breaks off just slightly beyond the passage quoted from the second chapter of Boethius's *De trinitate*. The work has six chapters and Thomas's commentary covers approximately one-fourth of the text.

It is not an interlinear or line-by-line commentary, like his commentaries on Scripture and on the works of Aristotle; rather, as is the case with his comments on the *Sentences* of Peter Lombard, he first gives a *divisio textus* and then discusses its content in a fairly independent series of questions in the style of a *Quaestio disputata* or of an article in the *Summa theologiae*. Furthermore, Thomas wrote his commentaries on Boethius early in his career.[6] The fifth question of his commentary bears on the passage quoted and is divided into four articles, the first of which asks whether the division of the speculative into three parts as Boethius has done is a good one. Among the considerations suggesting that it is not, we find this:

> *Objection 3.* Again, philosophy is commonly divided into seven liberal arts, which include neither natural nor divine science, but only rational and mathematical science. Hence natural and divine should not be called parts of speculative science.[7]

Here is Thomas's resolution of the difficulty.

> *Reply to obj. 3.* The seven liberal arts do not adequately divide theoretical philosophy; but, as Hugh of St. Victor says, seven arts are grouped together, leaving out certain other ones, because those who wanted to learn philosophy were first instructed in them. And the reason why they are divided into the trivium and quadrivium is that 'they are as paths introducing the eager mind to the secrets of philosophy.' This is also in harmony with what the Philosopher says in the *Metaphysics,* that we must investigate the method of scientific thinking before the sciences themselves. And the Commentator says in the same place that before all the other sciences a person should learn logic, which teaches the method of all the sciences; and the trivium belongs to the domain of logic. The Philosopher further says in the *Ethics* that the young can know mathematics, but not physics, which requires experience. So we are given to understand that we should learn mathematics, to whose domain the quadrivium belongs, immediately after logic. And so these are as paths preparing the mind for the other philosophic disciplines.[8]

The ambiance of the discussion is Aristotelian—we notice the now familiar epithets: Aristotle is *the* philosopher and Averroes is *the* commentator (contrast this with earlier identifications of Aristotle as *logicus* and Plato as *physicus!*) —but the reference to Hugh of St. Victor displays Thomas's penchant for ligature rather than rupture with the tradition. The liberal arts are neatly fed into the order of learning the philosophical sciences, an order gleaned from various passages in Aristotle, just as it is his authority that establishes what are the philosophical sciences. In his *expositio* of the *Liber de causis,* Thomas gives this statement of the *ordo addiscendi:*

> Thus the chief intention of philosophers was that they should come to knowledge of the first causes by way of all the things they learned about other things. That is why they put the science of first causes last, devoting the final period of life to its consideration, beginning first with logic, which teaches the method of the sciences, proceeding next to mathematics of which even boys are capable, then to natural philosophy which requires time for experience, fourth to moral philosophy, of which a youth is not an appropriate student, and coming finally to divine science which considers the first causes of beings.[9]

The terminology of the liberal arts tradition is taken to point to *paideia,* the introduction to learning, and the arts are thus seen to be instrumental, prerequisites for what is to follow. That the study or studies beyond themselves to which the arts point is/are diversely identified by a Hugh of St. Victor or a Thomas Aquinas goes without saying, but Thomas himself says nothing of this difference with the tradition because his tendency is to reconcile rather than to underline differences.[10]

In the continuation of the text, Thomas takes up a question that is at least as old as Cassiodorus[11]: why are some studies called both arts and sciences?

> We may add, too, that these are called arts among the other sciences because they involve not only knowledge but a certain work which is directly a product of reason itself; for example, producing a composition, syllogism or discourse, numbering, measuring, composing melodies and reckoning the course of the stars. Other sciences, like divine and natural sciences, either do not involve a work produced, but only knowledge, and so we cannot call them arts, because, according to the *Metaphysics,* art is called 'productive reason'; or they involve a material product, as in the case of medicine, alchemy and other sciences of this sort. These latter, then, cannot be called liberal arts because such actions belong to man on the side of his nature in which he is not free, namely, on the side of his body.[12]

This is an ingenious passage. In it, Thomas provides a reason why some of the philosophical sciences recognized by Aristotle are called arts while others are not, and he distinguishes the liberal arts from the mechanical arts which, according to Hugh of St Victor, are also seven in number.[13] Taking the Aristotelian conception of art as *recta ratio factibilium,*[14] an intellectual skill in making, Thomas suggests that, in its obvious sense, making is a transitive activity involving corporeal effort and resulting in a product that differs from, and is distinct from, the activity itself. Thus, art in its primary sense is servile or mechanical, and its result is a spatio-temporal entity, an artificial object taking up room among natural objects. Art therefore involves the natural as its material in the way that a statue is shaped marble that continues to take up space just as it did in its purely natural condition. If some of the sciences are called arts, this must be because, on an analogy with arts in the usual or primary sense, they have an opus, a product. The products Thomas lists proceed through the arts that make up the traditional liberal arts: grammar aims at syntax or construction; logic at the forming of syllogisms; rhetoric at the making of speeches; arithmetic at enumeration; geometry at measuring; music at the forming of melodies; and astronomy at the charting of the courses of heavenly bodies. The suggestion is that the works or products of the liberal arts are more spiritual, products of that in us which is the root of freedom, namely, mind.[15] Sciences that have such *opera* or products are called arts by way of analogy. Sciences that have no such products are not called arts. We notice that moral science is still unaccounted for. "And although moral science is directed to action, still that action is not the act of the science but rather of virtue, as is clear in the *Ethics*. So we cannot call moral science an art; but rather in these actions virtue takes the place of art."[16] The virtuous action with which moral science is concerned is neither a matter of knowledge alone nor, as such, a transitive activity producing a spatio-temporal object as its effect.

In this remarkable discussion, then, the liberal arts have entered the universe of Aristotelian philosophy. Rather than see the latter as replacing the former, as if they were rivals, Thomas interprets the liberal arts tradition as a *partial* and *inadequate* division of philosophical labor. Traditionally, the liberal arts had been regarded as propaedeutic —the terms trivium and quadrivium indicate this—but, if they were instrumental, they were more or less directly *ancillae theologiae,* that is, ways to the wisdom contained in Scripture. We will return to this. With Thomas, they are seen as propaedeutic and ancillary *to other philosophical sciences,* which for different reasons must be learned later than the trivium and quadrivium. Of course, philosophy taken as a whole, the sum of the liberal arts and the sciences that are not arts, continues to be regarded as *ancilla theologiae.*[17] The difference is that philosophy is a larger whole than it was when philosophy could be equated with the liberal arts.[18]

What do commentators writing prior to the influx of the integral Aristotle make of the text of Boethius? Gilbert of la Porée's commentary is included in the volume of Migne that contains the theological tractates of Boethius.[19] It is a running commentary. Having cited the Boethian remark *Nam cum tres sint speculativae partes,* et cetera, Gilbert explains it thus:

> There are many kinds of science. For some are theoretical, that is, spec-
> ulative, namely those whereby we see whether and what and how and
> why each created thing is; others are practical, that is, active, namely
> those whereby we know how to act rather than see, like medicine, magic,
> and the like. Putting the practical aside, the speculative lay claim to that
> appellation because through them we see, and some are called physical,
> that is, natural, others ethical, that is, moral, and others logical, that is,
> rational. If we now set aside the moral and rational, those which are
> called by the one term natural, and by common usage speculative, have
> three parts. . . .[20]

Gilbert identifies the practical by citing medicine, magic, and the like,
and sets it to one side; he then invokes the Stoic threefold division of
philosophy (physics, logic, and ethics), and presents it as a division of
speculative philosophy. The threefold division of the text is then discussed as a subdivision of one of the parts of speculative philosophy,
an oddity justified by appealing to common usage. The passage gives
evidence of acquaintance with the *Posterior Analytics* in its listing of
the four questions that the theoretical sciences put to created things.[21]
In the sequel, some display is made of Greek and it may be that Gilbert
has *akoristos* (unseparated) for *anupexairetos* (inseparable). The discussion of the criteria for distinguishing the three speculative sciences
is quaint. The matter-form couplet is discussed with references to Plato
and indeed there is something Platonic in the presentation of the objects
of these sciences.[22] Insofar as the text of Boethius refers to the Aristotelian natural writings and the *Metaphysics,* and not to the *Timaeus,* it
cannot be unpacked by Gilbert.

If we glance at the various commentaries on the *De trinitate* attributed to Thierry of Chartres by Häring,[23] we find a similar Platoniz-
ing explanation, one that makes explicit reference to the *Timaeus* but
that also employs[24] other passages from Boethius. The threefold division of philosophy into physics, ethics, and logic is altered to *logica,
ethica et speculativa,* these being distinguished as concerned, respectively, with arguments, actions, and causes.

Now what is noteworthy about these twelfth century commentaries
on the *De trinitate* of Boethius, that of Gilbert of la Porée, and all those
attributed to Thierry of Chartres by Häring, is that, in the supposed
heyday of the liberal arts tradition, they exhibit no interest whatsoever
in comparing the division of intellectual labor given in the texts with
that embodied in the liberal arts. Insofar as arts are alluded to, they
are immediately excluded from consideration. In the case of Gilbert,
the arts mentioned are not liberal (medicine and magic *et hujusmodi
alii*), but one can still be surprised at the failure to mention the liberal
arts.

On the basis of the twelfth century commentaries on Boethius of Gilbert and Thierry and the thirteenth century one of Thomas Aquinas, we would have to say that it is the earlier writers who, confronted by a division of intellectual labor apparently different from the liberal arts, gloss the text with reference to Plato and the *Timaeus* only, whereas Thomas is concerned to relate the Aristotelian division of speculative science to the liberal arts tradition. Let this serve as caveat, then, and a check to the tendency, if we feel it, to say that it is in the thirteenth century, with the rise of the universities and the introduction of the complete Aristotle, that the liberal arts are rudely cast aside or made subservient to other and alien ends. We have seen at least two twelfth century figures who completely ignore the liberal arts tradition when commenting on a text that invites mention of it.

But perhaps we have simply come up with bad or unrepresentative samples of these two centuries. Surely, as we have acknowledged, there is something to be said for the claim that there was a time when the liberal arts were considered an adequate division of secular learning and there was a subsequent time when the liberal arts were no longer so considered. Let us take a swift look at that earlier period, having in mind as we do so the first item on our *syllabus errorum*.

In recalling the tradition of the liberal arts, we could do worse than begin with St. Augustine. Having left his native Africa to take a post as teacher in the imperial rhetorical school in Milan, he listened to the sermons of St. Ambrose and then, one day, in his garden, he heard from over the wall the voices of children at play. *Tolle et lege,* take and read, and he picked up St. Paul and read the passage on which his eye fell.[25] Its application to himself seemed incontestable; he decided to prepare himself for baptism. Now how did he do this? He went into retreat at Cassiciacum and began to write works on the liberal arts! His *De musica* dates from this time and is one proof that he kept his intention. He also wrote (more accurately, dictated) the *De ordine* and the *De magistro,* the latter a dialogue with his son, Adeodatus, in whom Augustine took much justified paternal pride. We can see in these works some traces of what Augustine must have been like as a teacher and what the education of his time was like. In any case, he speaks of the liberal arts as a preparation for philosophy, the latter having as its two great concerns the soul and God.[26] The arts give one the skills necessary to discuss these great questions. And what are the liberal arts? Grammar, rhetoric, logic, arithmetic, geometry, music, and astronomy. With Augustine, the number of the liberal arts is fixed at seven, under the influence of Martianus Capella, whose allegorical work, *De nuptiis Mercurii et Philologiae* lopped off the medicine and architecture that

Varro had included along with the arts that were to become the traditional seven. Augustine himself sometimes and confusingly replaces astronomy with philosophy,[27] apparently because of his distaste for astrology which catered to superstition. Notice that, for Augustine, the liberal arts are taught and learned in order that, given them, something else, namely philosophy, might be done. Although it is not the case that we find in Augustine a clearcut and consistent distinction between philosophy as an activity in which a pagan might engage and philosophy as a reflection on Christian belief, to study the soul and God is to employ the liberal arts but to engage in something else.

Cassiodorus Senator, a contemporary of Boethius who survived, as Boethius did not, his association with the Ostrogoths, founded a monastery at Vivarium and wrote for its inhabitants a work called the *Institutiones*.[28] It is divided into two parts and may orginally have been two works, the first of which deals with the liberal arts, the second with Scripture. Here we have what will become a commonplace, namely, that the study of the liberal arts is a preparation for the reading of Scripture. The arts are seen as secular, even pagan attainments that the believer can redeem and put to a higher purpose.

We have already seen how the threefold Stoic division of philosophy was employed by two men in the twelfth century. This division of philosophy into logic, physics, and ethics could have been known by the medievals from book eight of Augustine's *City of God*. Alcuin, the teacher of Charlemagne, knows that the seven liberal arts are studied as preparations for the study of Scripture. If the trivium and quadrivium are ways to something, that something is wisdom and wisdom is to be found in Scripture; thus the arts are viewed as the seven pillars of wisdom. But if the pursuit of wisdom, i.e., philosophy, comprises three parts, these parts must be found in Scripture. They must be linked to books of the Bible. Where is physics to be found? In *Genesis*. Where is ethics to be found? In the sapiential books. Where is logic to be found? Alcuin's answer boggles the mind. Logic is contained in the *Song of Songs*.[29] Of course Alcuin's theory poses many difficulties. Is not logic one of the liberal arts that are presupposed to the pursuit of wisdom, one of whose parts is logic, improbably located in the *Song of Songs*?

It is tempting to consider Hugh of St. Victor in the twelfth century as the apotheosis of the liberal arts tradition. In his *Didascalicon*, he balances the liberal arts with a list of servile or mechanical arts, on the one hand, and with the wisdom contained in Scripture, on the other. Hugh knows the traditional divisions of philosophy; for him philosophy is not equated with the liberal arts but includes the mechanical arts and the wisdom of the word of God. He takes seriously the commodious traditional definition: *philosophia est disciplina omnium rerum hu-*

manarum atque divinarum rationes plene investigans (philosophy is a discipline that seeks understanding of all things both human and divine.[30] But philosophy is a whole within which the arts serve as stepping stones to the fullness of the Christian life. This can be seen as a reiteration of the views of Cassiodorus and of Alcuin and of other earlier figures in the liberal arts tradition, a reiteration intended to oppose what Hugh regarded as the growing secularization of the schools. That is, Hugh saw the move toward the autonomy of the liberal arts as a threat to their true value.

We need an interim summary of results. What is the historical cash value of the claim that a period when the liberal arts were pursued for their own sake and enjoyed autonomy was succeeded by a period in which the arts diminished in importance and were made subservient to other disciplines, this second period being identified with Scholasticism? While it is easy to concede that something significant happened as the twelfth century gave way to the thirteenth, the claim we are examining does not seem to be the best way of expressing that change. First, the standard way of regarding the liberal arts entailed from the beginning that they were viewed as propaedeutic, instrumental, *viae* to something else. Second, this something else in the early Middle Ages tended to be identified with the wisdom contained in Scripture. One wanted to study the liberal arts in order to be a better, more adroit reader of Holy Writ. Third, prior to the great change, when commentators confronted such a text as that of Boethius's *De trinitate,* where the Aristotelian division of speculative philosophy was reported, they did not immediately ask how such a division related to the liberal arts tradition. Gilbert of la Porée did not; Thierry of Chartres did not.[31] On the other hand, Thomas Aquinas in the thirteenth century was concerned to show how the liberal arts fitted into the Aristotelian scheme. So was Kilwardby in the *De ortu scientiarum.*[32] Fourth, in the earlier period, efforts to secularize the study of the arts, that is, to divorce them from their orientation to Scripture, were regarded as dangerous by such men as Hugh of St Victor. Fifth, there was little uniformity in the earlier period and "arts schools" differed considerably from one another in the arts they emphasized and the authors read. Of course, there would be general agreement as to the number and identity of the liberal arts.

What then is the cash value of the claim? This: prior to the thirteenth century, it was possible to employ the schema of the seven liberal arts as an adequate summary of secular learning, even if this required stretching a point or two; after the introduction of the complete works of Aristotle, the Arabic commentaries, et cetera, et cetera, the inadequacy of the liberal arts scheme as a net in which to catch the entirety of secular learning could scarcely be ignored. In the words of Van Steenberghen:

> La grande entrée d'Aristote au XIIIe siècle vint modifier de fond en comble la situation: pour la première fois, un système compact de disciplines scientifico-philosophiques forçait l'entrée du monde chrétien; l'aristotélisme, chef d'oeuvre de l'intelligence grecque, enrichi par les rapports du néoplatonisme grec, juif et arabe, se dressait soudain en face de la théologie; une sagesse paienne se trouvait tout à coup en présence de la sagesse chrétienne; le savoir profane n'était plus représenté par le cortège modeste et inoffensif des arts libéraux, mais par la puissante synthèse scientifique du péripatétisme.[33]

> (Aristotle's grand entry into the thirteenth century radically altered the situation: for the first time, a compact system of scientific-philosophical disciplines entered the Christian world; Aristotelianism, the masterpiece of the Greek mentality, enriched by its contact with Greek, Jewish, and Arabic Neoplatonism, suddenly confronted theology; a pagan wisdom found itself face to face with Christian wisdom; profane knowledge would no longer be represented by the modest and inoffensive parade of liberal arts but by the powerful scientific synthesis of Peripateticism.)

Now the classical divisions of philosophy that had been handed down through the early Middle Ages, labels without their corresponding packages, could be matched with a hitherto unsuspected library of works. Thus, it is the adequacy or inadequacy of the liberal arts to gather all secular learning that is the issue. The liberal arts are not rejected; they are placed in a wider scheme by a Thomas Aquinas or a Kilwardby (radically different from the wider schemes of a William of Conches or a Hugh of St. Victor). Indeed, one might say that the liberal arts were *returned* to what had been their native habitat prior to the Dark Ages. These arts had been subservient parts of *paideia* for Plato and Aristotle.[34] In Islam, we are told, the liberal arts never enjoyed the separate existence they led during the early Middle Ages in the West.[35] That separate existence was a function of the *partial* inheritance of the classical patrimony. When this was remedied at the end of the twelfth century and later, the status of the liberal arts was bound to change, to revert to what it had been in the classical setting.

It must also be stressed that we cannot differentiate our two periods by dubbing the second Scholasticism or the Scholastic Age. It is, of course, no easy matter to define Scholasticism.[36] As a term of abuse, it is doubtless well that it should be as commodious as possible, the better to encompass all one's enemies. The tired example of the angels and the pinhead has been used again and again to suggest the fatuity and vacuousness of medieval school discussions. And yet, in a recent introduction to philosophy, Stephan Koerner, no negligible figure on the contemporary scene, absolves that very discussion from blame. After all, it is a good illustration of a category mistake and we may take it that that was the point of the medieval discussion. That nonspatial entities are not circumscribed in place as are spatial ones is precisely the point. It is customary to refer to the exiguous and impersonal style of Scholastic writers as if this were the essence of Scholasticism. Well, one could equally well praise the care with which the medievals wrote and applaud the literalness of their style, seeing in it an apt instrument for a well-defined intellectual task. Philosophical styles change and it is a noteworthy fact that the philosophical style now dominant in English-speaking countries shares many characteristics with the philosophical (and theological) writings of the Middle Ages, early and late. Surely it is no accident that contemporary philosophers move easily into the analysis of medieval texts, feeling almost immediately at home with them. Doubtless this constitutes a subtle danger and one not always avoided. The very familiarity of the medieval style may deceive as to its burden, and knowledge of the historical setting, the origin of problems, of the evolution of the literary genre, is required if anachronisms are to be avoided.

We find in Chenu a criticism of the Scholastic style that, since it contains a fairly accurate description of it, can easily be taken as the basis for an opposite appraisal.

> Il est bien vrai que le style, extérieur et intéieur, du scholastique sacrifie tout à une technicité dont l'austérité le dépouille des ressources de l'art. Ou plutôt il se crée une rhétorique spéciale où les images, les comparaisons, les métaphores, les symboles sont immédiatement conceptualisés, hors tout complaisance sensible. Toutes les figures y sont ramenées à l'exemple, ou tournées à l'allégorie, procédés où la raison exploite crûment l'imagination, aux dépens de sa propre fécondité.[37]

> (To be sure, both the inner and outward style of Scholasticism sacrifices everything to a technical standard whose austerity is not hospitable to artistic nuance. Or rather it fashions a special rhetoric in which images, comparisons, metaphors, and symbols are immediately conceptualized with little eye to sensible effect. All its figures are led back to the example or turned to allegory, procedures in which reason cruelly exploits imagination at the expense of its proper fecundity.)

It is really difficult to know what Chenu is demanding. Surely there is a rhetoric appropriate to philosophical and theological discourse, one element of which he hints at. That the style does not always come off, that even an impersonal style remains the man, is scarcely an objection to it as such. Brand Blanshard is one of the few, if he is not the only contemporary philosopher who has devoted serious thinking to the question of philosophical style.[38] The striking thing about Chenu's down-putting remarks about "Scholastic style" is that he ties it to the influence of the arts. Glossing his own *mot* that "Penser est un métier, dont les lois sont minutieusement fixées" [thinking is an occupation with minutely defined laws], he writes:

> Lois de la grammaire, d'abord. Le premier des sept arts n'est pas relégué comme aujourd'hui dans la lointaine préparation de la culture; il en est le sol permanent, même en théologie, et il se trouvera au contraire quasi promu à la dignité de discipline philosophique, la grammaire spéculative. La scolastique médiévale demeure à base de grammaire, et son attention au langage est consciemment poussée à l'extrême, non pas seulement pour l'usage des *nominales* . . . mais en pleine substance philosophique et théologique.[39]

> (First of all, the laws of grammar. The first of the seven arts is not relegated, as it is today, to the distant preparation of culture; it is its permanent soil, even in theology, and it will even be promoted to the dignity of a philosophical discipline, speculative grammar. Medieval Scholasticism reposes on a base of grammar and its attention to language is consciously pushed to the limit, not simply in the practice of nominalists . . . but in the very substance of philosophy and theology.)

Chenu sounds like a certain kind of critic of contemporary philosophical style with its emphasis on language. It is very difficult to know what his quip about grammar being as it were promoted to the dignity of a philosophical discipline means; indeed, throughout this section, Chenu adopts an arch, condescending manner, and his reader constantly feels the writer's elbow in his ribs, as it were. But the thing to notice is the linking of arts and Scholasticism. Scholasticism, as a style, arises naturally out of the liberal arts tradition and can scarcely be opposed to it. Nonetheless, this apparent impasse brings us to the heart of the matter I have been asked to discuss.

I hope I have convinced you that we cannot regard the age of the universities, the age when an influx of classical and Arabic works changes the whole picture of the range and scope of human knowledge, as an age that pitched out the previous liberal arts tradition. After all, the base faculty of the university was the faculty of arts. From the age of fifteen to perhaps twenty-five, a man was engaged in pursuits that were the continuation of those previously studied in monastic and cathedral schools. Indeed, we are reminded by Delhaye of something important. There were perhaps twenty medieval universities all told, which is not a massive number when we think of the area over which they were scattered. Moreover, the monastic and cathedral schools continued to exist after the rise of universities and it appears that their curricula did not change radically.[40] Certainly there was preuniversity schooling. Siger of Brabant, for example, likely studied at Liège before coming to Paris at about the age of seventeen.[41] In the faculty of arts, though only after many vicissitudes, condemnations, and heated exchanges, there came about the sort of integration of the liberal arts and Aristotelianism we have seen urged programmatically by Thomas Aquinas. The struggle in the first century of the university (I am thinking, of course, of Paris) was between the arts faculty and the masters of theology.

Thomas Aquinas occupied a chair of theology at the University of Paris and it was from that perspective that he attempted the reconciliation of the liberal arts and Aristotelianism that we examined earlier. In the arts faculty itself there grew up what Van Steenberghen calls "heterodox Aristotelianism," that is, an acceptance of Aristotle as interpreted by Averroes even if this led to conflict with Christian faith. This is a complicated and fascinating story in its own right. Bonaventure, who ascended to a chair of theology on the same day as Thomas Aquinas, is one of our sources for the initial reaction to what was going on in the arts faculty. In his *Conferences on the Ten Commandments* and in his *Conferences on the Gifts of the Holy Ghost,*[42] lenten sermons, he inveighs against those who accept the pagan philosophical tenets that are in clear conflict with the Christian faith. The controverted points are several but three must appear on any list: the eternity of the world, the denial of providence, the denial of personal immortality. These three claims, and others like them, were taken, following Averroes, to be the clear sense of Aristotle's philosophy. Thomas Aquinas enters the fray with his *De unitate intellectus contra Averroistas,*[43] and matters come to a head with the Condemnation of 1270 and, when that did not settle it, the further Condemnation of 1277.[44] The latter, three years after the death of Aquinas, also condemned several Thomistic teachings.

Why are these matters pertinent to our inquiry? They provide us with a parallel to the twelfth century situation that exercised Hugh of St. Victor. Just as Hugh lamented the secularization of the liberal arts, so the great theologians of the thirteenth century objected to masters of arts who were teaching as philosophical truths claims clearly in contradiction with the faith. For a Bonaventure, such a conflict, when seen as such, was immediately resolved against the philosophical claim. Thomas, in his *De unitate intellectus,* quotes his adversary in the faculty of arts (who may have been Siger of Brabant) as saying:

> But what he says later is still more serious: 'I necessarily conclude through reason that the intellect is one in number; but I firmly hold the opposite through faith.' Therefore he thinks that faith is concerned with some propositions whose contraries can be necessarily concluded. But since only a necessary truth can be concluded necessarily, and the opposite of this is something false and impossible, it follows, according to his remark, that faith would be concerned with something false and impossible, that not even God could effect. This the faithful cannot bear to hear.[45]

That is Thomas's concluding remark. The burden of his work has been to show that it is historically, that is, textually, inaccurate to interpret the text of Aristotle as did Averroes and Siger of Brabant. Thomas is concerned to protect Aristotle from his interpreters, not to protect the faith from Aristotle.

But let me return to what I suggested is truly the heart of our matter. If Scholasticism is taken to mean a style of thought and of writing, then we must recognize its continued existence across the Middle Ages; it cannot be seen as a new departure from a previously dominant medieval style. When Boethius turns into Latin the *Isagoge* of Porphyry and some logical writings of Aristotle, he accompanies them with commentaries whose style conveys to the West what we might call Greek Scholasticism. Boethius had been trained in a milieu where one commented on the works of Plato and Aristotle. One of the prominent literary genres was the commentary and it had become, as Boethius makes clear, a very stylized genre. For example, he lists the points that should be made by the commentator in his proemium.[46] To brood over a text, to explain its meaning, to paraphrase and unpack it, to reveal its order and arrangement—it is by doing these things that an adept can aid a novice. This is how one exhibits his mastery. So it was that Boethius's commentary on Porphyry generated commentary after commentary during the Middle Ages. Here is a major component of any description of Scholasticism, and it cannot be said that it shouldered out some previously dominant style. Heeding *auctores,* seeming always to be looking backward to a golden age, trying to retrieve it through the documents that have been handed down—even when a medieval wanted to say something original, he could be constrained by the tradition of commenting on *auctores.* Thus, Abelard's *Dialectica* pursues the same course as the canonical works in logic. It is not a commentary on those books—Abelard had written any number of those—but it is haunted by them.[47] As we move into the thirteenth century and the university milieu, the *expositio textus* continues.

Needless to say, though its style is continuous with preceding centuries, the Scholasticism of the university introduces variations on and additions to the Scholastic method. The *lectio,* the reading of the texts set for a given term, occurred in a dramatic setting, with the master aided by bachelors who were his apprentices, but the written result does not amount to a stylistic innovation. It is rather of the *Quaestio disputata* and the *Quaestio quodlibetalis* that we think when we seek something peculiar to the Scholasticism of the university. These convey to us the dialectical setting of the university, the give and take prior to any magisterial resolution of the question. Of course these *quaestiones,* as they have come down to us, cannot be regarded as tapes or records of the debate itself, but as written they reflect their origin in a vital exchange before a "live audience." I suggested earlier that an article in the *Summa theologiae* has the same structure, simplified, as the disputed question. Thomas wrote the *Summa* in his cell, but it is as if he wished to engage in imaginary conversation, to write closet drama at least. Any strength is a potential weakness and it is easy to see how *amour propre,* the drive to win an argument rather than seize the truth, might take over and how subtlety might come to invite for its own sake or as a way to bedazzle an audience. Someone once wrote a piece on the vice of gambling and the virtue of insurance and I suppose one might alter this and speak of the vice of contention and the virtue of dialogue. It is the same activity that is done badly or well. There is no need nor justification for identifying Scholasticism with the bad employment of its methods.

Thus, while there are additions made to the method as we move into the thirteenth century, Scholasticism does not provide us with a way of distinguishing a later time from the earlier time when the liberal arts were dominant—where by 'dominant' we mean that they could be taken as adequately summarizing the range of secular knowledge.

The only sense we have so far been able to find for the claim that the liberal arts are replaced as we make the turn into the thirteenth century and into the fledgling university is that, with the introduction of the integral Aristotle, a new and wider conception of secular knowledge is gained such that the liberal arts must be seen as making up only a fraction of the *ancilla theologiae.* But surely, were we to content ourselves with this, we would be missing something terribly important, something that may not have been accurately expressed in the simple story with which we began but that, nonetheless, we *know* is there. Chenu's somewhat guardedly critical remarks about Scholastic style, which we cited earlier for their linking of the arts with the maligned style, hint at something else. In ticking off the supposed defects of Scholastic style, Chenu is obliquely expressing a preference for uses of language that, it could be argued, are not appropriate for the handling of philosophical and theological subjects. What is really at issue is a reappearance of that ancient quarrel between the philosopher and poet of which Socrates speaks in the *Republic.*

What is at issue, that is to say, and what I will have seemed disingenuous for ignoring so studiously, is what Van Steenberghen calls *l'exil des belles-lettres,*[48] the leitmotif of Ernst Robert Curtius's *European Literature and the Latin Middle Ages.*[49] Already in the twelfth century, creativity and vitality in logic seem bought at the expense of grammar in the sense of a prolonged immersion in the works of the great writers; so too, as the fortunes of philosophy rise, literature—belles-lettres—and poetry feel neglected, feel themselves the object of hostility, feel themselves engaged in battle. Gilson makes succinctly the point Chenu was hinting at in a passage cited earlier: "On voit apparaître une culture de type nouveau, fondée sur le minimum de grammaire exigé pour l'usage courant d'un latin tout scolaire, constituée par l'étude de la logique et de la philosophie d'Aristote et couronnée par celle d'une théologie dont la technique s'inspire de cette logique et de cette philosophie."[50] The fate of grammar may seem to sum up the sort of evolution that is a result of the study of grammar altering from a study of a Latin, as exemplified in the writings of its best practitioners, to the study of rules and parts of speech and this latter eventually becoming the phenomenon called speculative grammar. In this evolved form of grammar, one attempts to see beneath the flesh of any living language the essential structure that any language must possess. Both Chenu and Gilson cite speculative grammar as an *exemplum horribile,* and Van Steenberghen seems in agreement. How swiftly fashions change. Few things are "hotter" at the moment and one is no longer surprised to see analogies drawn between medieval speculative grammarians and Chomsky and his school.[51] But however appraisals of its upshot differ, there can be agreement on the evolution mentioned. A case can be made for the assertion that literary studies, to say nothing of the composing of literary works, do not flourish where logic and philosophy thrive. Personally, I suspect that this can be overstated. We need a careful presentation of precisely what historical data sustain the case. It is doubtless overly dramatic to speak of belles-lettres being exiled. Can John of Garland and Henry Andeli be taken as sober historians of the matter? Moreover, pleasant as it is to wallow in the Teutonic erudition of Curtius, I think he is a bad guide on the question. This is never more evident than when he discusses poetry and philosophy, notices that Jean de Meun speaks of writing poetry as "travailler en philosophie"[52]—doing philosophy, as we might say—and considers this a confusion. In summary of his discussion, Curtius writes:

Scholasticism put an end to the confusion of philosophy with poetry, rhetoric, proverbial lore, and the various learning of the schools. The old connection between *artes* and philosophy is severed at a blow. The blow lay in Thomas's dictum: 'Septem artes liberales non sufficienter dividunt philosophiam theoreticam.' Yet Leopardi can still write: 'La scienza del bello scrivere e una filosofia, e profondissima e sottilissima, e tiene tutti i rami della sapienza.'[53]

This passage can be taken as a retrospective justification of my procedure in this paper. The remark of Aquinas, which Curtius quotes from Grabmann,[54] simply cannot bear the freight Curtius wants to put upon it. (The allusion to Leopardi baffles me; is he being cited as a backslider or as someone who failed to get the news of history as Curtius reads it?) Nevertheless, Curtius's reader begins to discern what he is really after. He wants to get literary studies, considered as bearing on the status of the poet and the act of writing poetry, recognized as wholly autonomous, as having won freedom from faith, philosophy, and other alien masters.[55] But that cannot be illuminatingly discussed as a severing of the liberal arts from philosophy, or vice versa.

To have written a paper on the fortunes of poetry in the Middle Ages would not have been, perhaps, to connect with what my predecessors at this podium have had to say, assuming of course that I am capable of writing on that topic. Ready or not, I am prompted to make, by way of conclusion, some animadversions on the relationship between poetry and philosophy.

The style, the language, the latinity of Scholasticism are frequent topics of discussion and, in introducing a remark of Chenu, I alluded to the familiarity many contemporary philosophers feel when they turn to medieval sources. The so-called analytic style of philosophizing finds resonance in the Scholastic. Indeed, one would not have to look far to find analogues of Thomas's description of poetry as *infima doctrina*[56] in contemporary discussions where the language of the poet is said to possess at best emotive meaning. It would be entertaining to lay side by side passages from medievals like Thomas, Ockham, or Abelard with passages from G. E. Moore, J. L. Austin, or Wilfrid Sellars. A family resemblance could be described, I think, though there is hardly a question of influence. I will not try to characterize this common style except to say that it is above all *literal* and that it strives with a moral passion for clarity of expression. Now it would be possible to think of a continuum of linguistic usage that would move from the literal at one extreme to the figurative and/or metaphorical at the other. Something like this is suggested by Aristotle when he sees philosophy as arising out of myth. Within the tradition of Aristotelian logic, we find a spectrum running from poetry through rhetoric through dialectic to the apodictic, the demonstrative, with works of Aristotle to represent the different styles of argument or discourse: the *Poetics,* the *Rhetoric,* the *Topics,* the *Analytics.*[57] Imagine that we developed a similar theory to the effect that there is a mode of language (call it literalness, for want of a better term) that is appropriate to the philosopher. A companion claim, I suspect, would be that there is also an appropriate literary genre in which to express philosophical thought. Don't we feel that we can immediately identify a piece of philosophical prose? Isn't there a sameness about the offerings in any given issue of a philosophical journal and indeed a sameness about journals? We may react to this as would John of Garland (or perhaps Roger Bacon), but the shock of recognition there would be.

Very well. Once one feels one has a manageable notion of philosophical style and the appropriate literary genre in which it expresses itself, one will be tempted to rank other styles and other genres as perhaps falling away from this austere ideal. Of course the assessment can be reversed. One isolates the essence of poetic language and ranks other uses of language as falling away from this golden ideal, with philosophical prose, *ca va sans dire,* ranking low, even lowest.[58]

Here is the source of the battle, a battle between poet and Scholastic, that is alluded to in the simple story with which I began. That it is not a fabrication, the passage from Curtius shows. I have myself felt the attraction of the view that there is a peculiar philosophical style, a use of language appropriate to the peculiar tasks the philosopher sets himself, easily distinguished from the uses to which poet and imaginative writer, historian and moralist, put language. I have been tempted by the notion that these differences exhibit themselves in a corresponding variety of literary genres. Well, whatever may be said for this as theory, it has little to do with the history of philosophy. For one thing, if we consider the genres in which recognized philosophers have expressed themselves, we are confronted with a bewildering variety: verse, aphorisms, meditations, dialogues, prayers, commentaries, *summae,* disputed questions, treatises, essays, et cetera.[59] Nor can it be maintained that these genres can be sorted out chronologically, as if the history of its literary genres matches the supposed history of its struggle toward the light, that is, our time. Consider the styles and works of Heidegger and Wittgenstein, perhaps the two most influential philosophers of this century. Consider Nietzsche and Kierkegaard in the last. Santayana wrote a little book called *Three Philosophical Poets* in which he discussed Lucretius, Dante, and Goethe.[60] It is a fascinating book though one may doubt that he succeeded in isolating the essence of the philosophical poet. I doubt that one could isolate the essence of the poetic philosopher, a genus that would include Parmenides and Plato as well as Nietzsche and Kierkegaard. We could draw a lesson from the synthesizing efforts of William of Conches, Hugh of St. Victor, Thomas Aquinas: we do not have to choose between poetry and philosophy, between the humanities and philosophy, between the arts and theology. What we want is a view that will embrace them all, not in an eclectic mishmash, but by seeing continuity and overlap as well as distinctions between the various uses of language, the various activities of mind.

I began with a quotation, "One ought not grow old in the study of the arts." The arts are part of a larger whole, a whole that, as Thomas Aquinas sees it, is capped by theology, and we may, it is permitted, grow old in the study of ultimate causes. Does wisdom entail a repudiation of the arts? Surely it is the mark of the wise man that he remains true to the dreams of his youth.

NOTES

1. Cf. Fernand Van Steenberghen, *Maître Siger de Brabant,* Louvain, 1977, p. 31 and note 2.

2. Cf. Boethius, *De arithmetica,* Liber Primus, caput primum, in Migne, PL 63, 1079D-1083A.

3. Cf. Heinrich Roos, "Le *Trivium* à l'Université au XIIIe Siècle," *Arts Libéraux et Philosophie au Moyen Age,* Actes du Quatrième Congrès International de Philosophie Médiévale (Montreal, 1969) , pp. 192-93. Hereafter, this collection will be cited as ALPAMA.

4. Fernand Van Steenberghen, *Aristotle in the West* (Louvain, 1955) . *Idem, La Philosophie au XIIIe Siècle* (Louvain, 1966) , pp. 72-117.

5. "Nam cum tres sint speculative partes, *naturalis,* in motu inabstracta anupexairetos . . . *mathematica,* sine motu inabstracta . . . *theologica,* sine motu abstracta atque *separabilis." De trinitate,* caput 2, in *Boethius,* Loeb edition, edited by H. F. Stewart and E. K. Rand (London and New York, 1918) , p. 8.5-15.

6. In 1948 Paul Wyser published a partial edition, the commentary on chapter 2, so far as Thomas got, comprising questions 5 and 6. *Thomas von Aquin In Librum Boethii De Trinitate Quaestiones Quinta et Sexta,* Fribourg and Louvain. Bruno Decker published a complete edition a decade later: *Sancti Thomae de Aquino Expositio Super Librum Boethii De Trinitate* (Leiden, 1959) . Wyser, in his *einleitung,* gives the correct title: "Der in vielen, auch ältesten Werkkatalogen angeführte Titel *Expositio in librum Boethii de Trinitate* entspricht daher dem Inhalte nur teilweise. Die mittelalterliche Expositio literalis ist eine Form des sog. Commentums oder Commentarius, die —zum Unterschiede von der zweiten scholastischen Kommentarform der Glossen und Paraphrasen—den zu erklärenden Text in ein logisches Einteilungs-

schema bringt und sodann Wort für Wort, Satz für Satz erklärt. Der Thomas-kommentar in librum Boethii de Trinitate ist aber nur zum kleinsten Teile Literalkommentar des Boethiustextes. Er verbindet nämlich die Divisio und Expositio textus mit der Quaestio, die aber in Umfang und Inhalt die Expositio literalis bei weitem übertrifft." Wyser, p. 4.

7. Translation from Armand Maurer, *St Thomas Aquinas: The Division and Methods of the Sciences* (Toronto, 1958), p. 4: "Praeterea, communiter dividitur philosophia in septem artes liberales, inter quas neque naturalis neque divina continetur, sed sola rationalis et mathematica. Ergo naturalis et divina non debuerunt poni partes speculativae."

8. Maurer, pp. 10-11: "Ad tertium dicendum quod septem liberales artes non sufficienter dividunt philosophiam theoricam, sed ideo, ut dicit Hugo de Sancto Victore in III sui *Didascalicon*, praetermissis quibusdam aliis, septem connumerantur, quia his primum erudiebantur, qui philosophiam discere volebant. Et ideo distinguuntur in trivium et quadrivium, 'eo quo his quasi quibusdam viis vivax animus ad secreta philosophiae introeat.' Et hoc etiam consonat verbis Philosophi qui dicit in II *Metaphysicorum*, quod modus scientiae debet quaeri ante scientias; et Commentator ibidem dicit, quod logicam, quae docet modum omnium scientiarum, debet quis addiscere ante omnes alias scientias, ad quam pertinet trivium. Dicit etiam in VI *Ethicorum*, quod mathematica potest sciri a pueris, non autem physica, quae experimentum requirit. Et sic datur intelligi, quod post logicam consequenter debet mathematica addisci, ad quam pertinet quadrivium; et ita his quasi quibusdam viis praeparatur animus ad alias philosophicas disciplinas."

9. "Et inde est quod philosophorum intentio ad hoc principaliter erat ut, per omnia quae in rebus considerabant, ad cognitionem primarum causarum pervenirent. Unde scientiam de primis causis ultimo ordinabant, cuius considerationi ultimum tempus suae vitae deputarent: primo quidem incipientes a logica quae modum scientiarum tradit, secundo procedentes ad mathematicam cuius etiam pueri possunt esse capaces, tertio ad naturalem philosophiam quae propter experientiam tempore indiget, quarto autem ad moralem philosophiam cuius iuvenis esse conveniens auditor non potest, ultimo autem scientiae divinae insistebant quae considerat primas entium causas."—*Sancti Thomae de Aquino Super Librum De Causis Expositio,* ed. H. D. Saffrey (Fribourg and Louvain, 1954), p. 2.15-24. It was Thomas who saw that the *Liber de Causis* had been compiled from *The Elements of Theology* of Proclus; see Saffrey's introduction, p. xxiv. Perhaps the most striking thing about Thomas's *expositio* of this Neoplatonic work is the fact that he reads it through an Aristotelian lens. It is Aristotle who provides standards of acceptance, rejection, interpretation. Much interest has recently been shown in the Platonism of Thomas, by Geiger, Fabro, Klaus Kremer. This is a large subject, but the conclusion that Thomas remains basically an Aristotelian seems inescapable. Not only is this true of his reading of Boethius's *De hebdomadibus,* early in his career, but also with his exposition of the *Liber de Causis* in the last years of his life. In short, there is nothing unusual about his reduction of the liberal arts to Aristotelianism.

10. On Hugh of St Victor, see the introduction to Jerome Taylor's *The Didascalicon of Hugh of St. Victor* (New York, 1961).

11. See Ralph McInerny, *A History of Philosophy,* vol. II, *Philosophy From Augustine to Ockham* (Notre Dame, 1970), p. 77.

12. Maurer, p. 11: "Vel ideo haec inter ceteras scientias artes dicuntur, quia non solum habent cognitionem, sed opus aliquod, quod est immediate ipsius rationis, ut constructionem, syllogismum vel orationem formare, numerare, mensurare, melodias formare et cursus siderum computare. Aliae vero scientiae vel non habent opus, sed cognitionem tantum, sicut scientia divina et naturalis, unde nomen artis habere non possunt, cum ars dicatur ratio factiva, ut dicitur in VI *Metaphysicorum*, vel habent opus corporale, sicut medicina, alchimia et aliae huiusmodi, unde non possunt dici artes liberales, quia sunt hominis huiusmodi actus ex parte illa, qua non est liber, scilicet ex parte corpus." This is the continuation of q. 5, a. 1, ad 3m.

13. Cf. McInerny, pp. 190-94. I use *Didascalicon*, ed. C. H. Buttimer (Washington, 1939).

14. Thomas must have had in mind *Metaphysics*, E.1.1025b22, but he could equally as well have cited *Nicomachean Ethics*, 1140a8-10.

15. The sciences not called liberal arts are nonetheless liberal and may be more so than the sciences that are called liberal arts.

16. Maurer, pp. 11-12. "Scientia vero moralis, quamvis sit propter operationem, tamen illa operatio non est actus scientiae, sed magis virtutis, ut patet in libro *Ethicorum*, unde non potest dici ars, sed magis in illis operationibus se habet virtus loco artis." *In Boethii de trinitate*, q. 5, a. 1, ad 3m.

17. *Summa theologiae*, Ia, q. 1, a. 5.

18. Thomas discusses the different senses the theoretical/practical contrast has applied to philosophy as a whole, to the arts, and even to different aspects of a practical art like medicine. *In Boethii de trinitate*, q. 5, a. 1, ad 4m.

19. Migne, PL 64. The commentary on *De trinitate* runs from 1255B to 1300C.

20. *Ibid.*, 1265B-C: "Scientiae multorum sunt generum. Aliae namque sunt theoricae, id est speculativae, ut illae quibus intuemur an sint et quid sint et qualia sint, et cur sint singula creata; aliae vero sunt practicae, id est activae, ut illae quibus potius inspectionem scimus operari: ut medici, magi, et hujusmodi alii. Ut autem de practicis taceamus, speculativae ex his quae per ipsas inspicimus contrahunt appellationem, et vocantur aliae quidem physicae, id, est naturales; aliae vero ethicae, id est morales; aliae autem logicae, id est rationales: et ut item morales atque rationales praetereamus, illarum quae uno nomine naturales dicuntur, quae etiam usu majore speculativae vocantur, tres partes sunt. . . ."

21. Cf. *Posterior Analytics*, II, 1, 89b24-25.

22. Etienne Gilson, *History of Christian Philosophy in the Middle Ages* (New York, 1955), pp. 140-44.

23. See Nikolaus Häring, "A Commentary on Boethius' *De trinitate* by Thierry of Chartres (Anonymous Berolinensis)," AHDL (1956), pp. 257-325; "The Lectures of Thierry of Chartres on Boethius' *De trinitate*," AHDL (1958), pp. 113-226; "Two Commentaries on Boethius (*De trinitate* and *De hebdomadibus*) by Thierry of Chartres," AHDL (1960), pp. 65-136. L.-J. Bataillon has disputed some of these attributions to Thierry. See his "Bulletin d'histoire des doctrines médiévales: Le douzième siècle," *Révue des Sciences Philosophiques et Théologiques* (1978), Tome 62, No. 2, p. 245 and his "Sur quelques éditions de textes platoniciens médiévaux," in the same journal, Tome 61, No. 2 (1977), pp. 253-60.

24. For example, AHDL (1960), p. 93, no. 7.

25. "Dicebam haec et flebam amarissima contritione cordis mei. Et ecce audio uocem de uicina domo cum cantu dicentis et crebro repetentis quasi pueri an puellae, nescio: 'Tolle, lege; tolle, lege.' Statimque mutato uultu intentissimus cogitare coepi, utrumque solerent pueri in aliquo genere ludendi cantitare tale aliquid, nec occurrebat omnino audisse me uspiam repressoque impetu lacrimarum surrexi nihil aliud interpretans diuinitus mihi iuberi, nisi ut aperirem codicem et legerem quod primum caput inuenissem." *Saint Augustin Confessions*, Livres I-VIII, ed. Pierre de Labriolle, Paris, 1956, Liber octavus, note 29, p. 200. See *Retractationes*, I, 6.

26. *Soliloquies*, I, ii, 7. See McInerny, pp. 12-15.

27. *Retractationes*, I, 6.

28. *An Introduction to Divine and Human Readings*, trans. L. W. Jones (New York, 1946).

29. "In his quippe generibus tribus philosophiae etiam eloquia divina consistunt.—C. Quomodo?—A. Nam aut de natura disputare solent, in Genese et in Ecclesiaste; aut de moribus, ut in Proverbiis et in omnibus sparsim libris; aut de logica, pro qua nostri theologiam sibi vindicant, ut in Cant. Cant. et in sancto Evangelio." *De dialectica*, in Migne, PL 101, 952. Alcuin's interlocutor in this dialogue is none other than Charlemagne.

30. Cf. *Didascalicon*, ed. C. H. Buttimer (Washington, 1939).

31. In fairness, it should be pointed out that Thierry of Chartres did write an *Eptateuchon*, on the liberal arts. The prologue to this work has been edited by E. Jeaneau in *Mediaeval Studies*, 16 (1954), p. 174ff., and the work itself is discussed by A. Clerval in *Les Ecoles de Chartres* (Paris, 1895). Another 12th century figure, William of Conches, suggested the following division of knowledge that finds room for the liberal arts.

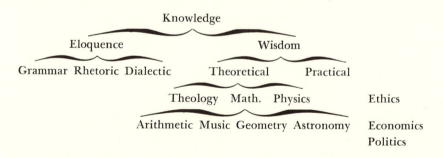

See McInerny, pp. 167-69.

32. Cf. Robert Kilwardby, *De Ortu Scientiarum*, in Auctores Britannici Medii Aevi, vol. 4, edited by Albert G. Judy, O.P. (London, 1976).

33. Fernand Van Steenberghen, *La Philosophie au XIIIe Siècle* (Louvain and Paris, 1966), p. 287.

34. See the magnificent introduction by Ludwig Baur to his edition of Gundissalinus's *De divisione philosophiae* in Bauemker's *Beitrage*, vol. 4, II/III, 1903.

35. See Majid Fakhry, "The Liberal Arts in the Mediaeval Arabic Tradition From the Seventh to the Twelfth Centuries," in ALPAMA, pp. 91-97.

36. Cf. Chenu, *Introduction à l'étude de Saint Thomas d'Aquin* (Montreal and Paris, 1954), pp. 51-60; Gilson, *History of Christian Philosophy in the*

Middle Ages (New York, 1955), pp. 246-50; M. De Wulf, *Histoire de la philosophie médiévale,* 6 ed., 1934, vol. 1, p. 15, note 2; M. Grabmann, *Die Geschichte der scholastischen Methode,* 2. vols. Fribourg, 1909-1911); Astrik Gabriel, "The Cathedral Schools of Notre Dame and the Beginning of the University of Paris," in *Garlandia* (Frankfurt, 1969), pp. 39-64.

37. Chenu, p. 52.

38. Brand Blanshard, *On Philosophical Style* (Bloomington, Ind., 1954).

39. Chenu, pp. 52-53.

40. Cf. Philippe Delhaye, "La Place des Arts Libéraux dans les Programmes Scolaires du XIIIe Siècle," in ALPAMA, pp. 161-73.

41. Cf. Van Steenberghen, *Maître Siger de Brabant* (Louvain and Paris, 1977), pp. 28-30.

42. "Ex improbo ausu investigationis philosophicae procedunt errores in philosophis, sicut est ponere mundum aeternum, et quod unus intellectus sit in omnibus. Ponere enim mundum aeternum, hoc est pervertere totam sacram Scriptuzam et dicere, quod Filius Dei non sit incarnatus. Ponere vero, quod unus intellectus sit in omnibus, hoc est dicere, quod non sit veritas fidei nec salus animarum nec observantia mandatorum; et hoc est dicere, quod pessimus homo salvatur, et optimus damnatur." *Collationes de Decem Praeceptis,* Collatio II, note 25, in *Obras de San Buenaventura,* Tomo Quinto (Madrid, 1948). In the same volume, see *Collationes de Septem Donis Spiritus Sancti,* Collatio VIII, and, on the historical setting of these sermons, see Fernand Van Steenberghen, *Maître Siger de Brabant,* pp. 40-46.

43. *Sancti Thomae Aquinatis Tractatus De Unitate Intellectus Contra Averroistas,* editio critica, Leo W. Keeler, S. J. (Rome, 1946). English translation by Beatrice H. Zedler, *On the Unity of the Intellect Against the Averroists* (Milwaukee, 1968).

44. Cf. Roland Hissette, *Enquête sur les 219 Articles Condamnés à Paris le 7 Mars 1277* (Louvain and Paris, 1977); John Wippel, "The Condemnations of 1270 and 1277," *Journal of Medieval and Renaissance Studies,* 7, (1977), pp. 169-201.

45. Zedler translation of Keeler, note 123: "Adhuc autem gravius est quod postmodum dicit: 'per rationem concludo de necessitate, quod intellectus est unum numero; firmiter tamen teneo oppositum per fidem.' Ergo sentit quod fides sit de aliquibus, quorum contraria de necessitate concludi possunt. Cum autem de necessitate concludi non possit nisi verum necessarium, cuius oppositum est falsum impossibile, sequitur secundum eius dictum quod fides sit de falso impossibili, quod etiam Deus facere non potest: quod fidelium aures ferre non possunt."

46. Cf. Boethius, *In Porphyrium Dialogi,* PL 64, 9B-C: "Tunc ego: Sex omnino, inquam, magistri in omni expositione praelibant. Praedocent enim quae sit cujuscunque operis intentio, quod apud illos *skopos* vocatur. Secundum quae utilitas, quod a Graecis *kresimon* appellatur. Tertium qui ordo, quod Graeci vocant *taxin.* Quartum si ejus cujus opus dicitur, germanus propriusque liber est, quod *gnesion* interpretari solet. Quintum quae sit ejus operis inscriptio, quod *epigraphen* Graeci nominant. . . . Sextum est id dicere, ad quam partem philosophiæ cujuscunque libri ducatur intentio. . ." Discussion in Pierre Courcelle, *Late Latin Writers and Their Greek Sources,* trans. Harry E. Wedeck (Cambridge, Mass., 1969), pp. 286-95.

47. Petrus Abaelardus, *Dialectica,* 2nd revised edition, L. M. De Rijk (Assen, 1970). See Maria Teresa Beonio-Brocchieri Fumagalli, *La Logica de Abelardo*

(Firenze, 1969), infelicitously translated in the Synthese Historical Library, *The Logic of Abelard* (Dordrecht, 1970).

48. Van Steenberghen, *La Philosophie au XIIIe Siècle,* pp. 527-29.

49. Translated by Willard R. Trask in the Bollingen Series (Princeton, N.J., 1953).

50. E. Gilson, *La Philosophie au Moyen Age des Origines Patristiques à la fin du XIVe Siècle,* 2 ed. (Paris, 1944), p. 401.

51. Cf. G. L. Bursill-Hall, *Speculative Grammars of the Middle Ages* (The Hague, 1971), and J. Pinborg, *Die Entwicklung der Sprachtheorie in Mittelalter* (1967).

52. Curtius, p. 208.

53. *Ibid.,* p. 213. The quote from Leopardi is from *Zibaldone,* note 2728.

54. *Mittelalterliches Geistesleben,* vol. 1 (Munich, 1926), p. 190.

55. Cf. Curtius, p. 480.

56. Cf. *Summa theologiae,* Ia, q. 1, a. 9, obj. 1; *In Libros Posteriorum Analyticorum Expositio,* proemium, note 6. For an interesting defense of Thomas's description of poetry, see Otto Bird, *Cultures in Conflict: An Essay in the Philosophy of the Humanities* (Notre Dame: University of Notre Dame Press, 1976), p. 70.

57. What I am suggesting here is found in Thomas's proemium to his commentary on the *Posterior Analytics.*

58. Bird's book, cited above, is important for this whole discussion.

59. See Julian Marias, *Philosophy as Dramatic Theory* (University Park: Pennsylvania State Press, 1971).

60. George Santayana, *Three Philosophical Poets* (New York: Doubleday Anchor, 1953).

BIBLIOGRAPHY

Congar, Y. "Scolastique" in *Dictionnaire de théologie catholique,* 15:1, 346-447.

Forest, A. *Le mouvement doctrinal,* vol. 13 of Fliche et Martin, *Histoire de l'Eglise.* Paris, 1956.

Gilson, E. *The Spirit of Medieval Philosophy.* New York, 1940.

———. *History of Christian Philosophy in the Middle Ages.* New York, 1955.

Grabmann, M. *Die Geschichte der scholastischen Methode,* 2. vols. Friberg, 1909-1911.

Knowles, D. *The Evolution of Mediaeval Thought.* Baltimore, 1962.

McInerny, R. *History of Western Philosophy,* vol. 2. Notre Dame, 1970.

———. *St Thomas Aquinas.* Boston, 1978.

New Catholic Encyclopedia, articles on "Scholastic Method," "Scholastic Philosophy," and "Scholasticism."

Van Steenberghen, F. *Aristotle in the West.* Louvain, 1955.

———. *La philosophie au xiiie siècle.* Louvain, 1966.

———. *Maître Siger de Brabant.* Louvain, 1977.

The Contributors

MARTIN CAMARGO is assistant professor of English at the University of Missouri-Columbia. He has published essays on Middle English lyrics and medieval rhetoric.

JEFFREY F. HUNTSMAN is associate professor of English at Indiana University. His fields of research include the theory and practice of grammar, lexicography, and translation in the Middle Ages.

THEODORE C. KARP is chairman of the Department of Music History and Literature at Northwestern University. He has published widely in the subjects of medieval secular song, twelfth-century polyphony, and Gregorian chant.

CLAUDIA KREN is professor of history at the University of Missouri-Columbia. She has published extensively in medieval astronomy.

RALPH McINERNY, director of The Medieval Institute, University of Notre Dame, has published widely in the field of medieval philosophy. His latest book is *Ethica Thomistica*.

MICHAEL MASI is associate professor of English at Loyola University, Chicago. He has translated Boethius's *De arithmetica* and is the editor of *Boethius and the Liberal Arts*.

KARL F. MORRISON is professor of medieval history and of New Testament and early Christian literature at the University of Chicago. His latest book is *The Mimetic Tradition of Reform in the West*.

LON R. SHELBY is professor of sociology and history at Southern Illinois University at Carbondale. He is the author of numerous articles on medieval building techniques and has published the design booklets of Mathes Roriczer and Hanns Schmuttermayer.

ELEONORE STUMP is associate professor of philosophy at Virginia Polytechnic Institute and State University. She was associate editor of *The Cambridge History of Later Medieval Philosophy* and has published a translation of Boethius's *De topicis differentiis*.

DAVID L. WAGNER is associate professor of history and coordinator of the Medieval Studies Program at Northern Illinois University. He has begun work on the seven liberal arts in the Renaissance.

Index